The Un-Civil War

Shattering the Historical Myths

Leonard M. Scruggs

Published by *Universal Media, Inc.*

One Boston Way

Asheville, NC 28803

www.thetribunepapers.com

Layout and cover design by *Drawing Distinction.*

―――――――――――――――○-□-○――――――――――――――――

The Un-Civil War, Shattering the Historical Myths is available in quantity for promotional and educational use. For information:

Write to:

Director of Special Sales

Universal Media

P.O. Box 5615

Asheville, NC 28813

Call:

828-674-9103

Email:

publications@thetribunepapers.com

―――――――――――――――○-□-○――――――――――――――――

ISBN: 978-0-9834356-0-0

Library of Congress Control Number: 2011927689

Printed in the United States of America

DEDICATION

This book is dedicated to the Southern people and to all those of every section, race, or nation who have, with persevering courage, striven for truth and the good of their people. Let us go and do likewise.

Soli Deo Gloria
lms
January 7, 2011.

───────────────○□○───────────────

ACKNOWLEDGEMENTS

I owe thanks to many friends and readers for encouraging me to write this book, which first appeared in a series of articles on the "Un-Civil War" in the *Asheville Tribune* and the *Hendersonville Tribune* in North Carolina, and later in the *Times Examiner* in Greenville, South Carolina. A special thanks goes to the editors and publishers of those papers: David Morgan and Katrina Morgan, Bill Fishburne, Mark White, and Bob Dill.

I also owe a special thanks to those who at one time or another toiled in the tedious and sometimes frustrating work of editing my writing nd who made many helpful comments: Ken Bachand, Jan Kral, Ben Moon, and Amy Shook.

In addition, I have greatly appreciated the many readers and friends who encouraged me with emails, phone calls, and letters. They often enhanced my knowledge and understanding of the War for Southern Independence by recommending important contacts and reference materials.

Finally, I would like to thank the authors of the many books and articles that I used as references. Though I have only met a few of the most recent authors, and many have long passed from this life, having written as much as two hundred years ago, they have become like familiar and cherished friends.

Soli Deo Gloria
January 7, 2011
Hendersonville, North Carolina
Leonard M. (Mike) Scruggs

"At a time when liberty is under attack,
decency under assault, the family under
siege, and life itself is threatened, the good
will arise in truth; they will arise in truth
with the very essence and substance of their
lives; they will arise in truth never shying
from the Standard of Truth, never shrinking
from the Author of Truth."

—Henry Laurens,
South Carolina patriot,
and 5th President of the
Continental Congress
(1777-1778).

THE UN-CIVIL WAR
Shattering the Historical Myths

CONTENTS

Appendix Chapters

"SOUTHERN ILIAD"
P.S. Worley, 1867

"The grand old bard that never dies,
Receive him in our English tongue!
I send thee, but with weeping eyes,
The story that he sung."

"Thy Troy is fallen—thy dear land
Is marred beneath the spoiler's heel—
I cannot trust my trembling hand
To write the things I feel."

"The widow's moan, the orphan's wail,
Come round thee; but in truth be strong!
Eternal Right, though all else fail,
Can never be made wrong."

******

These three verses are from a special translation of *The Iliad* presented to Robert E. Lee by British writer, P.S. Worley in 1867.

FOREWORD
The Battle for Historical Truth

Shortly before his death at the Battle of Franklin, Tennessee, on November 30, 1864, Confederate Major General Patrick Cleburne reminded his comrades in arms of the possible cost of surrender:

"Surrender means that the history of this heroic struggle will be written by the enemy, that our youths will be trained by Northern school teachers; learn from Northern school books THEIR version of the war; and taught to regard our gallant dead as traitors and our maimed veterans as fit subjects of derision."

This was particularly true during the Reconstruction years from 1865 through 1877. Not only was the South exploited economically, it was also subjected to continuous political despotism in an attempt to remold its social and political structures in the image of Northern radicalism. The concomitant objective of this tyrannical reign was to maintain the dominant national party in power without serious opposition. In addition, many Northern politicians campaigning at home "waved the bloody shirt," reminding Northern voters how much invading the South had cost in Northern blood and treasure. Demonization of the South and the cause of Southern independence continued to be a dominant feature of Northern politics for many decades.

In an address to the graduates of Hampden Sidney College in Virginia in 1887, prominent theologian Robert L. Dabney advised them that Northern interests were straining every nerve to falsify or misrepresent history in order to justify the late war and sustain Northern national dominance. He warned them that:

"With a gigantic sweep of mendacity, this literature aims to falsify or misrepresent everything; the very facts of history, the principles of the former Constitution as admitted in the days of freedom by all statesmen of all parties....The whole sway of their commercial and political ascendancy is exerted to fill the South with this false literature. Its sheets come up, like the frogs of Egypt, into our houses, our bed chambers, our very kneading troughs."

Union propaganda generally served up a self-justifying misrepresentation of the war as a morality play in which a noble Union Army marched forth to battle for the glorious purpose of emancipating downtrodden slaves from evil Southerners. This explanation has been continued in an even more strident and self-righteous form in modern political correctness. These often-repeated assertions attempt to claim the moral high ground for Northern aggression and to discredit the South's resistance to that aggression as "morally wrong."

No serious student of the "Civil War" believes that the Union invaded the South to emancipate the slaves. Such ignorance, however, is commonplace. This propagandistic version of the war is commonly taught in public schools, and, in ignorance, even in many Christian schools. Yet it has little basis in fact. Slavery was an issue between North and South, but not in the propagandistic, fabricated moral sense usually assumed. The extension of slavery into new territories was an issue. The Northern States wanted to preserve the new states for free labor without unfair competition from slave labor, but they also feared the possible social consequences of bringing in large numbers of blacks into the new territories. Most Northern legislatures severely restricted the entry of blacks, slave or free, into their states. Southern political leaders, on the other hand, felt that legislation preventing Southern immigrants from bringing their slaves into the new territories violated their property rights and was designed to assure Northern dominance in the new states and the national Congress. It was in the latter sense a matter of political numbers—part of an ongoing struggle for legislative dominance in Congress. It was the fear of unfettered Northern political dominance that made limited Constitutional government and States Rights paramount to the interests of Southern states.

President Woodrow Wilson was once asked how the role of slavery became so distorted and exaggerated as a cause of the "Civil War." Wilson gave this succinct answer:

"It was necessary to put the South at a moral disadvantage by transforming the contest from a war waged against states fighting for their independence into a war waged against states fighting for the maintenance and extension of slavery..."

In the decades before the "Civil War," the political parties that dominated North and South had come to have almost opposite interpretations of the Constitution. The Republican Party that emerged as the dominant party in the North in 1860 was essentially a big-business-big-government party willing to sacrifice the Constitution to national industrial and political greatness. Yet the South believed Constitutional government, and especially States Rights, were essential to its political and economic well-being. At that time, the terms "Conservative," and "Democrat" were virtual political synonyms. How things have changed!

Southerners also believed they were being forced to submit to a government whose character had been sacrificed to sectionalism. This sectionalism had been most flagrant in the protective tariffs passed to benefit Northern industry and imposed against strong Southern opposition beginning in 1824. This culminated in the passage of the Morrill Tariff, signed into law on February 2, 1861, which imposed tremendous hardship on the South for the benefit of Northern industry. This legislation nearly tripled the tariff burden on the South and virtually compelled the cotton producing states to secede. The immediate cause of armed conflict beyond the bloodless Fort Sumter confrontation was, however, Lincoln's call for 75,000 troops on April 15 to put down the "rebellion" of seceding states and assure the tariff was collected.

Few modern writers recognize that there was also an underlying religious conflict between North and South that went to more fundamental depths than the debate over slavery. Secular propaganda has succeeded in framing the issue as a debate over slavery, but the truly essential issue was a debate over the authority and interpretation of Scripture, with the South taking the conservative side of the debate. Southern Biblical conservatives had their allies in the North, but one Southern cleric remarked that North and South had fundamentally different interpretations of the Constitution and the Bible.

There were a several decades from the late 1890s until the end of 1950s that saw a reconciliation of North and South. This was largely the result of efforts by the veterans on both sides of the war. Despite differences, each side treated the other with respect and even admiration. Southern cultural symbols thrived in a relatively friendly atmosphere of mutual understanding.

In the early 1960s, however, legitimate civil rights issues began to be pushed beyond the pale of Constitutional government, sound judgment, and fairness. Liberal politicians and demagogues then began to use the slavery and race issues again as a weapon to shout down debate on issues like school-busing for the purpose of racial balance, racial quotas and preferences, and other coercive methods of social change reminiscent of Reconstruction. This eventually led to tyrannical social and academic political correctness being imposed on discussion of issues related to race, slavery, and the "Civil War." These intellectual chains have also spread to any issue that conflicts with the now dominant philosophy of secular humanism. Unfortunately, the chains of political correctness are most heavily forged in academia. Degrees, grants, scholarships, promotions, publication opportunities, and academic prestige are often dependent on adherence to politically correct dogma and presuppositions. This has been inimical to truth and courage, without which, no nation or people can long remain free.

One purpose of this book is to expose the historical errors and myths about the War for Southern Independence that have been imposed on a public largely unaware that historical truth has been considerably obscured by modern political correctness. Fortunately, this can be done without using a single Southern source. However, I have made it a point to use Northern, Southern, and British sources to get a three-line navigational fix on the truth.

The historical concern of this book touches both the causes and the conduct of the war. In the latter regard, I have included some guidance on the historical development of Just War Theory. This was generally adhered to by Southern political and military leaders but was flagrantly violated by the Lincoln Administration as a matter of unspoken policy.

The primary purpose of this book, however, is to rescue the South from decades of slanderous propaganda. Americans, of all sections and races, have not been well served by whitewashed or propagandistic history. True unity cannot be imposed by guns and bayonets or enhanced by false versions of history. True and lasting unity must be founded on a mutual respect for truth. Truth is the surest foundation for liberty.

INTRODUCTION

My first knowledge of the so-called "Civil War," which I now prefer to call *The War for Southern Independence*, was learned at my grandfather's knee. My great grandfather, John Berry Scruggs and his brother, James, served in the 2nd Kentucky Cavalry, CSA. They also had a brother, Thomas, in the 19th Alabama Infantry and another, Sterling, in the 26th/50th Alabama Infantry. All three regiments saw considerable combat, but all the brothers survived the war. My great grandfather was wounded and along with his brother captured in Ohio during John Hunt Morgan's great raid into Indiana and Ohio in July 1863. They spent the rest of the war as prisoners at Camp Douglas near Chicago. The other brothers were in the same Alabama infantry brigade and saw action from Shiloh to the bloody defeats at Franklin and Nashville.

When my grandfather, G. B. Scruggs, was a boy, he and his brothers, sisters, and cousins loved to sit on the stairs of the two story, white frame Scruggs home in North Alabama and listen, sometimes late into the evening, to the brothers and their father talk about the war. My grandfather passed many of these stories directly to me, when I was a boy. My father often repeated them to me as well.

During the Vietnam War I myself saw combat as an Air Force crewmember of an A-26K attack-bomber designed for close air support and armed reconnaissance. In February of 1967, I was shot down over Laos in a gun duel with four North Vietnamese anti-aircraft guns. I was rescued within an hour, but spent more than five months in hospitals recovering. During that recovery time I began to read extensively on military and political history.

Some years later I decided to write an account of my own Vietnam War experience and the experience of my great grandfather and his brothers in that devastating war of 1861 to 1865 that Ludwell Johnson has called *The American Iliad*. I wrote mainly for my sons and nephews but was encouraged to write more.

It was the Sons of Confederate Veterans of the Joe Wheeler Camp in Birmingham, Alabama, that ignited my curiosity in many aspects of the "Civil War" and gave me much encouragement and many opportunities to write still more. I was also very moved by the command given to the Sons of Confederate Veterans by Confederate General Stephen D. Lee to defend the honor of the Confederate soldier.

Eventually my interests gravitated more to the character of the men and women of that era and to the political issues that motivated them rather than the battles of the war. All this occurred just as the NAACP launched an all out attack on the Confederate Battle Flag. That is when I researched and wrote the first piece of this series outlining the historical background of the Confederate Battle Flag and the true issues that motivated the South to secede from its union with the North.

Never since Reconstruction has our country been so chained by political correctness. Yet there are many modern scholars like Charles Adams and Thomas DiLorenzo who have risen to the defense of historical truth. In writing these essays I have also discovered many a buried treasure in older books written in times more amenable to truth. Many of these, suppressed by the Eastern establishment publishers for decades, are now being reprinted.

There were many causes of the war. One of the most heinous political crimes in history was the Morrill Tariff, which made secession of the major cotton producing states almost inevitable. But the most important underlying causes were Constitutional in nature. The war was not really very much about slavery. It was over strong differences on the meaning and obligations of Constitutional government. The South held the traditional position of limited government and strict adherence to the protections of the Constitution, especially States Rights. The North favored a strong, centralized government and material and social progress unfettered by Constitutional limits. These issues are not dead.

One aspect of the war that has been suppressed is the Union conduct of the war. The "Civil" War was the first modern and large scale use of "total war strategy." Total war is war against both military combatants and civilian non-combatants in blatant contrast to the Christian Just War Doctrine. Most of the really good sources on this are older.

Following the war, came Reconstruction from 1865 to 1877. The defeated South was subjected to plunder by Northern carpetbaggers and almost unbelievable despotism and tyranny by the Radical Republicans. It was during this period that the invisible empire of the Ku Klux Klan arose. It was largely the Klan, born of desperate circumstances but noble purposes, that defeated Reconstruction and rescued the people of the South— both white and black—from corrupt and exploitive carpetbagger governments and Radical Republican tyranny and brutality. This is hard to reconcile with the more recent historical versions of the Klan, but readers should keep in mind that the original Klan and corrupted modern copies were very distinct in motivation and operation. Most good sources on Reconstruction and the Klan are older.

In tackling the subject of slavery I have first tried to give a worldwide historical perspective. Then I described how New England shippers developed the slave trade. Next I have tried to show what Southern slavery was really like as opposed to the usual politically correct views. I have attempted to do justice to the little known story of the sterling loyalty and contributions of black Confederates to the Southern war effort. Finally, I have commented on the remarkable spiritual heritage and connections of both black and white Southerners.

This book is a consolidation of several series of articles published in the *Asheville* and *Hendersonville Tribunes* in North Carolina and the Greenville, South Carolina, based *Times Examiner*. Several series were consolidated in October 2006 to make *The Un-Civil War: Truths Your Teacher Never Told You*, published in tabloid form. Since then several other series and articles have been published in all three papers on related topics of the war. These are among others that have been consolidated into this volume.

Of the additional material, three important series have been placed among the appendix chapters. This is not because they are by any stretch of the imagination dry or overly statistical. These three are treatments of important subjects that have a bearing on the entire North-South conflict rather than fitting neatly into the chronology of the war. Appendix Chapter 2 covers the "Un-civil War in Missouri," which is important to understanding the origins of the war and the development of Union "total war" policies. Appendix Chapter 3, entitled "Fighting Joe Wheeler" is helpful in understanding the role of cavalry and mounted infantry in the war and at the same time deals with many of the issues with Sherman's destructive march through Georgia and South Carolina. Wheeler also inflicted the greatest cavalry defeat on the Union Army during the war. Appendix Chapter 4, entitled "Find the *Alabama*," deals with the Confederate Raider, *CSS Alabama*. Many astute scholars of the war have credited Union victory to the fact that they had one of the strongest navies in the world and were able to cut off Confederate war materials before they reached the battlefield. Union gunboats operating along the inland rivers were also important in squeezing the life out of the Confederacy.

Amazingly, a mere handful of Confederate raiders severely curtailed Union shipping and nearly rendered the vastly superior Union Navy ineffective in maintaining its blockade of Southern ports. *The Alabama*, under Raphael Semmes, became the most effective commerce raider in the history of the world, unsurpassed by any German submarine during World War I or II.

Appendix Chapter 1 describes the development of Just War Theory from Augustine to the present. This has an important bearing on evaluating Union war policy.

In combining essays of a series into a single chapter, some of the transitional language connecting the essays has been left in place. This is not meant to burden the reader but to drive home important points and impress them more indelibly on the mind.

These essays have two main objectives: to rescue truth from decades of oppression and to uphold the honor of the Confederate soldier and the Southern cause.

CHAPTER 1

Beneath the Southern Cross

The Confederate Battle Flag, sometimes called the Southern Cross, is held in disfavor by many who are unfamiliar with its origin and true symbolism. Many have been taught to treat it as an object of moral horror and political infamy. A deadly combination of ignorance and arrogant self-righteousness is constantly engaged in shouting down its true history and meaning. Demagogues freely defame it, while moral cowardice acquiesces to their outrageous distortions of the truth. The apathetic allow its true history to be buried under decades of slanderous propaganda. It is incumbent upon those who value truth, fairness, goodwill, reasonable tolerance, and charity in society to educate themselves on the true history and meaning of this famed banner.

In order to understand and fully appreciate the meaning and heritage of the Confederate Battle Flag it is necessary to reach back far into history and then come forward to the battlefields of its fame. Finally we must visit the hallowed resting-places of the fallen and of the veterans of that historic struggle.

The prominent design feature of the Battle Flag is its diagonal cross or saltier. This has for many centuries been a preeminent Christian symbol. In the Greek alphabet the name of Christ begins with the letter "X" or "Chi." Thus it became a symbol for Christ and Christianity.

The symbol was reinforced when the Apostle Andrew was martyred on a diagonal cross in 60 AD. This was later to influence the Christian symbolism of far-off Scotland. About 357 AD, during the reign of Constantine, some of the bones and relics of Andrew were brought to Constantinople.

St. Andrews Cross (Scotland)   St. Georges Cross (England)   St. Patricks Cross (Ireland)

According to various legends some of these were eventually moved to a monastery near a small Pictish village on the East Coast of Scotland, probably about 733 AD. The town that grew up there was renamed St. Andrews and became the ecclesiastical capital of Scotland and a center of learning. Hence there began to be an identification of Scotland with St. Andrew and the diagonal cross on which he was martyred.

In a battle about 832 AD, Angus MacFergus, King of the Picts, with a combined army of Picts and Dalriada Scots, drove the Northumbrian Angles out of Scotland. Various legends attend this battle, including the appearance of a white diagonal cross in the blue sky on that day. Whatever is behind the legends, the bottom line was that Angus, the Picts, and the Scots attributed their victory and rout of the Angles to the intercessory assistance of Saint Andrew. All this is clouded in the fog of history and legend. Saint Andrew was eventually recognized as the Patron Saint of Scotland. Since early in the 12th century the Scottish national flag, also called the St. Andrews Cross, has been a white diagonal cross or saltier on a field of blue.

The important thing about the St. Andrews flag to the Scots was that it was an identification of themselves as a Christian people. Many European nations chose the cross in various designs to identify themselves as Christian nations.

The English flag is a red perpendicular cross, called St. Georges Cross, on a field of white. The British national or union flag contains the English St. Georges Cross with the diagonal St. Andrews Cross of Scotland, and the red diagonal St. Patricks Cross representing Northern

British Union Jack   South Carolina   South Carolina Sovereignty

First National   Army of Northern Virginia
Battle Flag   Army of Tennessee Battle Flag

Ireland. All the Scandinavian countries including Finland and also Greece and Switzerland use a cross in their flags.

The Southern Cross or Confederate Battle Flag with its white trimmed blue diagonal on a red field is a descendent of the Scottish St. Andrews Cross. As we shall see it was meant to be a preeminently Christian self-identification of the Southern people.

On December 20, 1860, the elected delegates of the South Carolina Secession Convention met in St. Andrews Hall in Charleston. One of the 169 delegates was U. S. Congressman and future Confederate Congressman, William Porcher Miles. Miles had a very keen interest and knowledge of heraldry. Besides their famous Palmetto Flag, the South Carolinians had prepared a special South Carolina Sovereignty Flag for the occasion. This flag, which probably had the touch of William Miles, was a blue St. Georges Cross on a field of red, with a white South Carolina Palmetto and Crescent in the upper left canton. The 15 white stars on the cross probably represented the hope of a 15 state Confederacy. Again, the important thing about this flag was that its symbolism identified with Christianity.

One of the underlying causes of the war was the growing religious difference between North and South. By 1850 the original Calvinism of the New England Puritans had been in steep decline for generations. The Calvinism and orthodox Christianity of the Puritan fathers was being eroded and displaced by Deism, Unitarianism, Universalism, and Transcendentalism, the antecedents of modern liberalism. A few strong bastions like Princeton remained, but the authority of Scripture, the sovereignty of God, and the centrality of Christ's redeeming grace were fighting a rear guard battle against secularism and numerous heresies. In addition, the man-centered preaching of Charles G. Finney further weakened the theology of Northern Christianity. The godly zeal of the first Puritans had been replaced by zeal to reform society by government force.

The South on the other hand was not only holding fast to traditional Christian teachings, but was experiencing dramatic revival, culminating in more than 150,000 conversions in the Confederate Army alone during the war. These growing religious differences caused considerable anxiety and mistrust of Northern goodwill in the South, especially after John Brown's 1859 raid on the arsenal at Harper's Ferry, now in West Virginia. John Brown, a fanatical abolitionist and cold-blooded murderer of innocent Kansas farmers in 1856, was hanged by federal authorities, but he was made a hero and martyr in the North by the press, and most alarmingly, many influential abolitionist preachers. Many famous Northern personalities compared John Brown's hanging to the martyrdom of Christ. Here for example are the words of Unitarian Transcendentalist, Julia Ward Howe, who composed the words of *The Battle Hymn of the Republic*: "John Brown will glorify the gallows like Jesus glorified the cross." A few other famous admirers of this terrorist who became important in the liberal propaganda version of American history and culture were Reverend Henry Ward Beecher, Henry David Thoreau, and Ralph Waldo Emerson. Many statements glorifying such lawless violence in the name of abolition alarmed the South and intensified their desire to disassociate themselves with the North. It also further intensified in Southerners their desire to identify themselves as a distinctively Christian people.

Because of his knowledge of heraldry, Miles, a now Confederate Congressman from South Carolina, was appointed Chairman of the congressional committee to select a national flag for the newly formed Confederate States of America. On the deadline date of March 4, 1861, the work of the committee was presented to the Confederate Congress. Out of numerous suggestions the committee had narrowed the field down to four choices.

One of these choices was William Miles' own. It was essentially the South Carolina Sovereignty Flag except that the cross was changed from a St. Georges Cross to a diagonal St. Andrews Cross, and of course, without the Palmetto canton. There were only seven stars on it, however, because on March 4th only seven states had properly seceded and joined the Confederacy. This made it asymmetrical and was one of the reasons it was rejected as the new National Flag. The flag chosen was the "Stars and Bars" which had a circle of seven white stars on an upper left, blue canton and three horizontal bars red, white, and red.

One of the main reasons this flag was chosen over Miles' St. Andrews Cross was that the "Stars and Bars" was close in resemblance to the

United States Flag. At that time the Confederate Congress wanted to keep its identification with the 1787 U. S. Constitution. They believed they had been faithful to it, but the Northern states, especially the Northeastern industrial states had continually tried to undermine it for Northern profit at Southern expense.

This is itself a clue to two other important causes of the war. The Southern belief was in a government of Law and strict constitutionalism versus majoritarian rule and manipulation of the Constitution. In addition the North had imposed enormous tariffs on manufactured goods that protected Northern industry at considerable expense to Southern agriculture, trade, and the Southern economy. The Confederate Congress passed over Miles' St. Andrews Cross for the Stars and Bars, but Miles did not give up promoting his choice for some honorable Southern use.

In the early battles of the Civil War, it was noted that there was often confusion on the battle-field because of the similarity of the Stars and Bars flag to the U. S. flag. After the First Battle of Manassas at Bull Run Creek both Generals P. G. T. Beauregard and his commander, Joseph E. Johnston were convinced that there was a need to change the flag. Battlefield commanders needed to be able to identify their troops and positions on the field without confusion, despite the smoke and dust.

As it happened Congressman William Miles was now serving on Beauregard's staff, and was also now Chairman of the House Military Affairs Committee. As the Confederate Congress did not favor changing the national flag, Miles suggested the Army of the Potomac, later renamed the Army of Northern Virginia, should have a special battle flag. Hundreds of suggestions were received from Confederate officers and officials. Most of these were crosses of some sort. Miles prevailed in his suggestion that his original St. Andrews Cross choice for the national flag be used as the needed battle flag for the regiments of the Army of Northern Virginia (ANV). It was modified by putting a white border around the edges. Now that there were more states in the Confederacy the stars were more symmetrical, and the flag was very attractive.

Johnston determined that the ANV battle flag would be square in order to save cloth and money. The Southern Cross was officially accepted as a battle flag on October 1, 1861. It was not used as the battle flag by every regiment in the ANV, however. Some already had battle flags they wished to keep. The first battle flags had only 12 stars, but the 13th was added in early 1862, making its symmetry complete. The ANV battle flag eventually spread to the Army of Tennessee and other Confederate Armies.

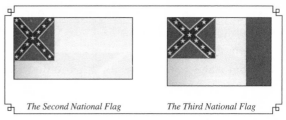

The Second National Flag   *The Third National Flag*

The Army of Tennessee typically used a rectangular version without the white edging. This also became the Confederate Naval Jack and is the most common Confederate Battle Flag seen today.

There can be no doubt that the Confederate Battle Flag or Southern Cross was intended to be a banner signifying the Christian heritage of the Southern people. The saltier or diagonal cross is the signal feature of that symbolism and is connected with the Christianity of ages past and of the martyrdom of the Apostle Andrew. The red field signifies courage. The blue of the saltier signifies truth. The white stars and bordering of the cross signified the purity of their cause. One of the heraldic meanings of the saltier is strength, connected to the meaning of Andrew. A letter written by William Miles to Samuel Barrett of Georgia during the summer of 1861 clearly indicates the reasoning and intent of its principal designer and sponsor:

"The flag should be a token of humble acknowledgement of God and be a public testimony to the world that our trust is in the Lord our God."

This meaning was widely understood by Confederate soldiers and the Southern people. That is why they frequently referred to it as "our Southern Cross."

On May 1, 1863 the Confederate Congress changed the national flag to "The Stainless Banner." This flag featured the Battle Flag in the top, left canton on a field of white. There was so much white in the flag, however, it was feared it might easily be mistaken for a flag of surrender or truce. On February 27, 1865, just weeks before the end of the war, The Confederate Congress added a wide, vertical, red bar to the fly end of the Stainless Banner. This was the third and final CSA national flag and contained the Battle Flag in the canton.

The Southern Cross then had a very strong Christian association to Confederate soldiers and the Southern people. As celebrated Southern historian, Shelby Foote, has said, it also came to stand for Law, in the sense of a government of Law rather than a government subject to the whim of tyrants or majorities. In that regard it stood for a strict rather than opportunistic interpretation of Law and Constitutions. It also came to be a symbol of defiance against tyranny and the right of a free people to determine their own destiny. This may be one of its most enduring meanings. The Confederate Battle Flag has been seen all over the world in this regard, on the Berlin Wall, and in the capitals of the Baltic republics and Eastern Europe, wherever free people must resist tyranny and the modern scourge of political correctness. It stood for limited government and States Rights against the dangers of concentrated and centralized power. It stood for the principles of the constitutional federal republic of 1787 that the South felt were threatened by Northern political philosophies and economic ambitions. It stood for the Rights gained and blood-sacrifices their forefathers had made in the Revolutionary War. If there was one word used more often than any other in the secession conventions, it was "Honor." The Confederate Battle Flag came to signify the honor of the Confederate soldier and the Southern people. It has come to symbolize the South itself with all its culture. These are not dead issues. More than anything it must forever symbolize the sacrifice of fallen Confederate soldiers on the battlefields of their War for Southern Independence and also to the veterans of those fields of honor.

The Confederate Battle Flag is frequently slandered and treated with contempt by those who have uncritically accepted the prevailing perversion of Civil War history. Those who have broken the chains of political correctness and unsnarled the many decades of propaganda justifying that war come to a different conclusion. The Confederate Battle Flag deserves the honor and respect of all Americans, indeed the whole world.

Yet even in the South there are those who are willing to accept an ignominious degradation of truth and venomous slander against the honor of the Confederate soldier in order to maintain social peace. There are those who are willing to trample on the honor of noble ancestors in order to promote such a social peace. There are those to whom heritage and honor mean nothing compared to present favor with the media and powerful political constituencies.

The Reverend James Power Smith, the last surviving member of Stonewall Jackson's staff, had this to say in 1907:

"No cowardice on any battlefield could be as base and shameful as the silent acquiescence in the scheme which was teaching the children in their homes and schools that the commercial value of slavery was the cause of the war, that prisoners of war held in the South were starved and treated with barbarous inhumanity, that Jefferson Davis and Robert E. Lee were traitors to their country and false to their oaths, that the young men who left everything to resist invasion, and climbed the slopes of Gettysburg and died willingly on a hundred fields were rebels against a righteous government."

But how long would a prosperity or social peace based on such disrespect for truth last? How long would a peace based on suppression of a people's cherished heritage last? How long would a peace built upon suppressing the memory, valor, and virtue of the revered forebearers of a great number of the Southern people last? Does anyone outside of a madhouse believe such reckless villainy would not in a very short time reap a whirlwind of social destruction?   What could possibly be a surer cause of immense strife, bitterness, and economic and political turmoil? Can anyone believe that peace and prosperity can be achieved by discarding the heritage of a numerous people to gain the political favor of another? It is more likely to shatter all hope of peace. Can a society set itself against tolerance and mutual respect and have peace? No fair-minded person can accept such corrupt reasoning.

There are those who say that the display of the Confederate Battle Flag is insensitive. They say it is a symbol of slavery and offends many people. But their offense is based on ignorance of its true origin and history. Their offense is based on decades of unquestioned propaganda attempting to justify an unjust war and its deplorable tyranny and conduct. The men who carried the Southern Cross into battle never meant it to be a symbol of slavery. Their letters and diaries prove it was far from their minds. Not many of them owned slaves or favored its continued existence for very long in the future. Less than 25% of Southern households owned slaves. So far as slavery was concerned they only wanted the right to deal with it in their own way in their own time state by state, just as the Northern states, all of which had slavery in 1776, had done. The Union Army did not invade the South to free slaves. They invaded the South to prevent its political and economic independence. Lincoln's Emancipation Proclamation came after more than 19 months of war and did not actually free any slaves in the Union or Union held areas of the Confederacy. It was done as a war measure in hopes of causing disorder in the South. Only later was the slavery issue used in an attempt to give tyranny a pious justification.

The right to define the meaning of the Confederate Battle Flag, or any flag, belongs to those who, by their history and shed blood, own its heritage. Radical and lawless groups often display the United States flag, but this does not change its true meaning to fair-minded people. Nor should fair-minded people rightly associate the Confederate Battle Flag with evil because the very same groups expropriate and display it. Groups such as the NAACP and SPLC have no right to define the meaning of Confederate flags any more than the French have the right to define the meaning of the Italian flag or any flag but their own. Redefining and slandering someone else's heritage and symbols is incredibly arrogant and stirs up needless strife. Honorable people pursuing a just and civil society do not seek to dishonor and marginalize the heritage and symbols of others.

To Southern solders and their families the Confederate Battle Flag symbolized their Christian heritage and resistance to tyranny. They were fighting for the right of Southern States and their people to determine their own political destiny, just as their Revolutionary War forefathers had fought the British. They were fighting against the evil of unjust taxation and many other abuses of power perpetrated by Northern political factions. They were fighting to free themselves of a Northern political dominance that had enriched the Northern states and oppressed Southern states. After many years of hardship and blood spent on the battlefield, the Southern Cross came to symbolize the courage and blood sacrifice of the Confederate soldier and Southern people. They believed in the justice and righteousness of their cause, and when the surrender at Appomattox came, they gave up their regimental banners with tears and weeping.

We must ourselves honor the memory of our fallen heroes and of all that served in that great struggle beneath our Southern Cross. The words of the South Carolinian journalist and poet Henry Timrod (1829-1867) in his moving *Ode at Magnolia Cemetery* should move our hearts to resolve:

"Sleep sweetly in your humble graves, sleep martyrs of a fallen cause, Though yet no marble column craves the pilgrim here to pause.

In seeds of laurel in the earth, the blossom of your fame is blown, And somewhere, waiting for its birth, the shaft is in the stone.

Meanwhile, behalf the tardy years, which keep in trust your storied tombs,
Behold! Your sisters bring their tears, and these memorial blooms.

Small tributes! But your shades will smile, more proudly on these wreaths
today, than when some cannon-moulded pile shall overlook this bay.

Stoop, angels, thither from the skies! There is no holier ground
than where defeated valor lies, by mourning beauty crowned."

But now there are many who for political or economic gain would
rather see every memory and symbol of that noble army destroyed and
desecrated. There are still others who though being descendents of those
noble soldiers by their indifference and moral cowardice would acquiesce
to that destruction. In dishonoring the Southern Cross and suppressing a
noble Christian heritage they heap dishonor on themselves.

Yet I cannot believe that Providence will suffer the memory and sacred honor of valiant men and righteous principles to be blotted out. I
cannot believe their heroic banner will be suffered to be discarded and forgotten. I cannot believe that the blood of valorous heroes, still coursing in
the veins of their sons and daughters and their future generations, will not
continue to inspire and encourage the friends of liberty everywhere. Whatever storms may come, we will not surrender the honor or our gallant flag.

CHAPTER 2

<small>◁◈▷</small>

The New South and the Frogs of Egypt

Robert L. Dabney

On June 15, 1882, the Reverend Robert L. Dabney delivered a discourse at the Annual Commencement of Hampden Sidney College in Virginia, entitled, "The New South." Dabney was a Presbyterian theologian, seminary teacher, pastor, and author of numerous and diverse works on theology, philosophy, ethics, history, and political economy. Although frequently quoted by scholars, historians and theologians, he is unfortunately little known today by the general public. He was, however, among the most prominent men of his era. His service in the Confederate Army as a Chaplain and for a time as Stonewall Jackson's Chief of Staff was by no means the limit of his great accomplishments. He was a scholar and social commentator of enormous breadth and penetrating insight. Much of Dabney's writing is as relevant today as it was in the late nineteenth century. While he is long dead, he yet speaks with near prophetic clarity on issues facing the nation and especially the South today. His words are particularly relevant to the present discussion of the heritage and future of the South. In our own time as in his, Southern Heritage is being constantly battered by politically correct propaganda. Today as never before, there are powerful organizations and ambitious power seekers who butter their political and economic bread by purveying historical ignorance and misinformation as a form of olic righteousness. Politicians, educators, businessmen, churchmen, and whole states are cowered and blackmailed into accepting outrageous distortions of history. We suffer a time of too little knowledge and too little courage. Our own generations would do well to heed Dabney's passionate and fiery exhortation on that day in 1882, a few paragraphs of which are here quoted:

"It behooves the New South, in dismissing the animosities of the past, to see to it that they retain all that was true in its principles or ennobling in its example. There are those pretending to belong to this company who exclaim: 'Let us bury the dead past. Its issues are all antiquated, and of no more practical significance. Let us forget the passions of the past. We are in a new world. Its new questions alone concern us.' I rejoin: Be sure that the former issues are dead before you really bury them! There are issues that cannot die without the death of the people, of their honor, their civilization, and their greatness. Take care that you do not bury too much, while burying the dead past: that you do not bury the inspiring memories of great patriots, whose actions, whether successful or not, are the eternal glory of your race and section; the influence of their virtues, the guiding precedents of their histories. Will you bury the names and memories of a Jackson and Lee, and their noble army of martyrs? Will you bury true history whose years are those of the God of Truth?"

"There is one point on which you insist too little, which is vital to the young citizens of the South. This is, that he shall not allow the dominant party to teach him a perverted history of the past contests. This is a mistake of which you are in imminent peril. With all the astute activity of their race, our conquerors strain every nerve to pre-occupy the ears of all America with the false version of affairs which suits the purposes of their usurpation. With a gigantic sweep of mendacity, this literature aims to falsify or misrepresent everything; the very facts of history, the principles of the former Constitution as admitted in the days of freedom by all statesmen of all parties; the very essential names of rights and virtues and vices. The whole sway of their commercial and political ascendancy is exerted to fill the South with this false literature. Its sheets come up, like the frogs of Egypt, into our houses, our bed chambers, our very kneading troughs. Now, against this deluge of perversions I solemnly warn young men of the South, not for our sakes, but for their own. Even if the memory of the defeated had no rights; if historical truth had no prerogatives; if it were the same to you that the sires whose blood fills your veins, and whose names you bear, be written down as traitors by the pen of slanderous history, still it is essential to your own future that you shall learn the history of the past truly."

Today as equaled only in the days of Reconstruction, there are those who would bury truth and honor to gain peace and prosperity. The perversion of history that Dabney warned of in 1882 prevails as never before in our media, our educational institutions, the halls of government, in the giant business corporations with their vast economic power, and even in many of our churches. It is time we resurrected Dabney's words and with them the courage to insist that our children and future generations learn history free of outrageous distortion and propaganda, that they learn the history of the past fully and truly.

The Secession Declarations

Four seceding Southern states published some form of declaration of their reasons for secession. These were South Carolina, Georgia, Mississippi, and Texas. Many modern academic allies of the Northern War to Prevent Southern Independence have recently taken up the cry that because these declarations have many references to slavery that they are proof that the war was all about slavery. First of all, however, there is a difference between the cause of the war and the causes of secession. The cause of the war was Lincoln's call for 75,000 troops to invade the Southern states. This invasion immediately triggered four more state secessions—Virginia, North Carolina, Tennessee, and Arkansas—in addition to protests from the governors of Kentucky and Missouri, and unrest in Maryland.

continued on next page

The Secession Declarations

continued from previous page

In addition, the substance of the secession declarations must be interpreted in their political/economic and constitutional contexts. The Northern Union had become an oppressive government dedicated to Northern regional dominance and almost exclusively Northern economic prosperity. States Rights were the primary bulwark against this Northern regionalism. Many modern apologists for the Union cause also fail to recognize that these declarations, following South Carolina's example, were building a legal case against Northern breaches of the Constitution. Moreover, much of the language of these declarations was a protest against the constant inflammatory distortions and repeated attacks on Southern honor by radical abolitionists in Congress and in the Northern press.

The Mississippi declaration included an admission of its economic dependence on slave labor. However, over-dramatizing this admission in accusatory terms fails to recognize a genuine dilemma. Many Southerners, probably a majority, would have gladly rid themselves of slavery. But how could it be done without destroying the economies of the major cotton producing states and severely damaging New York banking and shipping interests? Many also saw the necessity of preparing the slaves to compete in a free economy before emancipation. Many would have followed the British model of gradual emancipation with compensation to slave owners.

What the secession declarations prove is that Southerners had strong reasons to believe that their political rights and economic welfare were unsafe under Northern political dominance.

CHAPTER 3

cx/cx

Politically Correct History

Making Slavery the Cause of the Un-Civil War

Abraham Lincoln

What was the cause of the so-called American "Civil War"? Post war Union propaganda generally served up a self-justifying misrepresentation of the war as a morality play in which a noble Union Army marched forth to battle for the glorious purpose of emancipating downtrodden slaves from evil Southerners. This explanation has been continued in an even more strident and self-righteous form in modern political correctness. This is usually supplemented with assertions that the South also had to be conquered (and hundreds of thousands of people killed) to "save" the Union. These often repeated assertions attempt to claim the moral high ground for Northern aggression and to discredit the South's resistance to that aggression as "morally wrong," as one incredibly arrogant editorial in a nominally Southern newspaper put it. This is insulting to those Southerners who have not surrendered mind and soul to the truth suppressing tyranny of modern reconstruction. It should also be disconcerting to anyone who values truth and eschews politically motivated distortion.

No serious student of the "Civil War" believes that the Union invaded the South to emancipate the slaves. Such ignorance, however, is common place. This propagandistic version of the war is commonly taught in public schools and in ignorance even in many Christian schools. Yet it has little basis in fact. Slavery was an issue between North and South, but not in the propagandistic, fabricated moral sense usually assumed.

First of all, the thinking of most Northerners about race and slavery before and after the war was not of the high moral tone usually believed. The Free State versus Slave State controversy was not over the moral question of slavery. It was, as Lincoln said regarding Kansas and Nebraska in 1854, about preserving these states **"for the homes of free white people."** When Pennsylvania Congressman David Wilmot introduced his famous 1846 proviso that slavery would be excluded from territories acquired after the Mexican War, he explained his motivation:

"I would preserve to free white labor a fair country, a rich inheritance, where the sons of toil, of my own race and color, can live without the disgrace which association with Negro slavery brings upon free labor."

Most Northern states did not want blacks within their borders, and Indiana, Ohio, Illinois, and Oregon had strict laws to enforce this bias. As an Illinois Legislator, Abraham Lincoln fully approved of such laws. The "underground railroad" for escaped slaves went to Canada because the intervening Union states did not want blacks in their territory. Even after the war, voters in Ohio, Michigan, Minnesota, and Kansas refused to extend the right to vote to blacks.

Some of Lincoln's public and private remarks are shocking to those who have been taught the whitewashed version of American history that lifts up Lincoln as the Great Emancipator. Lerone Bennett, Jr., Editor of *Ebony Magazine*, has pointed out that:

"On at least fourteen occasions between 1854 and 1860 Lincoln said unambiguously that he believed the Negro race was inferior to the White race."

In the September 1858 debate with Stephen Douglas in Ottawa, Illinois, Lincoln insisted vigorously that:

"I will say that I am not...in favor of making voters or jurors of Negroes, nor of qualifying them to hold office, nor to intermarry with white people...Anything that argues me into his (Douglas's) **idea of perfect social and political equality with the Negro is but a specious**

and fantastic arrangement of words, by which a man can prove a horse chestnut to be a chestnut horse."

Lincoln was for gradual, slave-owner compensated emancipation of slaves, a common sentiment in both North and South. But he did not believe the black and white races could coexist in the same country. He favored deporting them and colonizing them to the Caribbean, Central America, or Africa. Lincoln was a very strong admirer of Henry Clay, a slave owner and one of the founding members of the American Colonization Society. In his 1852 eulogy of Clay, Lincoln quoted Clay's words on colonization of blacks back to Africa approvingly:

"There is a moral fitness in the idea of returning to Africa her children...they will carry back to their native soil the rich fruits of religion, civilization, law and liberty."

In his famous Cooper Union speech on February 27, 1860, he advocated the peaceful **"deportation"** of blacks so that **"their places be... filled up by free white laborers."**

In 1862 Lincoln met with a deputation of free blacks in the White House intending to persuade them of the benefits of colonization. His words, severely criticized by Horace Greeley in the *New York Tribune*, are astonishing in the light of his near deification by civil rights groups and most political leaders today:

"You and we are of different races. Your race suffers very greatly by living among us while ours suffers from your presence. Even when you cease to be slaves, you are yet far removed from being on equality with the white man...Go where you are treated the best, and the ban is still upon you. I do not propose to discuss this, but to present it as fact. It is better for us, therefore, to be separated."

Later Lincoln suggested to the occupation Governor of Louisiana in regard to elective franchise that some blacks, the very intelligent and those who had served in the Union ranks, "be let in."

Much to the constant dismay of the abolitionists, slavery was imbedded in the U.S. Constitution and could not be removed without a Constitutional Amendment. In early 1861, to ensure the South that slavery would not be endangered, the U. S. Congress, now composed of only Northern states, passed a prospective Constitutional Amendment that would have forever prohibited any Constitutional change that interfered with slavery in any state, and this was endorsed by Lincoln in his inaugural speech. This Amendment, however, became a moot issue after Lincoln's call for 75,000 troops to invade the South following Confederate occupation of Fort Sumter in South Carolina.

Of course, Lincoln also stated unequivocally in his first inaugural address what he had previously written to *New York Tribune* Editor, Horace Greeley:

"I have no purpose, directly or indirectly, to interfere with the institution of slavery in the States where it exists. I believe I have no right to do so, and I have no inclination to do so."

Furthermore, the Northern Congress passed a Resolution on July 22, 1861, stating specifically that preserving the Union and maintaining the supremacy of the Constitution and not interfering with slavery were the purposes of the war. Their statement about maintaining the supremacy of the Constitution was truth and logic turned on its head, and the role of the South in this involuntary Union was comparable to the subjugated status of the Baltic States under the Soviet Union, but they were emphatic that they had no intention of overthrowing the institution of slavery.

Like Lincoln, the vast majority of Northern whites did not have very sympathetic attitudes towards blacks. Lincoln and most Northerners, like most Southerners, thought emancipation should be gradual. Only a tiny minority of radical abolitionists wanted an immediate end to slavery regardless of the economic consequences to the South or the freed slaves. Northerners actually feared that emancipated Southern slaves might emigrate to the North.

The abolitionists, although representing less than two percent of the Northern population, did have a tremendous impact on Southern thinking. The Free State versus Slave State Controversy erupted into border warfare between Missouri and Kansas in the 1850's. Missouri came into the Union as a Slave State. Approximately 80 percent of its people were of Southern origin. Not many Missourians owned slaves, but they were sympathetic to the South and were of conservative Democrat political persuasion. The North hoped to make Kansas a Free State, and New England abolitionists encouraged emigration there to secure Northern Republican domination. Many Southerners, however, also desired to take advantage of new land opportunities in Kansas. The result was "bleeding Kansas," where there was frequent armed conflict between Northern immigrants and Southern immigrants from Missouri. Southern sympathizers in Missouri began to engage in reprisals for injustices to Missouri settlers in Kansas, and bands of Kansas "Jayhawkers" or "Redlegs" began to raid, burn, loot, and kill in Missouri. Missouri raiders responded by sacking the Northern abolitionist stronghold of Lawrence, Kansas in 1856.

Into this volatile situation New England abolitionists were sending money and arms. One man they financed and sent with arms was the radical abolitionist and Bible quoting Unitarian, John Brown. In May of 1856, near Pottawatomie Creek, Kansas, John Brown and six of his followers, including four of his sons, paid a night visit to several farms owned by Missouri men. They roused five men and their families from bed and brutally hacked the five men to death with swords. This was a heinous crime, but John Brown was praised in much of the Northern press where abolitionism had a strong foothold. Even today John Brown is admired by some civil rights extremists, and it is amazing to see how many short biographies of Brown completely omit the Charles Manson style Pottawatomie killings. In 1859 John Brown would show up at the armory at Harper's Ferry, Virginia, with twenty-one men intending to lead a slave revolt far wider in scope and deeper in blood than his famous crimes in Kansas. Brown was captured and hanged in Virginia, but the Northern press, and many influential Northern clergy and political leaders proclaimed John Brown a hero comparable to Christ. This enraged the South and made Southerners very suspect of Northern good will.

Because Northern abolitionists constantly engaged in propaganda campaigns to encourage bloody slave revolts in the South, Southerners had a fear and loathing of abolitionism. There had not been many slave revolts in the South, but the memory of the Nat Turner Rebellion in 1832 in which sixty whites, mostly women and children, were savagely murdered, was still fresh on the mind of Southerners. This fear for their families and loathing of abolitionist ideology was amplified by frequent abolitionist misrepresentation of the conditions of slavery in the South, their insulting and morally arrogant characterization of everything Southern, and their vicious verbal attacks on Southern leaders.   Hence an important way in which slavery was a cause of the war was Southern fear of abolitionist influence on Southern slaves and on Northern politicians. As it turned out, their fear of abolitionist influence on Northern politicians was not without justification. Following the war the abolitionists, aligning themselves with the Radical Republicans, made an immense contribution to the vengeful despotism of Reconstruction.

Only about 20% of Confederate soldiers owned slaves, and only about one-third came from slave-holding families. So far as slavery was concerned they only wanted the right to deal with it in their own way in their own time state by state, just as the Northern states, all of which had slavery in 1776, had done.

When Union Armies invaded the South in 1861, they had no intention of freeing the slaves. They invaded the South to enforce political unity and Northern economic and legislative dominance by bayonets. Lincoln's Emancipation Proclamation, on January 1, 1863, came after more than 19 months of war and did not actually free any slaves in the Union or Union held areas of the Confederacy. It was a complete fraud that has been turned into a modern civil rights icon. The Proclamation was according to Lincoln himself done as a war measure in hopes of causing disorder in the South. Only later was the slavery issue used in an attempt to give tyranny a pious justification.

A major cause of the war was the tariff system that exploited the South unmercifully for the benefit of Northern commercial and industrial interests. The final blow was the Morrill Tariff, passed by the U.S. House on May 10, 1860, and signed into law on March 2, 1861. Only one Southern Congressman had voted for this enormous tariff increase that would benefit Northern interests and impoverish the South. The Morrill Tariff was so disparate in its generous benefits for the North and severe burdens for the South that it left no recourse but secession to the cotton producing Gulf States. Other Southern states joined them, when Lincoln revealed his plans to subjugate the South by armed force. The Morrill Tariff was notable for its shameless regional partisanship and greed. Its egregious disregard for the welfare of Southern states is a very important historical issue that has been suppressed by those who wish to present the Northern cause as a glorious crusade for human rights and national unity.

Preserving the Union was the principal purpose of the war stated by the North. That might be called noble; if forcing states to bear an exploited status in an unwanted and to them unprofitable Union by gunpoint can be called noble. Was Germany's annexation of Austria just before the Second World War noble? Was the Soviet Union's totalitarian grip on Estonia, Latvia, and Lithuania noble? Should the American Colonies in

1776 have submitted gladly to continued exploitation and unjust taxation by the British? The North had more than just territory in mind when preserving the Union. Loss of the Southern States would mean loss of most tax revenues, of which over 90% were from the tariff that so burdened the South. They would also have to compete with the South's proposed free trade policies, which would have wreaked economic havoc in the North, just as the tariff had wreaked economic havoc in the South. A unity of territories can be accomplished by might. But might does not make right. Union enforced by bayonets is despotic hypocrisy. Such a coerced union is tyranny and the enemy of liberty.

How did the role of slavery become so distorted and exaggerated as a cause of the "Civil War"? In the words of President Woodrow Wilson:

"It was necessary to put the South at a moral disadvantage by transforming the contest from a war waged against states fighting for their independence into a war waged against states fighting for the maintenance and extension of slavery..."

The "Civil War" was not really a civil war. For the North it was a War to Prevent Southern Independence. It was not a glorious crusade to free slaves. Unfortunately, most Americans today accept the pious fraud that the "Civil War" was all about ending slavery and "preserving" the Union. Lincoln's own words, the proceedings of Congress, and a multitude of other records provide shattering documentary evidence disproving that cherished humbug.

Cleburne's Warning

"Surrender means that the history of this heroic struggle will be written by the enemy; that our youth will be trained by Northern school teachers; will learn from Northern school books their version of the War; will be impressed by all the influences of history and education to regard our gallant dead as traitors, and our maimed Veterans as fit subjects for derision"

—*Major General Patrick Cleburne, CSA, shortly before his death at the Battle of Franklin, Tennessee, November 30, 1864*

CHAPTER 4

The Morrill Tariff

Understanding the Real Causes of the War

Justin Morrill

Most Americans believe the U. S. "Civil War" was over slavery. They have to an enormous degree been miseducated. The means and timing of handling the slavery question were at issue, although not in the overly simplified moral sense that lives in postwar and modern propaganda. But had there been no Morrill Tariff there might never have been a war. The conflict that cost the lives of 620,000 Union and Confederate soldiers and perhaps as many as 50,000 Southern civilians and impoverished many millions for generations might never have been.

A smoldering issue of unjust taxation that enriched Northern manufacturing states and exploited the agricultural South was fanned to a furious blaze in 1860. It was the Morrill Tariff that stirred the smoldering embers of regional mistrust and ignited the fires of Secession in the South. This precipitated a Northern reaction and call to arms that would engulf the nation in the flames of war for four years.

Prior to the U. S. "Civil War" there was no U. S. income tax. In 1860, approximately 95% of U. S. government revenue was raised by a *tariff* on imported goods. A *tariff* is a tax on selected imports, most commonly finished or manufactured products. A high tariff is usually legislated not only to raise revenue, but also to protect domestic industry form foreign competition. By placing such a high *protective tariff* on imported goods it makes them more expensive to buy than the same domestic goods. This allows domestic industries to charge higher prices and make more money on sales that might otherwise be lost to foreign competition because of cheaper prices (without the tariff) or better quality. This, of course, causes domestic consumers to pay higher prices and have a lower standard of living. Tariffs on some industrial products also hurt other domestic industries that must pay higher prices for goods they need to make their products. Because the nature and products of regional economies can vary widely, high tariffs are sometimes good for one section of the country, but damaging to another section of the country. High tariffs are particularly hard on exporters since they must cope with higher domestic costs and retaliatory foreign tariffs that put them at a pricing disadvantage. This has a depressing effect on both export volume and profit margins. High tariffs have been a frequent cause of economic disruption, strife, and war.

Prior to 1824 the average tariff level in the U. S. had been in the 15 to 20% range. This was thought sufficient to meet federal revenue needs and not excessively burdensome to any section of the country. The increase of the tariff to a 20% average in 1816 was ostensibly to help pay for the War of 1812. It also represented a 26% net profit increase to Northern manufacturers.

In 1824 Northern manufacturing states and the Whig Party under the leadership of Henry Clay began to push for high protective tariffs. These were strongly opposed by the South. The Southern economy was largely agricultural and geared to exporting a large portion of its cotton and tobacco crops to Europe. In the 1850's the South accounted for anywhere from 72 to 82% of U. S. exports. They were largely dependent, however, on Europe or the North for the manufactured goods needed for both agricultural production and consumer goods. Northern states received about 20% of the South's agricultural production. The vast majority of export volume went to Europe. A protective tariff was a substantial benefit to Northern manufacturing states, but meant considerable economic hardship for the agricultural South

Northern political dominance enabled Clay and his allies in Congress to pass a tariff averaging 35% late in 1824. This was the cause of economic boom in the North, but economic hardship and political agitation in the South. South Carolina was especially hard hit, the State's exports falling 25% over the next two years. In 1828 in a demonstration of unabashed partisanship and unashamed greed the Northern dominated Congress raised the average tariff level to 50%.

Despite strong Southern agitation for lower tariffs the Tariff of 1832 only nominally reduced the effective tariff rate and brought no relief to the South. These last two tariffs are usually termed in history as the *Tariffs of Abomination.*

This led to the Nullification Crisis of 1832 when South Carolina called a state convention and "nullified" the 1828 and 1832 tariffs as unjust and unconstitutional. The resulting constitutional crisis came very near provoking armed conflict at that time. Through the efforts of former U. S. Vice President and U. S. Senator from South Carolina, John C. Calhoun, a compromise was effected in 1833 which over a few years reduced the tariff back to a normal level of about 15%. Henry Clay and the Whigs were not happy, however, to have been forced into a compromise by Calhoun and South Carolina's Nullification threat. The tariff, however, remained at a level near 15% until 1860. A lesson in economics, regional sensitivities, and simple fairness should have been learned from this confrontation, but if it was learned, it was ignored by ambitious political and business factions and personalities that would come on the scene of American history in the late 1850's.

High protective tariffs were always the policy of the old Whig Party and had become the policy of the new Republican Party that replaced it. A recession beginning around 1857 gave the cause of protectionism an additional political boost in the Northern industrial states.

In May of 1860 the U. S. Congress passed the Morrill Tariff Bill (named for Republican Congressman and steel manufacturer, Justin S. Morrill of Vermont) raising the average tariff from about 15% to 37% with increases to 47% within three years. Because more items were covered, tariff revenues were approximately tripled. Although this was remarkably reminiscent of the Tariffs of Abomination which had led in 1832 to a constitutional crisis and threats of secession and armed force, the U.S. House of Representatives passed the Bill 105 to 64. Out of 40 Southern Congressmen only one Tennessee Congressman voted for it.

U. S. tariff revenues already fell disproportionately on the South, accounting for 87% of the total even before the Morrill Tariff. While the tariff protected Northern industrial interests, it raised the cost of living and commerce in the South substantially. It also reduced the trade value of their agricultural exports to Europe. These combined to place a severe economic hardship on many Southern states. Even more galling was that 80% or more of these tax revenues were expended on Northern public works and industrial subsidies, thus further enriching the North at the expense of the South.

In the 1860 election, Lincoln, a former Whig and great admirer of Henry Clay, campaigned for the high protective tariff provisions of the Morrill Tariff, which had also been incorporated into the Republican Party Platform. Thaddeus Stevens, the most powerful Republican in Congress and one of the co-sponsors of the Morrill Tariff, told an audience in New York City on September 27, 1860, that the two most important issues of the Presidential campaign were preventing the extension of slavery to new states and an increase in the tariff, but that the most important of the two was increasing the tariff. Stevens, a Pennsylvania iron manufacturer, was also one of the most radical abolitionists in Congress. He told the New York audience that the tariff would enrich the northeastern states and impoverish the southern and western states, but that it was essential for advancing national greatness and the prosperity of industrial workers. Stevens, who would become virtually the "boss' of America after the assassination of Lincoln, advised the crowd that if Southern leaders objected, they would be rounded up and hanged.

Two days before Lincoln's election in November of 1860, an editorial in the *Charleston Mercury* summed up the feeling of South Carolina on the impending national crisis:

"The real causes of dissatisfaction in the South with the North, are in the unjust taxation and expenditure of the taxes by the Government of the United States, and in the revolution the North has effected in this government, from a confederated republic, to a national sectional despotism."

With the election of Lincoln and strengthened Northern dominance in Congress, Southern leaders in South Carolina and the Gulf states began to call for secession. The U.S. Senate finally passed the Morrill Tariff on March 2, 1861, on an outrageously partisan vote. Not a single Southern Senator voted for it. It was immediately signed into law by President James Buchanan, a Pennsylvania Democrat. Lincoln endorsed the Tariff in his March 4 inaugural speech and promised to enforce it even on seceding Southern states. The South was filled with righteous indignation.

At first Northern public opinion as reflected in Northern newspapers of both parties recognized the right of the Southern States to secede and favored peaceful separation. A November 21, 1860, editorial in the *Cincinnati Daily Press* said this:

"We believe that the right of any member of this Confederacy to dissolve its political relations with the others and assume an independent position is absolute."

The *New York Times* on March 21, 1861, reflecting the great majority of editorial opinion in the North summarized in an editorial: "There is a growing sentiment throughout the North in favor of letting the Gulf States go."

Northern industrialists became nervous, however, when they realized a tariff dependent North would be competing against a free-trade South. They feared not only loss of tax revenue, but considerable loss of trade. Newspaper editorials began to reflect this nervousness. Events in April would engulf the nation in cataclysmic war.

Lincoln met secretly on April 4, 1861, with Colonel John Baldwin, a delegate to the Virginia Secession Convention. Baldwin, like a majority of that convention would have preferred to keep Virginia in the Union. But Baldwin learned at that meeting that Lincoln was already committed to taking some military action at Fort Sumter in South Carolina. He desperately tried to persuade Lincoln that military action against South Carolina would mean war and also result in Virginia's secession. Baldwin tried to persuade Lincoln that if the Gulf States were allowed to secede peacefully, historical and economic ties would eventually persuade them to reunite with the North. Lincoln's decisive response was,

"And open Charleston, etc. as ports of entry with their ten percent tariff? What then would become of my tariff?"

Despite Colonel Baldwin's advice, on April 12, 1861, Lincoln manipulated the South into firing on the tariff collection facility of Fort Sumter in volatile South Carolina. This achieved an important Lincoln objective. Northern opinion was now enflamed against the South for "firing on the flag." Three days later Lincoln called for 75,000 volunteers to put down the Southern "rebellion". This caused the Border States to secede along with the Gulf States. Lincoln undoubtedly calculated that the mere threat of force backed by a now more unified Northern public opinion would quickly put down secession. His gambit, however, failed spectacularly and would erupt into a terrible and costly war for four years.

Shortly after Lincoln's call to put down the "rebellion;" a prominent Northern politician wrote to Colonel Baldwin to enquire what Union men in Virginia would do now. His response was:

"There are now no Union men in Virginia. But those who were Union men will stand to their arms, and make a fight which shall go down in history as an illustration of what a brave people can do in defense of their liberties, after having exhausted every means of pacification."

The Union Army's lack of success early in the war, the need to keep anti-slavery England from coming into the war on the side of the South, and Lincoln's need to appease the radical abolitionists in the North led to increased promotion of freeing the slaves as a noble cause to justify what was really a dispute over fair taxation and States Rights.

Writing in December of 1861 in a London weekly publication, the famous English author, Charles Dickens, who was a strong opponent of slavery, said these things about the war going on in America:

"The Northern onslaught upon slavery is no more than a piece of specious humbug disguised to conceal its desire for economic control of the United States."

Karl Marx, like most European socialists of the time, favored the North. In an 1861 article published in England, he articulated very well what the major British newspapers, *The Times, The Economist, and Saturday Review,* had been saying:

"The war between the North and South is a tariff war. The war, is further, not for any principle, does not touch the question of slavery, and in fact turns on the Northern lust for power."

The Tariff question and the States Rights question were therefore strongly linked. Both are linked to the broader issues of limited government and a strong Constitution. The Morrill Tariff dealt the South a flagrant political injustice and impending economic hardship and crisis. It therefore made Secession a very compelling alternative to an exploited and unequal union with the North.

How to handle the slavery question was an underlying tension between North and South, but only one of many tensions. It cannot be said to be the cause of the war. Fully understanding the slavery question and its relations to those tensions is beyond our scope here, but numerous historical facts demolish the propagandistic morality play that a virtuous North invaded the evil South to free the slaves. Five years after the end of the War, prominent Northern abolitionist, attorney and legal scholar, Lysander Spooner, put it this way:

"All these cries of having 'abolished slavery,' of having 'saved the country,' of having 'preserved the Union,' of establishing a 'government of consent,' and of 'maintaining the national honor' are all gross, shameless, transparent cheats—so transparent that they ought to deceive no one."

Yet apparently many today are still deceived and even prefer to be deceived.

The Southern states had seen that continued union with the North would jeopardize their liberties and economic wellbeing. Through the proper constitutional means of state conventions and referendums they sought to withdraw from the Union and establish their independence just as the American Colonies had sought their independence from Great Britain in 1776 and for very similar reasons. The Northern industrialists, however, were not willing to give up their Southern Colonies.

In addition to the devastating loss of life and leadership during the War, the South suffered considerable damage to property, livestock, and crops. The policies of "Reconstruction" and "carpetbagger" state governments further exploited and robbed the South, considerably retarding economic recovery. Further, high tariffs and discriminatory railroad shipping taxes continued to favor Northern economic interests and impoverish the South for generations after the war. It is only in relatively recent history that the political and economic fortunes of the South have begun to rise.

Unjust taxation has been the cause of many tensions and much bloodshed throughout history. The Morrill Tariff was certainly a powerful factor predisposing the South to seek its independence and determine its own destiny. As outrageous and unjust as the Morrill Tariff was, its importance has been largely ignored and even purposely obscured. It does not fit the politically correct images and myths of popular American history. Truth, however, is always the high ground. It will have the inevitable victory.

Had it not been for the Morrill Tariff there would have been no rush to secession by Southern states and very probably no war. The Morrill Tariff of 1860, so unabashed and unashamed in its short-sighted, partisan greed, stands as an astonishing monument to the self-centered depravity of man and to its consequences. No wonder most Americans would like to see it forgotten and covered over with a more morally satisfying but largely false version of the causes of the Un-Civil War.

CHAPTER 5

⊙ℨ⊙

The Abolitionists

John Brown

Several years ago, the guests on a popular Christian radio program tried to make the point that the pro-life movement was comparable to the abolitionist movement of the Civil War era. This is a colossal historical error resulting from a complete misunderstanding of the abolitionists and a shallow understanding of the causes and politics of that war.

The term "abolitionist" had a radical connotation in that era that distinguished those so described from the great bulk of people who favored the emancipation of slaves. Most Americans, both North and South, favored the gradual emancipation of slaves. Reasonable people believed that prior to emancipation some training and education would be necessary to assure the economic success and social adjustment of newly freed slaves. They also reasoned that slave owners should be compensated for their loss. In addition, they were cognizant of the social and economic dangers inherent in making such huge changes abruptly. The abolitionists, however, insisted on the immediate emancipation of slaves no matter what the consequences might be to the Southern economy, the slave owners, and the slaves themselves.

Many of the abolitionist leaders were ordained clergy, but they were predominantly Unitarian rather than Christian. Moreover, abolitionist clergy of Christian denominations tended to embrace many of the theological tenets of their Unitarian brethren.

The principal difference between Unitarians and Christians is that Unitarians do not believe in the Trinity or the divinity of Christ. They also reject a high view of Scripture, disdaining any claim of its divine inspiration. They generally believe in the innate goodness and perfectibility of man in contrast to the biblical and traditional Christian concept of original sin and the natural depravity of men. Hence Unitarians see no need of redemption or a Savior. Consequently, their worldview tends to be more humanistic than theistic and leans toward abstract idealism rather than realism in dealing with the complexities and contingencies of life and social order.

The Unitarianism of the Civil War era was closely associated with universalism and transcendentalism. Universalism is a belief in the universal salvation of all mankind. Transcendentalism involved such things as séances and extrasensory perception. Not all abolitionists were Unitarians, but Unitarian theology was pervasive among its leaders and activists.

The theological framework of the abolitionist worldview resulted in a fanatical and self-righteous zeal willing to change society by whatever means. Not every abolitionist was characterized by the ruthless and sometimes savage extremes of its most famous activist leaders, but in its rank and file there was an underlying sympathy that rejoiced whenever bloody and despotic retribution was inflicted on their enemies. Their enemy was not only the institution of slavery, but also the South. Because slavery and States Rights were institutionalized in the U.S. Constitution of 1787, they despised that Constitution.

The most famous abolitionist, whose murderous rampages helped create an underlying regional distrust so strong as to be a major cause of the Civil War, was John Brown. In 1855, Brown was sponsored by six wealthy New England abolitionists to move to Kansas with the purpose of arming abolitionists there. One of these sponsors was Thomas Wentworth Higginson, a Unitarian minister whose radical leftist career stretched until 1911. Brown also became a raider into pro-Southern settlements in western Missouri. At Pottawatomie Creek, Kansas, on May 24, 1856, he led four of his sons and two other men in a midnight massacre of Missouri immigrants in that area. Five men were rousted from their homes in the middle of the night and then brutally slaughtered and mutilated with swords. Rather than condemning this Charles Manson-style murderer and terrorist, much of the Northern press made him into a hero of the anti-slavery movement.

Julia Ward Howe

In 1858, Brown led 21 followers in a brief raid on the Federal arsenal at Harpers Ferry, (West) Virginia, hoping to start a bloody slave revolt in the South. Several innocent people were killed, the first of whom was black. Ten of Brown's followers were killed when a detachment of U.S. Marines, under the command of U.S. Army Col. Robert E. Lee and Lieutenant Jeb Stuart, arrived on the scene. Brown was wounded and captured with the rest of his men. He was tried and hanged at Harpers Ferry on December 2, 1858. Again, he became a national hero of the abolitionist movement. What really disturbed Southerners was that so many newspapers and prominent citizens were praising Brown for his heinous atrocities and actions that might have resulted in thousands of deaths in an armed slave revolt.

John Brown was very fond of quoting the Old Testament, but his attitude toward biblical authority was typical of the abolitionists. They believed in higher truth than Scripture. Rev. H. D. King, who once talked with Brown about his religious beliefs, quoted his attitude toward the Bible:

"If any great obstacle stands in the way, you may properly break all the Decalogue (Ten Commandments) **to get rid of it."**

King noted that for Brown, **"there was only one wrong and that was slavery."**

In general, the abolitionists were anti-biblical and hostile to orthodox forms of Christianity. Yet they set themselves up as expositors of the Will of God. The theology of abolitionism can be seen clearly in statements by Unitarian transcendentalist Julia Ward Howe, author of the words to the *Battle Hymn of the Republic:*

"Not until the Civil War did I officially join the Unitarian Church and accept the fact that Christ was merely a great teacher with no higher claim to preeminence in wisdom, goodness, and power than many other men."

"Having rejected the exclusive doctrine that made Christianity and special forms of it the only way of spiritual redemption, I now accept the belief that not only Christians but all human beings, no matter what their religion, are capable of redemption."

Mrs. Howe and her husband, Dr. Samuel Gridley Howe, were early and radical enthusiasts for the abolition movement. Just before John Brown was hanged, Mrs. Howe had this to say about him:

"John Brown will glorify the gallows like Jesus glorified the Cross."

Another famous Unitarian transcendentalist, Ralph Waldo Emerson, called Brown a saint and a martyr and echoed Mrs. Howe's comparison of John Brown's hanging with the crucifixion of Christ.

Fellow abolitionist and transcendentalist, Henry David Thoreau, made this connection between Christ and the merciless terrorist, John Brown:

"Some eighteen hundred years ago Christ was crucified; this morning, perchance, Captain Brown was hung. These are the two ends of a chain which is not without its links. He is not Old Brown any longer; he is an angel of light."

It is not without significance that these last two apostate abolitionist writers are usually required reading in public high schools.

The abolitionist philosophy that the end justifies the means was also found in the Radical Republicans. The Radical Republicans were often radical abolitionists as well but with a slightly different twist. Though they used idealistic rhetoric in abundance, most of them had little real interest in the welfare of slaves or freed slaves. More typically they were interested in manipulating them to gain political power and to plunder the conquered Southern States. This became most evident during Reconstruction.

The Radical Republicans knew that the Republican Party, coming into power only by a plurality vote because of a split in the Democratic Party in 1860, would lose power if the Southern States were readmitted to the Union—unless there was a radical change in their polity. Therefore, they disenfranchised all Confederate veterans and enfranchised blacks in the Southern States. They had no intention, however, of giving blacks in the Northern States the right to vote. The Radical Republicans were noted for their hypocrisy, corruption, ruthless political tactics, and hatred for the South.

President Lincoln was not an abolitionist himself. In fact, he hated both the abolitionists and the Radical Republicans, but he had to pay them considerable regard to manage his majority in Congress. Unfortunately, his Secretary of War, Edwin Stanton, turned out to be a leading Radical Republican collaborator. Both Lincoln and Congress had stated that ending slavery was not the purpose of the war. But Stanton thought it was necessary to destroy Southern society and replace it with a Radical Republican society. Stanton even wanted to prolong the war to further devastate the South. In George B. McClellan's autobiography, he quotes Major Charles Davies, who was part of a delegation that met with Stanton at the White House early in the war:

"Mr. Stanton stated that the great end and aim of the war was to abolish slavery. To end the war before the nation was ready for that would be a failure. The war must be prolonged, and conducted so as to achieve that."

In Congress the leading abolitionist and Radical Republican was Thaddeus Stevens. In a December 1865 speech, he made very clear his objective in reconstructing the South:

"…and so as to secure ascendancy to the party of the Union."

In other words, he wanted a one-party State. Stevens believed that all the social foundations of the South had to "be broken up and relaid." Southerners had to be treated as a conquered people and held in subjugation.

The abolitionists were infatuated with every socially destructive fashion known to man: socialism, communism, feminism, egalitarianism, and a host of other "isms." Coercion and fanaticism were their trademarks.

Theologian Robert L. Dabney spoke the truth about the abolitionists, when he noted:

"Your true abolitionist is then, of course, a Red-Republican, a Jacobin."

He went on to connect them philosophically with the French Revolution and the "reign of terror." At the root of abolitionism was not freedom or liberty, and certainly not any orthodox form of Christianity. It was apostasy. They should not be known by their propaganda but by their fruits. Those fruits were violence, vengeance, cruelty, corruption, greed, deception, bloody revolution, despotism, tyranny, and rebellion against God, marked by arrogant self-righteousness.

Presbyterian leader James Henley Thornwell was equally direct, describing the abolitionists as "atheists, socialists, communists, red republicans, (and) Jacobins" The contest, he said, was between the forces of atheistic radicalism and "the friends of order and regulated freedom."

There was a great political and philosophical overlap between the abolitionists and the Radical Republicans. Their common objective was radical change in society and government. The old Constitutional Republic, with its decentralized and limited federal powers, would be replaced by a centralized democracy with almost unlimited coercive federal powers capable of making sweeping social and political changes. This, thought the big-business dominated Radical Republicans, was the true path to national greatness. To accomplish such radical changes and maintain political power, the conservative and Democratic South had to be destroyed and reconstructed in such a way that Radical Republican political dominance could never be seriously challenged.

"Woe to those who call evil good and good evil, who put darkness for light and light for darkness...Woe to those who are wise in their own eyes and clever in their own sight." (Isaiah 5: 20a, 21 NIV)

CHAPTER 6

c8x0

Constitutional Issues of the Un-Civil War

Union, Liberty, Secession, States Rights and the Republic

Andrew Jackson

In 1830, President Andrew Jackson, through Senator Thomas Hart Benton of Missouri, arranged for an elaborate Democratic Party dinner to celebrate on April 13, the birthday of Thomas Jefferson and the Jeffersonian principles of the new Democratic Party. This was held at Brown's Indian Queen Hotel in Washington. Political tension was increasing because of the effects of the substantial and controversial tariff increases that had been passed in 1828. These tariffs favored Northern manufacturers and punished farmers, especially those exporting agricultural products.

The tariffs were having the most devastating economic impact on the cotton producing states of the South. Among these, South Carolina, was suffering the most.

Jackson's Vice President, John C. Calhoun of South Carolina, one of the guests of honor, had become one of the leading spokesmen against the "Tariff of Abomination." He, along with many Southern leaders, believed that the tariff of 1828 was unconstitutional because it subsidized one branch of industry, manufacturing, at the expense of commerce and agriculture. Calhoun maintained that a tariff should not tax one section of the economy or one region of the country for the benefit of another. He also believed that a tax on all the people should not be levied for the exclusive enrichment of only a part of the people. There was talk in the South

John C. Calhoun

Carolina legislature of Nullification, refusing to comply with such an unconstitutional, unfair, and very damaging law. There was even talk of Secession.

Senator Robert Hayne of South Carolina was to be the speaker that evening. After his remarks would come both voluntary and special toasts. Besides unifying the Party, Jackson looked upon the toasts as an opportunity for him to promote national and Democratic Party unity and to indicate his displeasure with any talk of Nullification.

Senator Hayne spoke, denouncing the tariff but avoiding any mention of Nullification. But when the voluntary toasts began, they took on an increasingly anti-tariff tenor, and the Pennsylvania delegation walked out.

When it came time for the special toasts, the tension was high. President Jackson rose, holding his glass before him. Rather than sweeping his eyes across the audience, he stared sternly at Calhoun alone and said,

"Our Union, it must be preserved."

The Vice President was next to give his toast. The room was deadly quiet and the tension building even higher. Slowly Calhoun stood, lifted his glass, and in a firm voice directly addressed the President:

"The Union, next to our liberty, most dear."

He paused for a moment and then to make his point unmistakably clear continued,

"May we all remember that it can only be preserved by respecting the rights of the states and by distributing equally the benefits and burdens of the Union."

We may draw a lesson from this famous drama. Union or unity is a beneficial condition of like minded men, but it is not a condition so beneficial that it outweighs every other condition, principle, or virtue. Unity by no means outweighs in their various degrees considerations of liberty, truth, honor, justice, high moral principle, or spiritual fidelity. It cannot outweigh essential human dignities and unalienable rights. If unity does not serve mutual benefit, virtue and principle, its value is nullified. Furthermore, real unity cannot be coerced. Union forced at the point of a bayonet is tyranny and the enemy of liberty and all its virtues and blessings.

Thomas Jefferson

John C. Calhoun is little remembered today by the general public outside of his home state of South Carolina and is often denigrated in politically correct academic circles. He was a slave owner and is identified with the political doctrines of nullification, States Rights, and the right of secession—all doctrines that PC liberals have been taught to hate. But he was one of the giant intellects of political theory in his time, and to the more knowledgeable political historians and political theorists today, he is still a giant, recognized not only in the United States but throughout the entire free world.

It was Thomas Jefferson who first spoke of the doctrine of nullification in American politics. It was also Jefferson who was the strongest advocate of States Rights in the early days of the American republic. Both concepts are solidly grounded in the Magna Carta of 1215. But it was Calhoun who fully developed both doctrines in the 1830's and was very successful in using the doctrine of nullification to negotiate a critical relief for South Carolina and other Southern states from oppressive tariffs that were benefiting the North but devastating the South.

Calhoun also developed an important doctrine called "the concurrent majority." This differs from a simple numerical majority in that it must constitute a majority of all the major divisions of a political polity. Today this might be called a form of consensus government that takes into account the special needs and rights of major political or regional minorities. Switzerland's long life as a multi-ethnic republic is usually attributed to the concurrent majority concepts incorporated into its constitution. The concept of the concurrent majority has uses that go beyond politics. It is also a very useful concept for business, social, and community leadership.

In addition to his political genius, Calhoun was amazingly advanced in his analysis and understanding of economic theory. Consequently, many foreign leaders and political scholars visit South Carolina to study Calhoun's thinking and political theories.

To the extent that Calhoun is denigrated by modern academics and politicians in America we can be sure that liberty is threatened. The doctrine of States Rights is particularly crucial to constitutional government in the United States. Without States Rights the protection of our liberties from centralized despotism is greatly weakened. The great issues of liberty or union and of States Rights or centralized Federal power would culminate in the secession crisis of 1860 and 1861, followed by four years of terrible war.

WAS SECESSION LEGAL?

On July 4, 1776, thirteen British colonies announced their Secession from Great Britain and declared to the world their just reasons:

"When in the Course of human Events, it becomes necessary for one people to dissolve the Political Bands which have connected them with another, and to assume among the Powers of the Earth, the separate and equal Station to which the Laws of Nature and of Nature's God entitle them, a decent Respect to the Opinions of Mankind requires that they should declare the causes which impel them to Separation."

The Declaration of Independence goes on to say that,

"...Governments are instituted among Men, deriving their just powers from the Consent of the Governed, that when ever any Form of Government becomes destructive to these Ends, it is the Right of the People to alter or abolish it, and to institute new Government..."

The Declaration goes on to list numerous grievances against the British Crown and Parliament. Most of these have to do with the British Crown and Parliament usurping the powers of the colonial legislatures. Among the most prominent of these are unjust taxes and taxation without representation. The next most common group of grievances is that the British Crown and Parliament would not listen to their complaints and pleas for relief. In other words, the colonists felt the Crown and Parliament had usurped their States Rights.

In the closing paragraph the signers declare that the colonies are "**Free and Independent States.**" This paragraph also contains the words, "**appealing to the Supreme Judge of the World**" and "**with firm Reliance on the Protection of divine Providence.**" Note that the United States of America were not formed into a single national state, but a confederation of independent and sovereign states.

Previous to the Declaration of Independence, both North Carolina (May 15, 1775) and Virginia (early 1776) had already declared their independence from Great Britain.

The right of self-determination for people seeking independence is firmly established in international law. With U.S. backing, Panama seceded from Colombia in 1903. Norway seceded from Sweden in 1905. In the United States, the right of self determination and therefore secession is supported by the precedence of the Declaration of Independence which declared our own secession from Great Britain.

While the Declaration of Independence is of immense importance as a founding document, it is the Constitution of 1787 and the Bill of Rights ratified in 1791 that are the official founding documents. The Constitution was made official by the approval of the people of each state acting independently in convention, not by the people of the United States in general. Nor did these states surrender their sovereignty to the United States. Only limited governmental powers were delegated to the Federal Government and every state reserved the right to withdraw these powers. In fact, three states—Rhode Island, Virginia, and New York—specifically stated in their ratifications that they reserved the right to withdraw. Other states had less strongly worded reservations, but no state would have ratified the Constitution if they believed that in doing so they would be surrendering their newly won independence. It was to guarantee the sovereignty of the states that the ninth and tenth amendments were added to the Bill of Rights.

The Ninth Amendment: "**The enumeration in the Constitution of certain rights shall not be construed to deny or disparage others retained by the people.**"

The Tenth Amendment: **"The powers not delegated to the United States by the Constitution, nor prohibited by it to the States, are reserved to the States respectively, or to the people."**

Since the Constitution was ratified by sovereign states who desired to retain their sovereignty, it is in essence a compact or contract between the states and the Federal Government acting as their delegated agent. The nation's first Chief Justice, John Jay, although a proponent of a strong central government, in the case of Chisholm versus the State of Georgia, expressly declared that the U.S. Constitution was a compact. The right of withdrawal or secession is inherent in the basic document, but the Ninth and Tenth Amendments further establish it as a right of each state. It is thus the option of each State, not the Federal Government, whether it shall remain in the Union or withdraw. The right of secession was almost universally accepted until Lincoln came up with a new theory of the Constitution based on an 1833 text by Supreme Court Justice Story.

New Hampshire's constitution of 1792 contains very strong words reserving its sovereign powers as a state. In 1798 Thomas Jefferson and James Madison circulated the Kentucky and Virginia Resolutions among the states. These resolutions strongly supported the Doctrine of States Rights and thus also the right of secession. Together these Resolutions became known as the "Principles of '98."

The Kentucky Resolution, the work of Thomas Jefferson, asserts States Rights in very strong terms:

"This Commonwealth is determined to submit to no undelegated and consequently unlimited power, in no man, or body of men on earth, even the President...When powers are assumed which have not been delegated, a nullification of the act is the rightful remedy; and every state has a natural right in cases not within the compact...to nullify of their own authority all assumptions of power by others within their limits...In the questions of power then, let there be no more heard of confidence in man; but bind him down from mischief by the chains of the constitution."

No states disagreed. The Principles of '98 were the principles of the Constitution and Bill of Rights.

The New England states threatened secession on five occasions: in 1803 because they feared the Louisiana Purchase would dilute their political power; in 1807 because the Embargo Act was unfavorable to their commerce; in 1812 over the admission of Louisiana as a state; in 1814 (the Hartford Convention) because of the War of 1812; and in 1814 over the annexation of Texas (which had seceded from Mexico). From 1803 to 1845, any time New England felt their political power or commercial dominance might suffer, they threatened secession. Many New England abolitionists favored secession because the Constitution allowed slavery.

As early as 1825 the right of secession was taught at West Point. William Rawle's *View of the Constitution* specifically taught that secession was a right of each state and was used as a text at West Point in 1825 and 1826 and thereafter as a reference. Rawle was a friend of both George Washington and Benjamin Franklin, and his 1825 text was highly respected and used at many colleges. A subsequent text by James Kent maintained the same position and was used at West Point until the end of the war in 1865. Several Union and Confederate generals were at West Point during the time Rawle's text was used. Rawle even spelled out the procedure for a state to secede, explaining:

"The secession of a state from the Union depends on the will of the people of each state. The people alone...hold the power to alter their constitution."

The right of secession was very well stated by none other than by Congressman Abraham Lincoln himself in 1848:

"Any people anywhere, being inclined and having the power, have the right to rise up and shake off the existing government and form a new one that suits them better. This is a most valuable and most sacred right, a right which we hope and believe is to liberate the world."

That same year Lincoln further stated:

"Any people that can may revolutionize and make their own of so much territory as they inhabit."

But in 1861, Lincoln adopted a view of secession more expedient to holding the Southern states in the Union against their will. He discovered the theory of Supreme Court Justice Joseph Story concocted in 1833, asserting that there was an American nation in the minds of the people before the states were formed. This humbuggery had been strengthened by Daniel Webster's eloquent but emotional rather than factual speeches in Congress.

So Lincoln characterized the orderly secession conventions of South Carolina and the Gulf States, conducted in accordance with Rawle's text on the Constitution, as a rebellion perpetrated by a small minority and proceeded on a path every member of his cabinet knew meant war.

KEEPING A CONSTITUTIONAL REPUBLIC:
THE IMPORTANCE OF THE TENTH AMENDMENT AND STATES RIGHTS

The United States is not a democracy; it is a constitutional republic. The founding fathers of our Republic mistrusted pure democracy. They had learned from history that pure democracy could become as tyrannical as any monarchy or dictatorship. They also knew that even the noblest men are vulnerable to corruption and especially the temptations of power. Therefore they eschewed a government of men and sought to create a government of law that would endure as a gift to their posterity. They believed that the rights of free men and the principles of liberty must be protected by a constitution. After the Constitutional Convention of 1787, someone asked Benjamin Franklin what kind of government had been instituted. His response was:

"A Republic, if we can keep it."

The function of the Constitution is to define and limit the powers of the Federal Government. It was ratified by the people of the States. From this ratification and consent by the people of the respective States, the Constitution derives its validity. The Tenth Amendment was meant as a final reinforcement and written guarantee that the powers of the Federal Government would be limited to those enumerated in the Constitution. This was a safeguard against the infringement of rights and powers retained by the States and their people. It was also a safeguard against the tyranny, despotism, and abuses which have so often evolved from unchecked centralized power. Let us examine the wording of this Amendment more closely:

"The powers not delegated to the United States by the Constitution, nor prohibited by it to the States, are reserved to the States respectively, or to the people."

Thus the executive, legislative, and judicial branches and subsidiaries of the Federal Government have only those powers and those powers alone that are delegated to them by the Constitution. All other powers are reserved to the States or the people and are thereby prohibited to the Federal Government except by amendment to the Constitution, which would require not only the approval by two thirds of both houses of Congress but also by three-fourths of the States.

It is important to note here that the people of the States do not derive their rights from the federal judiciary, nor have they by any means delegated that power to federal judges. The people of the States have reserved the power to determine their unalienable rights to themselves. The Tenth Amendment thus cannot be left to the Federal Government and its courts to ignore or interpret for themselves. A defining characteristic of a constitutional government is that power must not be allowed to define its own limits. Power must be checked and restrained by an equal or greater power.

A major victory against judicial tyranny has been won in the recent appointments of two strict-constructionist judges to the United States Supreme Court. But still there are only four conservative judges of the nine on the court, and the judicial philosophies of the latest two have not been fully tested. This is not a time for complacency. The people's liberty will never be safe if we depend on the judiciary alone to protect us. Congress and the States must continually insist that federal judges abide by the Constitution.

Failure to honor and enforce the Tenth Amendment by the Judiciary, Congress, the States, and the People has spawned ever-escalating abuses of power, social nonsense, and political chaos. In its misguided and unconstitutional zeal to impose a liberal and godless social agenda on the American people, the Federal Judiciary has overstepped its powers so often that judicial tyranny is now accepted and defended as "The Rule of Law." There is an enormous difference, however, between the true Rule of Law, which in the U.S. is constitutionally based, and the rule of judges legislating their own agenda. Federal judges who flout the Tenth Amendment, distort the First Amendment beyond recognition, and create federal powers not enumerated in the Constitution are not upholding the Rule of Law. They are destroying law and have become tyrants.

The American people have been lulled into complacent surrender of the principles we inherited as a constitutional and federal republic. The majority of our elected officials do not seem to possess the political and moral courage to defend our Republic and our rights. Who then will defend them?

There are historical, Christian precedents and traditions going all the way back to the Magna Carta in England in 1215 that call for "interposition" of civil magistrates against unlawful decrees and usurpations by rulers. This approach was endorsed by Calvin, Knox, Rutherford, and many others in the 16th century and provided much of the rationale for the American Revolution.

Federal judges who give decrees that are transparently unconstitutional or which overstep their constitutional jurisdiction are acting unlawfully. It is thus the duty of other civil magistrates to say, "No, this must be contested." This could be done by Congress or State governments. Again, the very essence of preventing tyranny in a republic is that power must not be able to define its own limits. The federal judiciary must be kept in check by Congress and the States. The horizontal separation of powers in the Constitution between the executive, legislative, and judicial branches is well known to most people. What is less known but tremendously important is the vertical separation of powers between the federal and state governments.

This is why the States Rights issue is so important. It is the people's last bulwark against executive, congressional, and judicial tyranny. States Rights and the Tenth Amendment were largely ignored by the Republican

Party previous to the "Civil" War and absolutely ignored during the War. There were several very important underlying causes of the War, but the ultimate issue enveloping all others was States Rights. Republican disrespect for the Constitution became even more flagrant during the despotic and disgraceful period after the War which historians call "Reconstruction."

In his book, *Coercing Virtue, the Worldwide Rule of Judges*, Robert Bork traces the transformation of American culture by liberal judges hell bent on imposing a radical and anti-Christian humanism on society by means of judicial fiat. Bork notes that this trend began in the 1950's and has been successful in displacing the older American traditions with the new socially engineered leftist agenda. The progress of this judicially imposed radicalism has been steady and is now gaining unprecedented momentum. It reminds one of the old Mark Twain story about boiling frogs. If you heat the water slowly, the frogs are cooked before they realize what has happened to them. Around the world, free or formerly free peoples have shown a tendency not to resist or even to recognize judicial tyranny.

But the trend that Bork points to, beginning in the 1950's, is the legacy of Federal tyranny that began with the "Civil" War. When States Rights were defeated on the battlefield in 1865, the Constitution and the legal structures to resist tyranny and despotism were decisively weakened. This left the door to executive, judicial, and congressional tyranny open wide and the ultimate guardians of liberty, the Tenth Amendment and States Rights, bound and gagged.

One prominent example of judicial tyranny in recent years is Roe versus Wade. This case was not just about abortion and right to life, it was about the right of states to regulate abortion. In this case the Federal Judiciary usurped the power of state legislatures and state courts to make abortion laws and in so doing violated the Tenth Amendment of the U.S. Constitution and the principle of States Rights.

But the Tenth Amendment has not been repealed, and in recent years the importance of States Rights to liberty and constitutional government is regaining recognition. The Federal Judiciary and Congress are growing more receptive to States Rights arguments. However, the battle for States Rights and constitutional government is far from won, and it is ultimately up to the States to insist on their own rights and enforce compliance by every legal means at their disposal.

Elected state officials, legislatures, and local civil magistrates must stand up and say, "No," when the Tenth Amendment and States Rights are being violated by any branch of the Federal Government. Alexander the Great once remarked that:

"The peoples of Asia were slaves because they would not learn to pronounce the word 'No'."

Let that not be the epitaph of the American Republic and the rights and liberties of free men.

A more recent and flagrant violation of both the Tenth and the First Amendments by a Federal District Judge involved the removal of a large stone display of the Ten Commandments in the Alabama State Judicial building. A great opportunity to insist on both States Rights and religious liberties was forfeited when the Governor and most of the Alabama Supreme Court failed to back Alabama Chief Justice Roy Moore in his resistance to Federal judicial tyranny. The First Amendment states that:

"Congress shall make no law respecting an establishment of religion, or prohibiting the free exercise thereof;"

Note that it is Congress that is prohibited from establishing religion or interfering with its practice, and not the States. According to both the First and Tenth Amendments, that Federal Judge appointed by Jimmy Carter had no legal or constitutional authority to order the state of Alabama to remove the Ten Commandments from its Supreme Court Building.

It takes courage to stand up against federal judges and government officials who are violating the Constitution and usurping the powers delegated to the States and the people. Every failure to resist unconstitutional tyranny tightens the noose around freedom's neck a bit tighter. The frog has been heated a bit closer to the point of death. Judges, governors, and other civil magistrates must stand up and say, "No," even at the risk of their removal—this is in keeping with the Doctrine of Interposition that dates back to the Magna Carta. Free men must stand. Going along with tyranny in hopes of getting in a few licks for justice and good government is flawed reasoning. Otherwise just judges and other state and local officials will find their ability to render justice increasingly hampered and overturned by a federal judiciary legislating a radical liberal agenda unfettered by sound constitutional interpretation. The Rule of Law is not the rule of judges. It is the rule of the people through Federal and State Constitutions, duly authorized by them in their respective states and interpreted according to their original and common-sense meaning. The Federal Government and its courts are constantly violating the Tenth Amendment and the true Rule of Law. These transgressions against the Constitution and the people cannot be tolerated. It is time for Americans to rediscover the neglected and suppressed Tenth Amendment and the Doctrine of Interposition and for our state and local officials to show the courage to use them.

Courage is the virtue most needed to save our Republic. It would be well to remember the words of Samuel Johnson (1709-1784):

"Where courage is not, no other virtue can survive except by accident."

Let us hope and pray that courage will not be in such short supply among our elected officials that our Republic and our liberties should perish and be swept into the dust bin of history. Let us hope that the words of South Carolinian Henry Laurens (1724-1792) will prove as true of our time as in his:

"At a time when liberty is under attack, decency under assault, the family under siege, and life itself is threatened, the good will arise in truth; they will arise in truth with the very essence and substance of their lives; they will arise in truth never shying from the Standard of Truth, never shrinking from the Author of Truth."

The South was right in defending States Rights. States Rights and the Tenth Amendment are essential to our liberties. We cannot allow the First Amendment, which guarantees freedom of religion, speech, and the press, or the Tenth Amendment, which is the ultimate guarantee of our political liberty, to be turned upside down by black-robed tyrants or political despots.

Judge Roy Moore of Alabama has raised a banner of truth and courage. To very roughly paraphrase the words of Robert Burns, attributed to Robert the Bruce of Scotland:

"Let those who would fill a coward's grave turn and flee, but let the true and the brave join in striking a blow for liberty."

Southern Secession Dates

South Carolina ....December 20, 1860
Mississippi ....January 9, 1861
Florida..................................January 10, 1861
Alabama................................January 11, 1861
Georgia.................................January 19, 1861
Louisiana..............................January 26, 1861
Texas ....February 1, 1861
Virginia ....April 17, 1861
Arkansas ....May 6, 1861
Tennessee ....May 7, 1861
North Carolina ....May 20, 1861

Union Occupied Border States
Secessions and Attempted Secessions

Maryland...............................September 17, 1861
Scheduled but blocked by arrest of pro-secession legislators
Missouri* ....October 31, 1861
Legislature meeting at Neosho, Missouri
Kentucky* ....June 16, 1862
Convention at Russellville, representatives from 65 counties.

....

Territories
S. Arizona & S. New Mexico March 16, 1861
   Ratified by CSA on February 14, 1862
Oklahoma July 10-12, 1861 ....Choctaw, Chickasaw,
                                                                   Creek treaties
                  August 1, 1861 ....Seminole Treaty
                  October 7, 1861 ....Cherokee Treaty
                  October 28, 186 ....Cherokee Declaration

Note: **The 12ᵗʰ and 13ᵗʰ stars in the Confederate Battle
Flag are for Missouri and Kentucky*

CHAPTER 7

⟨∞⟩

The First Thirteenth Amendment

Contradicting the Union Myth of a Holy Cause

Ludwell H. Johnson used the words, *The American Iliad,* in the subtitle for his comprehensive book on the American "Civil War," *North Against South.* The *Iliad* analogy is very appropriate for two reasons. First, the War was a traumatic, bloody, and nation changing event. The enormous casualties and destruction alone would sear its battles, personalities, and tales of heroism into American memory. Second, what most Americans know about the causes of the War is a pious myth.

But in history Americans seem to prefer whitewashed myth to truth. So much so that any truth that contradicts the ruling myths of academia and the dominant media and political class is apt to be shouted down or suppressed. One of the most important and persistent myths of American history is that the primary cause of the American "Civil War" was slavery, and that the War was morality play in which virtuous Northern armies crushed the wicked South in order to free the slaves. This myth is so enduring that it is taught as unassailable truth in American public schools and even in most Christian schools. The myth thus has widespread emotional if not factual support. The first 13th Amendment is one of several uncomfortable truths that demolish this much cherished propaganda.

Most Americans are at least vaguely aware that the 13th Amendment to the U. S. Constitution passed by Congress and approved by the States in December 1865 following the "Civil War" prohibited slavery. But this was actually the second 13th Amendment. The U. S. House of Representatives had passed with the required two thirds majority, a 13th Amendment on February 28, 1861. This same amendment was passed by the U. S.

Senate on March 2, 1861. It was then sent to the States for final approval. Three-quarters of the States must approve before an amendment becomes a validated part of the U. S. Constitution. Two days after Senate approval the newly elected President of the United States, Abraham Lincoln, promised to support this first 13th Amendment in his inaugural speech.

But what was this first 13th Amendment and what became of it? Here is the wording:

"No amendment shall be made to the Constitution which will authorize or give to Congress the power to abolish or interfere, within any State, with the domestic institutions thereof, including that of persons held to labor or service by the laws of such State."

The first 13th Amendment would have forever prohibited any Constitutional change that interfered with slavery in any state!

Lincoln endorsed this amendment, which would have permanently engraved slavery into the Constitution by two statements in his inaugural address: First, self quoting what he had written to *New York Tribune* Editor, Horace Greeley:

"I have no purpose, directly or indirectly, to interfere with the institution of slavery in the States where it exists. I believe I have no right to do so, and I have no inclination to do so."

Later in the speech he specifically promised to support this first 13th Amendment with these words:

"I understand a proposed amendment to the Constitution...has passed Congress, to the effect that the Federal Government shall never interfere with the domestic institutions of the States, including that of persons held to service. To avoid misconstruction of what I have said, I depart from my purpose, not to speak of particular amendments, so far as to say that, holding such a provision to now be implied Constitutional law, I have no objection to its being made express and irrevocable."

In other words Lincoln had no problem with an amendment which would have prohibited the Federal Government from interfering with slavery in the States! In addition, he felt the Constitution already prohibited the Federal Government from interfering with slavery in the States! The reason for this first 13th Amendment was, of course, to reassure Southern States that were threatening to leave the Union that there was not and never would be danger of any Congressional or Federal interference with slavery in the States. The slavery question was a concern to Southern States. The Northern States had gradually phased out slavery, but there had been few slaves in the North. Phasing out slavery in the North was a much less daunting social and economic endeavor. The calls of radical abolitionists in the North for immediate abolition of slavery regardless of the economic cost to the South and heedless of the hardship it would suddenly inflict on the slaves themselves, though not really a prevalent Northern sentiment, was a worry to the South. Slavery was by no means universally popular in the South, and many Southern States and individual Southerners were already struggling with how they might phase out the institution of slavery without devastating the Southern economy. But Southern States preferred to handle the slavery question when, if, and however they saw fit. Like Lincoln and many other political leaders in the North, the South considered how to handle the slavery question to be the Constitutional right of each state respectively.

Slavery was an issue that caused tensions between North and South, but it was by no means the only issue. If slavery was the only crucial issue, the South had no reason to secede. The first 13th Amendment would have guaranteed the question in their favor.

There were other important issues to the South. One enormous issue was the question of tariffs and in particular the Morrill Tariff that had been passed by the predominantly Northern Congress with the support of only one Southern Congressman. This tariff like others in the past was an economic hardship to the agricultural South, but a protective benefit for Northern manufacturers. To make matters worse, most of the revenue was collected at Southern ports but substantially used to the benefit of Northern States. Southern States were furious over this tariff, which had just been raised from an average under 20% to an average which would reach 47%. The Morrill Tariff was part of Lincoln's and the Republican Party's campaign platform. In fact, Lincoln further endorsed the Tariff in his inaugural speech and strongly implied that even if the South seceded the tax would be collected by the Union Navy at Southern ports.

There were other issues as well. North and South had developed different views of government. The South favored the limited and decentralized federal government of the Constitution, but the North was strongly trending toward a powerful centralized government, especially with the election of Lincoln. Early in the years of the American Republic the South and especially Virginia had dominated national politics. Massive waves of immigration to Northern manufacturing states now made them much more populous and politically dominant. The South simply did not want to stay in a Union dominated by Northern interests. Besides the economic injustice to the South, the Morrill Tariff proved to Southerners that Southern interests would be disregarded and completely subservient to Northern interests in the future. There was even a growing religious rift caused by Southern Biblical orthodoxy versus what was to Southerners an alarming increase in unbiblical "isms" in the North such as unitarianism, universalism, transcendentalism, and other forms of religious or Biblical liberalism. This was particularly aggravated by the adulation of John Brown, radical abolitionist and Charles Manson style murderer of Kansas farmers suspected of Southern sympathies, in Northern pulpits and the Northern press. The radical abolitionists' unmitigated hatred of everything Southern and constant insulting language directed against the South and its leaders also kept aggravating tensions. The first 13th Amendment would have relieved political tension over slavery, but not the Morrill Tariff and other very important political, economic, and cultural questions.

The first 13th Amendment became a moot issue after the firing on Fort Sumter and Lincoln's call for 75,000 volunteers to invade the South. The outbreak of the" Civil War" that would claim the lives of 620,000 Union and Confederate soldiers and as many as 50,000 Southern civilians effectively cancelled the first 13th Amendment.

On March 2, 1861, the same day the first 13th Amendment passed the Senate, another Amendment to the Constitution was also proposed. This amendment would have outlawed secession. This is a good indication that most of Congress realized that the right of secession was implied when the Constitution was originally approved by the States and effectively reinforced by the Tenth Amendment. In fact, textbooks used at West Point for years before the war had explained the validity of secession rights.

On July 22, 1861, the now Northern only Congress passed a joint resolution stating the purpose of the war:

"Resolved...That this war is not being prosecuted upon our part in any spirit of oppression, not for any purpose of conquest or subjugation, *nor purpose of overthrowing or interfering with the rights or established institutions of those states*, but to defend the maintain the supremacy of the Constitution and all laws made in pursuance thereof and to *preserve the Union*, with all the dignity, equality and rights of the several States unimpaired; and that as soon as these objects are accomplished the war ought to cease." (*Italics for emphasis are mine.*)

In other words the Northern Congress stated in resolution that Union and not interfering with the institution of slavery was the purpose of the war.

Later, on August 22, 1861, Lincoln explained his thinking on the war to the abolitionist editor of the *New York Tribune*, Horace Greeley:

"My paramount object in this struggle is to save the Union, and it is not either to save or destroy slavery. If I could save the Union without freeing any slave, I would do it; and if I could save it by freeing some and leaving others alone I would also do that. What I do about slavery, and the colored race, I do because I believe it helps save the Union."

Nearly two years into the War Lincoln found it expedient to issue in September 1862, the Emancipation Proclamation. This actually freed no slaves in any territory under Union control. It was done primarily as a war measure. Lincoln hoped that the Proclamation would encourage slave uprisings in the South, thus causing Confederate troops to be diverted. The overwhelming majority of the slaves, however, proved remarkably loyal to the families of their Southern masters, most of which were away in the Confederate Army. Some say that it was also to please the anti-slavery British and thus keep them from coming into the War on the side of the South. The British did not come into the War on the side of the South, but they were not so stupid as to be fooled by this ruse. Though the Proclamation had disappointing military results, and only made the British more skeptical of Northern intentions, it did please those radical abolitionists who did not seem to mind the hypocrisy of a document that did not free a single slave in Southern territory occupied by the Union Army. After a period of discontent in the North and in the Union Army over the Proclamation, the abolition of slavery began to be used to bolster the moral purpose of the war. Ever since then it has been a prime propaganda tool justifying and glorifying the War as a just and noble cause.

However, as can easily be seen in the first 13th Amendment, Lincoln's speeches, and Congressional resolutions, slavery cannot be said to be the cause of the Civil War. It was an issue causing much tension, but it was not the cause of the War. These tensions are very much misunderstood today. Contrary to current misinformed public opinion, most Northern objections to slavery were not really of a high moral tone. Many Northern States, such as Illinois, severely restricted the possibility of any Blacks, free or slave, taking up residence within their borders. Ohio and Indiana even prohibited free Blacks from entering their states. Northern attitudes toward Blacks that drove much of the Free State versus slave state controversy can best be summarized by an October 16, 1854, quote from Abraham Lincoln, himself:

"Whether slavery shall go into Nebraska, or other new territories, is not a matter of exclusive concern to the people who may go there. The whole nation is interested that the best use shall be made of these territories. We want them for the homes of free white people. This they cannot be, to any considerable extent, if slavery shall be planted with them"

A common, but highly impractical solution of what to do with emancipated slaves was colonization. That meant sending them back to Africa or to Central America. Lincoln, himself was strongly in favor of colonization. Lincoln was a great admirer of Henry Clay, who first proposed the colonization solution in 1827. Lincoln frequently stated his advocacy of colonization, and on December 1, 1862, in a message to Congress stated:

"I cannot make it better known than it already is, that I strongly favor colonization."

This was undoubtedly spoken to reassure Northern politicians who were uneasy with the possible migratory consequences of the Emancipation Proclamation.

Lincoln opposed slavery and was in favor of gradual, compensated emancipation and colonization. But he obviously considered Union and Northern business interests a much higher priority than eliminating slavery. To his credit he recognized and hated the dangerous fanaticism of the radical abolitionists. But all the late and post War talk and modern propaganda about the War being a noble crusade to free the slaves and of Lincoln being the Great Emancipator is a shameless fraud. Preserving the Union was the principal purpose stated by the North. That might be called noble; if forcing states to bear a subservient and exploited status in an unwanted and to them unprofitable Union by gunpoint can be called noble. The North had more than just territory in mind when preserving the Union. Loss of the Southern States would mean loss of most tax revenues, of which over 90% were from the tariff that so burdened the South. They would also have to compete with the South's proposed free trade policies, which would have wreaked economic havoc in the North, just as the tariff had wreaked economic havoc in the South. The South would have gained economically by independence, whereas the North would have lost considerably both in tax revenues and trade. The "Civil War" was not really a civil war. Two titles for the war are more appropriate. For the South it was the War for Southern Independence. For the North it was the War to Prevent Southern Independence. It was not a glorious crusade to free slaves. Unfortunately, most Americans today accept the pious fraud that the "Civil War" was all about ending slavery. The first 13th Amendment, however, provides shattering documentary evidence disproving that cherished humbug.

Percent of Southern Households Owing Slaves

State	Percent
Alabama	34.0
Arkansas	20.1
Florida	34.1
Georgia	37.4
Kentucky	23.2
Louisiana	29.5
Maryland	12.5
Mississippi	49.1
Missouri	12.7
North Carolina	27.7
South Carolina	45.5
Tennessee	24.7
Texas	28.5
Virginia	25.9
Total	**26.3**

Source:
John C Perry, see Reference Resources.

CHAPTER 8

∞

The Cherokee Declaration of Independence
Why the Cherokees Allied with the South in 1861

General Stand Watie

Many have no doubt heard of the valor of the Cherokee warriors under the command of Brigadier General Stand Watie in the West and of Thomas' famous North Carolina Legion in the East during the War for Southern Independence from 1861 to 1865. But why did the Cherokees and their brethren, the Creeks, Seminoles, Choctaws, and Chickasaws determine to make common cause with the Confederate South against the Northern Union? To know their reasons is very instructive as to the issues underlying that tragic war. Most Americans have been propagandized rather than educated in the causes of the war, all this to justify the perpetrators and victors. Considering the Cherokee view uncovers much truth buried by decades of politically correct propaganda and allows a broader and truer perspective.

In 1861 there were two principal groups of Cherokees in the United States, the Western Band with a population slightly over 20,000 and the smaller Eastern Band in North Carolina with a population of only abut 2000. Both sided with the Southern Confederacy, but the larger Western Band made a formal declaration of independence from the United States.

On August 21, 1861, the (Western) Cherokee Nation by a General Convention at Tahlequah (in Oklahoma) declared its common cause with the Confederate States against the Northern Union. A treaty was concluded on October 7th between the Confederate States and the Cherokee Nation, and on October 9th, John Ross, the Principal Chief of the Cherokee Nation called into session the Cherokee National Committee and National Council to approve and implement that treaty and a future course of action.

The Western Cherokees had at first considerable consternation over the growing conflict and desired to remain neutral. They had much common economy and contact with their Confederate neighbors, but their treaties were with the government of the United States. The Northern conduct of the war against their neighbors, strong repression of Northern political dissent, and the roughshod trampling of the U. S Constitution under the new regime and political powers in Washington soon changed their thinking.

The Cherokee were perhaps the best educated and literate of the American Indian Tribes. They were also among the most Christian. Learning and wisdom were highly esteemed. They revered the Declaration of Independence and the U, S Constitution as particularly important guarantors of their rights and freedoms. It is not surprising then that on October 28, 1861, the National Council (of the Western Cherokee) issued: *A Declaration by the People of the Cherokee Nation of the Causes Which Have Impelled them to Unite Their Fortunes With Those of the Confederate States of America.*

The introductory words of this declaration strongly resembled the 1776 Declaration of Independence:

"When circumstances beyond their control compel one people to sever the ties which have long existed between them and another state or confederacy, and to contract new alliances and establish new relations for the security of their rights and liberties, it is fit that they should publicly declare the reasons by which their action is justified."

In the next paragraphs of their declaration the (Western) Cherokee Council noted their faithful adherence to their treaties with the United States in the past and how they had faithfully attempted neutrality until the present. But the seventh paragraph begins to delineate their alarm with Northern aggression and sympathy with the South:

"But Providence rules the destinies of nations, and events, by inexorable necessity, overrule human resolutions."

Comparing the relatively limited objectives and defensive nature of the Southern cause in contrast to the aggressive actions of the North they remarked of the Confederate States:

"Disclaiming any intention to invade the Northern States, they sought only to repel the invaders from their own soil and to secure the right of governing themselves. They claimed only the privilege asserted in the Declaration of American Independence, and on which the right of Northern States themselves to self-government is formed, and altering their form of government when it became no longer tolerable and establishing new forms for the security of their liberties."

The next paragraph noted the orderly and democratic process by which each of the Confederate States seceded. This was without violence or coercion and nowhere were liberties abridged or civilian courts and authorities made subordinate to the military. Also noted was the growing unity and success of the South against Northern aggression. The following or ninth paragraph contrasts this with ruthless and totalitarian trends in the North:

"But in the Northern States the Cherokee people saw with alarm a violated constitution, all civil liberty put in peril, and all rules of civilized warfare and the dictates of common humanity and decency unhesitatingly disregarded. In the states which still adhered to the Union a military despotism had displaced civilian power and the laws became silent with arms. Free speech and almost free thought became a crime. The right of habeas corpus, guaranteed by the constitution, disappeared at the nod of a Secretary of State or a general of the lowest grade. The mandate of the Chief Justice of the Supreme Court was at naught by the military power and this outrage on common right approved by a President sworn to support the constitution. War on the largest scale was waged, and the immense bodies of troops called into the field in the absence of any warranting it under the pretense of suppressing unlawful combination of men."

The tenth paragraph continues the indictment of the Northern political party in power and the conduct of the Union Armies:

"The humanities of war, which even barbarians respect, were no longer thought worthy to be observed. Foreign mercenaries and the scum of the cities and the inmates of prisons were enlisted and organized into brigades and sent into Southern States to aid in subjugating a people struggling for freedom, to burn, to plunder, and to commit the basest of outrages on the women; while the heels of armed tyranny trod upon the necks of Maryland and Missouri, and men of the highest character and position were incarcerated upon suspicion without process of law, in jails, forts, and prison ships, and even women were imprisoned by the arbitrary order of a President and Cabinet Ministers; while the press ceased to be free, and the publication of newspapers was suspended and their issues seized and destroyed; the officers and men taken prisoners in the battles were allowed to remain in captivity by the refusal of the Government to consent to an exchange of prisoners; as they had left their dead on more than one field of battle that had witnessed their defeat, to be buried and their wounded to be cared for by southern hands."

The eleventh paragraph of the Cherokee declaration is a fairly concise summary of their grievances against the political powers now presiding over a new U. S. Government:

"Whatever causes the Cherokee people may have had in the past to complain of some of the southern states, they cannot but feel that their interests and destiny are inseparably connected to those of the south. The war now waging is a war of Northern cupidity and fanaticism against the institution of African servitude; against the commercial freedom of the south, and against the political freedom of the states, and its objects are to annihilate the sovereignty of those states and utterly change the nature of the general government."

The Cherokees felt they had been faithful and loyal to their treaties with the United States, but now perceived that the relationship was not reciprocal and that their very existence as a people was threatened. They had also witnessed the recent exploitation of the properties and rights of

Indian tribes in Kansas, Nebraska, and Oregon, and feared that they, too, might soon become victims of Northern rapacity. Therefore, they were compelled to abrogate those treaties in defense of their people, lands, and rights. They felt the Union had already made war on them by their actions.

Finally, appealing to their inalienable right to self defense and self determination as a free people, they concluded their declaration with the following words:

"Obeying the dictates of prudence and providing for the general safety and welfare, confident of the rectitude of their intentions and true to their obligations to duty and honor, they accept the issue thus forced upon them, unite their fortunes now and forever with the Confederate States, and take up arms for the common cause, and with entire confidence of the justice of that cause and with a firm reliance upon Devine Providence, will resolutely abide the consequences."

The Eastern Band of Cherokee made no formal declaration, but considered themselves North Carolinians and were anxious to join Confederate forces in defending their state and the Southern cause. The Eastern Band Chief, Col. William H. Thomas, a North Carolina State Senator, gathered two hundred Cherokee braves to form the core of what later became the Thomas Legion consisting of slightly over four hundred Cherokees and about 1,900 North Carolina mountain men. Thomas, of Welsh descent, was the adopted white son of the late Eastern Band Chief, Yana-guska (Drowning Bear). He is said to have spoken the Cherokee language better than any white man that ever lived. The Cherokees had come to have great respect for his wisdom and relentless hard work in their behalf in North Carolina. It should be noted that the approximately 416 Cherokee braves that served in the Thomas Legion represented almost every male of military age of their small population. They served very faithfully with only about a dozen known to have deserted.

Both Cherokee bands proved their courage and loyalty. The last shot fired in the war east of the Mississippi was May 6, 1865. This was in an engagement at White Sulphur Springs, near Waynesville, North Carolina, of part of Thomas' Legion against Kirk's infamous Union raiders that had wreaked a murderous terrorism and destruction on the civilian population of Western North Carolina. It took some effort at the end of the war for

Thomas to persuade his Cherokee braves to surrender rather than continuing guerilla warfare against the Union.

In the West, Confederate Brigadier General Stand Watie's mounted infantry regiments became a legend for their guerilla cavalry tactics, baffling and diverting far greater numbers of Union troops. On June 23, 1865, in what was the last land battle of the war, Confederate Brigadier General and Cherokee Chief, Stand Watie, finally surrendered his predominantly Cherokee, Oklahoma Indian force to the Union.

The issues as the Cherokees saw them were 1) self defense against Northern aggression, both for themselves and their fellow Confederates, 2) the right of self determination by a free people, 3) protection of their heritage, 4) preservation of their political rights under a constitutional government of law, 5) a strong desire to retain the principles of limited government and decentralized power guaranteed by the Constitution, 6) protection of their economic rights and welfare, 7) dismay at the despotism of the party and leaders now in command of the U. S. Government, 8) dismay at the ruthless disregard of commonly accepted rules of warfare by the Union, especially their treatment of civilians and non-combatants, 9) a fear of economic exploitation by corrupt politicians and their supporters based on observed past experience, and 10) alarm at the self-righteous and extreme, punitive, and vengeful pronouncements on the slavery issue voiced by the radical abolitionists and supported by many Northern politicians, journalists, and social and religious leaders, of which the Unitarians were the most numerous and vocal. It should be noted here that some of the Cherokees owned slaves, but the practice was not extensive.

The Cherokee Declaration of October 1861 uncovers a far more complex set of "Civil War" issues than most Americans have been taught. Rediscovered truth is not always welcome. Indeed some of the issues here are so distressing that the general academic, media, and public reaction is to rebury them or shout them down as politically incorrect.

The notion that slavery was the only real or even principal cause of the war is very politically correct and widely held, but historically ignorant. It has served, however, as a convenient ex post facto justification for the war and its conduct. Slavery was an issue, and it was related to many other issues, but it was by no means the only issue, or even the most important underlying issue. It was not even an issue in the way most people think of it. Only about 25% of Southern households owned slaves. For most people, North and South, the slavery issue was not so much whether to keep it or not, but how to phase it out without causing economic and social disruption and disaster. Unfortunately the Southern and Cherokee fear of the radical abolitionists turned out to be well founded.

After the Reconstruction Acts were passed in 1867, the radical abolitionists and radical Republicans were able to issue in a shameful era of politically punitive and economically exploitive oppression in the South, the results of which lasted many years, and even today are not yet completely erased.

The Cherokee were and are a remarkable people who have impacted the American heritage far beyond their numbers. We can be especially grateful that they made a well thought out and articulate declaration for supporting and joining the Confederate cause in 1861.

Un-Civil War Casualty Statistics

Northern Forces

Number Serving	Battle Deaths	Other Deaths	Total Deaths
2,213,000*	140,000	224,000	365,000

Southern Forces

1,000,000 (est.)	94,000	164,000	258,000

Total

234,000	388,000	623,000

*Of the Union forces, approximately 500,000 or 24 percent were foreign born, many recruited in Europe—total foreign born: German, 175,000; Irish, 150,000; British, 100,000; other, 75,000. In addition, approximately 193,000 blacks served in the Union Army and Navy, including 93,000 from Southern States.

Over 2,800 black Union soldiers were killed in action or died of wounds. Estimates of deaths from disease and other causes range from 30 to 65 thousand. According to Scott K. Williams, approximately 65,000 blacks (estimates range from 40 to 90 thousand) served the Confederate Army in some capacity. There are no reliable estimates of black Confederate casualties.

Sources:
1. Stonewall Jackson Memorial, Lexington, Virginia.
2. Scott K. Williams, website, Black Confederates in the Civil War.
3. Wikipedia website: United Stated Colored Troops.
4. Wikipedia website: Military History of African Americans in the Civil War.
5. John C. Perry, see reference resources.

CHAPTER 9

෧෨෨

Fort Sumter and the War Conspiracy

Fort Sumter

Who started the so-called "Civil War" in 1861? Many high school textbooks declare that the South started the war by firing on the American flag at Fort Sumter in the harbor of Charleston, South Carolina. Abraham Lincoln often referred to the South as having started the war as in his December 6, 1864, address to Congress:

"I mean simply to say that the war will cease whenever it shall have ceased on the part of those who began it."

The beginning of the War Between the States is wrapped in Union propaganda justifying the war. There was much more to it than Confederate guns firing on the Union held fort in Charleston harbor. It is a story filled with intrigue, secret orders, political deception, and conspiracy.

The election of Abraham Lincoln as President of the United States in November 1860 set off a series of state secession conventions that resulted in seven states leaving the Union by his inauguration on March 4, 1861. These Confederate states, even volatile South Carolina, hoped to leave the Union in peace. The desire for a peaceful separation was so central that it was specifically included in Section 2, Article VI, of the Confederate Constitution:

> "The Government...hereby declaring it to be their wish and earnest desire to adjust everything pertaining to the common property, common liability, and common obligations of that Union upon the principles of right, justice, equity, and good faith."

In late 1860, most of the people of the North believed that secession was a natural right based on the consent of governed and that the Southern states should be allowed to secede peaceably. Historian Howard Cecil Perkins compiled 495 Northern newspaper editorials dated from late 1860 to mid-1861 and concluded that the great majority of them assumed secession was a constitutional right and opposed the use of force against seceding states. *The Bangor Daily Union* stated on, November 12, 1860, that:

> "Union depends for its continuance on the free consent and will of the sovereign people of each state, and when that consent and will is withdrawn on either part, their Union is gone. A state coerced to remain in the Union is 'a subject province' and can never be a co-equal member of the American Union."

Supreme Court Justice Samuel Nelson of New York after studying the President's war powers reported to Secretary of State William Seward that the President could not use coercion against states without serious violation of both the Constitution and statutory law.

Of particular immediate concern for peaceful separation was the disposition of several coastal forts, the most important of which were Fort Sumter in Charleston harbor and Fort Pickens near Pensacola. In that regard, on December 9, eleven days before the South Carolina Secession Ordinance, South Carolina Congressmen met with President Buchanan on the Fort Sumter issue. At that meeting there was an informal agreement that Forts Moultrie and Sumter in Charleston would not be attacked by South Carolina forces so long as they were not reinforced and did not act aggressively toward South Carolina.

On December 12, seven weeks before his inauguration, Lincoln sent E. B. Washburne to Army Chief Winfield Scott with instructions to prepare to hold or retake the forts after his inauguration on March 4. The Commander of the Union garrison in Charleston, Major Robert Anderson, at that time was situated at Fort Moultrie and Fort Sumter was unoccupied except for construction crews. Following the December 20 secession of South Carolina, feeling that Fort Moultrie was too vulnerable to attack from shore, on the night of December 26, Anderson moved his eighty-two men to Fort Sumter in the middle of the bay. This caused a stir in both Charleston and Washington. South Carolina regarded the move suspiciously and several of President Buchanan's cabinet members felt the move violated their informal agreement with South Carolina. In fact, Secretary of War Floyd, a Virginian, resigned over the matter. Major Anderson, however, had made the move on his own initiative.

Shortly after his move to Sumter, Anderson reported to Army Headquarters in Washington that he had four months of provisions, enough to last until around April 26. A few days later, he wrote to a trusted friend in Charleston that he had five months supply, enough to last until around May 29. Charleston authorities also allowed Anderson to continue purchasing provisions in Charleston. Meanwhile on December 31, General Scott secretly and unbeknown to President Buchanan, had the Navy ship, *Brooklyn*, outfitted to supply and reinforce either Fort Sumter or Fort Pickens. Besides supplies and ammunition, it was to carry 200 artillery soldiers under Army Captain Vogdes.

Also under orders from General Scott, a merchant steamer, *The Star of the West*, left the Norfolk area on January 7, with supplies for Fort Sumter. It concealed 200 troops below deck. On arriving in the Charleston harbor two days later and making for Fort Sumter, the Charleston batteries fired a warning shot across her bow. She kept coming, but after the Charleston batteries began to fire in earnest, she turned away. This incident was an embarrassment to the Buchanan administration, who hoped to avoid war and keep faith with the South.

On January 10, Florida seceded. That night the Union commander at Fort Barrancas on Pensacola Bay moved his men during the night to the larger facility of Fort Pickens. On January 21, the *Brooklyn*, carrying Army Captain Vogdes and his artillery reinforcements arrived at Pensacola and was joined by the *Sabine* and *Wyandotte*. Following some tension and negotiations with Confederate civil authorities and General Braxton Bragg, on January 29, an Armistice was signed by Union Secretary of War

Holt and Navy Secretary Toucey, agreeing that Fort Pickens would not be attacked unless reinforced or engaging in aggression against Confederate forces in the area. Back in Washington on February 7, retired Navy Captain G. V. Fox presented an aggressive plan using supporting warships to General Scott and Secretary of War Holt to reinforce Fort Sumter. The next day President Buchanan doused the plan. The cabinet agreed that reinforcing Fort Sumter or Fort Pickens was an act of war and would be likewise interpreted by the South. Unexpectedly, on February 20, General Scott renewed the Sumter reinforcement plan. On February 25, Confederate President Jefferson Davis appointed three high ranking Peace Commissioners to go to Washington for the purposes of negotiating the disposition of Forts Sumter and Pickens and other issues.

President Davis also assigned Brigadier General P. G. T. Beauregard as Confederate Commander in Charleston on March 3. Beauregard had been a student of Robert Anderson at West Point, and the two men were close friends. Anderson was himself a Southerner from Kentucky, married to a Georgia girl. Anderson was a loyal Unionist, but he did not want war.

Lincoln was inaugurated on March 4, promising to collect the tariff regardless of secession. It was also evident that unlike all his predecessors and most other Americans, he did not regard secession as legal, and he was willing to use military force to prevent states from leaving the Union. He would not see the Confederate Peace Commissioners. They were, however, able to negotiate indirectly through Supreme Court Justices John A. Campbell and Samuel Nelson, who had volunteered to interposition with Secretary of State William Seward for the cause of peace. Seward continuously promised them that Fort Sumter would be evacuated.

On March 9, Lincoln proposed to his Cabinet that Fort Sumter be reinforced. Only two supported him in this. They thought it would mean war and could end in a military and naval disaster. Somewhat surprisingly, since he had secretly been doing Lincoln's bidding even before his inauguration, General Scott, who was a Virginian and who did not want war, was the plan's most vocal opponent. He believed it would take a force of 20,000 men, and no such force was now available. The Navy men were more hopeful of success, claiming that the reinforcement squadron would not come under fire for long.

General Scott, however, on March 12, ordered reinforcement of Fort Pickens in Florida. Lincoln again polled his cabinet on March 15 with negative results. Captain Fox was sent on a special mission to see Major Anderson and South Carolina Governor Pickens on March 21 to assess the possibilities. On March 29 Lincoln's Cabinet was finally persuaded to approve Lincoln's plan to reinforce Fort Sumter, although they knew it meant war.

Many Northern businessmen were now reassessing their positions on secession. They began to realize that a free trade South would take business away from a high tariff North. They also realized they would lose their principal source of tax revenue. More Northern newspapers began to reflect a distaste for secession.

There was also serious talk of California and Oregon seceding to form a Pacific nation. Democratic controlled New Jersey was also considering secession to escape Republican national dominance. New York City was sympathetic to the South and was considering secession to become a free trade zone. Lincoln believed a brief war was necessary to put down the Southern rebellion and to discourage others from the same path. But general public opinion in the North did not favor war.

On April 1, Lincoln issued six different secret orders directly to various naval personnel without consulting Secretary of the Navy Gideon Welles or Secretary of War Cameron. All pertained to outfitting and manning the *Powhatan*, one of the Navy's fastest and most heavily armed ships for a secret mission to Fort Pickens in Florida. The most unusual was direct to Navy Captain Porter to relieve Captain Mercer and take command of the *Powhatan*.

Meanwhile on April 1, Army Captain Vogdes finally delivered the March 12 order from General Scott to reinforce Fort Pickens to the squadron commander at Pensacola, Navy Captain H. A. Adams. Adams, however, refused to comply, since it would violate the Armistice and mean war. Instead, on April 6, he sent a letter to Navy Secretary Welles to authenticate the orders. Adams received orders from Welles confirming that Fort Pickens must be reinforced immediately on the 12th. By this time the Pensacola task force had been joined by a ship deceptively steaming into Pensacola Bay flying British colors, the *Powhatan*, under the command of Captain Porter. Under cover of night they succeeded in reinforcing Fort Pickens without a fight. They were unaware of developments at Sumter.

Confederate General Bragg took no immediate action as the Confederate government was still hoping for peace.

Major Anderson received notification on April 4 that a reinforcement expedition should arrive in Charleston by the 15th. He and his officers did not regard it as a happy prospect. Like General Scott, they believed that reinforcement could not occur without a Union army of 20.000 men first taking Charleston and its batteries from behind.

On April 6, Lincoln gave the final order for reinforcing Fort Sumter. Three warships, the *Pocahontas, the Pawnee,* and the *Harriet Lane* were assigned to the task force commanded by Captain Fox aboard the steamer *Baltic,* which would carry 200 soldiers. The *Powhatan* (that Lincoln had sent to Pensacola) was also listed as part of the task force.

The Confederate Peace Commission was still in Washington on April 7 listening to Seward's promise that Sumter would be evacuated. But they had grown suspicious of all the activity of the last weeks and had surmised that a battle fleet was on its way to reinforce Sumter.

South Carolina Governor Pickens received an envoy from Washington on April 8 with a message announcing:

"I am directed by the President of the United States to notify you to expect an attempt will be made to supply Fort Sumter with provisions only, and that if such an attempt be not resisted, no effort to throw in men, arms, and ammunition, will be made without further notice, or in case of an attack on the fort."

Governor Pickens passed the unsigned communication to President Davis and his Cabinet in Montgomery.

In the meantime, Lincoln had planted in the Northern press, the misinformation that the garrison at Fort Sumter was starving and in desperate need of provisions. Judging from his communications in late December, Anderson probably had anywhere from two to six weeks provisions in store, not counting the provisions the Confederates had allowed to be purchased in Charleston up until April 7.

President Davis knew all along that Lincoln was maneuvering to get the South to fire the first shot. But Davis knew that legally the aggressor in war and other law is not the first to use force, but the first to render force necessary. Davis also recognized that Lincoln did not care about legal technicalities. He was maneuvering for the favor of Northern public opinion, which he would need behind him to successfully wage a short war to put down the Confederacy. Lincoln's public relations pitch would be that the Confederates fired first on the flag to prevent starving men from receiving provisions.

Realizing that the Union war fleet was already nearing Charleston and not wanting to risk the prospect of fighting the fort and a Union war flotilla at the same time, Beauregard sent former Senator and now Col. James Chesnut and Captain Stephen D. Lee on April 9 to demand surrender of the fort and evacuation of Federal troops. Anderson indicated that he was honor bound to resist, but that he would be starved out in a matter of days anyway.

This message was sent back to Montgomery. An offer was made to Anderson to let him choose the day of evacuation at which time he and his men could salute their colors. Anderson named the 15th, probably based on Captain Fox's promise of reinforcement by that date. By April 11, however, warships of the Union reinforcement squadron could be seen within striking distance of Fort Sumter and Charleston. At 3:20 am on the 12th, Beauregard sent messengers to announce that the fort would be bombarded within one hour. At 4:30 am the Confederate batteries encircling Fort Sumter commenced its bombardment.

The outline of the dark harbor was dotted with a line of twinkling lights while bursting shells illuminated the sky above. Fort Sumter did not begin to return the fire for two hours. Although the Union flotilla could be seen from Sumter and Charleston, they did not engage the Confederate guns and held their distance.

The Union Naval Commander Captain Fox arrived on the *Baltic* and boarded the *Pawnee*. The Captain of that ship, the senior officer of the task force except for Fox, however, refused to engage the Charleston batteries or move to support Fort Sumter, telling Captain Fox that his sealed orders stated specifically to wait for the arrival of the *Powhatan* before initiating the reinforcement action, which he knew meant inaugurating war. This was a shock to Fox as he had been led to believe by the Secretary of War that the Captain of the *Pawnee* would have orders to allow his entire force to open a passage to Sumter if needed. The *Powhatan* was at that very moment at Fort Pickens under secret orders from Lincoln. The warship *Pocahontas* arrived early on the 13th.

At about 7:30 am on the morning of April 13, seeing that the fort was on fire, the Confederates stopped firing and offered the use of a small fire engine to contain the fire, which might threaten the fort's ammunition and powder supplies. Although his men were having to stay low to the ground and breathing through wet handkerchiefs to deal with the smoke, Anderson refused the help, saying the fire was almost burned out. Later a shell knocked down the flag, and bombardment ceased, the Confederate commanders thinking surrender was imminent. The flag was quickly replaced by a Union sergeant, to the cheers of the Confederates, who expressed constant admiration for their brave and embattled enemies, many of whom were personally known to them. At about 2:00 pm in the afternoon a white flag was displayed, and the nearly thirty-four hours of bombardment ended.

Amazingly, there had been no casualties on either side. Beauregard allowed the gallant defenders of Fort Sumter to assemble and salute their flag before being picked up by a transport and delivered to the Union flotilla just outside the Charleston bar. Unfortunately, while Anderson was firing a fifty-gun salute to his flag, an ember fell into some powder and one man was killed and five injured. In a final show of respect for the weary defenders of Fort Sumter, Confederate soldiers lined the beaches and removed their caps in salute as a steamer silently passed out of the harbor to the Union Navy expeditionary force.

Lincoln had achieved what he wanted. The news of Confederate firing on the flag at Fort Sumter and its "half-starved" defenders rallied the North. In a May 1 letter to Captain Fox, Lincoln said,

"You and I both anticipated the cause of the country would be advanced by making the attempt to provision Fort Sumter, even if it should fail; and it is no small consolation now to feel that our anticipation is justified by the result."

That result was the rallying of Northern patriotism and war fever to punish the South for firing on Fort Sumter. The Confederates had been placed in a position of either firing the first shot or risking the loss of Charleston and the credibility of Confederate resistance to Northern coercion. President Davis shouldered that responsibility in his statement to his cabinet:

> **"The order for the sending of the fleet was a declaration of war. The responsibility is on their shoulders, not on ours. The juggle for position as to who shall fire the first shot in such an hour is unworthy of a great people and their cause. A deadly weapon has been aimed at our heart. Only a fool would wait until the first shot has been fired. The assault has been made. It is of no importance who shall strike the first blow or fire the first gun."**

General Beauregard had the Confederate Stars and Bars raised over Fort Sumter on April 14 to the salute of Confederate guns ringing the harbor. The next day Lincoln called on the state governors for 75,000 volunteers to put down the Southern rebellion.

Although Lincoln was successful in rallying Northern support by maneuvering the Confederates into firing on the flag at Fort Sumter, his call for troops to coerce Southern states back into the Union had a disastrous impact on the Border States. Union sentiment in those states quickly evaporated, and Virginia, Tennessee, Arkansas, and North Carolina seceded. Governor Ellis of North Carolina declared that his state would:

> "be no party to this wicked violation of the laws of the country and this war upon the liberties of a free people."

Lincoln was truly shocked when he received wires from the Governors of Kentucky and Missouri. Governor Magoffin of Kentucky replied that:

> "I say emphatically Kentucky will furnish no troops for the wicked purpose of subduing her sister Southern states."

Governor Jackson of Missouri was even harsher in his reply to Lincoln:

"Your requisition is illegal, unconstitutional, revolutionary, inhuman, diabolical, and cannot be complied with.

Lincoln immediately sent Federal troops to occupy Kentucky, Missouri, and Maryland to make sure that they had no opportunity to secede.

Thus began four years of bloody, destructive, and bitter war that would take the lives of 620,000 Union and Confederate soldiers and destroy forty percent of private property in the South.

Who started the War? It was not the South. Technically, it was not the North either. It takes Congress to declare war, and Congress did not convene until July 1861. It was Lincoln's war to prevent Southern independence.

CHAPTER 10

ᢙᣛᣩ

Maryland, My Maryland!

"The Despot's Heel Is on Thy Shore."

Chief Justice Taney

Following the bombardment and surrender of Fort Sumter at Charleston on April 9, 1861, Lincoln ordered Governors of the remaining Union states to call up their state militias and supply an army of 75,000 to invade and subdue the seven Southern states that had seceded. While this was received enthusiastically in many northern states, the Border States viewed this order as a tyranny they would not follow. Consequently, the border states of Virginia, Tennessee, North Carolina, and Arkansas seceded and secession efforts were underway in Missouri and Kentucky. The order was likewise not well received in Maryland.

One of the first steps of the Lincoln administration was to secure the capitol in Washington, although the Southern states wished to secede peacefully and had indicated no aggressive intentions against the Northern capitol. In order to get to Washington the mustered Union regiments had to come through Baltimore. As the railroad did not go through the city of Baltimore, they had to disembark their troop trains north of the city and proceed by wagon, horse, and foot through the city, and then embark by train again on the other side. Unfortunately, on April 19th, the 6th Massachusetts chose to march through the city fully armed and in military formation. They were jeered by unsympathetic crowds of bystanders.

Furthering the misfortune, the troops fired on the crowds killing twelve people. Fire then began to be returned from the crowd, and four soldiers were killed. These twelve civilians and four Union soldiers, whose blood flecked the streets of Baltimore, were the first battle deaths of a war that would take the lives of 620,000 Union and Confederate soldiers and an estimated 50,000 Southern civilians from all causes.

By May of 1861 Lincoln, his cabinet, and generals had already begun to close down dissenting newspapers all over the country from Chicago to New York. Lincoln also took it upon himself to suspend the Writ of Habeas Corpus, a constitutional guarantee of the Bill of Rights with precedent dating back to the English Magna Carta. Habeas corpus is a fundamental liberty which prevents arbitrary arrest and imprisonment indefinitely without defined charges, trial, or means of release. Suspension of habeas corpus under conditions of civil disorder can only be temporary and must be authorized by Congress within 30 days.

In that same month of May a resident of Baltimore, John Merryman, who had been arrested on the order of Union General George Cadwallader and held at Fort McHenry without charges or trial, petitioned U. S. Chief Justice Roger B. Taney for a writ of habeas corpus. Taney granted a writ and set a date for a hearing, but it was ignored by Lincoln and his generals. Cadwallader responded by letter that Lincoln had suspended habeas corpus, so there would be no compliance with the Supreme Court. Taney ordered a federal marshal to Fort McHenry to enforce the writ, but Union Army officials refused his entrance.

Taney responded by writing a blistering court opinion, a constitutional classic, that held Merryman's arrest to be unlawful and a violation of the Constitution, and that only Congress could suspend the Writ of Habeas Corpus. The Chief Justice stated that if Lincoln's actions were allowed to stand,

"…the people of the United States are no longer living under a government of laws, but every citizen holds, life, liberty, and property at the will and pleasure of the army officer in whose military district he may happen to be found."

Lincoln not only ignored the Supreme Court's ruling, he wrote out an order for the arrest of Chief Justice Taney. This arrest, however, was in the end not actually carried out for fear of extremely adverse public opinion and political consequences.

With these developments, a sizeable portion of the Maryland public was becoming sympathetic not only to the South, but even secession. Therefore, there was much talk of it among Maryland State Legislators. Consequently, Northern informers were asked to identify members of the Maryland Legislature that might support secession in the coming legislative session. Secretary of War Simon Cameron then issued an order to Major General Banks in Maryland that **"all or any part of the Legislative members must be arrested to prevent secession."**

On the night of September 12-13 all suspected Southern sympathizers in the Maryland Legislature were arrested and imprisoned in Fort McHenry. In all, fifty-one persons were arrested and imprisoned. Ironically, among those arrested and imprisoned was the grandson of Francis Scott Key, the author of the Star Spangled Banner.

To further tighten Union political hold on Maryland, all members of the Union armed forces were allowed to vote in the November election, although they were citizens of other states. Voters had to walk through platoons of soldiers with rifles and fixed bayonets to reach their polling place. The London *Saturday Review* noted:

"It was as perfect an act of despotism as can be conceived. It was a *coup d'etat* in every essential feature."

Hence the lines of Maryland's state song, from the poem written by James Ryder Randall in 1861, that few now realize were directed against Abraham Lincoln, his cabinet, and generals. These are the most famous verses:

> "The despot's heel is on thy shore,
> Maryland, My Maryland!
> His torch is at thy temple door,
> Maryland, My Maryland!
> Avenge the patriotic gore,
> That flecked the streets of Baltimore,
> And be the battle queen of yore,
> Maryland, My Maryland!

> Dear Mother! Burst the tyrant's chain,
> Maryland, My Maryland!
> Virginia should not call in vain,
> Maryland, My Maryland!
> She meets her sisters on the plain,
> 'Sic simper!' 'Tis the proud refrain
> That baffles minions back amain,
> Maryland, My Maryland!
> Arise in majesty again,
> Maryland, My Maryland!

Twenty thousand of Maryland's sons were able to escape the Union occupation of their mother state and distinguish themselves in the Confederate Army.

CHAPTER 11

⊙⅊⅁⊙

The Union's Total War Policy

Starving and Terrorizing Civilians

Abraham Lincoln

According to Romans 13, governments are ordained by God for the public good. Among the benefits of a just government we surmise from the Commandments are the protection of life, property, and responsible freedom. Governments are given the power of the sword to assure its ordained purposes are sustained. That sword may be used to enforce its ordained purposes within the limits of its geographical sovereignty or to defend itself and its people from foreign intrusion or harassment. War is thus sometimes necessary to maintain peace, safety, justice, and liberty. Categorical pacifism is unbiblical, unrealistic, and unloving.

The concepts of Just War Doctrine were developed principally by the Christian churches on biblical grounds, but many aspects of Christian Just War Doctrine can also be found in Jewish, Greek, Roman, and even Germanic and Celtic warrior societies. There are a number of criteria for a just war, but the most essential is that it must be for a just cause. That would include protecting, restoring, or recovering a nation's territorial integrity, the identity of its people, and its legitimate government—as well as the lives, properties, and freedoms of its citizens. In actual practice the concept of Just War is sometimes complex on its fringes. Certainly, state sponsored terrorism is unjust war, and defensive and even preemptive measures against state sponsored terrorism would be just.

General William T. Sherman

The Christian concept of war requires not only a just cause but also just conduct and just means in its prosecution. A principal require-ment of just conduct is that military action must discriminate between combatants and noncom-batants. Targeting innocent civilians or their pri-vate property is an unjust means of warfare. Just conduct requires that noncombatants, prisoners of war, and wounded be treated humanely. The food supplies, shelter, clothing, medical sup-plies, harmless personal properties, and peaceful means of livelihood of noncombatants should be respected. Any military means and action must be proportionate to the threat. Minor incidents do not justify massive re-taliation.

For several centuries before the U.S. Civil War, Western nations adhered fairly closely to the Christian concept of just conduct in war, if not always just cause. Confederate forces, with only a few exceptions, conducted military operations according to the Western and Christian tra-dition of just conduct and means. Union forces, however, soon began a systematic escalation to a Total War concept. Total War differs from the Christian concept of limited war in its erosion of the distinction between combatants and noncombatants. Total War is war on an entire society, often escalating by degree according to military or political expediency or desire for vengeance on a demonized enemy. Total War pursues victory and dominance by whatever means without regard to moral or humanitar-ian considerations.

Many people familiar with the Bible may recall that God ordered on several occasions the destruction of entire tribes. But such decrees belong to an all-wise and perfectly just God alone and most emphatically not to human leaders. Total War decreed and practiced by human leaders finds no sanction in the Bible.

General William T. Sherman, perhaps the most famous practitioner of Total War, summed up the Total War philosophy that prevailed in Wash-ington:

"This war differs from other wars, in this particular. We are not fighting armies but a hostile people and must make old and young, rich and poor, feel the hard hand of war."

Edwin Stanton, U.S. Secretary of War and chief advocate for Total War strategy

Southern civilians, especially Southern women, were adamantly unsympathetic to Northern invasion and occupation of the South. Sherman, who believed that **"fear is the beginning of wisdom,"** thought it very important to humble the South and put a fear and dread of Union might and power in their hearts. In June of 1864 he wrote to like-minded Secretary of War Edwin Stanton that:

"There is a class of people, men, women and children, who must be killed or banished before you can hope for peace and order."

TOTAL WAR POLICY IN MISSOURI

Some of the first indications of Union leanings toward a Total War philosophy occurred in Missouri. A majority of Missouri's population was of Southern origin and sympathy. One of the thirteen stars in the Southern Cross honors Missouri. Union forces quickly occupied Missouri before secessionist sentiment could be marshaled in the state legislature. Pro-secessionist Governor Claiborne Jackson and former Governor Sterling Price left to form the Missouri State Guard and join with Confederate forces in Arkansas. Other Southern sympathizers engaged in partisan warfare in Missouri. These Confederate partisans were generally treated as outlaws by Union officials. This outlaw status and mistreatment of their families and other Missouri civilians by Federal troops spawned the bloody vengeance raids of William Quantrill and William Anderson. This extended into the Reconstruction era with the exploits of the James and Younger brothers.

More than one thousand military engagements took place in Missouri during the war. Missouri was the scene of the most drastic and repressive military action directed against civilians in U.S. history. The Palmyra Massacre of October 1862 is only one of many incidents.

THE PALMYRA MASSACRE

In September of 1862 Col. Joseph Porter, commanding a Missouri Confederate cavalry unit, moved into Northeastern Missouri to recruit volunteers and to achieve some limited military objectives. On September 12th Porter raided Palmyra, rescuing 45 Confederate prisoners and capturing among others, Col. Andrew Allsman. A recently retired Union cavalry leader in his sixties, Allsman had been assisting the Union Provost Marshall in Palmyra in identifying Southern sympathizers. Porter apparently released Allsman within a few days, but Allsman disappeared on the road back to Palmyra. On October 8th, suspecting foul play against a valuable Unionist informant, the Union commander in the area, Col. John McNeil, acting through Provost Marshall William Strachan, posted a notice to Col. Porter that if Allsman was not returned safely by October 18th, ten of the several dozen Southern sympathizers then held in the Palmyra and Hannibal jails would be selected for execution on that day. McNeil's action was probably influenced by his instructions from Brigadier General J. W. Schofield on June 12th not to rest **"until you have exterminated the rascals"** (Southern partisans).

No one knew if Col. Porter was still in Missouri, and by the 17th no one had come forth with any news of the missing Unionist informant. Though many doubted that such an order would be carried out, ten men were selected that evening to die by firing squad at 1:00 p.m. the next day. One of these, Willis Baker, was suspected of murdering a Union neighbor. Another, Captain Thomas Sidener, who was soon to be married to a local girl, was a captured Confederate cavalry officer. According to the local Palmyra newspaper, *The Missouri Courier*, except for their Southern sympathies, the crimes of the other eight were unknown. Later that night at the Palmyra jail, Rev. James Green prepared them to meet their maker on the next day.

On the next morning, according to Judge Henry Clay Dean and Cole Younger, the young wife of William Humphrey, the mother of several small children, went to Col. McNeil to plead for her husband's life. When he cursed her, she fled in fear to Provost Marshall Strachan to persuade him to intercede. Strachan said it could be done for $300, and so through the kindness of two gentlemen she quickly raised the money. But when she returned, Strachan also demanded that she submit to his lustful desires. Mrs. Humphrey collapsed before him and was found later in a state of physical exhaustion and mental incoherence. Strachan then went to the jail and demanded that a substitute replace Humphrey. At first Humphrey adamantly refused to be replaced, but reminded that he was the sole provider to his young family by nineteen-year-old orphan, Hiram Smith, at last agreed to the change. And so it was that courageous young Hiram Smith took Humphrey's place among the condemned men.

Three wagons carrying the ten condemned men and their coffins left the jail shortly before 11:00 a.m. and proceeded to the fairgrounds about a half mile east of town. Captain Sidener was wearing the suit he had purchased for his wedding. At the fairgrounds a small military band played. Then the prisoners knelt in prayer and were briefly attended by Rev. R. M. Rhoades. Provost Marshall Strachan shook their hands, and they were seated on their coffins. They were offered blindfolds, but only a few took them. Facing them were 30 riflemen from the 2nd. Missouri Militia. To each side were reserves. Only a few of the condemned men seemed to show any sign of fear. At the command to fire the volleys did not occur simultaneously. Three of the prisoners including Captain Sidener were killed more or less instantly. Six wounded lay writhing and moaning on the ground, and one was not hit at all. The reserves dispatched the six wounded men and finally the seventh with pistol shots to the head. This ghastly series of executions took fifteen minutes.

The pro-Union *Missouri Courier* justified the execution of the ten Southern sympathizers, who had not received the benefit of formal charges, hearing, or trial, with these words:

"It seems hard that ten men should die for one. Under ordinary circumstances you would hardly be justified. But severe diseases demand severe remedies. The safety of the people is the supreme law. It overrules all other considerations. The madness of rebellion has been so deep seated that ordinary methods of cure are inadequate. To take life for life would be little intimidation to men seeking the hearts blood of an obnoxious enemy. They would well afford to make even exchanges under many circumstances. It is only by striking the deepest terror in them, causing them to respect the lives of loyal men that they can be taught to observe the obligation of humanity and of law."

Union Gen. George McClellan opposed Lincoln's Total War Strategy

The *Missouri Courier's* appalling and arrogant self-righteous philosophy was typical of the Radical Republicans and radical abolitionists of that era. It does not stem from any legitimate form of Christian morality, but from the abstract morality and expedient pragmatism of secular humanism. This was shameless self-justifying brutality masquerading as patriotism. But it was not patriotism. It was totalitarian statism.

To their credit, many other Northern newspapers including the then conservative *New York Times* were outraged. The bad publicity from the Palmyra executions was discussed in at least two of Lincoln's Cabinet meetings. Less than six weeks later, after attempting to suppress further news and outcry, President Lincoln promoted Colonel McNeil to the rank of Brigadier General. A fellow Union officer brought charges against Provost Marshall William Strachan, finally resulting in his conviction in 1864. However, Union General William Rosecrans overturned the conviction.

Palmyra was not the only demonstration of Total War philosophy in Missouri. Two similar mass executions involving a total of 26 Confederate POWs and civilians occurred in the northeastern Missouri towns of Kirksville in August and Macon in September. Under Union Generals Ewing and Schofield, more than four-fifths of the families of three western Missouri counties were forced from their homes and lands and made to flee the state because of their sympathy and aid to Confederate partisans. Burning and pillaging of the homes and farms of Southern families elsewhere in Missouri were commonplace. Torture by strangulation became a standard method for forcing civilians to reveal the location of money and valuables or for deriving information on Confederate partisans. The stepfather of Jesse and Frank James was strangled to the point of brain damage.

Many courageous Union officers, including General George B. McClellan, opposed the Lincoln administration's Total War policies, but they did not prevail. Many Northern politicians also opposed these policies, but were unable to prevail in Congress. In 1907 the people of Palmyra, Missouri, erected a monument honoring their ten Southern patriots.

More on the Un-Civil War in Missouri can be found in Appendix Chapter 2.

DEVELOPMENT OF UNION TOTAL WAR POLICY

Before the arrogant and bombastic Major General John Pope was summoned by President Lincoln to command a combination of reorganized forces called "the Army of Virginia," in June of 1862, he had distinguished himself as a ruthless opponent of Confederate partisans in Missouri and as an aggressive commander in Mississippi. He encouraged his troops to plunder civilian food sources, burn homes in any area of Confederate resistance, hang civilians suspected of aiding Confederate forces, and shoot civilians in reprisal for Confederate guerilla attacks. He continued his severe philosophy of war in Virginia, drawing the resolute enmity of Confederate Generals Lee and Jackson. But during his rise to fame and favor with Lincoln, he received much praise in the Northern press until his ignominious defeat in September 1862 at the hands of Jackson and Longstreet at Second Manassas. Pope's praise in the Northern press prior to Second Manassas for his ruthlessly effective Total War tactics was noted by other Union officers of similar tactical inclinations. One of these was the Russian émigré, Col. Ivan (John) Turchin.

In the spring of 1862, the Army of the Ohio under Union Major General Don Carlos Buell was occupying Kentucky and Tennessee and raiding into North Alabama. In April, Huntsville, Alabama, was occupied by Col. Turchin, Commander of the 19th Illinois and temporarily in command of the 8th Brigade, consisting of Illinois and Ohio regiments. He quickly gained the reputation in North Alabama as the "Robber" Colonel for his rampant pillaging and indignities of all kinds heaped upon its citizens. His thievery and violence against civilians had been a matter of official record since July of 1861.

THE RAPE OF ATHENS, ALABAMA

In the middle of April, the 18th Ohio under Turchin's command occupied Athens, Alabama, a prosperous town of about 1,200 population. On May 1, however, they were driven out by a combined regular and partisan Confederate cavalry force of only 112 men and retreated back to Huntsville. The Confederate cavalry was greeted with cheers and waving handkerchiefs by the citizens in the streets. Reports indicate that some Athens civilians may have fired on the Union troops from their homes as they left. The Confederate forces, however, quickly pulled out of town.

The next morning Turchin marched into Athens unopposed with at least three regiments of his brigade. The townspeople, including the ladies, turned their backs to him as he rode into town. Turchin was furious with this gesture of impertinence and told his troops he would close his eyes for a few hours while they took their pleasure in looting the town and terrorizing its citizens. He then left them to their depredations for the rest of the day. At least some of Turchin's troops stayed a few weeks.

Later testimony indicated that numerous homes, offices, and stores were pillaged. Money, jewelry, dishware, silver, watches, clothes, shoes, medical supplies, medical instruments, and anything else of value were stolen. Furniture, carpets, artwork, and fixtures were destroyed. Books and especially Bibles were viciously destroyed. Numerous testimonies indicated that the soldiers' language to women was rude, insulting, threatening, and vulgar. One white woman, the pregnant wife of a Confederate cavalryman, was singled out and gang-raped, shortly thereafter dying from a miscarriage. Several black servant girls were raped, and several more had to fend off attempted rapes. The commander made his headquarters in the home of a prominent citizen and refused to let his sick daughter receive any medical treatment. She subsequently died. Shots were fired into homes and terror reigned. Some of the troops billeted themselves in the slave quarters on a nearby plantation for weeks, debauching the females. They roamed with the males over the surrounding country, plundering and pillaging.

Some Union officers of integrity among Turchin's troops, however, reported this to his Division Commander, Major General O. M. Mitchell. Mitchell immediately rebuked Turchin and notified General Buell and Secretary of War Stanton. After some delay on the part of Stanton, General Buell, a very effective officer of high integrity who was especially concerned that his soldiers conduct themselves with honor, stepped in and relieved Turchin of command, insisting on his court-martial.

Most of the information in the previous paragraphs was taken from the court-martial proceedings of August 1862. Brigadier General James A. Garfield, a future President of the United States, presided over the court-martial. Turchin and one of his regimental commanders, Col. Gazlay, were found guilty and dismissed from the Army. Charges against several other officers were dropped on proof they were only acting on Turchin's orders. General Buell approved and signed the verdict.

The proceedings of Turchin's court-martial received considerable national attention and became the focus of a debate on the prosecution and conduct of the war. The Chicago newspapers bitterly condemned Buell for Turchin's dismissal and court-martial. Their howl for harsh policies including devastation and plundering by Union armies was picked up by many other papers. The Radical Republicans in Congress were especially pushing for a more vigorous and punishing war policy.

Turchin's wife, evidently a very formidable woman in many regards, personally went to see Lincoln and persuaded him that not only should Turchin be reinstated but that he should also be promoted to Brigadier General. Hearing of this, General Buell protested to Secretary of War Stanton that:

"If as I hear, the promotion of Colonel Turchin is contemplated I feel it is my duty to inform you that he is entirely unfit for it. I placed him in the command of a brigade, and now find it necessary to relieve him from it in consequence of his utter failure to enforce discipline and render it efficient."

But within a few days of the court-martial, President Lincoln reinstated Turchin and promoted him to the rank of Brigadier General. A few months later Lincoln would make a similar promotion. In November Lincoln promoted Col. John McNeil, one of the senior officers responsible for the October 1862 Palmyra Massacre in Missouri, to Brigadier General. It was obvious that Total War policy had many advocates in Washington.

Brigadier General Turchin and his wife returned to their home in Chicago to cheering crowds. He was presented a sword, and a band played "Lo, the Conquering Hero Comes." On August 30, General Buell was informed that a large part of Athens, Alabama, had been burned by Union troops passing through the town.

MCCLELLAN AND BUELL OPPOSE
TOTAL WAR POLICY IN VAIN

Major General Don Carlos Buell was soon to be shoved aside, as would be his friend, George B. McClellan. Both generals were adamant

Union Gen. Don Carlos Buell opposed Lincoln's Total War strategy

advocates of the rules of conventional warfare and vigorous opponents of the Total War concept. General Buell was shoved aside by the War Department after the Battle of Perryville in Kentucky in October 1862 for failing to pursue Braxton Bragg's divisions in their forced withdrawal. Buell could not have safely pursued Bragg, however, because his supply lines had been cut and severely devastated by Confederate General Joe Wheeler's Cavalry.

McClellan was a conservative Democrat with strong views on how to win both the war and afterwards the peace. These ideas were in substantial disagreement with the Radical Republican dominated Committee on the Conduct of the War and especially Secretary of War Edwin Stanton. Stanton undermined him at every opportunity. McClellan was also grievously disappointed that Lincoln did not seem to take seriously a strict code of honor and conduct in prosecuting the war. In assuming command of the Army in November 1861 McClellan told Lincoln this:

"This rebellion has assumed the character of a war, as such it should be regarded, and it should be conducted upon the highest principles known to Christian civilization…In prosecuting the war, all private property and unarmed persons should be strictly protected…"

McClellan was shoved aside by Lincoln and Secretary Stanton in November of 1862. Thereafter occurred a series of Union Army disasters, most notably at Fredericksburg and Chancellorsville.

Federal war policy was increasingly dominated by Total War advocacy as the conflict continued. In 1864 and early 1865, Total War had left the Shenandoah Valley in Virginia and wide swaths of Georgia and South Carolina in smoking ruins. By the end of the war over 40 percent of all private property in the South was destroyed. An estimated 50,000 homeless refugees and displaced slaves perished of hunger, disease, and exposure. Political despotism reigned in both the North and the now subjugated South.

DEVASTATION OF THE SHENANDOAH VALLEY OF VIRGINIA

General Robert E. Lee

On June 27, 1863, near Chambersburg, Pennsylvania—just days before the momentous Battle of Gettysburg—Confederate General Robert E. Lee issued a general order to the Army of Northern Virginia, praising them for their honorable conduct thus far in their march into Union territory, but cautioning them on their continuing responsibility to respect all private property and the lives of all noncombatants.

"The commanding general considers no greater disgrace could befall the army, and through it our whole people, than the perpetration of the barbarous outrages upon the unarmed and defenseless and the wanton destruction of private property, that have marked the course of the enemy in our own country...It must be remembered that we make war only upon armed men, and that we cannot take vengeance for the wrongs our people have suffered...without offending against Him to whom vengeance belongeth, without whose favor and support our efforts must all prove in vain."

With few exceptions, the Confederate armies managed to conduct themselves honorably during the war. One of the major exceptions, however, was at Chambersburg a little more than a year after the Battle of Gettysburg. On August 30, 1864, Confederate Brigadier General John McCausland tried to exact a tribute in cash or gold from the city of Chambersburg as payment in retaliation for Union General David Hunter's burning crops and homes in the southern part of the Shenandoah Valley of Virginia and shelling the ungarrisoned and unprotected town of Lexington in the previous two months. When the town officials refused, he evacuated the 3,000 inhabitants and then set the downtown business district on fire, which resulted in about half the town being destroyed. This was unbeknown to General Lee. According to Jubal Early, McCausland's immediate superior, McCausland had gone beyond the scope of his orders. Even so, this action was taken to deter further depredation of Virginia towns and farms by Hunter, and considerable precaution was taken to prevent civilian casualties.

Gen. Joshua Lawrence Chamberlain, Gettysburg hero. opposed Lincoln's Total War strategy

Misconduct occurred on both sides, but with a significant difference. Southern misconduct was infrequent and not sanctioned by high levels of Confederate leadership. It usually resulted in discipline. Six Confederate soldiers were shot for plundering during the Gettysburg campaign in 1863. Union misconduct was frequent and—especially in the last two years of the war—was employed as part of a systematic policy of devastation to break the will of the Southern people by starvation and terror.

There were notable exceptions to this, Union generals George B. McClellan and Don Carlos Buell, being among the most prominent. But these generals were unable to prevail against the Total War thinking of Lincoln, Secretary of War Stanton, and the Radical Republicans in Congress. Many lower-ranking Union officers were heart-sick at having to carry out orders to torch the homes of women and children. Among these was General Lawrence Chamberlain, hero of Little Round Top at Gettysburg, and Col. Robert G. Shaw, commander of the 54th Massachusetts, depicted in the movie, *Glory*. Chamberlain wrote to his sister during the Petersburg campaign, late in the war: **"I am willing to fight men in arms, but not babes in arms."** The highest level of Union military leadership would fall into the hands of those generals willing and sometimes eager to practice the devastation and inhumanity of Total War.

In September 1864, General Grant sent General Philip Sheridan with 40,000 men to reinforce Hunter's 22,000 men and severely punish the much smaller forces of Jubal Early and Wade Hampton. But their primary purpose was to destroy the entire Shenandoah Valley. Up to that point the Union's Total War policy had been on a relatively small scale, but now it would be practiced on a grand scale. Union troops under the command of Sheridan and Hunter devastated a 92 mile strip of the Shenandoah Valley from Winchester to Staunton, in some places 40 miles wide. This had been the breadbasket of the Confederate Army and the Southern people. The remaining railroads were destroyed. Crops of all kinds were burned. Homes were looted and burned. The Federal troops destroyed more than 2,000 barns and all the farm equipment in them. A destroyed barn was a destroyed livelihood for farm families. They destroyed seventy mills, 4,000 horses, 11,000 cattle, 12,000 sheep, and other livestock. Anything the Union troops could not use themselves, they destroyed. Even pump handles were destroyed so families could not draw water from their wells. One of Jubal Early's staff officers wrote of this tragic and appalling scene:

"I rode down the Valley after Sheridan's retreating cavalry beneath great columns of smoke...I saw mothers and maidens tearing their hair and shrieking to Heaven in their fright and despair, and little children, voiceless and tearless in their pitiable terror."

Sheridan had made good on Grant's order "**to eat out Virginia clear and clean.**" As Grant had suggested, a crow flying over the Shenandoah Valley would have to carry its own lunch. One might ask what sort of a "Union" practices such deliberate barbarity on those it claims should be partners in the "Union." What sort of thinking allows such inhumanity in the name of "Saving the Union"? It is the twisted thinking of secular humanism with its sanctimonious and totalitarian pragmatism. It is the moral perversion that insists that the means justifies the end. It is the contorted philosophy that might makes right.

General Sherman, perhaps the grand champion of Total War, said in January of 1864:

"The government of the U. S. has any and all rights which they choose to enforce in war—to take their lives, their homes, their land, their everything—war is simply unrestrained by the Constitution...to the persistent secessionist, why death is mercy, and the quicker he or she is disposed of the better."

Sherman and Sheridan would both attain the position of Commanding General of the U. S. Army in later years. Both are credited with the famous saying that "**the only good Indian is a dead Indian.**" Sherman elaborated his Total War philosophy with these words:

"The more Indians we can kill this year the fewer we will need to kill the next, because the more I see of the Indians the more convinced I become that they must either be killed or be maintained as a species of pauper. Their attempts at civilization are ridiculous."

Some people sympathize with Sherman's famous words that cruelty makes wars shorter, and since shortening a war will bring peace sooner, cruelty in war is justified. But this is a corrupting and convoluted doctrine that would justify anything in the pursuit of victory. Just warfare must be proportionate in its response to enemy action and threats. An appropriate level of force to bring a quick peace would be justified. But deliberate cruelty, especially that targeting noncombatants, prisoners of war, and wounded can never be justified. Wanton destruction of the food supplies and shelter of noncombatant civilians is neither justified nor honorable. It only multiplies violence and future grievances and morally corrupts those who succumb to such a brutal philosophy. One thing Sherman said is more agreeable to sensible people:

"War is at best barbarism. Its glory is all moonshine...War is hell."

The devastation of the Shenandoah Valley, so appalling in its grand scale of Total Warfare, would pale in comparison with Sherman's operations in Georgia and South Carolina in late 1864 and early 1865.

MISSISSIPPI AND GEORGIA BURNING

When Confederate General John Brown Gordon entered the town of York, Pennsylvania, during the Gettysburg campaign of 1863, he found the population in a state of panic, fearing retaliation for Union atrocities against Southern civilians. He gathered a large crowd of women in the street and told them this:

"Our Southern homes have been pillaged, sacked, and burned; our mothers, wives, and little ones driven forth amid the brutal insults of your soldiers. Is it any wonder that we fight with desperation? A natural revenge would prompt us to retaliate in kind. But we scorn to war on women and children. We are fighting for the God given rights of liberty and independence as handed down in the Constitution by our fathers. So fear not. If a torch is applied to a single dwelling or an insult offered to a female of your town by a soldier of this command, point me out that man and you shall have his life."

General Gordon, a future Governor and U. S. Senator from Georgia, had in those few words articulated the just cause of Southern secession and had distinguished between honorable warfare and the dishonorable and indiscriminate brutality of Total War.

This was not the style of Union Major General William T. Sherman. Before leaving Mississippi for his new assignment to capture Atlanta, he would leave much of northern Mississippi burning. In July of 1863 his troops burned half of the state capital of Jackson. In August he left only three buildings standing in Oxford. In early February of 1864 two wings of Sherman's command stationed in Vicksburg and Memphis converged on the Confederate supply depot at Meridian. After some skirmishing on February 14, his troops moved into Meridian as General Polk's Confederates withdrew to the south. For the next five days, 10,000 of Sherman's men worked like demons, pulling down every structure in Meridian, including homes, businesses, army supply warehouses, hospitals, churches, everything. The civilian refugees moved south seeking the protection and sustenance of Polk. On the sixth day, Sherman's troops pulled out of Meridian, setting fire to the debris. There was nothing left of Meridian but a blackened scar on the earth.

May 1864 found Sherman in North Georgia at the head of a vast army advancing toward Atlanta. Sherman continued his practice of destroying livestock, food supplies, crops, and every means of agricultural production—leaving women, children, the disabled, and elderly exposed to the threat of starvation. His orders to his troops were to **"make Georgia howl."**

Sherman also decided to destroy the factories in North Georgia that were important to the Confederate war effort. The towns of Marietta, Roswell, and New Manchester took the brunt of his destructive wrath. His men first proceeded to reduce the factories. Then the houses were either pulled down or burned, but not before the townspeople were robbed of their jewelry and valuables. Even wedding rings were forced from the hands of tearful wives. Fearing that the factories might somehow survive, he took the unprecedented step of rounding up the factory workers to be shipped north of the Ohio River by rail. The great majority of these workers were women and older children. Nevertheless, they were pulled from their sobbing loved ones to await transportation. Before departure about 400 women and children were forced to stay in the town square of Roswell day and night for a week in the sweltering July heat. Altogether more than 2,000 women and children carrying very few belongings were put on trains and shipped north. One train with 249 destitute looking women and children was seen as it stopped briefly at Louisville, Kentucky. Few of the 2,000 women and children involved in this criminal inhumanity were ever seen again. Neither did the U. S. government make any attempt to reunite the families after the war. The town of New Manchester was so completely devastated that it was no more.

Sherman's forces finally forced the Confederate Army to withdraw from Atlanta, and the Mayor surrendered the city to him on September 2. Shortly after Lincoln's reelection in November, Sherman ordered the evacuation of the city. Much to the protest of Confederate General John B. Hood, several thousand Atlanta civilians became homeless and starving refugees. In a letter to Sherman he protested:

"And now, sir, permit me to say that the unprecedented measure you propose transcends, in studied and ingenious cruelty, all acts ever before brought to my attention in the dark history of war."

Most of the refugees headed south to Macon. On November 15, with refugees still streaming from the city, Sherman had everything but homes and churches set on fire. Many of these were, nevertheless, enveloped in the flaming holocaust. According to one of Sherman's staff officers, drunken soldiers cheered, danced, and sang as large flaming buildings collapsed. When the fires subsided, only about 200 homes and a few other buildings were left standing.

The next day Sherman proceeded on his famous 300-mile, 60-mile-wide march through Georgia with the two wings of his 62,000 man army looting and burning homes and barns, and stealing or killing horses, mules, and livestock. As they left the smoking city of Atlanta a band struck up Julia Ward Howe's *Battle Hymn of the Republic,* and the men began to sing "Glory, glory, hallelujah." The right wing of two corps was commanded by the pious young abolitionist, Oliver O. Howard, who would become

chief of the Freedmen's Bureau during Reconstruction. The left was commanded by Henry Slocum. Sherman's cavalry was led by young Judson
Kilpatrick, considered perfectly obnoxious by his fellow Union officers,
his Confederate opponents, and especially the women of the South. Constant criticism of Kilpatrick did not bother Sherman, saying of him:

"I know he's a hell of a damned fool, but I want just that sort of man
to command my cavalry on this expedition."

Most of Hood's Confederate forces had moved northwest toward
Nashville, where he hoped to cut Union supply lines and throw the Union
Army into confusion by striking a devastating blow at Nashville and Franklin. That left only 13,000 Confederates of Hardee's Corps and Wheeler's
cavalry to harass Sherman's advance.

Sherman's foragers, often called "bummers" for the German word
meaning an "idle wastrel," went about their work with devilish enthusiasm. They looked upon their work as a treasure hunt, discovering where
Southern families had hidden valuables and food and sometimes even
livestock. They particularly craved gold and jewelry and often resorted to
threats and violence to discover their whereabouts. Frequently they would
hoist a home owner or trusted slave up on a rope thrown over a tree limb
and strangle them until they revealed the location of their valuables. Some
white women were raped, but young black slave girls received most of the
abuse and attention of rapists and womanizers. Whether or not they were
assigned to foraging duty, most soldiers participated in looting and wanton destruction given an opportunity. Officially, much of this was strictly
forbidden, but it was generally winked at. Many Union soldiers began to
see pillaging and the spoils of war as a right and as just punishment for the
"rebellious" South. As the army marched farther to the southeast toward
Savannah and the sea, they became less and less disciplined. Sherman's
officers also set another new precedent of war by forcing Confederate prisoners of war to clear mine fields for Union troops.

By December 2, against comparatively light resistance, Sherman
managed to occupy Savannah and telegraphed Lincoln that the city was
secure. This was published in Northern newspapers with great acclaim, re-
assuring Congress and the public that victory was at long last at hand. His
triumphant march through Georgia was heralded as a spectacular military

achievement. Congress passed a joint resolution of praise and gratitude, and Sherman became the hero of an admiring press and public. His next great thrust would be through South Carolina, which would be an even more devastating demonstration of Total War.

SOUTH CAROLINA UNDER THE TYRANT'S HEEL

Encountering only token resistance from Hardee's much smaller Confederate forces, Sherman's troops occupied Savannah on December 21, 1864. Sherman spared the city for personal, political, and military reasons. He then prepared to cut a destructive path through South Carolina with its capital, Columbia, as the major target. A letter from Union General Henry Halleck suggested that he consider the destruction of Charleston, adding:

"and if a little salt should be sown upon the site it may prevent the growth of future crops of nullification and secession."

Charleston, however, was far off the route of Sherman's plan. Columbia was to be the special target of his destructive designs. He replied to Halleck that he would keep his suggestion in mind, adding:

"The truth is, the whole army is burning with an insatiable desire to wreak vengeance upon South Carolina. I almost tremble at her fate, but feel that she deserves all that seems in store for her."

As it turned out, Charleston was to be shelled and partially burned by other Union forces.

Sherman's general order for launching his march through Georgia and then South Carolina called for **"liberal foraging."** Horses, mules, and wagons were to be appropriated freely. Should any community resist, the order called for **"devastation more or less relentless."** This was a warrant for a high degree of confiscation, looting, or destruction of private property. Indeed, South Carolina would suffer a loss of more than 50 percent of all private property, exceeding that of any other state.

The prohibition against community resistance effectively meant that even skirmishing by Confederate militia or cavalry could be punished by punitive property damage, executions of Confederate prisoners of war, and occasionally even shooting down a few random civilians. Sherman gave his cavalry leader, Judson Kilpatrick, instructions to execute as many as five prisoners for each "murdered" Union soldier.

Resistance was to be put down by instilling fear in Southern women and children, as well as in fighting men. Southern women, however, often proved to be steel magnolias. One young Georgia farm wife was standing at the door of her home with two small boys by her side when a Yankee soldier carrying two of her chickens asked whether she thought the war would end soon. She looked at the column of blue on the road and said quietly,

"Our men will fight you as long as they live, and these boys'll fight you when they grow up."

Sherman moved into South Carolina with more than 50,000 men. Opposing him were "Old Reliable" William Hardee with scarcely 10,000 men and Joe Wheeler and Wade Hampton with a few thousand cavalry. As they moved toward Columbia, Sherman's northern wing under Oliver Howard's troops looted and burned the towns of Buford's Bridge, Barnwell, Blackville, Graham, Bamberg, and Midway. Farther to the south, Henry Slocum's wing obliterated Purysburg, Robertsville, Lawtonville, and McPhersonville. At the village of Hardeeville every building was dismantled. When the spire of the village church came crashing down, one of the soldiers yelled out, **"There goes your damned old gospel shop."**

The farms and homes along the way suffered the now standard depredation and burning. Any means of sustenance including livestock was either carried away or destroyed. As Sherman's troops approached Columbia, the towns of Orangeburg and Lexington were partially burned, and the surrounding farms subjected to the same sweeping destruction.

Confederate commanders did not intend to defend Columbia with more than a cavalry skirmish. They considered it too risky to the civilian population and too costly in Confederate casualties. The Confederacy was in desperate straits now. General Hardee was instructed to conserve his manpower. Confederate strategy was to concentrate forces at some more advantageous position to deliver a major punishing blow to Federal forces.

Meanwhile the population of Columbia was swollen with refugees from the Low Country and Charleston. As the meager Confederate garrison at Columbia began to withdraw on February 16, Union artillery began to pound the city. No warning or summons to surrender had been given. On the next day, Mayor T. J. Goodwyn and a delegation of aldermen, carrying a white flag, surrendered the city and received assurances for its safety. But by late morning the pillaging and robbery had begun in earnest. An estimated twelve hundred watches were transferred from the pockets of elderly men to the pockets of the blue-coated invaders. About the same number of purses were yanked from ladies' hands. Some fires began to break out, including some cotton piled in a street, but they were extinguished by Columbia firemen.

The citizens of Columbia were robbed and abused on the streets, and felt unsafe in their homes as squads of soldiers pillaged and ransacked home after home. The soldiers used the usual method of hanging and strangulation, often to a point near death, to discover the location of valuables. Some white women were raped, but as usual the sexual depredations were more commonly visited on young black girls. Scores endured unwanted ravage by wave after wave of Union soldiers. Some were approached with more finesse, but refusal often brought brutal violence. At least two were beaten to death and left lying face down in the street.

Many citizens had been warned by sympathetic soldiers that the city was doomed, regardless of any promises to the contrary by General Sherman. The most horrendous terror began at night. Commencing with signal flares, twenty fires around the city broke out almost simultaneously. Swarms of drunken soldiers proceeded with pots of flammable liquids, balls of cotton, and matches to wreak a flaming havoc. They prevented the Columbia firemen from their duty and cut the fire hoses of their equipment. Streams of refugees, almost all women, children, and elderly men, crowded the streets of Columbia seeking to escape the spreading fires. Even what belongings they carried were yanked from them by abusive and threatening soldiers.

Nothing was sacred to the mobs of drunken soldiers that roamed, pillaged, and torched Columbia. A group of Catholic nuns and their sixty female students sought refuge in the chapel of the Ursuline Convent. In the dark night they could see the flames of burning buildings as they prayed and said the rosary. With a crashing banging at the door, a mob of drunken soldiers swarmed the altar, stripping it of sacred gold vessels. A priest rescued the nuns and girls and took them to a nearby church. A few hours later they witnessed the burning convent collapse into a mass of fiery debris. Laughing soldiers taunted the nuns. Rudely blowing cigar smoke in their faces, one scoundrel jeered,

"Oh, holy! Yes, holy! We're just as holy as you are! Now, what do you think of God? Ain't Sherman greater?"

Novelist William Gilmore Simms came to Columbia as a refugee after his home in Orangeburg was burned. As an eye-witness, he wrote a short book on the destruction of Columbia. According to Simms, the soldiers reveled and played fiddles and accordions as they smashed and robbed. Ladies were hustled from their chambers with taunts and foul language as their jewelry was plucked from their very persons. As the soldiers burned and looted they asked such questions as,

"And what do you think of Yankees now? Do you not fear us now? and What do you think of secession now?"

According to Simms, even General Oliver Howard, known by some as "Old Prayer Book," expressed a callous and punitive attitude toward a woman complaining of the monstrous crimes of his army, telling her,

"It is only what the country deserves. It is her fit punishment; and if this does not quit the rebellion, and we have to return, we will do this work thoroughly. We will not leave woman or child."

Despite all this, Simms noted that many Union soldiers gave what help they could to protect women, children, elderly men, and their property, often at the risk of their own lives. He cites by name several who heroically tried to protect the Ursuline Convent. It seemed to Simms that instances of kindness, sympathy, and protection generally came from the Western men--those from Ohio, Indiana, Illinois, and Iowa--while the Easterners were more likely to express punitive attitudes.

Leaving Columbia, Sherman's troops destroyed the towns of Allston, Pomaria, Winnsboro, Blackstock, Society Hill, Camden, and Cheraw before advancing into North Carolina. Two occurrences of gang-rape murder on young white girls started a reprisal war between Wheeler and Kilpatrick. In both cases, Wheeler's cavalry quickly caught up with the culprits and executed them on the spot. They also began tracking down and killing some of the worst foraging predators. Sherman would not have Wheeler administering justice to Union soldiers, and thus the reprisal war escalated. In Cheraw, Federal troops executed a gray-haired Confederate prisoner chosen by lot as retaliation for the "murder" of a Union soldier. The Confederate prisoner was a Methodist minister with nine children.

Sherman blamed the burning of Columbia on Confederate General Wade Hampton and on accident. In later years, writing his autobiography, he admitted blaming Hampton was only a ruse to discredit Hampton and damage Confederate morale. Sherman's famous march through Georgia and South Carolina made him the most lauded Union general in the war.

REPORTS OF BARBARIC HORDES

By March 11, 1865, Union General Sherman's troops had occupied Fayetteville, North Carolina. General Sherman instructed his officers to go easier on North Carolina than South Carolina. By this he hoped to drive a wedge of mistrust between the two states. But advancing on Raleigh from the South and East, Sherman's troops could not restrain themselves from the usual plunder and depredations. Wilmington, Goldsboro, and Greenville were terrorized, and most of the homes and farms on the roads to Raleigh were left in smoking ruin. Thousands of women, children, and elderly were left without food, shelter, medical supplies, and adequate clothing. Pillaging and robbery were rampant. Reports of rape and murder were common.

Sherman's earlier letter to Major R. M. Sawyer in Huntsville, Alabama, gave some insight into the general's thinking about the Union cause and the treatment of Southerners. Beginning with,

"We of the North are beyond question, right in our lawful cause..."

He then details his assertion that the Union Army had the right to take their lives, homes, land, and everything they own. Sherman continued,

"Next year their lands will be taken; for in war we can take

them, and rightfully, too; and in another year they may beg in vain for their lives."

In his official report on his march through Georgia, Sherman stated that 20% of Georgia's property loss was to provision the Union Army, and the other 80% was "**simply waste and destruction.**" But many of the Union officers accompanying Sherman on his march through Georgia and the Carolinas were not so proud of that destruction. Captain Daniel Oakley of the 2nd Massachusetts commented that,

"It was sad to see the wanton destruction of property, which was the work of the 'bummers,' who were marauding through the country committing every sort of outrage...At the very beginning of the campaign in Dalton, the Federal soldiery had received encouragement to become vandals. When Sherman cut loose from Atlanta everybody had license to throw off restraint and make Georgia 'drain' the bitter cup..."

Speaking of the area along the route of the march, Captain Oakley also asserted that a traveler will:

"...hear stories from the lips of women that would make him ashamed of the flag that waved over him as he went into battle. When the army passed nothing was left but a trail of desolation and despair. No houses escaped robbery, no woman escaped insult, no building escaped the firebrand...War may license an army to subsist on the enemy, but civilized warfare stops at livestock, forage, and provisions. It does not enter the houses of the sick and helpless and rob women of their finger rings and carry off their clothing."

Both Generals Grant and Sherman turned more magnanimous at the end of the war. Grant gave Lee's men gracious terms of surrender at Appomattox. Union General Joshua Chamberlain even had his men present arms in a salute respecting the renowned bravery of the vanquished Confederates as they marched in final review. Sherman, on Grant's instructions, gave the same terms to Joe Johnston's army surrendering in North Carolina, and for it came under criticism by Stanton and the Radical

Republicans. Sherman, however, defended the terms on his own, saying that the South had received enough punishment. When the Radical Republicans howled for the imprisonment or execution of Lee, Grant made it very clear that he would not permit it. General Lee, to the end of his life, would never allow anyone in his presence to speak ill of Grant. The gracious terms of surrender, however, would be betrayed by the Radical Republicans during Reconstruction.

Following Grant's election to the presidency in 1868, Sherman would become Commander-in-Chief of the U.S. Army for over fifteen years. He was tremendously popular in the North, and many wanted to make him President. In that regard, he made his famous remarks, **"If nominated, I will not run; if elected, I will not serve."** Sherman even became more popular in the South because of his opposition to ruthless Radical Republican policies during Reconstruction.

General Sheridan became military governor of Louisiana and Texas after the war. President Johnson considered Sheridan so repressive that he transferred him to Missouri, where he took command of the Indian Wars. Sheridan found success in the Indian Wars by the same methods he used to suppress resistance in the Shenandoah Valley of Virginia, only even more ruthlessly. Sheridan destroyed Indian food supplies and on a few occasions massacred whole villages including women and children. As his superior officer, Sherman must also bear part of that responsibility. In 1870, Sheridan was assigned as an observer with the Prussian Army during the Franco-Prussian War. His influence there was to have a lasting legacy on the conduct of war. On Sherman's retirement in 1884, Sheridan replaced him as Commander-in-Chief of the U.S. Army.

LINCOLN'S DESPOTISM AND WAR AGAINST DISSENT IN SIX NORTHERN STATES

The whitewashed versions of American history prevailing today seldom inform us that Lincoln was fighting a ruthless war on two fronts. Lincoln waged one war against the Confederacy and another against dissent within the Union. In some aspects the Un-Civil War might be considered not only a regional war, but a war between the Republican and Democratic parties. Northern Democrats held a conservative philosophy of government in common with Southern Democrats. In those days the words

"Democrat" and "Conservative" were almost political synonyms. (How different it is today!) A majority of Northern Democrats also favored a negotiated peace to end the war. Many Democratic newspapers and politicians voiced strong reservations about the justice and wisdom of the war and strong criticism of Lincoln's conduct of the war. This dissent was particularly strong in six Northern states controlled by the Democratic Party: New York, Pennsylvania, Ohio, Indiana, Illinois, and Wisconsin.

Abraham Lincoln

Lincoln and his Cabinet reacted to this dissent with ruthless despotism, beginning with suppression of dissenting newspapers. Over three hundred newspapers critical of Lincoln, the government, or the conduct of the war, were closed down. Dissenting editors, political leaders, clergy, influential persons critical of the Lincoln administration, and anyone suspected of disloyalty were imprisoned without formal charges or trial. Secretary of State, William Seward, who boasted to the British ambassador of his power to ring a bell and have a man arrested anywhere, normally directed the Lincoln Administration's secret police functions. But Lincoln sometimes acted directly, as in May 1864, when he gave a direct order to General John Dix to close two influential New York newspapers:

"You will take possession by military force, of the printing establishments of the *New York World* and *Journal of Commerce*...and prohibit further publication thereof...you are therefore directed to arrest and imprison...the editors, proprietors and publishers of aforesaid newspapers."

Many newspapers, such as the very influential, *New York Daily News*, were driven out of business by denying them use of the Postal Service. Some newspapers, such as the *Brooklyn Eagle,* were allowed to resume publication contingent on favorable coverage of Lincoln. In addition, clergymen were barred from preaching because they refused to support Lincoln in their sermons and public prayers. Freedom of the press and freedom of speech ceased to exist.

An estimated 14,000 to 38,000 Northern civilians were arrested and taken to unknown places of confinement. Some simply disappeared. Early in the war, a large portion of the Maryland legislature was arrested and imprisoned. Clement Vallandigham, a leading Congressional Democrat and candidate for governor of Ohio, was arrested and deported. Federal armies were used to influence elections.

In July 1863, an army of 50,000 New York State and citizen militia battled Federal troops and New York City Police over Federal despotism and federalization of conscription. This was organized resistance, not a spontaneous "draft riot." It took Federal troops four days to suppress the revolt. Thousands were killed or wounded. General Sherman complained that half the strength of the Federal Army was tied up suppressing dissent in six Union states.

DIRTY UNION LAUNDRY:

THE REAL STORY OF ANDERSONVILLE, THE HANGING

OF MARY SURRATT, AND HOPES FOR A BLOODY SLAVE REVOLT

Union propaganda in its postwar and modern forms characteristically treat the Andersonville tragedy as a Confederate atrocity. It was actually a self-inflicted Union atrocity against its own soldiers that culminated in a postwar political atrocity. The Andersonville POW camp was established in early 1864 when the Union Navy blockade, called Anaconda, was becoming increasingly successful at squeezing the life out of the Confederacy. There was a shortage of everything in the Confederacy. But Union prisoners at Andersonville received the same food rations and medical attention as their guards. The guards died of malnutrition and disease at the same rate as the prisoners. The Confederate government did everything possible to relieve the suffering of Union prisoners at Andersonville. To that end they made every effort to exchange these prisoners. But Union Secretary of War Stanton repeatedly refused to compromise his policy of attrition on the much smaller Confederate Army. He repeatedly refused to ship medical supplies and assistance to the prisoners despite Confederate guarantees that these supplies would be used exclusively for Union POWs. The Confederates even released 3,000 prisoners, but they were turned back by Union commanders. Stanton, astonishingly insensitive to the suffering of his own soldiers, thought it more important that the prisoners be a burden to the Confederate Army. At the end of the war, Andersonville's Commandant, Henry Wirz, who tried very hard to relieve the suffering of his prisoners, was convicted in a travesty of legal justice on the basis of perjured and bribery-tainted testimony for conspiring in the death of Union prisoners. Despite the fact that he had even given half his salary to the relief of the prisoners, he was falsely demonized and hanged. This cruel miscarriage of justice satisfied the Northern cry for vengeance and directed the blame away from Stanton. See Chapters 17 and 18.

Another postwar political atrocity involving Stanton was connected to the trial of alleged conspirators in the assassination of Abraham Lincoln. Mary Surratt, the middle-aged and devoutly Catholic owner of the boarding house frequented by several conspirators, was convicted on largely circumstantial evidence. Besides her boarding house connection, she had a son in Canada suspected of being a Confederate agent. The chief government prosecutor, Joseph Holt, obscured the complication that there were really two plots, one to kidnap Lincoln and the other to assassinate him. The prosecution also withheld key evidence on the existence and content of John Wilkes Booth's diary. This diary placed the origin of the assassination plot only three days before Lincoln's death. That information would have exonerated Mrs. Surratt in the assassination conspiracy. Two key witnesses that had been held in hooded solitary confinement (a form of torture) testified against Mrs. Surratt in exchange for their own release and exoneration. The military tribunal, although convicting her of being part of a conspiracy to assassinate Lincoln, recommended mercy in her case. There was also much public pressure for mercy. However, Secretary Stanton failed to inform President Johnson of the military tribunal's recommendation for mercy. Mary Surratt was hanged with the other conspirators. See Chapter 19 for more details on this tragic story.

Even Lincoln's Emancipation Proclamation anticipated atrocities. The Proclamation actually only freed slaves in Confederate held territory and not in Union held territory. The Proclamation, though an obvious political swindle, would have its diplomatic advantages. But Lincoln himself stated that the Proclamation was primarily a war measure to encourage a slave revolt in the South. Such a revolt would force many Confederate troops out of the field to protect their families. The Proclamation also appeased the Radical Republicans, who had been crying for such a measure and putting considerable pressure on Lincoln for more successful prosecution of the war. Past slave revolts had seen bloody atrocities against white families. Some thought was given to including a specific exhortation to rise up in revolt in the Proclamation, but it was rejected for diplomatic reasons. Fortunately, Lincoln and the Radical Republicans underestimated the loyalty of Southern slaves to their master's families. There were no slave revolts or bloody atrocities.

Total War philosophy, often wrapped in the flag, prevailed until Appomattox. In the form of Reconstruction it revived and prevailed until 1877.

TOTAL WAR: LEGACIES AND WORLDVIEWS

In 1870 Union General Philip Sheridan was assigned as a guest of the King of Prussia to observe the Franco-Prussian War. At a dinner honoring Prussian Chancellor Otto von Bismarck, he shared some of his military experience and philosophy with Prussian Army officers:

"First, deal as hard blows to the enemy's soldiers as possible, and then cause so much suffering to the inhabitants of the country that they will long for peace and press their government to make it…Nothing should be left to the people but eyes to lament the war."

Even many of the Prussian Army officers were shocked. But Sheridan's teachings would be remembered and practiced by some units of the German Army once under the control of Adolph Hitler and indoctrinated with the statist ideology of National Socialism during the Second World War. They found Sheridan's model, perfected against American Indians, particularly useful against French, Greek, Polish, Czech, and Serbian partisans.

What causes men to make Total War on a whole people? How do they justify callous depredations and violence against unarmed civilians, even their fellow countrymen? Aleksandr Solzhenitsyn in his book, *The Gulag Archipelago*, describing the oppressive and brutal prison system of the former Soviet Union, makes the statement that:

"To do evil a human being must first of all believe that what he's doing is good."

Solzhenitsyn also understood the critical underlying question of his statement. By what moral compass should good or right be determined?

Should right be determined by Marxism, National Socialism, an elite judiciary, popular fashion, majority vote, or by some more transcendent standard?

Earlier in this chapter, we noted that Romans 13, in agreement with numerous other Scriptural passages, declares that government is ordained by God. All government is accountable to Him, and He is the only underlying legitimate source of law. Church and State must operate in their separate spheres of authority and influence, but they are both accountable to God. God's Law may be seen clearly in Scripture, supremely in Christ, but also in nature. The constant error of mankind is to make themselves rather than God the source and standard of all law. This error has sometimes flourished even in the Church due to careless, distorted, or corrupt interpretations of Scripture. Man by himself is a spinning and unreliable moral compass. Refusing God as the source of law, man will fashion for himself idols. The State often becomes the chief idol of societies that have forgotten God.

Statism is a philosophy that embraces the State rather than God as the ultimate source of all law. Whatever advances the State is good. The values of statism are expansion of the wealth, territory, power, and authority of the State. The leaders of the State determine what is right without reference to any higher moral law or source of authority. The State becomes the supreme lawgiver and judge. Statism naturally tends ultimately toward totalitarian forms of government, but its initial forms are often democratic. In fact, nominal democratic form and language are frequently essential propaganda tools of the State. This can be seen in such national titles as, "The People's Democratic Republic of Vietnam."

Statism in one form or another is a common engine for convincing its adherents that whatever they do in the service of the State is right and good. Statism is easily wrapped in the flag, so its adherents can more easily twist enormous evil into "patriotic" themes. Statism also tends to rationalize lies with distortions of patriotism. The Communists had a saying that "A lie in the service of Marxism is the truth." Islam has a similar saying and philosophy. But statist philosophies often permeate parliamentary democracies and constitutional republics to some extent. Unless checked, statism is a poison that undermines the foundations of all constitutional, democratic, and republican forms of government. Even worse, it undermines all morality and values that contradict or impede the advancement of the State.

Statism is not patriotism. Patriotism is a love of one's own people and country that is inseparable from their history and cultural, social, and religious traditions and values. Statism is often ready to jettison any of these except territory to advance or defend its power and authority. The "Union" has often been glorified as a transcendent cause. But what is meant by "Union"? If "Union" is not accompanied by mutual consent and mutual good, what are its values? It is only a territorial imperative. It is only a euphemism for statism. Union is good when it advances the common good and enhances and defends liberty. Only in the mindset of statism does Union trump liberty.

In the long annals of history, statism has often been the underlying ideology used to justify incredible violence against dissenters. Stalin and Mao killed more of their fellow countrymen stifling dissent than were killed in the Second World War. Statist violence must, however, wear a mask of virtue and patriotism. In order to do great evil men must first convince themselves that what they do is righteous and what they have done is good and patriotic.

Therefore, unjustly perpetrated and unjustly waged war must be made into a noble crusade. Truth must be buried beneath more palatable legend. Once men have done great evil they will also go to great lengths to justify it. It may take the form of enormous monuments or enormous lies. It may take the form of even greater evil in suppressing the truth and persecuting the truthful. Solzhenitsyn also remarked of his experience with Soviet statism that:

"Violence can only be concealed by a lie, and the lie can only be maintained by violence."

How could numerous Union political leaders and generals direct a campaign of terror and devastation against Southern civilians? How could Union armies destroy civilian food supplies, homes, farms, medical supplies, wells, hospitals, schools, and libraries over large areas of the South? How could they mock, dance, and laugh as they burned down churches? How could they execute civilian hostages and prisoners of war as reprisals for partisan resistance? How could they condone looting, pillage, and rape as a strategy to crush Southern resistance? Forty percent of all private property in the South was destroyed. An estimated 50,000 homeless civilians died from malnutrition and disease as a result. How could Americans do this to Americans? It was a pervading and terrible distortion of patriotism that we have identified as statism. Statism holds to no higher law than the advancement and defense of the State.

The South is still being subjected to an outrageous tyranny. When the victors occupy the territory of the defeated for a long period, they are able to reshape history so well as to glorify enormous evil and shame righteous courage. It is a form of tyranny more evil even than the initial conquest. Ignorance and cowardice enshrine as good what in truth was enormous evil. Truth and courageous dissent from lies and distortions are not celebrated in societies where might has come to mean right. Truth is displaced by self-justifying propaganda. Nobility is crushed by outrageous slander.

There are more books written about the "Civil War" than any other topic except Christianity. Yet most of the real causes of the war have been buried under twenty feet of propaganda. Self-justifying propaganda is now the prevailing staple of "Civil War" history in public and unfortunately even in most Christian schools. It presents as a noble struggle against slavery what was really an unconstitutional military aggression to prevent Southern Independence. This prevailing cover of propaganda serves both to bury uncomfortable history and as a tool for modern political agendas.

Slavery was an issue that caused many serious tensions, but the full scope and nature of these tensions are largely unknown and badly misunderstood today. The war was about the right of the Southern people to self-determination and government by the consent of the governed versus being held involuntarily to a Union which experience was proving not to be in their best political and economic interests.

Has our society been in a moral tail-spin for too long to value truth? Are Americans still morally capable of dealing honestly with the causes and conduct of the "Civil War"? Once you have built your worldview on a lie, it is very difficult to see the truth, much less to embrace the truth. But truth, however uncomfortable and unpopular or however deeply buried and trampled, is still truth. It has a tendency to resurrection, though truth is hard to face after decades of believing lies. Truth is hard to bear when you have for many years justified yourself and an idolized State with lies.

The standard school texts and teaching on the "Civil War" in both public and Christian schools perpetrate enormous dishonesty as history.

We now have a generation of Americans including most Southerners who are shamelessly ignorant of their own history. What history they do know is laced with political deception. How many high school teachers in the South in both public and Christian schools know anything but propaganda on the causes and conduct of the "Civil War"? How many know the full truth about the Reconstruction era? What are the penalties for them, if they step outside the chains of political correctness in their study and teaching?

Yet there are reasons for optimism. With the internet and many advances in computer technology in publishing, the Eastern liberal establishment is no longer as dominant in the publishing industry as it once was. The truth about the war is seeping out into the public in newly published works and the republication of many older works. I am optimistic that despite near fanatical opposition to the true history of that war, that courage will eventually rescue truth.

Where are we today? As a former Air Force intelligence officer I am always sensitive to claims of American misconduct or atrocities. These claims are in the vast majority of cases false and usually based on politically motivated sources of distortion and propaganda. As a combat veteran of Vietnam, I must say that our government and Armed Forces went to extraordinary lengths to avoid civilian casualties and private property damage during that period. I believe the same can be said of the Iraq wars. There have been tragic exceptions and a few shameful moral relapses, but during the twentieth and twenty-first centuries, the United States has been a leading advocate and conscientious practitioner of the Geneva Conventions, which closely approximate standards of Christian Just War conduct. The U.S. was not a party to the first Geneva Convention signed in 1864.

Yet the danger of statism is always with us. In the last forty years it has become rampant in the courts and increasingly pervades government and society at many levels. When the people have forgotten God, and government has removed Him as lawgiver, our country flirts with cruel tyranny and mortal danger.

When I see in recent newspapers that our Air Force and Navy chaplains are discouraged from speaking the name of Christ in public prayer, I fear for my country.

CHAPTER 12

The Atlanta Campaign

April 24 to November 16, 1864

Atlanta after destruction

Many historians date the Atlanta campaign from late April 1864 to September 2, 1864, the September 2 date coinciding with the withdrawal of General Hood's Confederate forces from Jonesboro and the official surrender by Atlanta Mayor, James Calhoun. However, that leaves out an important part of the history. It was not until November 12 that Sherman destroyed Atlanta by ordering all buildings except homes and churches to be burned. Many homes and churches, however, were caught up in the conflagration.

Union forces had begun to probe Confederate strength south of Ringgold, Georgia on April 24 with the objective of a major advance on Atlanta, an important Confederate railroad center and supply depot. Up until the middle of May, General Joe Wheeler's Confederate cavalry were able to frustrate Sherman's enormous army of over 100,000 men attempting to advance toward Atlanta.

After a two-day battle at Resaca, Georgia on May 14 and 15, Sherman's overwhelming numbers forced General Johnston's Army of Tennessee to withdraw. Sherman's better than two to one numerical superiority constantly threatened Johnston with flanking or encirclement. Johnston's Army, however, was able to inflict some stinging defeats on Sherman at

Pickett's Mill in late May and at Kennesaw Mountain from June 19 to 27. Union General McPherson's flanking movements, however, forced Johnston to withdraw to Smyrna.

On July 17, President Davis, frustrated with Johnston's defensive caution and continued withdrawals, replaced Johnston with John B. Hood. On July 21, after repulsing Hood at Peachtree Creek the previous day, Sherman was in position to bombard downtown Atlanta with artillery. A fierce battle occurred the next day on July 22 that cost the Confederates about 8,500 casualties. This is the date usually given for the Battle of Atlanta. Union General McPherson was killed on that day. However, the Confederates did not withdraw as Sherman had expected.

Sherman then sent General George Stoneman for a cavalry raid on Macon in an attempt to cut Hood's main southern supply line. He was supported by cavalry divisions under Garrard just southeast of Atlanta and McCook swinging to the south from Newnan southwest of Atlanta. A total of 9,000 Union cavalry pressed to cut off Hood from the major supply depot at Macon.

When Stoneman's cavalry arrived in front of Macon, however, they met unexpectedly fierce resistance by Confederate militia, composed mostly of older men, disabled veterans, and young boys, commanded by politician-General Howell Cobb. This resistance and the delay it caused may have seemed at first a mere nuisance to Stoneman, but it was a nuisance that contributed to a completely unexpected tactical outcome. Neither did Stoneman anticipate the sheer audacity, speed, and fighting spirit of Confederate cavalry forces opposing him. Hood's cavalry commander, the young, serious-minded and normally soft-spoken Joe Wheeler, was not inappropriately nicknamed "Fightin' Joe."

On July 29-30 Wheeler's cavalry force of only 5,000 dealt Sherman's cavalry forces of 9,000 men a series of stunning, one might even say, astonishing defeats. Wheeler's cavalry defeated all three divisions of Sherman's cavalry, mauling and vanquishing McCook at Newnan, routing and capturing Stoneman at Macon, and forcing back Garrard. For the Union, this was the most disastrous cavalry defeat of the war. In all, the Confederates took 3,200 prisoners including Major General Stoneman and five brigadier generals in addition to numerous supply wagons and artillery batteries.

Unfortunately, the overwhelming manpower resources of the Union would be able to replace Sherman's losses within months and supply them down to the last tent peg. In August, Hood ordered Wheeler to take 2,000 cavalry on a raid into central Tennessee. This reduction of Confederate cavalry in the Atlanta area had the unfortunate effect of leaving Hood unable to gather intelligence effectively or to successfully hinder the build-up of Union forces around the city. By August 30, Sherman's forces were in position to cut off the last railroad supply line to Atlanta at Jonesboro.

From August 30 to September 1, Hardee's Corps with portions of Stephen D. Lee's Corps and elements of Wheeler's cavalry attempted to parry a death blow to the strategic city of Atlanta by defending the remaining railroad connection between that city and Macon to the south. This valiant effort was against odds of nearly three to one. On September 2 General Hood was forced to evacuate Atlanta. Hardee had succeeded, however, in delaying Jonesboro's capture long enough to allow for Hood's orderly retreat to Lovejoy, Georgia, just south of Jonesboro. Henry Slocum's Union XX Corps moved into Atlanta and accepted the surrender of the city from Mayor James Calhoun.

At Jonesboro today, a Confederate Battle Flag still flies over the Patrick Cleburne Memorial Cemetery near the railroad. The area once marked a Confederate field hospital. The cemetery contains the remains of Confederate soldiers killed at Jonesboro or dying of wounds from other battles around Atlanta. There are several hundred grave stones there, only seven of which can now be identified. It is estimated that a total of 600 to 1,000 Confederate soldiers lie there in either marked graves or mass burials.

Seeing that Confederate Battle Flag there is a marvelous sight but brings sadness to the heart. The Confederates suffered about 2,000 casualties at Jonesboro. Union losses were about 1,100 for the two-day battle. The Union's most devastating losses in the Atlanta campaign were suffered in June at Kennesaw Mountain and July 29-30 at the hands of Fighting Joe Wheeler's cavalry.

On September 4, General Sherman ordered civilian evacuation of Atlanta, much to the protest of Hood and other Confederate leaders. On November 8, Lincoln was reelected President, and on November 12, Atlanta was destroyed by Sherman's troops.

On November 16, Sherman departed the Atlanta area with his men singing *The Battle Hymn of the Republic*. His force of 60,000 men proceeded to devastate a 60 mile-wide swath of farms and communities on his march through Georgia to Savannah. Then he turned to destroy 50% of the private property in South Carolina, including the burning of Columbia and about a dozen smaller towns.

CHAPTER 13

Real Memories of a Not So Civil War

Family History

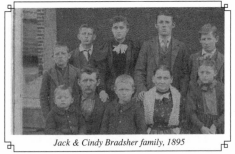

Jack & Cindy Bradsher family, 1895

My mother, Wanda Bradsher Scruggs, passed away not long ago at the age of 91, but a few years ago she shared with me some memories of the "Civil" War related to her by her grandparents, Jack and Lucinda Ross Bradsher. My mother was the daughter of the youngest of their seven sons, W. C. Bradsher. They also had four daughters. Both the Bradsher and the Ross families were farmers whose parents had come to northeastern Arkansas in covered wagons in the late 1840's. The Bradsher family had come from North Carolina, and the Ross family had come from Kentucky. Jack Bradsher, being a hard worker, very astute, and affable became a very successful farmer whose sons became successful community leaders in medicine, pharmacy, farming, business, education, and the ministry. Jack Bradsher's farm was near Marmaduke, Arkansas, named for the Confederate General, who later became Governor of nearby Missouri.

One thing my mother remembers about Jack Bradsher is that he was a great storyteller, loving to share his stories with children, grandchildren, and guests at Sunday dinner in their home. His wife and her grandmother, Lucinda or Cindy, she remembers as always cheerful and continually singing hymns. She sang hymns in the kitchen as she worked, and she sang hymns to her grandchildren. She often had a little spiritual guidance to assert here and there in Jack's stories.

Once when my mother was a young girl attending public school, she asked Grandmother Lucinda if she remembered Abraham Lincoln. Her usually cheerful grandmother allowed in a more serious tone that she did remember him, but that she never thought much of him. Very surprised at her grandmother's response, she asked the reason for her disdain.

Grandmother Lucinda answered: "Because when the Yankees came, they took away everything we had."

Grandmother Lucinda had other memories of the war. Her father, James Alexander Ross, was in the 15th Arkansas Rifles. He served only from late July 1861 to December 20, 1861. He had taken a severe cold from exposure and became very ill. He died at home shortly thereafter.

Later in the war, when Grandmother Lucinda was about eight-years-old, she remembered Yankee soldiers came to their home foraging for food. They had searched the whole house and were beginning to search the cellar, when her widowed mother, Mary Joiner Ross, confronted the Yankee Lieutenant in charge.

Her mother stood up to this Yankee officer, asking him, "Do you want to be the one responsible for the starvation of these children?" Her bold appeal had its affect. The Union Lieutenant ordered his men to stop searching the cellar. Mary Ross and her four children were left with a little food hidden in the cellar, but little else. Grandmother Lucinda never forgot the incident and never had a very high opinion of Yankee soldiers or Abraham Lincoln.

With a little more home schooling from her grandparents, my mother also learned that the Bradsher family had also suffered in those times. Her great-grandfather, Thomas Jefferson Bradsher, was killed by a band of bushwhackers in the summer of 1865. They came to T. J. Bradsher's house one night and demanded money. He insisted he had none, and they left, but returned the next night. In full view of his family and in front of their house, the leader drew a large pistol and threatened to shoot him unless he told them where he kept his money and valuables. When T. J. Bradsher refused, and the bushwhacker cocked his revolver and was about to shoot him, his twelve-year-old daughter, Deanie (Martha), jumped on the gunman's back to try and stop him, but he shook her off and fired the fatal shot, hitting T. J. Bradsher in the head, killing him. This was also witnessed by his wife, Sarah Wisdom Bradsher, thirty-weeks pregnant with their daughter, Callie. At least two of their other three children, Elizabeth and nine-year-old Jack Bradsher, also witnessed this brutal murder. The newly appointed Yankee carpetbagger sheriff made no effort to bring these marauders to justice.

After Grandmother Lucinda and Grandpa Jack's eye-witness home schooling lessons, my mother realized there could be quite a difference between public school history and real history. And this was around 1925! She also learned from their eye-witnesses accounts about the suffering of Southern families and the courage of Southern women during the "Civil" War. I believe my mother received not only a history lesson from her grandparents, but also a far more important character lesson about suffering and courage. I believe those lessons stuck. Others have said of my mother that she was remarkable in her unselfish generosity, cheerful patience, and on occasions, fearless courage. She was devoted to Truth and the Faith of our Fathers.

Truth and courage are sorely needed in today's morally disintegrating society. It is especially important in recovering these virtues to know our true history. Much of what is published and taught in public schools and colleges today is either a sanitized whitewash or perverted political propaganda. But I have confidence that even in today's politically correct climate, truth will not be blotted out We cannot, as R. L. Dabney said, "bury true history whose years are those of the God of Truth." William Cullen Bryant put it a little differently, "Truth crushed to the ground shall rise again; the eternal years of God are hers." We should also remember the words of Samuel Johnson: "Where courage is not, no other virtue can survive except by accident." No republic can long survive whose people and leaders are not both devoted to truth and resolute in their courage to maintain it. Ultimately all courage, including political courage and courage in battle, is moral courage. Moral courage, more often than not, is tested principally by time, often a long period of time. I believe we can recover both truth and courage, but we had better get busy, for we are well on the way to destruction.

As a step along the way to recovering truth and courage, I would like to recommend some strong historical medicine, an eye-opening new book, *War Crimes Against Southern Civilians* by Walter Brian Cisco, just published by Pelican. Dr. Clyde N. Wilson, Distinguished Professor

Emeritus of History at the University of South Carolina has said of the book, "Americans who read *War Crimes Against Southern Civilians* will have a more sober and true, and less self-righteous, understanding of our country."

My hope is best expressed in the words of South Carolina Revolutionary War patriot, Henry Laurens, who was a delegate to the first Continental Congress in 1777 and served as President of the Second Continental Congress from November 1777 to December 1778:

"At a time when liberty is under attack, decency under assault, the family is under siege, and life itself is threatened, the good will arise in truth; they will arise in truth with the very essence and substance of their lives; they will arise in truth though they face opposition by fierce subverters; they will arise in truth never shying from the Standard of Truth, never shirking from the Author of Truth."

CHAPTER 14

∞

Clement Vallandigham and the Copperheads

Clement Vallandigham

"Copperhead" was a derogatory term applied by pro-war Lincoln loyalists to Northern advocates of a peaceful resolution to the conflict between North and South. Although there were many "War Democrats" in the North, the underlying differences between "Copperheads" and "Union loyalists" were essentially the same differences that distinguished Northern Republicans from Northern Democrats. The Copperheads, however, did support the Union. But like Southern Democrats, they supported States Rights and a conservative and straight-forward interpretation of the U.S. Constitution. In those days, Democrat was a virtual synonym for conservative in both sections of the country.

Also like Southern Democrats, they favored free trade and opposed protective import tariffs, especially the outrageously high Morrill Tariff. This tariff was part of the Republican Party Platform and was strongly supported by Lincoln. Tripling import tariffs to 47 percent, it was a boon to Northern manufacturers but hurt farmers, particularly Southern cotton exporters.

The Copperheads opposed the Emancipation Proclamation primarily because it was unconstitutional. Like many Northern Republicans, they also feared that former slaves would flood into their states. Copperhead sympathies were most common in the agricultural states in the western part of the Union—Ohio, Indiana, and Illinois. Although Lincoln was from Illinois, these states had strong Democratic parties that often held a majority in their state legislatures. Before the war, congressmen from these states frequently aligned with Southern congressmen against Northeastern industrialist interests.

Yet the Copperheads opposed Secession, and they did not support helping the Confederacy to the harm of the United States. However, they were against keeping the Union together by force of arms. Hence they were strongly opposed to the draft.

When Confederate cavalry leader, Major General John Hunt Morgan crossed the Ohio River into southern Indiana and Ohio with 2,000 mounted raiders in June and July 1863, he hoped he would be aided and joined by many Copperheads. This was not the case. They were conservative Democrats, but they had no intention of helping Confederate conservative Democrats.

The Copperheads vehemently opposed the government's shut down of more than 300 newspapers that criticized Lincoln or his policies. Like Southern Democrats, they believed in limited government and resisted Lincoln and Republican efforts to ignore constitutional limits to federal power.

Being strong advocates of the Constitution, the Copperheads were strongly opposed to Lincoln's suspension of the constitutionally guaranteed *Writ of Habeas Corpus* and the arbitrary arrests of over 14,000 civilians. They likewise opposed military tribunals for civilians. Following the war, the U.S. Supreme Court ruled that these arrests were illegal because neither the President nor Congress has the right to suspend Habeas Corpus, even in wartime, as long as civil courts are in operation—and they were.

But Lincoln was not a constitutional conservative and not for limited government. He believed national greatness called for strong centralized government power and that force and harsh measures were necessary to both preserve the "Union" and reestablish American government in a more powerful and centralized form. He believed any wartime dissent or obstruction of these goals justified severe countermeasures. Lincoln declared that all secessionists and peace advocates were traitors who did not deserve the protection of federal laws.

Lincoln's Secretary of State, William Seward, bragged:

"I can touch a bell on my right hand, and order the arrest of a citizen of Ohio.

I can touch the bell again, and order the imprisonment of a citizen of New York; and no power on earth except that of the President, can release them. Can the Queen of England do so much?"

Seward's statement was perhaps a not so subtle suggestion that Democratic Ohio Congressman Clement Vallandigham and Democratic New York Governor Horatio Seymour risked arrest for their public criticism of the Lincoln government. Many less prominent people were arrested and held without charges or trial on the mere suspicion of disloyalty to "the Union."

Clement Vallandigham was a principled conservative and one of the Democratic Party's most eloquent defenders of the Constitution, limited government, and States Rights. He believed in Union, but he was strongly opposed to the use of force to subdue the Southern States, Lincoln's conduct of the war, and the draft. Most appalling to him were Lincoln's usurpation of congressional and judicial powers and suspension of Habeas Corpus, which led to a despotic abridgement of civil rights, free speech, and freedom of the press. Vallandigham vociferously opposed the Morrill Tariff as unjust.

While a newspaper editor in Ohio and later in Congress, Vallandigham ridiculed the former Whig and new Republican Party agenda of high protective tariffs, corporate welfare, and a currency inflating national banking system. Vallandigham viewed Lincoln's actions as a deliberate conspiracy to overthrow the existing constitution and republican system of government and replace it with a powerful, highly centralized national government, in which the states were mere administrative divisions.

Vallandigham criticized Lincoln for starting an unconstitutional war without Congressional consent, disregarding the Second Amendment by confiscating firearms in the Border States, and his unlawful arrest of Maryland legislators before they could deliberate on secession. He railed against Lincoln's ingenuous use of the words "saving the Union" and "freeing the slaves" to advance the cause of national banks, railroads, and expanded government. He further blasted Lincoln for implementing high taxes and unjust tariffs and promoting reckless spending and stupendous public debt. He called Lincoln's suspension of Habeas Corpus "treasonous" and referred to his actions as "cunning," and "wicked."

The Lincoln Administration argued that Vallandigham's speeches were discouraging Union enlistment and that was the real treason.

At 2:30 a.m. on the morning of May 4, 1863, Union soldiers under the command of General Ambrose Burnside knocked down the doors of Vallandigham's Dayton, Ohio, home, arrested him without civil warrant, and threw him into a military prison in Cincinnati. He was subsequently deported to the Southern States from where he was removed to Canada. Nevertheless, Ohio Democrats nominated Vallandigham for Governor.

Lincoln, of course, took an interest in the election and endorsed Republican candidate John Brough. Following an intensive campaign by the Republican Party and the Union League, which spared no scruple in scandal mongering and smearing and misrepresenting Vallandigham in his absence, Brough, with the help of a closely monitored and intimidated press and the votes of Federal soldiers stationed in Ohio, defeated Vallandigham 288,000 to 187,000.

In 1871, Vallandigham accidentally shot himself while demonstrating to other attorneys in Lebanon, Ohio, how a pistol could accidentally discharge. He died the following day.

CHAPTER 15

⊂⊃⊂⊃

The Kilpatrick-Dahlgren Raid

The Attempted Assassination of Jefferson Davis and his Cabinet

Ulric Dahlgren

In early February 1864, Union Major General Benjamin Butler proposed to President Lincoln and Secretary of War Edwin Stanton a plan for a surprise cavalry raid on Richmond with the objectives of destroying prime military targets, releasing Union prisoners of war, and capturing Confederate President Jefferson Davis and his Cabinet. Lincoln and Stanton approved, but Confederate field commanders were somehow forewarned, and Butler's force was easily turned back on February 7.

However, the ambitious young cavalry commander, Brigadier General Judson Kilpatrick, saw in Butler's failure an opportunity. In a cavalry action several months previous, he had found the defenses on the south side of Richmond relatively weak. Having considerable political connections, Kilpatrick got word to Lincoln and Stanton that he had a better plan. The twenty-eight-year-old Kilpatrick had made a name for himself as a daring cavalry raider. Because of his reckless disregard for the lives of his own men, he had earned the unofficial sobriquet, "Kill-Cavalry." But the ruthless Kilpatrick was just the sort of man Stanton wanted for the job. On February 12, outside of the chain of command, he was invited directly to the White House to meet with Lincoln and Stanton.

The official record of that meeting indicates that Lincoln was primarily interested in freeing the POWs at Belle Isle and Libby Prison, severing Confederate communications, and distributing amnesty proclamations aimed at persuading Southerners to return to the Union fold. The prisoners could have been easily released, however, by exchange. The Confederates had been begging for a prisoner exchange, but this would undermine the Union policy of attrition on the badly outnumbered Confederate Army, which was growing desperate for additional manpower. The Union claimed the exchange impasse was due to Jefferson Davis's refusal to exchange black Union soldiers who had been slaves. But most of these soldiers had previously been returned to their masters, making their exchange infeasible. The race issue was a public ruse to still Northern public sentiment that was demanding a prisoner exchange for the sake of their suffering relatives and friends—a sentiment which was in conflict with Union military strategy focused on shutting off any source of Confederate manpower. Of course, official meeting records do not always reveal whatever secret agendas are discussed.

On February 16, Kilpatrick met privately with Stanton at the War Department. It was there that an expanded agenda must have been revealed. Later events strongly suggest that this expanded agenda called for the assassination of President Jefferson Davis and his Cabinet and for the burning of Richmond.

Stanton then notified Major General George Meade, Commander of the Army of the Potomac and recent victor at Gettysburg, that Kilpatrick had a secret mission. Meade was given little detail other than that the plan involved a surprise raid on Richmond. He felt uneasy about the plan, but considered he had no real choice but to approve. His cavalry chief, Major General Alfred Pleasanton, objected, but to no avail.

The plan was for Kilpatrick and 3,100 cavalry to skirmish on the north side of Richmond while a detachment of 500 cavalry under a deputy commander penetrated the weaker defenses on the south side of Richmond and released the 1,500 officer prisoners at Libby Prison and the nearly ten thousand POWs on Belle Isle. The released prisoners were to burn Richmond. Bureau of Military Intelligence (BMI) officers would accompany the cavalry detachment and direct them to their targets, including the location of Davis and his Cabinet. Davis and his Cabinet were to be "killed on the spot."

A few days later, twenty-one-year-old Ulric Dahlgren, the youngest colonel in the Union Army, showed up sporting a new wooden leg and volunteered for the adventure. Dahlgren had been commissioned as a Captain in 1861 at the age of nineteen. His bravery in subsequent combat actions had won him the praise of three Union generals. His lower right leg was lost in a cavalry action just after Gettysburg. For that action he had received a personal visit from Lincoln and Stanton and was made a full colonel.

Ulric Dahlgren was the son of Admiral John Dahlgren, a close friend of Lincoln and inventor of the Dahlgren gun. In fact, it was Lincoln that arranged for Ulric Dahlgren's commissioning as a Captain in 1861. Despite the young colonel's splendid combat record and exploits in cavalry reconnaissance, he had almost no command experience. Nevertheless, he was given the important assignment of commanding the 500 cavalry troopers that would penetrate the back door to Richmond. The younger Dahlgren was much like Kilpatrick. He was daring, reckless, and had no qualms about breaking the ordinary rules of war.

Early on the morning of February 28, under the cover of infantry and cavalry diversions by Meade and Custer, Kilpatrick and Dahlgren led their 3,600 troopers across the Rapidan River toward Richmond. Dahlgren, accompanied by BMI Captain John McEntee, would penetrate the weaker southern defenses, while Kilpatrick demonstrated on the northern defenses, ready to support Dahlgren, if he broke through. Unfortunately for Dahlgren, nothing went according to plan. Winter rains had swollen the rivers, and he was met with stiff resistance by Richmond Home Guard and Confederate cavalry units.

North of Richmond, Wade Hampton's Confederate cavalry drove Kilpatrick off, leaving Dahlgren to his fate. Faced with the swollen rivers and freezing rain, his men became separated as they retreated to the northeast. Frustrated because he was unable to cross the James River, Dahlgren turned on his guide, a free black man, and had him hanged on the riverbank. On March 2, Dahlgren and one hundred troopers were ambushed by units of the 9th Virginia Cavalry and the Richmond Home Guard. Dahlgren was hit several times by the first volley and fell dead from his horse. Most of his men were captured.

When he inspected Dahlgren's body, William Littlepage, a thirteen-year-old Home Guard member, found two folded documents and a small notebook which he gave to Captain Edward Halbach, his teacher and company commander. These documents were Dahlgren's notes on Kilpatrick's orders and the orders he was to give his men once they had penetrated Richmond. The latter order was continued on the back of the first page and signed, U. Dahlgren. Confederate officers were shocked by the following statements and phrases:

"The released prisoners (are) to destroy and burn the hateful City and do not allow the Rebel leader Davis and his traitorous crew to escape...(Richmond) must be destroyed and Jeff Davis and his Cabinet killed...Gut the City...Jeff Davis and his Cabinet must be killed on the spot."

These documents were also witnessed by Halbach's immediate superior, Captain Richard Hugh Bagby, a minister, who later made a verbal affidavit of their contents. By evening, the documents had also been witnessed by Lieutenant Pollard and Col. Richard Beale of the 9th Virginia Cavalry. On March 4, Pollard delivered the papers and Dahlgren's wooden leg to Major General Fitzhugh Lee, nephew of Robert E. Lee, who immediately took them to President Davis.

Davis was not alarmed by the assassination plans, but others in his Cabinet were. It was decided to photograph them and release lithograph copies to the press and the British and French. Some in the Cabinet felt that the Dahlgren Raid prisoners should be shot, but the influence and words of Robert E. Lee dissuaded them:

"I do not think that reason and reflection could justify such a course. I think it better to do right, even if we suffer in so doing, than to incur the reproach of our consciences and posterity."

Lee had copies sent to Union General Meade, asking him to investigate the truth of the matter. Meade instructed Kilpatrick to "make careful inquiries" among Dahlgren's men to determine what, if anything, Dahlgren had instructed them. Dahlgren probably had not intended to give his men final instructions until they had broken through Confederate defenses. But asking Kilpatrick to find the truth was like asking a fox to guard chickens. Kilpatrick admitted approving Dahlgren's instructions to his men but claimed there was nothing in them about killing Jeff Davis and his Cabinet or burning Richmond. He claimed the Confederates had doctored the documents and that the whole thing was a fraud and a Confederate plot to stir up anti-war Democrats and Copperheads (Southern sympathizers) in the North. Meade was uncomfortable with Kilpatrick's testimony as he knew the man's character, but he responded to Lee that:

"Neither the United States Government, myself, nor General Kilpatrick authorized, sanctioned, or approved the burning of the city of Richmond and the killing of Mr. Davis and Cabinet..."

Privately, Meade confided to his wife that Kilpatrick's reputation for unethical conduct concerned him and that "collateral evidence" indicated Kilpatrick was lying. That collateral evidence was probably Captain McEntee of the BMI, who had accompanied Dahlgren on his mission and was the only member of the force taken into his confidence. Apparently, Captain John Babcock of the BMI also contradicted Kilpatrick's testimony.

The Northern press, however, erupted into a frenzy of accusations of Confederate fraud and forgery. The Southern press painted Dahlgren as "Ulric the Hun." Many Northern "court historians" still claim that the Confederates forged the Dahlgren Papers, but the overwhelming evidence now available indicates they are authentic. But who in the Union chain of command bears the ultimate responsibility?

The Kilpatrick-Dahlgren Raid on Richmond in March of 1864 might have gone down in history as a minor Union defeat had not Col. Dahlgren been killed and had not Confederate officers recovered from his body instructions not only to free Union prisoners of war, but also to burn Richmond and kill Confederate President Jefferson Davis and his Cabinet. Within 24 hours of receiving the documents in Richmond, the Confederate Government had them photographed for immediate release to the press in Richmond and Confederate envoy John Slidell in London. Slidell had lithograph copies made for distribution in Europe.

Brigadier General Kilpatrick admitted that he had seen and approved Dahlgren's instructions to his men but claimed the Confederates had tampered with the documents. He claimed that the documents were just as printed in the Richmond papers but without any instructions to burn Richmond and kill Davis and his Cabinet. When Admiral John Dahl-gren, father of Col. Dahlgren, received a copy of one of the London litho-graph copies, he immediately proclaimed them a fraud. The lithograph copy had misspelled Dahlgren's signature, transposing the letters "H" and "L" to form "Dalhgren." Furthermore, the Admiral claimed that his son always signed his full name rather than "U. Dahlgren." Based on Admi-ral Dahlgren's assertions the Northern press exploded with denunciations of Southern "fraud." The Southern press, however, continued to allege Washington's involvement in a deplorable assassination attempt beyond the pale of ethical warfare.

In 1879, former Confederate General Jubal Early noted that the Dahlgren instructions were written in ink on both sides of thin paper. He theorized that the writing on the front of the page showed through and made Dahlgren's signature difficult to interpret. A century later, historian James D. Hall proved Early's theory. On investigation he discovered that the London lithographer had touched up his lithograph copies for a more readable presentation. As a result of this process, Dahlgren's name appears to be misspelled. The Northern press had access only to the lithograph copies. Hence much of the Northern outrage was based on the error of the London lithographer. As for not signing his full name, the standard practice in the Union Army was for officers to use their first initial and surname.

In December of 1865, Francis Lieber, who was in charge of captured Confederate archives, delivered on request all documents related to the Dahlgren Affair to Secretary of War Stanton. They have never been seen since. Only one badly faded set of photographs made by the Confederate government now remains in the National Archives, along with copies of the London lithograph and the Richmond newspapers. Stanton most likely consigned the original documents to his office fireplace.

The most inflammatory sentence in Dahlgren's proposed instruc-tions to his men, calling for arson and the murder of Jefferson Davis and his Cabinet, is found toward the bottom of the first page of the document. A forgery, inserting the most inflammatory sentence into the middle of other detailed instructions for the raid on Federal Cavalry Corp letter-head and duplicating the document's folding, would have been a major technological achievement in 1865. Accomplishing such a forgery in the less-than-24-hour-period between the presentation of the documents to

Jefferson Davis and their release to the Richmond press would have been impossible.

Furthermore, as to the authenticity of the Dahlgren Papers, we have the testimonies of the Confederate officers who witnessed them before they were delivered to the Confederate Government in Richmond. These testimonies are unanimous that the documents called for the burning of Richmond and the killing "on the spot" of President Davis and his Cabinet. These witnesses were Captain (and teacher) Edward Halbach, Captain (and minister) R. H. Bagley (who swore a verbal affidavit), Lieutenant Pollard and Col. Richard L. T. Beale of the 9th Virginia Calvary, and Major General Fitzhugh Lee, the nephew of Robert E. Lee. These were all men of excellent reputation. There is no reason to question the truthfulness of their testimonies.

The testimony of Union Captain John McEntee, the BMI officer who rode with Dahlgren but managed to escape the Confederate ambush, is also compelling. General Marsena Patrick, Provost Marshall for the Army of the Potomac and BMI chief, recorded in his diary after interviewing McEntee that:

"...Captain McEntee had a contempt for Kilpatrick...He further says that he thinks the papers are correct that were found on Dahlgren, as they correspond with what **D.** (Dahlgren) **told him...**"

This was probably part of the collateral information that caused General Meade to suspect that Kilpatrick was lying in dissociating himself from an assassination plan. Meade also had previous reservations about Kilpatrick's character. It is not surprising then that Meade managed to relieve "Kill-Cavalry" of his position as cavalry commander and had him sent to the western theater before the spring campaign of 1864 opened.

Kilpatrick was, however, welcomed by General Sherman, who put him in charge of his cavalry. Kilpatrick further enhanced his reputation as a ruthless and disreputable officer during Sherman's march through Georgia and South Carolina. That military campaign is famous for its suspension of ordinary military and humanitarian ethics in accomplishing the South's devastation. Sherman said of his new cavalry commander, "**I know that Kilpatrick is a hell of a damned fool.**" But Sherman considered he was just the sort of officer he needed to cut a burning swath through Georgia and the Carolinas.

Despite the impressive array of evidence that the Dahlgren Papers are authentic, there is a strong reluctance to accept their authenticity among Lincoln scholars. In a 1998 book, *The Dahlgren Affair: Terror and Conspiracy in the Civil War*, author Duane Schultz makes a case for Confederate conspiracy rather than the authenticity of the Dahlgren Papers. Schultz's reasoning and evidence were, however, badly mauled in an article by historian Stephen W. Sears that year in *MHQ: the Quarterly Journal of Military History*. The article is still online in the internet archives of that journal. A splendid analysis of the evidence also appears in Sears' own 1999 book, *Controversies and Commanders*.

Lincoln scholars have a tendency to be overprotective of the Lincoln legend. They even become nervous, when his Secretary of War, Edwin Stanton, is implicated in ruthless and deceptive conduct. In the case of the Dahlgren Papers, it is likely, considering his previous approval of Benjamin Butler's failed plan to capture Davis and some of his Cabinet, that Lincoln at least restated his enthusiasm for apprehending the leaders of the Confederacy in his meeting with General Kilpatrick and Secretary Stanton on February 12. There is no proof that Lincoln directly endorsed killing Davis and his Cabinet.

It was the character of Secretary of War Edwin Stanton, however, to act on important matters without consulting President Lincoln and later President Andrew Johnson. Stanton was himself ambitious to become President and had a well-deserved reputation for backstabbing, double-crossing, ruthlessness, and deceptive practices within the Cabinet and top levels of the Government and Army. He was also the principal spokesman for the Radical Republicans in the Cabinet. Like the Radical Republicans, he championed and often authored the Total War practices that made Sherman, Sheridan, Pope, Kilpatrick and others infamous. Secretary of the Navy Gideon Welles reluctantly reported some of Stanton's questionable dealings to Lincoln. Probably others did, too. Lincoln realized Stanton's ways were disconcerting to many government and military officials but never seriously considered removing him.

It was probably his inexperience in commanding such a large detachment of cavalry and the importance of the mission that caused Dahlgren to make copious notes of Kilpatrick's instructions for the raid. It was foolish for him to carry them into Confederate territory. Dahlgren's own ruthless character can be seen in his unjust hanging of Martin Robinson, the free black guide so highly recommended by the BMI.

As ruthless, ambitious, and sometimes foolish as both Brigadier General Kilpatrick and Col. Dahlgren proved themselves to be, it seems unlikely that either would have undertaken measures to assassinate Davis and his Cabinet on their own. We are left with the usual suspect, Secretary of War Edwin Stanton. There is no way of knowing for sure the degree of Lincoln's involvement. It can definitely be said that he trusted Edwin Stanton too much.

Many historians theorize that the Dahlgren Affair prompted the later assassination of Lincoln by John Wilkes Booth. No evidence, however, has ever connected Booth to Confederate authority. The most prevalent theory, which I favor, is that the egotistical and highly dramatic Booth took it upon himself to kill Lincoln. There is another popular theory, with considerable circumstantial evidence but lacking definitive proof, that Booth was manipulated into assassinating Lincoln by agents of Stanton. Stanton and the Radical Republicans were unhappy with Lincoln because of his lenient Reconstruction plans for the South. This same motivation was behind the impeachment of Andrew Johnson in 1868.

On States Rights

"Nothing could so far advance the cause of freedom as for state officials throughout the land to assert their rightful claims to lost state power; and for the federal government to withdraw promptly and totally from every jurisdiction which the Constitution reserved to the states." — Barry Goldwater, 1960.

"I believe in state's rights; I believe in people doing as much as they can for themselves at the community level and at the private level. And I believe that we've distorted the balance of our government today by giving powers that were never intended in the constitution to that federal establishment. And if I do get the job I'm looking for, I'm going to devote myself to trying to reorder those priorities and to restore to the states and local communities those functions which properly belong there."

—Ronald Reagan,
Neshoba County, Mississippi,
August 3, 1980

CHAPTER 16

Camp Douglas—Eighty Acres of Hell

The Shameful Treatment of Confederate Prisoners of War

Camp Douglas

According to Union Army records, 4,454 Confederate prisoners of war died at Camp Douglas, located on the South Side of Chicago. These records are incomplete, however, and the actual number is estimated at more than 5,600. According to the Sons of Confederate Veterans, there are about 6,000 graves in the cemetery there. Of the 30,218 Confederate soldiers who died in POW camps, Camp Douglas was first in the list of infamy. Other names topping this dismal list were Point Lookout, Maryland (3,584); Elmira, New York (2,933); Fort Delaware, Delaware (2,466); Rock Island, Illinois (1,960); Camp Morton, Indiana (1,763); and Gratiot Street in St. Louis, Missouri (1,140).

Historian Thomas Cartwright has described Camp Douglas as "a testimony to cruelty and barbarism." Because of its miserable living conditions and increasing degrees of deliberate cruelty toward Confederate prisoners of war, the camp gained the title, "Eighty Acres of Hell." Prisoners were intentionally deprived of adequate rations, clothing, and heating as punitive measures. From September 1863 to the end of the war, many were subjected to brutal tortures that often resulted in permanent maiming and death.

Camp Douglas was originally a fairground. At the start of the war it was used as a center for training and quartering Union regiments raised in the Chicago area. It was named for Illinois statesman, presidential candidate, and U. S. Senator Stephen A. Douglas. The camp consisted of 64 barracks, a small hospital, and other prison buildings. The top capacity of the prison was about 6,000, but eventually over 12,000 would be crowded into its confines.

On February 21, 1862, the first group of 3,200 Confederate prisoners arrived in Chicago by train. As they were marched to their quarters at Camp Douglas, crowds of onlookers, enraged by Union war propaganda, cursed them, and some even hurled rocks at them. But the captured Southerners would soon face the far more deadly ravages of nature and disease.

Unfortunately, Camp Douglas was situated on low ground, and it flooded with every rain. During the winter months, whenever temperatures were above freezing for long, the compound became a sea of mud. Less than a handful of the barracks had stoves. Overcrowding and inadequate sanitation measures soon made the camp a stinking morass of human and animal sewage. Henry Morton Stanley, of the 6th Arkansas, who later in his illustrious career as an African explorer and journalist uttered the famous words, "Doctor Livingstone, I presume," had this to say of Camp Douglas: "Our prison pen was like a cattle-yard. We were soon in a fair state of rotting while yet alive." He later remarked that some of his comrades "looked worse than exhumed corpses."

Steadily, sickness and disease began to increase. By early 1863 the mortality rate at Camp Douglas had climbed to over 10 percent per month, more than would be reached in any other prison, Union or Confederate. The U.S. Sanitary Commission (now the Red Cross) pointed out that at that rate, the prison would be emptied within 320 days. One official called it an "extermination camp." The fall and winter of 1862-63 were very wet, cold, and windy. The majority of deaths were from typhoid fever and pneumonia as a result of filth, bad weather, poor diet, lack of heat, and inadequate clothing. Other diseases included measles, mumps, catarrh (severe sinus and throat infection), and chronic diarrhea.

Somewhere in excess of 317 Confederate soldiers escaped from Camp Douglas, over 100 of them being men of Morgan's 2nd Kentucky Cavalry. Hundreds of Morgan's men had been sent to Camp Douglas after being captured on their famous raid through Indiana and Ohio in July

1863. However, the daring escape of these Morgan cavalrymen resulted in retaliatory action. A reduction of rations and removal of the few barracks' stoves were ordered from Washington. Eventually all vegetables were cut off. This resulted in an epidemic of scurvy described by R. T. Bean of the 8th Kentucky Cavalry. "Lips were eaten away, jaws became diseased, and teeth fell out." Before authorities could correct the situation, many succumbed to the disease. In addition, an epidemic of smallpox raged through the camp. Lice were everywhere. Many prisoners had to supplement their diet by catching, cooking, and eating the all too abundant rats.

The first commander of Camp Douglas as a POW camp was Col. James Mulligan of the 23rd (Irish) Illinois Infantry. The prisoners respected Mulligan, even though an enemy, because of his heroic war record and honesty. He was a strict disciplinarian but always fair. With more prisoners pouring into Camp Douglas than could possibly be handled with efficiency and mounting administrative and sanitary problems, he was glad to take his regiment back to the field in June 1862. Though he felt his record had been sullied by the problems at Camp Douglas, his valor and leadership in battle soon won him a promotion to Brigadier General. Sadly, he was killed in action at Winchester, Virginia, in July 1864. His last words were, "Lay me down and save the flag," while being carried from the field. His monument dominates the western entrance to Calvary Cemetery in Evanston, Illinois.

Being commandant of a prisoner of war camp was not considered a desirable position by most Union officers. During its four year history the camp had eight commanders. Most of these were honorable men, who later proved their worth in battle and in peace. The punitive policies and directives to reduce prisoner rations and impose other deprivations had come from the War Department. Early in the war President Lincoln and Secretary of War Edwin Stanton termed all captured Confederates as "traitors" and refused to recognize them as prisoners of war. Nevertheless, public pressure resulted in a prisoner exchange program in July 1862. Camp Douglas was emptied twice by prisoner exchanges, in August 1862 and May 1863, just before Lincoln and Stanton seized the first opportunity to discontinue them. Prisoner exchanges were of more value to the badly outnumbered Confederates, and Lincoln and Stanton hoped by eliminating them to exhaust Southern manpower. This decision later resulted in much suffering for both Confederate and Union prisoners (most notably at Andersonville).

Nearly 8,000 Union soldiers on parole and awaiting official exchange were held at Camp Douglas rather than sent home on leave in late 1862. These frustrated soldiers, who quartered themselves just outside the camp, mutinied and burned down a third of the camp before order was restored by regular Union Army troops.

The commanders of Camp Douglas also had to put up with rampant military and political corruption. There was a scandal over the prices and quality of food rations. Orville Browning, a personal friend of Lincoln, taking advantage of his Presidential favor, sold prisoner releases to wealthy Confederate families for $250 each. The guards proved absolutely corrupt and eager for bribes. When the Chicago Police were brought in to clean up some of the corruption among guards, they used the opportunity to systematically rob the Confederate prisoners.

On August 18, 1863, Col. Charles DeLand was made commander at Camp Douglas, bringing with him the 1st Michigan Sharpshooters. In reprisal for escape attempts and other infractions and as a method of interrogation, he introduced several forms of torture, including hanging men by their thumbs for hours. Several died from this ordeal. He also introduced a torture called "riding the horse" or "riding Morgan's mule." Prisoners were forced to sit for many hours on the narrow and sharpened edge of a horizontal two by four and suspended by supports four to twelve feet high. Guards often hung weighty buckets of dirt and rock on their feet to increase the pain. This often caused permanent disabilities.

The Union Army frequently promised to release Confederate prisoners, if they would agree to join the Union Navy or Army units fighting Indians in the West. Sergeant-major Oscar Cliett of the 55th Georgia Infantry reported to DeLand that his men rejected an offer to join the Union Navy, "as we couldn't swim." Mulligan would have laughed, but DeLand had Cliett chained in a dungeon for 21 days on bread and water.

In March 1864, after a tour of duty at Camp Douglas distinguished by corruption and mismanagement as well as cruelty, DeLand and his regiment returned to the field. In May, during the Wilderness Campaign in Virginia, he was badly wounded and captured. Ironically, he was given every courtesy as a prisoner of war by his Confederate captors.

In May 1864, Colonel Benjamin Sweet, who lost his position in the famous "Iron Brigade" for trying to undermine the commander of the 6th Wisconsin, and who had been undermining DeLand for months, became commandant of Camp Douglas. The cruelties continued unabated, and rations were reduced even more, but the appearance of the camp improved. During the 1864 election campaign Sweet also managed to persuade Lincoln and the War Department to put Chicago, then a town of 110,000, under martial law to prevent a prison uprising supported by Southern sympathizers in Chicago. More than 100 civilians were arrested and jailed for criticizing Lincoln policies or on the mere suspicion of Southern sympathies without the benefit of hearing or trial. Twelve died in prison before the end of the war. The uprising threat was vastly exaggerated and largely fabricated, but Sweet was promoted to Brigadier General in December for saving Chicago. At the end of the war he received a commendation for a job well done.

Many people of Chicago and many Christian churches in the area offered relief to the prisoners at Camp Douglas. Until the Union government put a stop to the practice, many prominent people and local churches gave time, financial aid, and medicines to assist the post surgeon in the care of sick and destitute prisoners. The famous evangelist D. L. Moody was brought in to preach on several occasions. Some Confederate prisoners, however, complained of the high propaganda content of sermons by other preachers.

At the end of the war the Confederate prisoners were offered transportation home by train, if they signed the Union loyalty oath. Otherwise, they would have to walk home. Most of the prisoners at Camp Douglas elected to walk home. By July 1865, the last POW had left Camp Douglas. The disgraceful history of Camp Douglas has been largely forgotten. Nothing remains of the camp but a monument and 6,000 graves at nearby Oak Woods Cemetery.

Prisoners of War

	Total	Deaths	Percent
Union	270,000	22,576	8.4
Confederate	220,000	26,246	11.9

Union Prisons with one thousand or more Confederate deaths:

Camp Douglas, IL ....4,454+
Point Lookout, MD 3,587
Elmira, NY 2,933
Fort Delaware, DL 2,460
Camp Chase, Ohio 2,260
Rock Island, IL...1,960
Camp Morton, IN..1,763
 Auton, PA 1,508
Gratiot St., St. Louis, MO 1,140

Confederate Prisons with one thousand or more Union deaths:

Andersonville, GA 12,919
Salisbury, NC 3,700
Danville, VA...1,297

Typical causes of death for both Union and Confederate prisons:
Diarrhea, dysentery, pneumonia, influenza, extreme upper repertory infections, typhoid, small pox, tuberculosis, measles, scurvy, mumps, malaria, cholera, yellow fever, and hospital gangrene.

CHAPTER 17

The Andersonville Tragedy

Another Humanitarian Crisis Made in Washington

Andersonville prisoners

Near the tiny village of Andersonville, Georgia, are 13,714 graves, a testament to one of the greatest tragedies of the War Between the States and of American history. In fourteen months of 1864 and 1865, nearly 13,000 Union prisoners of war died there of malnutrition, disease, and despair. Union propagandists then and still today have branded it an atrocity. But what is the truth?

Late in the war, the Confederate government decided it needed to move its Union POWs to locations far removed from the most active areas of combat and vulnerability to attack. New locations also needed to be near railroad transportation and plentiful agricultural supplies to feed the prisoners and Confederate infantry units assigned to guard them. They found what they thought was an excellent location in southwest central Georgia at Station Number 8 on the Georgia Southwestern Railroad line. A small community of six buildings, called Andersonville, had grown up around that station.

The Confederates had planned to build a full scale prison with barracks and other facilities there, but by early 1864 the South was being strangled by the Union Navy blockade and Union Army advances that crippled railroad and other transportation. The area was heavily wooded, but due to the general lack of manpower and other building materials, it became impossible to build barracks. The Confederate government was forced to the cheapest and most expedient alternative, a stockade, a mere corral, initially encompassing just over 16 acres in which to confine prisoners. Slave labor from nearby plantations had to be requisitioned to complete the barricades.

The facility, meant to hold no more than 10,000 prisoners, was first called Camp Sumter. The first Union POWs were transferred from the upper South in late February 1864. Many of these prisoners were already in poor health. Colonel Alexander Persons of the 55th Georgia Infantry was placed in charge. Captain Henry Wirz, who was made responsible for the prisoners, and who later became the scapegoat for the Andersonville tragedy, did not arrive there until March 25 and was never in overall command.

By June, when General John Winder was placed in overall charge and expanded the compound to 27 acres, there were already over 22,000 prisoners there, and more than 2,600 had died. By August, 34,000 prisoners were crowded into the compound. This crowding caused many sanitation problems. Newly arriving prisoners often vomited from the smells. In addition, because of Union advances using the total-war tactics of burning crops and barns and either confiscating or killing domestic animals, food supplies were scarce everywhere in the South.

The first POW arrivals built huts with left over lumber, and subsequent arrivals put up tents within the compound. Food rations soon had to be reduced because of growing shortages. Union prisoners there, however, received the same rations as their Confederate guards throughout the war. Union forces also did everything possible to prevent medical supplies from reaching the South, severely handicapping treatment of sick and wounded prisoners.

The tragic situation at Andersonville could have been much relieved if prisoner exchanges had been allowed to continue. But Lincoln and Secretary of War Edwin Stanton decided that prisoner exchanges favored the Confederates too much, desperate as they were for manpower replacements against the increasing numerical superiority of Union forces.

James Madison Page of the 6th Michigan Cavalry, who was interned at Andersonville from its beginning until transferred in mid-September 1864 to Millen, Georgia, published his memoirs on Andersonville in 1908, entitled, *The True Story of Andersonville Prison*. He quotes an August 1,

1864 statement by Secretary of War Stanton that flattened the morale of Union POWs:

"We will not exchange able-bodied men for skeletons…We do not propose to reinforce the rebel army by exchanging prisoners."

Later the Confederates offered to give up their Andersonville prisoners without exchange, if only Union ships would pick them up. But despite their suffering, Stanton decided to leave them as a burden to Confederate forces.

The principal causes of death at Andersonville were dysentery, diarrhea, scurvy, typhoid, smallpox, and hospital gangrene. Of course, malnutrition greatly increased vulnerability to these diseases. Many of the men were very emaciated, and photos of them later enraged the Northern public. According to Page, about one half the prisoners suffered from scurvy. Page stated that:

"As bad as was the physical condition of the prisoners, their mental depression was worse and more fatal."

"Captain Wirz, on the advice of medical officers, put in operation the brewing of "corn beer." This was very effective in reducing scurvy in the camp and improved morale."

Nearly 45,000 Union prisoners spent time at Andersonville. Of these, 12,912, or about 29 percent, died. The Confederate guards, however, subject to the same diet and diseases, died at the same rate. Approximately 270,000 Union soldiers were held prisoner during the war, and 22,576, or just over 8 percent, died. More than half of the total Union POW deaths were at Andersonville. Of the 220,000 Confederates held prisoner during the war, in excess of 26,000 or nearly 12 percent died.

It should be noted that despite the tragedy at Andersonville, Southern POWs died at a rate at least 41 percent higher than Union POWs. At least 23 percent of Confederate prisoners interned at Camp Douglas in Illinois and approximately 25 percent of those held prisoner at Elmira, New York, died. George R. Farr, Historian for the Town of Elmira, clearly states the reason for the higher Confederate death rate:

"The prison records (at Elmira) **show that prisoners typically died from typhoid fever, chronic diarrhea, and pneumonia. What the records do not show is that the cause of death was often partly due to malnutrition. It is evident that military officials, many with a strong hatred for the South, from Secretary Stanton on down had some part in preventing adequate supplies of food being furnished to the prisoners. There can be no other explanation because this prison** (Elmira) **was located in a fertile, rich, agricultural part of New York State where food shortages just did not exist."**

Especially during the last part of the war, the Confederate armies were starving, while the Union armies were well fed and equipped to the last tent peg. Under the direction of Secretary of War Edwin Stanton, and with the complicit agreement of Abraham Lincoln and his highest ranking generals, the North pursued a policy of deliberate maltreatment of Southern prisoners, principally by lowering their food rations. At the same time, the Southern policy was to give the same rations to Union POWs as their own soldiers. Toward the end of the war, the entire corn reserve of the Army of Northern Virginia was transferred to Confederate prison camps.

There was little physical abuse of prisoners at Andersonville. After the first of 329 escapes at Andersonville, a "deadline" was marked 20 feet from the stockade walls. A few prisoners were shot crossing that line. This information was used to "wave the bloody shirt" in the Northern press, stirring up hatred for the South. What the War Department and Northern press did not reveal is that "deadlines" were common to all Northern and Southern POW camps.

Most of the few violent deaths of prisoners at Andersonville were the result of an internal struggle between an organized criminal band within the compound, responsible for robbing and murdering vulnerable prisoners, and a group of elected "regulators" that brought them to justice with the approval of Confederate authorities. The Union robbers were arrested and tried by the Union regulators. After trials, the Union regulators hanged six of the criminals. Another three were beaten to death in resisting arrest.

At the end of the war, Secretary of War Stanton was anxious to put the blame for Andersonville somewhere other than the War Department. He would have preferred to pin the responsibility on Confederate President Jefferson Davis, but that failed. Major Wirz was demonized by perjured testimony and made the scapegoat. Wirz, his lawyer, and his priest were told by representatives of **"a High Cabinet Official"** that he would be pardoned, if he would implicate Jefferson Davis. He did not and was hanged. In a shameful distortion of justice, the trial by Military Commission used perjury, bribery, and intimidation to force a predetermined guilty verdict. All charges of murder and other serious crimes brought against Wirz during the War Department trial have since been decisively refuted.

In a letter to Jefferson Davis in 1880, Father F. E. Boyle gave this testimony of Wirz:

"I attended the Major to the scaffold, and he died in the peace of God and praying for his enemies. I know that he was indeed innocent of all the cruel charges on which his life was sworn away, and I was edified by the Christian spirit in which he submitted to his persecutors."

Many people in the North were outraged by Wirz's shameless trial and execution. In December 1865, the *New York News* published a letter from Macon, Georgia, ending in these words:

"The radical conspirators against history may have the ear of the world just now, but sooner or later the truth will come out. 'The eternal years of God are hers."

The followers of Davis, Lee, and Jackson can bide their time, remembering what the great poet of Israel said: "I have seen the wicked in great power, and spreading himself like a green bay tree; yet he passed away, and lo! He is not." (Psalm 37: 35-36a)

Of the Charges Against Jefferson Davis

Following the war, the *New York Tribune* called for Confederate President Jefferson Davis to be tried for treason in regards to the secession of Southern States, and for murder for his alleged responsibility in Lincoln's assassination and the deaths of over 12,000 Union prisoners at Andersonville.

In 1866, New York attorney George Shea (afterwards Chief Justice of the Marine Court in New York) went to Canada to examine the secret records of the Confederate government on the prisoners of war issue. His report, which gained the backing of *Tribune* Editor Horace Greeley, Governor of Massachusetts John A. Andrew, "Commodore" Cornelius Vanderbilt, and Senator Henry Wilson (R, MA, and later Vice President under Grant), thoroughly exonerated Davis. In a January 24, 1876 letter to the Tribune, Shea summarized an important part of his 1866 report:

"...it conclusively appeared that the Rebel Senate believed the Southern prisoners were mistreated at the North, that they were eager for retaliation, and that Davis strenuously and to the end resisted these efforts, and that he attempted to send Vice-President Stephens North to consult with President Lincoln on the subject."

Shea was responding to speech of Representative James G. Blaine (R Maine) in Congress, in which Davis was charged with crimes compared to the 1572 St. Bartholomew massacre in France and the Spanish Inquisition:

"Mr. Davis was the author, knowingly, deliberately, guiltily, and willfully of the gigantic murders and crimes at Andersonville..."

Senator Ben Hill of Georgia responded:

If nine percent of the men in Southern prisons were starved and tortured to death by Mr. Jefferson Davis, who tortured to death the twelve percent of Southern men who died in Northern prisons?...See Secretary Stanton's Statistics."

After Jefferson Davis had been held in prison for two years after the war, Chief Justice Salmon P. Chase stated:

"If Jefferson Davis be brought to trial it will convict the North and exonerate the South."

CHAPTER 18

ᏟᎠᏇ

The Trial of Henry Wirz

Finding a Scapegoat for Shocking Union War Policies

Henry Wirz

Henry Wirz was a Swiss immigrant, who settled in Louisiana before the Civil War. He enlisted in the Confederate Army and by 1864 held the rank of Captain. Captain (later Major) Henry Wirz was appointed Commandant of the Confederate Prisoner of War (POW) camp at Andersonville, Georgia, a few months after it was established early in 1864. During its existence in 1864 and 1865, it was the largest Confederate prison, holding at one time nearly 33,000 Union POWs. Of the 45,000 Union soldiers there during its existence nearly 13,000 died. Most of these died of diarrhea, dysentery, typhoid, smallpox, scurvy, and hospital gangrene. Dysentery and diarrhea alone accounted for 4,500 deaths from March to August 1864.

Wirz's conviction and execution as a war criminal ranks as one of the most shameful miscarriages of legal justice in American history. After failing to link Confederate President Jefferson Davis to the Lincoln assassination, the Judge Advocate General of the Army sought to link Davis with the alleged war crimes at Andersonville along with Robert E. Lee, Confederate Secretary of War James Seddon, and Wirz. Lee's name was dropped from the final indictment. Wirz was pressured to save his own life by implicating Davis, but he adamantly denied the accusation against Davis and refused to save his own life with a lie.

At the insistence of radical Republicans in Congress, eager to punish the South and considerably more influential after the assassination of the more moderate Lincoln, Wirz was refused a jury trial. He would be tried by a Military Commission.

Wirz's civilian defense lawyers argued that the charges against Wirz were unconstitutionally vague and indefinite. From thirteen specific allegations of murder, not a single murder victim was named in the charges. These murders were supposed to have taken place in the presence of many witnesses. Yet, although there were carefully recorded lists of those who died at Andersonville, no names were given. The defense motion was denied without comment. After all defense motions were denied, three of the five defense counsels withdrew from the case.

The prosecution strategy was to create a parade of horrors on the terrible conditions at Andersonville. The disease, malnutrition, overcrowding, misery, and death were described in moving detail. The Prosecuting Attorney, Col. Chipman, introduced as evidence to show Wirz's knowledge of conditions, his letters to the Confederate Department of Prisons. But instead of showing a conspiracy to mistreat Union soldiers, these letters showed that the Confederate Government, despite all its problems late in the war, continued to regulate and inspect its prisons with the purpose of improving their conditions. Wirz's own letters to Richmond were filled with pleas for more food, tents, clothing, medicine, and supplies.

Over 160 witnesses were called for the prosecution. Of these 145 testified that they had no knowledge of Wirz ever killing or mistreating a prisoner. One prisoner gave the name of a prisoner Wirz had allegedly killed, but the date of the alleged murder did not correspond to any of the dates alleged in the indictment, so the indictment was changed to match the testimony.

The star prosecution witness was a man called Felix de la Baume. He testified that he personally saw Wirz shoot men. After the testimony, but before the trial was completed, he was given a commendation for a "zealous testimony" signed by all the Commission members and was given a job in the Department of the Interior. After the trial ended he was identified by veterans of the 7th New York as a deserter. They got de la Baume fired, at which time he admitted that he had committed perjury in the Wirz trial.

Prosecutor Chipman exercised extraordinary control over the entire proceedings. He required that all defense witnesses be interviewed by him before testifying, and determined whether they would testify. Several key defense witnesses were not allowed to testify, and one was arrested and jailed on presenting himself. When the defense attorneys objected to this, the Commission upheld Chipman without comment.

The defense attorneys showed that the Confederate Government did everything possible to exchange prisoners, but Secretary of War Stanton refused because prisoner exchange might be a military advantage to the numerically smaller Confederate Army. Despite Confederate pleas that they were unable to sustain the prisoners, Stanton refused the exchanges. He also refused requested humanitarian shipments of medical supplies to the prisoners on the ground that these supplies might fall into the hands of the Confederate Army and help sustain their war efforts. Wirz paroled a party of four prisoners to go to Washington, but Stanton would not listen to their pleas.

The Commission refused to hear any evidence by the defense on Southern offers to exchange prisoners and ruled such evidence irrelevant. The U. S. War Department's statistics showed more Southern prisoners died in prison camps than Northern prisoners, and that the death rate of Confederate soldiers in Northern camps was 12% versus 9% for Union solders in Confederate camps. This evidence was also kept out as irrelevant.

The defense was allowed to show, however, that Confederate guards at Andersonville had the same quantity and quality of rations as the prisoners, and the death rate of the guards was approximately the same as the prisoners. The 68 defense witnesses were former prisoners and their relatives. The consensus was that Wirz was a kind hearted man, anguished by the terrible conditions in the prison, who did all he could to alleviate the prisoners' suffering. A Catholic priest also gave testimony favorable to Wirz.

In November 1864, the South unilaterally released 13,000 prisoners who were seriously ill to the United States. The majority of these were from Andersonville. In February 1865, Wirz released 3,000 prisoners who were well enough to travel on their own to the Federal Commander at Jacksonville, Florida. They were refused and returned to Andersonville.

At the conclusion of the trial the defense was denied a request for time to prepare their closing argument. At this denial the remaining two defense attorneys quit the case in frustration and protest. The prosecution presented both their case and that of the defense.

On October, 24, 1865, the Commission gave a verdict of guilty of murder and conspiracy to harm Union prisoners, and Wirz was sentenced to be hanged. Union Judge Advocate General Holt, who had gathered evidence against Wirz, in his review, described Wirz as a "demon" whose work of death caused him "savage orgies" of enjoyment. After this show trial and hanging, the rest of the indictments were dropped.

The highly acclaimed 1990 PBS documentary on the Civil War took the position of the Commission. But here is what Henry Wirz said on November 10, 1865, as he stood on the gallows:

"I go before my God, the Almighty God. He will judge between us. I am innocent, and I will die like a man."

Much of the information in this chapter was extracted from papers at the University of Missouri School of Law.

CHAPTER 19

ⳠⳀⳡ

The Hanging of Mary Surratt

Mary Surratt

On July 7, 1865, forty-two year old Mary Surratt, an attractive, dark-haired widow, was hanged on the gallows at the Old Arsenal Penitentiary in Washington along with three others convicted of complicity in the assassination of Abraham Lincoln by a military court. Mary Surratt was the only woman of the four. She was, in fact, the first woman ever executed by the government of the United States. The execution of Mary Surratt was not a triumph of justice. It was a disgraceful political atrocity that still stains the national conscience and mars the American ideal of justice.

Americans have a strong tendency to whitewash history. It is more pleasant for us to believe and easier to teach our children that all our great leaders have been virtuous, that all our causes have been noble, and that all our courts have been just. No nation can long endure without a strong sense of patriotism. But genuine patriotism, a love of one's country and people that endures over many generations, is undermined when truth is mangled in the service of propaganda or political ambitions. Truth and love are inseparable. Patriotism without truth is a monstrous imposter.

The Lincoln assassination conspiracy trial was marked by judicial despotism, perjury, bribery, and even intimidation and torture of witnesses and defendants. The investigation, prosecution, trial, and sentences were all managed by the War Department under its ambitious Secretary, Edwin Stanton. Four of the eight defendants were hanged and the others sentenced to life imprisonment on an isolated island.

A principal objective of the conspiracy trial, conducted by nine high-ranking officers handpicked by Stanton, was the implication of Confederate President Jefferson Davis in Lincoln's assassination. But Stanton, like many of his Radical Republican allies in Congress and government, was also motivated by a consuming hatred for the South. Furthermore, he hoped to be elected President of the United States in 1868. According to the diary of Secretary of the Navy Gideon Welles and biographical statements by many other Union political and military leaders, Stanton was noted for his manipulative, and often treacherous, political dealings. He had often manipulated Lincoln and other Cabinet Members, and for a short time, he was very successful in persuading or manipulating President Andrew Johnson into supporting his schemes for vengeance on the South.

Mary Surratt, the devout Catholic mother of three children ranging in age from twenty to twenty-four, was the owner of a boardinghouse in Washington. She also owned her former residence, the Surratt House and Tavern, and some farmland in the tiny community of Surrattsville (now Clinton), Maryland, southeast of Washington. But when her husband, John Surratt, Sr., died in 1862, she was unable to manage the facilities and rented them to John Lloyd, a Southern sympathizer with a problematic drinking habit. The Surratts were Southern sympathizers. They came from the strongly pro-Southern agricultural area of southern Maryland, where in better times they had owned several hundred acres of land and as many as twelve slaves. Her 24-year-old son, Isaac, was a sergeant in the 33rd Texas Cavalry, and her 20-year-old son, John, had become a Confederate courier. Both John and her attractive 22-year-old daughter, Anna, lived at the boardinghouse in Washington. Although Mary Surratt was definitely pro-Southern, she was not very political. Especially by late 1864, she only wanted her two sons home and safe. For that reason she was not comfortable with John's courier trips and intrigues.

In December 1864, John ran into Dr. Samuel Mudd, who was visiting from southern Maryland. Dr. Mudd introduced him to John Wilkes Booth, one of America's most famous actors. John became good friends with the 26-year-old actor and soon became involved in Booth's plot to kidnap Abraham Lincoln in order to force a prisoner of war exchange or even end the war. The Confederate Government had considered such a plan in 1863 but rejected it. Jefferson Davis, in particular, was strongly opposed to such intrigues on both practical and philosophical grounds.

The wealthy and charismatic Booth generally stayed at the most expensive hotels in Washington, but he became a frequent visitor to the Surratt boardinghouse, where he befriended both the Surratts and their 20-year-old boarder, Louis Weichmann, a clerk at the Prisoner of War Commissariat. His planning and recruitment for his kidnapping plot were, however, mostly done at hotels and taverns. Booth managed to recruit six men for his daring abduction plot.

Through his many contacts, Booth discovered that Lincoln sometimes traveled Washington at night with very little accompaniment. Hoping to take advantage of this, he focused his band of recruits on abducting Lincoln on one of his customary routes. On March 17, he had them lying in wait at the most opportune point to intercept and abduct the President. However, Lincoln failed to show up. As a result of this disappointment, despite Booth's fame and charisma, several from the group began to be disillusioned with him. These included John Surratt and at least three of the conspiracy defendants: Michael O'Laughlin, Sam Arnold, and even George Atzerodt, who was executed along with Mary Surratt. Lee's surrender on April 9 further discouraged continuation with Booth's machinations.

Previous to that night, John Surratt had been amused that his sister, Anna, seemed a bit infatuated with Booth. Anna and Honora Fitzpatrick, a young boarder about the same age, had both purchased pictures of Booth. When her brother discovered hers, he told her to destroy it, but instead she hid it behind a picture that Weichmann had purchased for her. Later Anna admitted that she had been friendly with Booth and said that her brother told her that he thought Booth was crazy and should attend to his own business. In addition to his questions about Booth's reliability and good judgment, John Surratt was probably aware of the actor's reputation for having numerous romantic interests.

According to Booth's diary, he did not decide to assassinate Lincoln before April 13 and did not know that Lincoln was coming to the Ford Theater until late in the afternoon on April 14, the day of the assassination. At 8:00 p.m. that night he met with Lewis Powell (alias Paine), a strapping former member of Mosby's Confederate Rangers, David Herold, and

George Atzerodt and announced his plan to assassinate Abraham Lincoln. Powell would assassinate Secretary of State Seward, who was recovering at his home from a carriage accident, and Herold would assist with his getaway. Atzerodt would assassinate Vice President Johnson in his hotel, and Booth would shoot Lincoln at the Ford Theater.

Powell made a savage but unsuccessful knife attack on Seward with no help from Herold, who fled the scene early, leaving Powell to escape on foot. Atzerodt wandered around the town from bar to bar without any intention of assassinating Vice President Johnson. Booth, however, shot President Lincoln in the back of the head as he sat in his theater box. Lincoln died at 7:15 the next morning. The unfortunate Herold accidentally ran into the escaping Booth and was persuaded to assist him in escaping to Virginia.

Before the fall of Richmond early in April, John Surratt left Washington carrying important financial instructions to Confederate Commissioners in Montreal, Canada. From there he went to Elmira, New York, to investigate the possibility of rescuing Confederate POWs there. He never returned to Washington or knew until after the fact, that Booth had changed his plans from kidnapping Lincoln to assassinating him. When he heard of the assassination, he fled to Canada and then Europe.

Once on an early visit to the Surratt home, Lewis Powell had inadvertently blurted out something about the abduction plot. John Surratt firmly berated him, saying that neither his mother nor his sister knew anything about such plans and emphatically stressed that he did not want them to know anything. Lewis Powell later proclaimed to the military court, his religious and legal counselors, and to his executioners that Mary Surratt was completely innocent of the charges against her or any wrongdoing. No one in the War Department or political chain of authority would listen. Every effort was made to isolate and silence the accused conspirators.

The government's case against Mary Surratt was weak and largely circumstantial, but for some reason they made every effort not only to convict her of complicity in the assassination of Lincoln, but also to make sure she received the death penalty. To make their case, they bribed, threatened, and even tortured witnesses and defendants. They suppressed critical evidence and used completely unrelated emotional issues, such as "starving Union prisoners of war," to inflame the military court and the public against the defendants. There is substantial evidence that Secretary of War Stanton, Army Judge Advocate General Joseph Holt, and several Stanton and Holt associates deliberately deceived President Andrew Johnson in respect to a clemency plea for Mary Surratt, which had been urged by a majority of the officers on the military court.

The Surratt tavern and inn at Surrattsville was both a polling place and post office. John Surratt, Sr. had been the first postmaster there. During the war, it became a stopping place for Confederate and even Union agents and couriers traveling between Washington and Richmond. Naturally, it was an ideal first stopping place in Booth's plan to abduct Lincoln. Two days before the aborted abduction attempt on March 20, John Surratt, Jr., David Herold, and George Atzerodt visited there and deposited two carbines with the proprietor, John Lloyd. Lloyd was a Confederate sympathizer and occasional agent and courier when sober.

Much of the Military Commission's case against Mary Surratt revolved around her trips to Surrattsville on April 11 and April 14, the date of Lincoln's assassination.

On April 11, Mary Surratt, pressured by George Calvert, a creditor from southern Maryland, who held a $1,000 note on the Surrattsville properties, asked her favorite boarder, Lou Weichmann, to accompany her in a buggy to Surrattsville to collect $479 owed to her by John Nothey. On the way there, they happened to meet her Surrattsville tenant, John Lloyd, accompanied in his buggy by his sister-in-law, Emma Offutt. Mary spoke to them very briefly about a mutual friend, Gus Howell, a former Confederate courier, who had recently been arrested. She said she was going to encourage him to sign the Loyalty Oath, so he could be released. Later, Lloyd would testify (under duress) that Mary had told him to "get the shootin' irons ready." While in Surrattsville, Captain Bennett Gwynn, acting on Mary's behalf, spoke privately to Nothey about the debt, but they were unable to come to an agreement. Mary and Weichmann then returned to Washington.

On the morning of April 14, the day of Lincoln's assassination, Mary received an insistent letter from George Calvert stating that he had seen Nothey, who was now willing to settle his debt with Mary. That afternoon, Secretary Stanton had given War Department employees the afternoon off to celebrate Good Friday. When Weichmann returned home, Mary asked him to take her to Surrattsville again to see John Nothey. Mary suggested that perhaps they could borrow Booth's buggy. Booth had sold the buggy, however, and gave Weichmann some money to rent one. Just prior to Weichmann's return with the buggy, Booth showed up and asked if she would deliver a package to John Lloyd. She agreed to carry the small package, which contained a field glass, and immediately left with Weichmann for Surrattsville. On arriving in Surrattsville about 4:00 p.m. in the afternoon, they found neither Lloyd, Captain Gwynn, nor Nothey there. Having very poor eyesight, Mary asked Weichmann to write a letter to Nothey, threatening to sue him within ten days if he did not pay his debt. She signed and dated it *April 14, 1865*.

At that time, Mrs. Offutt arrived, and Mary gave her the package from Booth. In a few moments Captain Gwynn arrived, and she gave him the letter Weichmann had written for her, asking him to deliver and read it to Nothey. Because their buggy needed repairs, Mary and Weichmann were delayed from leaving. Just before they left, Lloyd also returned. According to Mrs. Offutt's later testimony, he was "very much in liquor, more so than I have ever seen him in my life." Lloyd had brought oysters and fish back with him from Marlboro and invited Mary and Weichmann to stay for dinner, but they declined and started for Washington in a drizzling rain.

They arrived at the boardinghouse by 7:45 p.m. to find Mary's daughter, Anna, and two of the young women renters sitting at the dining room table. By 10:00 p.m. all but Mary were in bed. Shortly afterwards, she heard loud voices outside. Opening a window, Mary heard a soldier shout that the President had just been shot. About 2:30 a.m., a persistent ringing of the doorbell introduced a team of detectives from the Metropolitan Police Department demanding to search the house. They told Weichmann that John Wilkes Booth had shot the President at Ford's Theatre. They were seeking John Surratt.

The next morning Lou Weichmann and boarder John Holohan went to the Metropolitan Police Station, where Superintendent Richards immediately placed Weichmann under arrest. Thereafter Weichmann took two detectives to see John Lloyd in Surrattsville. Asked if he had seen Booth, Lloyd lied and said that he had not. Holohan returned to the boardinghouse the next day, but Weichmann remained in custody.

On Monday evening, three detectives from the War Department arrived to place Mary Surratt and everyone else in the house under arrest and take them to the headquarters of the Washington area commander, General

Augur, for examination. Before they could leave, an untimely visitor arrived. It was the fugitive, Lewis Powell. He was very dirty, wearing a long coat and a skull cap, carrying a pick, and asking for Mrs. Surratt. He made the lame excuse that he had come to seek instructions for digging a gutter for her the next day. Mary raised her right hand and said, **"Before God, sir, I do not know this man, and I have not seen him before, and I did not hire him to come and dig a gutter for me."** Mary's eyesight was poor, especially in artificial light, and she was already quite upset, but several others there who knew Powell did not recognize him either. Much would be made at the trial over Mary's denying she had ever seen Powell.

At General Augur's office, Powell was immediately identified as the man who had attacked Secretary Seward. After being questioned, Mary, Anna, and the other two young women were taken to the infamous Old Capitol Prison. During her two week stay there, Mary Surratt gained a reputation for compassionate nursing and consoling of sick and downhearted prisoners. Anna and the other young women were soon released.

John Wilkes Booth was killed in Virginia on April 26 after a twelve-day manhunt. His reluctant fellow conspirator and fugitive companion, David Herold, surrendered.

By May 1, Mary Surratt and the other accused conspirators were imprisoned in the Old Arsenal Penitentiary. John Surratt would be at large in Europe for another two years. For all the alleged conspirators except Mary Surratt and Dr. Mudd, Edwin Stanton had invented a new torture. While in their cells, they were not only shackled, but forced to wear canvas hoods lined with cotton padding about one inch thick. Only a small opening at the mouth was left for feeding, and that was sometimes difficult. Some say that Stanton's purpose was to keep them from committing suicide, but his own statements indicated that it was for keeping them from communicating among themselves or with others. Several prison doctors noted that the hoods and isolation put men's sanity at risk. Weichmann, who was to be a star witness for the prosecution, was in and out of custody.

It is not a mystery how the Metropolitan detectives came to call on Mary Surratt immediately after the assassination. About a month before, Weichmann, who was putatively John Surratt's best friend and had come to know Booth and to know Atzerodt well, had shared his suspicions about a kidnapping plot with his War Department supervisor. What *is* a mystery is why the War Department failed to take immediate action. Perhaps they hoped to catch bigger Confederate fish by waiting. Another mystery is why Stanton advised Grant not to go to the theater the night of the assassination but did nothing to increase the President's protection. Grant had his own reasons for not wanting to go. Mary Todd Lincoln was subject to violent bursts of jealous temper, which had embarrassed Mrs. Grant in the past. Still, generals do not often reject invitations by Presidents.

On May 1, 1865, President Andrew Johnson--with the encouragement of Secretary of War Edwin Stanton and other members of the Radical Republican clique--announced that the Lincoln assassination conspirators would be tried by a military commission. There was an immediate outcry from a minority in Congress and the Administration over this unconstitutional order. The Constitution does not permit military courts to try civilians when civilian courts are in operation. The rules of evidence are much less rigorous in a military court: the rights of the accused are much abbreviated, and the court is a law unto itself with no appeal of its rulings, except to the President of the United States. The protests of shocked Congressmen, former Attorney General Edward Bates, Secretary of the Navy Gideon Welles, and countless attorneys were ignored, and on May 9, the Military Commission met for the first time.

Secretary Stanton appointed Major General David Hunter as President of the Court and Judge Advocate General Joseph Holt to act in a role that was somewhere between judge and prosecutor, most frequently the latter. But Stanton would take a keen day-to-day interest in the trial and an intense interest in its outcome. In the end, the cry for blood was louder than the cry for justice, and politics outweighed it all.

The Military Commission trial of the alleged conspirators in the Lincoln assassination convened on May 9, 1865. Court was held in a 30-foot-by-25-foot room at the Old Arsenal Penitentiary in Washington, near the cells of the accused. The weather was generally hot and humid and the ventilation of the makeshift courtroom was poor. This frequently challenged the span of attention of the military tribunal. The prisoners sat behind their defense attorneys on seats raised about one foot higher. The hoods of the male prisoners were removed, but they were not allowed to speak, except to their defense attorneys, or to move. Their restricted movement made it difficult to get the attention of their attorneys. Despite these restrictions, defendant Lewis Powell managed to shout once that Mrs. Surratt was innocent. On many days the press and a limited number of observers were allowed to attend the sessions. Mary Surratt seemed to be the center of public attention. Many of the observers indulged in conversations heaping humiliating verbal abuse on her within her hearing.

Booth's diary, recovered from his body in Virginia, clearly indicated that up to and including April 13, 1865, the conspiracy was not to assassinate Lincoln, but to abduct him and hold him as a bargaining chip to force a prisoner of war exchange or even to end the war. This extremely important evidence was withheld from the court and kept by Secretary of War Stanton. Although the abduction plan became known to the Military Commission, the prosecution and Judge Advocate General Joseph Holt continually tried to conflate the abduction plot with the assassination plot. Booth did not decide to attempt Lincoln's assassination until late in the afternoon on April 14. He did not organize it until 8:00 p.m. that night, only two and a quarter hours before he shot Lincoln at Ford's Theatre.

It should be noted that the U.S. War Department had refused to exchange prisoners since July 1863. Their objective was to deny the already badly outnumbered Confederate Army any source of desperately needed replacements. As a consequence, however, POWs on both sides were suffering. Hence there was actually a humanitarian factor associated with the abduction plot.

The main thrust of the prosecution in the case of Mary Surratt was to show that she was an active participant in the assassination plot. Thus they tried hard to convince the Military Commission and attending reporters that she coordinated with Booth by making sure that guns were ready for the assassins as they escaped through Surrattsville.

John Lloyd, her Surrattsville renter, gave perjured, but rather equivocal, testimony to that effect for the prosecution. Mrs. Surratt's boarder, Louis Weichmann, was more indirect in his insinuations, but his testimony, formed under great duress, was damaging.

Just after the trial, but a few days before the executions on July 7, Louis Weichmann went for a walk with two friends: John Brophy and Louis Carland. Saying that his conscience was troubling him, Weichmann told them that he had been arrested as one of the conspirators, and that both Stanton and Col. H. L. Burnett had threatened him with death unless he revealed all about the assassination. He then admitted that he had lied on the witness stand to save his own life and keep his government position. Weichmann said that he wanted to go to St. Aloysius Church and make a confession, but he would not, as suggested by Carland, make a statement under oath for fear of being indicted for perjury. On the day of the execution, John Brophy swore out an affidavit disclosing Weichmann's statements and copied the Washington *Constitutional Union*. Brophy took the affidavit to the White House and sent it in to President Andrew Johnson. He was told that Johnson thought it was "wholly without weight." Carland also testified to Weichmann's confession to them at the trial of John Surratt in 1867.

Weichmann later confided to John T. Ford, the owner of Ford's Theater, that he had been subject to great duress by Secretary Stanton, Col. H. L. Burnett, and their detectives to change a testimony favorable to Mrs. Surratt to one that more suited Stanton. Weichmann was brought before Stanton, who expressed in a very intimidating manner that Weichmann was as guilty of the President's death as Booth. In order to impress Weichmann further, the Secretary placed a rope around Weichmann's neck. Stanton then told him that if he didn't testify as the government wished, he (Weichmann) would be hanged.

Other testimonies indicate Weichmann was threatened with hanging more than once by War Department officials and detectives. On May 5, Weichmann wrote this to Col. Burnett from Carroll Prison:

"You confused and terrified me so much yesterday that I was almost unable to say anything."

Naturally, this note was not made available at the conspiracy trial. According to John Chandler Griffin's recent (2006) book, *Abraham Lincoln's Execution,* shortly after Weichmann's initial arrest as a conspirator, he was thrown into a cell where a rope was tossed over a rafter and a noose looped on his neck. He was then threatened with immediate hanging, if he did not tell them what they wanted to know. He was told that his death would be reported as a suicide.

Also according to John T. Ford, John Lloyd told him that he had agreed to testify against Mrs. Surratt only after he had suffered extreme duress in the hands of his captors. After Lloyd was arrested in Surrattsville on April 18, he was taken to Bryantown to be examined by Col. H. H. Wells. When Lloyd refused to say anything against Mrs. Surratt, he was hanged by his thumbs until he could no longer stand the pain. Only then, to spare himself from further torture, did he agree to give perjured testimony against his landlady.

In 1978, a written statement presumably made by George Atzerodt was found in the papers of General W. E. Doster, defense attorney for both Atzerodt and Lewis Powell. This statement, dated the evening of May 1, 1865, was given to Provost Marshall McPhail in the presence of detective John L. Smith. In that rambling document, Atzerodt made two conflicting statements: First he said that Booth told him,

"Mrs. Surratt went to Surrattsville to get out the guns which had been taken to that place by David Herold. This was Friday." Then a little farther on he stated,

"Booth never said until the last night (Friday) **that he intended to kill the President."**

In fact, Booth did not yet know that the President would be attending the play at Ford's Theater that night, when he spoke to Mrs. Surratt just before she and Weichmann left for Surrattsville.

Atzerodt's statement was not used by the prosecution, probably because of the revealing contradiction. Perhaps Atzerodt, desperate to save his own life, was promised leniency if he could reinforce the prosecution's attempt to connect Mrs. Surratt with arranging for the guns to be in place along the escape route. Undoubtedly, like Weichmann and Lloyd, Atzerodt was subject to the usual coercive methods of interrogation. Atzerodt failed to mention Booth assigning him to kill Vice President Johnson. But it is evident from various testimonies and his actions that Atzerodt had no intention of carrying out Booth's orders.

Secretary Stanton's Chief Detective, Col. Lafayette Baker, initially set the Government's mood for the conspiracy hunt. On taking charge of the pursuit of Lincoln's assassins, he released an astonishing official order urging his detectives "to extort confessions and procure testimony to establish the conspiracy…by promises, rewards, threats, deceit, force, or any other effectual means."

No wonder he was Stanton's most trusted lieutenant. And it is no wonder that there were numerous irregularities later discovered in the prosecution's conduct and securing of witnesses.

On May 13, the Military Commission heard testimony from a Canadian physician, James B. Merritt, that Booth, Surratt, and Atzerodt were parties in a previous scheme to kill Lincoln. The United States Government paid Dr. Merritt $6,000 for his testimony. After a prosecution witness named Von Steinacker, who had given a damaging testimony connecting Confederate officers with Booth, was found by the defense to have just been released from prison and to have a considerable criminal record, the court at first refused the defense the right to cross-examine him. After General Holt finally agreed to Steinacker's cross examination, the witness could not be found.

On May 25, the Military Commission suddenly introduced the subject of (alleged) Southern mistreatment of Union prisoners of war as an issue in the conspiracy trial.

This outrageous tactic was actually successful in raising the level of anger and resentment against the South, Jefferson Davis, and the defendants.

Probably the most damaging circumstantial evidence against Mary Surratt was the untimely arrival of a well disguised Lewis Powell at Mrs. Surratt's door on April 17.

This and her denial that she knew him created suspicions that were difficult to overcome. Numerous witnesses, however, testified to her poor eyesight. Many more testified of her sterling character and religious devotion. No fewer than five Catholic priests testified to her impeccable character.

The Lincoln assassination conspiracy trial was a shameful violation of due process. Only the Salem Witch Trials in 1692 and the autumn 1865 trial of Henry Wirz, commandant of the Andersonville prisoner of war camp, are comparable in their injustice, malice, and despotism. I do not believe that "Stalinist" is too strong a word for the conduct of Stanton and his inner council.

The Military Commission sentenced Atzerodt, Powell, and Herold to hang. The others were sentenced to long prison terms. Surprisingly, five of the nine officers on the Military Commission initially wanted either to acquit Mary Surratt or at least see that she did not get the death penalty. But Edwin Stanton and Joseph Holt, supported by others in the Radical Republican ring, would not stand for it.

On July 7, 1865, George Atzerodt, David Herold, Lewis Powell, and Mary Surratt were hanged for conspiring in the assassination of Abraham Lincoln. Samuel Arnold, Samuel Mudd, and Michael O'Laughlin were given life sentences of hard labor at Dry Tortugas Prison, off the Florida coast. Edward Spangler was given a lesser sentence. Years after the trial, Brigadier General William E. Doster, the attorney for George Atzerodt and Lewis Powell, said that

"...the trial had been a contest on which a few lawyers were on one side and the whole United States on the other — a case in which the verdict was known beforehand."

The rules of the Military Commission required six out of nine votes for conviction and sentencing. When they convened to consider their verdict and sentencing for Mrs. Surratt, they first proposed by a vote of five to four either to acquit her or at least to spare her life. Judge Holt and Secretary Stanton were expecting the death penalty. Outraged and alarmed, Holt immediately hastened to Stanton's office for consultation. Thirty minutes later Holt returned to the Commission with a compromise solution and intimidated the five dissenting officers — none of whom had any legal training — into accepting it. "For the sake of legal consistency," if the Commission would vote unanimously for the death penalty for Mrs. Surratt, they could draw up a petition asking the President for mercy in her case. Secretary Stanton would see to it that President Johnson received it favorably. With this compromise, the Commission could "save face" and yet spare the life of Mary Surratt. None of the defense counsels were consulted or made privy to this "compromise." Major General Hunter, the President of the Military Commission, later said that

"...this was done in violation of all principles of law and equity."

But Stanton had no intention of keeping his part of their mutual understanding. Having convinced the Commission, against their better judgment, to cast a unanimous vote to hang Mrs. Surratt, he would convince the President that it was absolutely necessary for her to hang. If an outraged public blamed Johnson for executing Mrs. Surratt, so much the better for Stanton's Presidential ambitions. This would be just one of the many double crosses that the highly manipulative Stanton got away with in his legal and political careers.

The existence of the clemency plea for Mrs. Surratt was not known except to several Cabinet members and a close circle in the War Department until the civil court trial of John Surratt, Jr. in 1867. Upon demand, General Holt delivered it to the court but quickly retrieved it, before it could be examined. Its existence was not publicly known until 1872. Below is the entire text, which was undersigned by Generals Hunter, Kautz, Foster, Ekin, and Col. Tompkins:

"The undersigned members of the Military Commission detailed to try Mary E. Surratt and others for the conspiracy and the murder of Abraham Lincoln, late President of the United States, do respectively pray the President in consideration of the sex and age of the said Mary E. Surratt, if he can upon all the facts in the case, find it consistent with his sense of duty to the country to commute the sentence of death to imprisonment in the penitentiary for life."

This petition was certainly not designed to be a convincing argument for commuting Mrs. Surratt's death sentence. Since Mrs. Surratt was 42 years-old, it would seem that making age a consideration in the petition weakened it considerably. Since none of the reasons are given that caused the undersigned officers to think that Mrs. Surratt's guilt was either questionable or insufficient to warrant the death penalty, the credibility and gravity of the petition was substantially debilitated. Considering that this "compromise" was concocted by Holt and Stanton and the heavy-handed manner in which it was recommended to the undersigned officers, it is logical to conclude that it was written by Stanton or Holt. It also seems rather obvious that it was designed to be of little consequence, thereby contributing to the government murder of Mary Surratt.

In 1872, when the existence of the clemency petition became public knowledge, President Johnson claimed he had never seen it. Neither Johnson nor anyone on his staff officially acknowledged its receipt or made a formal response advising the Commission of its disposition. General Holt, however, firmly insisted that it was properly delivered with the other verdicts and sentences, and that Johnson did see it. There is evidence that President Johnson received many written requests and personal pleas to commute Mrs. Surratt's sentence, and that it was discussed in at least one Cabinet meeting, perhaps of limited attendance.

James Harlan, Secretary of the Interior in 1865, in a letter dated May 23, 1875, remembered a Cabinet meeting just after the conspiracy trial at which clemency for Mrs. Surratt was discussed. He recorded the words of Stanton to Andrew Johnson:

"Surely not, Mr. President, for if the death penalty should be commuted in so grave a case as the assassination of the head of a great nation, on account of the sex of the criminal, it would amount to an invitation to assassins hereafter to employ women as their instruments, under the belief that if arrested and condemned, they would be punished less severely than men. An act of executive clemency on such a plea would be disapproved by the Government of every civilized nation on earth."

Thus the agreement for Mary Surratt's clemency that the petitioning officers thought they had with Stanton through Judge Advocate General Holt was betrayed.

In the two days that transpired between President Johnson's signing Mary Surratt's execution warrant and her actual execution on July 7, numerous people petitioned the President for mercy. It is not clear that any of them were able to speak directly to him during this time. When John Brophy and Anna Surratt tried to see him, he was protected by armed guards and Republican Senators James Lane of Kansas and Preston King of New York. Only his private secretary, Brigadier General R. D. Mussey, delivered messages and petitions to him or spoke directly to him. President Johnson was evidently not in a receptive mood for mercy. Reverend George Butler, who acted as chaplain for George Atzerodt and who made a social call on Johnson a few hours after the executions, gave this report on the President's disposition:

"Concerning Mrs. Surratt…very strong appeals had been made for the exercise of executive clemency…but he could not be moved, for in his own significant language, Mrs. Surratt 'kept the nest that hatched the eggs.' The President further stated that no plea had been urged in her behalf, save the fact that she was a woman, and his interposition upon that ground would license female crime."

This clearly indicates that either the President was lying or that he did not receive the petitions that presented evidence of confessed perjuries and witness intimidation by the government or the statements of Lewis Powell and John T. Ford. In a much later interview, he blamed his failure to commute Mary Surratt's execution on General Mussey, who had blocked communications to him. General Mussey was only assigned as Johnson's private secretary for a few months and may have been an appointment suggested by Stanton.

Col. William P. Wood, superintendent of the Old Capitol Prison while Mrs. Surratt was there, had become convinced of her innocence. Just before the execution, he rushed to the White House hoping to see President Johnson and make an appeal for mercy on her behalf. He was met there and blocked from entering by Col. Lafayette Baker, Stanton's chief detective, who held a signed order from Stanton specifically prohibiting Wood's admission to the premises. In an undated article that appeared in the *Washington Gazette* shortly after the death of Stanton in 1869, Wood revealed an interesting conversation with President Johnson:

"Some time after the execution of Mrs. Surratt, President Johnson sent for me and requested me to give my version of Mrs. Surratt's connection with the assassination of President Lincoln. I did so, and I believe he was thoroughly convinced of the innocence of Mrs. Surratt. He assured me he sincerely regretted that he had not given Mrs. Surratt the benefit of Executive Clemency, and strongly expressed his detestation of what he termed 'the infamous conduct of Stanton' in keeping these facts from him. I assured him of my unchangeable friendship for Mr. Stanton...while I regretted the course adopted by the Secretary of War towards Mrs. Surratt..."

In 1867, John Surratt, Jr. was brought back to the United States for trial as a Lincoln assassination conspirator. Stanton failed in his attempt to subject him to trial by a military commission. The rules of evidence, the introduction of previously suppressed evidence (such as Booth's diary), and the due process required by a civil court made it impossible to convict Surratt, and he was released. In 1866, the Supreme Court of the United States had decisively confirmed the Constitutional principle that military courts have no jurisdiction over civilian cases, if the civil courts are open. Had Mary Surratt been tried by a civil court, she would never have been convicted. Nor is it likely that George Atzerodt or David Herold would have received the death penalty. Nor would Dr. Mudd have been convicted of anything. The civil trial of John Surratt exposed many injustices that a free people must never again tolerate.

Before leaving office in 1869, President Johnson pardoned Dr. Mudd, Sam Arnold, and Edward Spangler. Michael O'Laughlin died of yellow fever in 1867 while imprisoned at Dry Tortugas.

There is a bronze plaque near the grave of Mary Surratt at Mt. Olivet Cemetery in Washington. It seems an appropriate epitaph for a woman who suffered enormous injustice, and whose public memory is still scarred by malicious and ignorant false witness:

"The souls of the just are in the hands of God, and the torment of malice shall not touch them. In the sight of the unwise they seemed to die, but they are at peace."

On Providence

"The truth is this: The march of Providence is so slow and our desires so impatient; the work of progress is so immense and our means of aiding it so feeble; the life of humanity is so long, that of the individual so brief, that we often see only the ebb of the advancing wave and are thus discouraged. It is history that teaches us to hope."

—Robert E. Lee,
a note found in his briefcase on his death

CHAPTER 20

Passage of the Fourteenth Amendment

A Tale of Corrupt Unconstitutional Political Manipulation

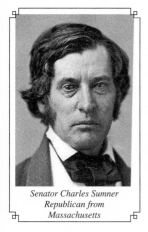

*Senator Charles Sumner
Republican from
Massachusetts*

Following the great tragedy of the "Civil War" and the assassination of President Lincoln in April of 1865, national leadership was largely in the hands of a Congress dominated by the Radical Republicans. They undermined the new President, Andrew Johnson, at every opportunity, and had little regard for the Supreme Court. They considered the Constitution to be an inconvenience and the Supreme Court to be an annoyance to the will of the people accomplished by Congress. States Rights, having been defeated by the coercion of bayonets, was no longer an effective check on federal power.

President Johnson planned to follow Lincoln's relatively benign plan for establishing loyal civil governments in the South and restoring them to the national family. Pursuant to this on May 29, 1865, he declared an amnesty for most Confederate veterans. By the middle of July many Southern state governments under the control of Union loyalists were functioning. But the Radical Republicans were bent on exacting vengeance and remaking the South. Johnson was uncomfortable with coercing the States into enfranchising former slaves, but the Radical Republicans, most of whom had been radical abolitionists, were insistent. Their motives in this were by no means pure. These included both political justice for blacks and exacting a humiliating vengeance on the South. But most importantly, they wanted to remake the South into an unassailable bastion of Radical Republican political support. That support would be used to guarantee the permanent political dominance of the Radical Republican faction over the nation and thereby guarantee the ongoing success of their economic and political agendas.

The Radical Republican hard core in Congress numbered only about thirty of some 230 Northern Senators and Representatives, but their influence was very powerful, and they had strong and widespread support in the Northern press. Five men exercised dominant leadership: Thaddeus Stevens, Representative from Pennsylvania; Benjamin Butler, Representative from Massachusetts; Charles Sumner, Senator from Massachusetts; Benjamin Wade, Senator from Ohio; and Secretary of War, Edwin Stanton.

In December 1865, the 13th Amendment abolished slavery. Included in the three-quarters of the states necessary for ratification were seven Southern States whose governments had been appointed and reconstituted by President Johnson. This, however, did not guarantee many civil rights for the former slaves, and as the Southern legislatures began to consist more of elected Democrats, they trended back to more traditional Southern thinking and far away from Radical Republican thinking. The Radical Republicans believed more amendments were needed to insure civil rights but also to advance their agenda for the South and the nation. Thus the 14th Amendment, which was really a combination of several amendments, was born in concept. Passing the 14th Amendment became a high priority for the Radical Republicans. In passing the 14th Amendment, they would ruthlessly violate the Constitution, engage in blatantly dishonest and despotic legislative manipulation, and impose a mean-spirited tyranny on the South that would poison race relations and regional trust for generations. Several aspects of the 14th Amendment would essentially turn the Constitution on its head and open the door for widespread Judicial and Congressional abuse and tyranny. The shameful coercion, blatant dishonesty, and numerous legislative and constitutional irregularities involved in passing the 14th Amendment place its legitimacy in extreme doubt.

The Amendment consists of five sections. The first section defines who is a citizen and overturns the Dred Scott v. Sanford Supreme Court decision that denied citizenship to blacks. It also prevented states from abridging the rights of citizens and denying any person due process and equal protection of the laws.

One reason for this section was to prevent Southern states from implementing "Black Codes" limiting the rights of former slaves. Some Mississippi legislation in particular was raising concern that the emancipation of slaves by the 13th Amendment was being circumvented.

At this very time, however, many Northern states had Black Codes more severe than any emerging in the South. Indiana law codes would not allow blacks and mulattos to come into the state. Illinois, the land of Lincoln, and Oregon were almost as restrictive of black immigration. Numerous other Northern states including Kansas, Michigan, Connecticut, Minnesota, and Wisconsin had rejected Negro suffrage and with it other rights and privileges of full citizenship.

Because Section 1 defines anyone born in the U.S. as a citizen, it has had vast unforeseen consequences in recent years. Each year, more than 300,000 children are born in the U.S. to illegal immigrant parents. This automatically makes these children citizens and entitles both the child and mother to many welfare benefits covering pregnancy and birth. The baby is entitled to Medicaid for an additional twelve months. In recent years this "anchor baby" provision of the 14th Amendment has seen much costly abuse. The writers of the 14th Amendment never intended it to be a benefit to illegal immigrants.

Section 2 eliminated the three-fifths rule for slaves in apportioning legislative representation. Each person was to be counted as a whole person. This section allowed for reducing representation as a penalty for its violation and left the door open to abridging the rights of those who had participated in "rebellion." Section 3 was the most objectionable to the South. It denied public office to any person who had supported the Confederacy during the war. This essentially limited civic leadership at any level to the planned constituents of the Radical Republicans. It was not only humiliating and debilitating to the South, but designed to guarantee Republican political hegemony in the South without significant opposition. Section 4 repudiated all Confederate debt and legitimized the obligation of all citizens to pay for U. S. debt incurred during and after the war. Section 5 gave Congress the power to enforce the other four sections by legislation. This was thought by many to be an open door to increasing federal power over the states, which turned out to be quite true.

The 39th Congress convened in December of 1865 just as the states, including seven Southern states, were finalizing ratification of the 13th

Amendment abolishing slavery.   The Radical Republicans knew that they could not depend on elected Southern Congressmen to achieve the two-thirds super majorities in the U. S. Senate and House to pass the 14th Amendment.   Consequently, they mustered a majority in both Houses of Congress and voted not to seat the 22 Senators and 58 representatives from eleven formerly Confederate, Southern states.   This was accomplished in part by "waving the bloody shirt" of Union losses during the war, impugning the patriotism of those willing to welcome the Southern states back into the Union fold, and appealing to partisan greed and lust for power.

However, in the U. S. Senate they could count only 33 of 50 votes, just one short, of that necessary for the two-thirds majority to pass a Constitutional Amendment.   To overcome this they devised a plan to retroactively unseat John P. Stockton of New Jersey, an outspoken opponent of the 14th Amendment.   It would have required a two-thirds vote to expel Senator Stockton for cause, but they could not muster the votes.   After several days of high pressure political maneuvering using the usual accusations and unseemly tactics, the Radical Republicans were able on March 27 to retroactively unseat Stockton.   The excuse was that the New Jersey Legislature had elected him by a plurality rather than a majority vote, but this was legal in New Jersey as well as several other states. In those days, U.S. Senators were elected by state legislatures rather than popular vote. Such a retroactive unseating for transparently political objectives was highly irregular, but the 14th Amendment was counted as having passed the Senate on June 13, 1866.   A few days earlier the Amendment had passed the U. S. House with 120 votes, easily more than two-thirds of the 152 that voted, but there were 30 abstentions.

The Amendment was then required to go to President Johnson before going to the States for approval. Johnson, an opponent of the Amendment, was somehow bypassed. The Amendment then went to the 37 States. A constitutional amendment requires ratification by three-quarters of the States, or in this case 28. A rejection or failure to ratify by ten States would have killed the amendment.

Tennessee was the first to ratify the amendment, but without a proper quorum of its legislature. Nevertheless, despite this irregularity, Tennessee was counted for ratification. By February 6, 1867, all ten of the remaining Southern states and three border states had rejected the amendment. California refused to consider it and later rejected it. In addition,

Ohio in January of 1868, and New Jersey in March of 1868, reacting to Radical Republican despotism and public displeasure thereof, rescinded their earlier ratifications. Oregon had ratified in September of 1866, but after settling a controversy over a few legislative seats, formally rescinded on October 15, 1868. The Oregon rescission was too late, however to effect the eventual outcome.

The Radical Republicans, however, had a radical plan to reverse Southern rejections of the 14th Amendment that fit their longer range agenda very well. Under their leadership on March 2, 1867, a Reconstruction Act was passed. Over the veto of President Johnson, this act revoked the legal status of the ten Southern states that had rejected the 14th Amendment and placed them under a military government administered through five U. S. Army districts.

The inconsistency, appalling capriciousness, and hypocrisy of the Radical Republican position should be noted here. If the Southern States were legal enough to have just ratified the 13th Amendment, how could Thaddeus Stevens now say that these same states were "without any legal authority?" It demonstrated once again the arbitrary and tyrannical mindset of the Radical Republicans. This would become increasingly evident during the years of Reconstruction. It was also certainly evident in their contrived attempt to impeach President Andrew Johnson for trying to dismiss his Secretary of War, Edwin Stanton. But as previously indicated, the Radical Republicans had little regard for the Constitution, legal precedent, any concept of fairness, or honest parliamentary procedure.

And what of the declared Union objectives of the War? Reunification of the states now became secondary to the vengeful and totalitarian will of a few men who proclaimed themselves to be the will of the people. The Radical Republican vision for the South can be clearly seen here. In effect, after a long and bloody war "to hold the Union together," Radical Republicans now kicked the South out of the Union for their own selfish, political purposes. Southern states were to be subjugated tools of Radical Republican ambitions. Every vestige of their culture, heritage, and political sovereignty would be subjected to a campaign of deliberate debasement and attempted eradication. It revealed that a strong underlying Northern motivation for the War was keeping the South under their economic and political control as subjugated territories stripped of their political rights. The purpose of the Reconstruction was to further subjugate and exploit the South, and this was done with a spirit of malice. Re-admission depended upon their declared acceptance of the 14th Amendment.

One of the provisions of the Reconstruction Act was to enfranchise black males and disenfranchise all Confederate veterans and former Confederate officials. Hence almost the entire white male population of the South except recent Northern immigrants and proven Union loyalists were without vote or voice in state, local, or federal government. Enflaming the hatred of former slaves against their former masters was to be an important Radical Republican tool for political dominance. Other sections of the act were designed to subdue Southern spirit and provide for continued economic exploitation of the South. This was to establish a permanent Republican dominance in the South and thereby the nation. The war had been ruinous, but military and "carpetbagger" governments would see to it that the ruin was increased and recovery was slow. Reconstruction was to be continued war by ruthless and unsavory political means.

Kentucky had not only rejected the amendment in January 1867, but by overwhelming majorities in a May 1867 election, sent a solid slate of nine Democrats to Congress. On July 3, the Radical Republican Congress voted not to seat them. On July 5, Senator Sumner of Massachusetts threatened to place Kentucky and Maryland under military government. No action was taken on this, however, as Republicans began losing off year elections to Democrats in Northern states.

It was now demanded of the ten Southern States under military government that statehood would not be regained unless they ratified the 14th Amendment. Six Southern states complied with the reconstructive coercion, and with the ratifications of South Carolina and Louisiana on July 9, 1868, Congress declared the 14th Amendment ratified, ignoring the rescissions of Ohio, and New Jersey, and the impending rescission of Oregon. By law, however, the official recognition of ratification of a constitutional amendment, rested with the Secretary of State, William H. Seward. Seward proclaimed ratification of the 14th Amendment on July 20, but in his written and oral proclamation he referred to the questionable status of the Ohio and New Jersey ratifications in view of their later rescissions. Congress was unhappy with this. The next day, assuming the function of the Secretary of State, Congress proclaimed by joint resolution that the 14th Amendment was officially ratified. On July 28, Seward bowed to the Congressional resolution of the 21st and proclaimed the Amendment ratified. With all the irregularities, frauds, and coercions involved, however, what fair minded person would recognize the 14th Amendment as constitutional? Yet it is accepted as such, and there are now many precedents in law based on the 14th Amendment.

The 14th Amendment in many senses turned the original Constitution and the first Ten Amendments on their head. With the 14th Amendment the nation has progressed from a philosophy of decentralized, limited government to a government increasingly characterized by highly centralized power. States Rights, once an essential check against excessive executive, judicial, and congressional power has been reduced to a meek whisper. Before the "Civil War" and the 14th Amendment no federal judge would have dared contemplate removing the Ten Commandments from the Alabama Supreme Court building or striking down state legislation on abortion, much less making laws that forced young children to be bused across a county to achieve an ideal racial balance, or prohibiting bibles in schools and prayer at high school athletic events. Congress now passes sweeping legislation that is clearly beyond the bounds of their enumerated powers in the Articles of the Constitution and in violation of the Bill of Rights, especially the 10th Amendment.

The 14th Amendment has some positives. More attention is paid to individual civil rights and due process, but it has come at the price of considerable loss of freedom and liberties to individuals, businesses, churches, civic, educational, and social organizations, and various spheres of local and state government. It also made us a coercive rather than a voluntary society. Every year under the penumbra of the 14th Amendment, we progress further toward totalitarian government with little accountability or responsiveness to the governed or any concern for constitutional limits of power.

The history of the passage of the 14th Amendment unveils a remarkable corruption of the spirit of liberty and flagrant despotism that has been covered with decades of politically correct whitewash. Such demonstrations of human depravity and coarse tyranny, though shameful, should not be covered up by a misguided sense of American patriotism. Few things are as necessary to a just society as truth. Hence a sine qua non of all genuine patriotism is a high regard for truth. Truth is always the high ground.

"Whoever conceals his transgressions will not prosper, but he who confesses and forsakes them will obtain mercy." Proverbs 28: 13, ESV.

Why the 14ᵗʰ Amendment to the U. S. Constitution Is Invalid

Twenty-three Senators* and fifty-eight Representatives were unlawfully excluded in securing the necessary two-thirds majority to adopt the Joint Resolution.

*(Twenty-two Senators from eleven Southern States and one from New Jersey)

(Violates Article I.3, I.2, and V of U. S. Constitution)

The joint Resolution was not submitted to the President for approval. (Violates Article I.5)

The proposed Amendment was rejected by more than one quarter of the States and never received the required approval three-fourths of all States in the Union.

(Violates Article V.1)

The governments and legislatures of ten States that had rejected the Amendment were unlawfully removed by military force and their reinstatement made contingent on approving the Amendment.

(Violates Article IV.4)

The Proclamation declaring the 14ᵗʰ Amendment valid included five States whose lawful legislatures had been replaced by unlawful puppet legislatures and two States (Ohio and New Jersey) whose legislatures had rescinded their initial approval.

(Violates Article IV.2 and V)

Remarkable Quotes:

In a post war interview with former Confederate Lt. General Richard Taylor (son of President Zachary Taylor), Thaddeus Stevens called the Constitution **"a worthless bit of old parchment."**

"The intent of the Reconstruction Act is to work a radical reorganization in Southern institutions, habits, and manners, and to break up the foundations of their institutions." — Thaddeus Stevens

"Greed of office, curse of democracies, will impel demagogues to grovel deeper and deeper in the mire in pursuit of ignorant votes." — Richard Taylor

CHAPTER 21

Reconstruction

The Tyranny and Corruption of the Radical Republicans

Thaddeus Stevens Republican Congressman from Pennsylvania "Boss of America" after Lincoln's death.

The South was as devastated by the un-civil war of 1861 to 1865 as much as any nation in the annals of warfare. By the end of the war one out of every four white men had been killed or died of wounds or disease. Over 40 per-cent of private property including homes, busi-nesses, livestock, and crops had been destroyed. In South Carolina, where Sherman's men had burned the capitol city of Columbia, over 50 per-cent of private property was destroyed. Most of this property damage was deliberately inflicted on the civilian population to deny the Confeder-ate Army the logistical means of resistance, but also to demoralize their families and supporters at home. It was ordered in cold calculation by Northern political and military leadership, but often executed with self-righteous religious zeal or criminal abandon. At the end of the war as many as 50 thousand homeless and displaced refugees, most-ly former slaves, died of famine and disease. Neither Christian teachings nor modern Geneva Conventions condone such total war. Reconstruction was an extension of that total war by political means.

To quote the eminent Southern historian, Clyde Wilson, Professor of History at the University of South Carolina, **"The purpose of Re-construction was not equality; it was plunder, plunder, plunder."** As the equally eminent Professor Emeritus of History at William and Mary,

Ludwell Johnson, has emphasized, the cardinal underlying objective of Reconstruction was to maintain and enhance the political dominance of the Republican Party, particularly that faction now referred to as the Radical Republicans.

To avoid a historical misunderstanding, it is necessary to point out that the Republican Party of the Civil War and Reconstruction bears little resemblance to the republicanism of Thomas Jefferson or Ronald Reagan. The Republican Party at that time was a party of big government serving big business. They believed in high protectionist tariffs to protect domestic manufacturing and supported generous government subsidies to powerful railroads, public works, and industrial interests. They were of the Hamiltonian philosophy of highly centralized government power and national banking. The Constitution and especially States Rights were frequently viewed as a hindrance to national prosperity and greatness. There were, however, more moderate and conservative factions in the party. The Radical Republicans were a minority faction within the party, but had strong support in the press and were not adverse to devious and despotic methods of maintaining and exercising power.

Neither did Democrats then much resemble Democrats today. They were more agrarian, socially conservative, and strongly committed to the decentralized, limited government outlined in the U. S. Constitution, including States Rights. During the Reconstruction years Conservative and Democrat were close political synonyms. Both parties at that time were generally conservative on social issues. Modern American liberalism, which is today most often associated with modern Democrats, ironically has its closest antecedents in the Radical Republicans, who often combined radical abolitionism with a strong belief in the efficacy of all-powerful government.

For more than a generation before the War radical abolitionists and their Republican political allies had stigmatized the South as a brutal and backward society in need of punishment, repentance, and remaking. A distorted understanding of the conditions of slavery in the South inflamed the preaching from many Northern pulpits, especially the radical abolitionist dominated Unitarian churches. Relentless Northern war propaganda magnified this twisted vision of the South into contempt and frenzied hatred for all things Southern. The Northern press seized upon every opportunity to fan the flames of sectional hatred. The devastating casualties endured by Union forces in conquering the South added a real and powerful emotional component to Northern animosity toward the South.

Nevertheless, near the end of the War in his second inauguration speech, President Lincoln had presented a generous vision for bringing the South back into the Union fold. His often quoted words, **"with malice toward none; with charity for all...to bind up the nation's wounds,"** were to set a new attitude and theme in the restoration of the South to the Union. Lincoln had instructed Grant in accepting Lee's surrender at Appomattox to **"let him up easy."** Union General J. L. Chamberlain ordered his battle seasoned troops at Appomattox to give a salute of honor to Confederate troops as they passed in final review at that surrender. Robert E. Lee had advised his men to go home and be good American citizens.

Following the assassination of Lincoln, however, goaded by the press and Radical Republicans in Congress, the flames of regional mistrust, hatred, and a desire for vengeance on the South erupted with vehement passion. Lincoln's Vice President, now President Andrew Johnson, a relatively conservative former Democratic Congressman from East Tennessee, had planned to follow the Lincoln plan for restoring the South to the Union. In this he would be vigorously opposed by the Radical Republicans led by Thaddeus Stevens of Pennsylvania in the House, Charles Sumner of Massachusetts in the Senate, and Edwin Stanton, Secretary of War. Their objective was permanent Republican Party dominance of the nation. A humiliating and vengeful subjugation of Southern States was to be an important instrument of the Radical Republican plan for continued national dominance. Southern States would be remade into Republican States fashioned and tightly controlled by Radical Republicans. Although civil rights idealism played a part in Radical Republican thinking and a very great part in their talk, the main role of former slaves would be insuring Republican political dominance in the South and suppressing any rising political opposition. This would have the effect of opening the South to economic exploitation and dominance by enterprising Northern fortune and office seekers.

Both Union war casualties and civil rights issues would provide fuel for demonizing the South. Waving the "bloody shirt' and exaggerated and even fabricated reports of racial injustice and disorder in the South became powerful instruments for gaining and maintaining political power in the North.

The Union loyalist state governments established by President Johnson quietly concentrated on economic recovery during the latter part of 1865 and early 1866. General Grant confirmed this in reports to the President. Just before the end of the War the Freedmen's Bureau had been established to aid in the economic adjustment of former slaves. By the end of 1865 the Thirteenth Amendment outlawing slavery had been ratified by seven Southern legislatures and became law. In July 1866, a Civil Rights Bill was passed to insure Southern blacks the full rights off citizens. Still the South was relatively quiet, but the Radical Republicans were stirring trouble both in the South and in Congress.

The Radical Republican leaders proposed a Fourteenth Amendment guaranteeing equal protection and due process under the law theoretically to all Americans, but also denying public office to former elected officials who had supported the Confederacy. This was not only punitive in spirit; but effectively eliminated the most likely source of any political opposition to Republican rule in the South. By February 1867, the Fourteenth Amendment had been temporarily derailed by the rejection of ten Southern and three Border State legislatures.

The Radical Republicans were ready for this. They had been stoking the flames of Northern outrage against the South by reporting numerous crimes and outrages against blacks. All this was contrary to the reports of General Grant. Few of these can now be substantiated. Most appear to have been either highly exaggerated or fabricated and some even incited. Many of the reports were telegraphed from Washington. In March 1867, over the veto of President Johnson, Republicans passed the first Reconstruction Act. **This act revoked the legal governments of ten Southern States and placed them under martial law, administered in five military districts.** This act gave the vote to adult black males and disenfranchised Confederate veterans and former elected officials. This disenfranchised over 85 percent of Southern white men. In addition, Union soldiers stationed in the South were allowed to vote. Ratifying the Fourteenth Amendment was made a contingency for readmission to the Union.

Another act greatly expanded the Freedmen's Bureau in both size and powers. These powers included rather arbitrary police and judicial powers and the ability to levy fines against "civil rights violators." Corrupt Freedmen's Bureau agents thereby made a good living.

UNION LEAGUE TERRORISM

In addition, Union Leagues were formed to insure the continued electoral success of carpetbagger Republican governments. These included largely black militia units that terrorized blacks and whites opposing Republican candidates. Little remembered by politically correct historians today, the Union League preceded the Ku Klux Klan in time and exceeded them in numbers and violence.

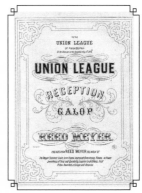

Most people today know something about the Ku Klux Klan, but very few are familiar with the Union League of America, also called the Loyal League. **Yet the Union League perpetrated far more violence against both blacks and whites in the post Civil War Reconstruction years of 1865 to 1877 than the Klan ever has.** The birth of the Klan was in fact a response to Union League bullying, violence, and murder. Why has the Union League been shoved into the memory hole of history? It is because the Union League was essentially a federal agency carrying out the policies of Reconstruction. The memory of such political despotism, corruption, and violence is just too embarrassing not to hide. This is even truer in today's hysterical political correctitude that chains modern academics to narrow bounds of subject, reasoning, and speech.

In 1862, many in the North had been demoralized by Confederate victories in the field. Also pro-States Rights Democrats made substantial political gains in six Northern states. Many Republicans felt that the success of Union war policies and efforts might be threatened by this. As a response, Union Clubs were formed in almost every town to support the war, the troops, and the Republican Party. These became the Union League of America. As the war was ending, Union League Clubs were also formed by Union loyalists in the South. These became a political arm of the Reconstruction or carpetbagger state governments. Their initial goal, shared with the Freedmen's Bureau, was to make sure that blacks registered to vote and voted Republican. Most of the loyalist whites soon dropped out of the League, and except for the carpetbagger politicians and Federal Army officers who formed its key leadership, the League was composed almost exclusively of former slaves and black soldiers of the Federal Army.

Radical Republican leaders in Washington realized during the war that if the South came back into the Union with Democrat Congressmen, the Republicans would lose the political dominance they had enjoyed since the 1860 election. This is why the Radical Republicans in Congress wanted to shove Lincoln's replacement, Andrew Johnson, aside. Johnson was a former Democrat, a constitutional conservative still sympathetic to States Rights, and committed to following Lincoln's lenient ideas about reconstructing the South. He was also incorruptible. They wanted control of Reconstruction. Their goal was first to punish and humiliate the South, and then to remake it into a powerful political tool for permanent national dominance by a Republican Party tightly controlled by a small, but ruthless faction. The core leaders of that faction were radical abolitionists Thaddeus Stevens, Charles Sumner, Edwin Stanton, Benjamin Wade, and Benjamin "Beast" Butler.

These ruthless radicals believed the key to making the South solid Republican was the black vote. Thus it was critical to insure that blacks voted Republican. The March 1867 Reconstruction Act disenfranchised Confederate veterans for the foreseeable future. Thus 85% of the white vote was eliminated. The Radical Republicans also thought it necessary to alienate blacks from white Southerners, Democrats, and especially their former masters. Previous to the war and especially immediately following the war, the relationships between former slaves and masters were cooperative and often affectionate. Most slaves in the South had been well treated, in many cases like family. The whites also appreciated the tremendous loyalty that most blacks had shown them during the war. The vast majority did not desert them during the war, and no Confederate Army in the field could have moved a mile without black wagon drivers and other logistical support. They served in many capacities. Some had proven their loyalty and combat effectiveness in Confederate infantry and cavalry regiments.

Union League meetings were conducted as a mystical secret society with secret rituals. Meetings were especially devoted to stirring up enmity between blacks and whites. A catechism written by Radical Republicans in Congress was used in Union League meetings to create an unreasonable sense of entitlement, grievance, and resentment. They were taught that Northern Republican whites were their friends and allies and that white

Southerners and Democrats were enemies to be hated and despised. They were frequently promised that they would receive land and livestock confiscated from the whites. In some cases they were even promised racial dominance that would entitle them to the wives and daughters of their white enemies. This led to a number of violent racial incidents. Such racial incidents were frequently used by carpetbagger governments to demonstrate to Washington and the Northern press and public the continued need for Southern reconstruction. Other promises were in the form of threats of a death penalty by hanging to any black who betrayed the League by voting Democrat.

With the coming of Radical Reconstruction and martial law the role of the Union League became more aggressive. Union League militias were formed and were an enforcement arm of the carpetbagger governments. The militia was composed of former slaves and black troops stationed in each state. The Union League had 250,000 men in ten Southern States. North Carolina's Scalawag Governor William W. Holden had a Union League militia of 80,000 at his bidding. The primary role of the Union League was now to keep the corrupt carpetbagger governments in power. This included suppression of competing carpetbagger factions.

In order to insure that all blacks voted Republican, the Union League bullied and beat other blacks into submission. Even flogging with the lash was used. If that did not work, they exacted the death penalty, frequently by lynching. In order to intimidate whites from seeking power or influencing black voting, they conducted terror campaigns. Barns and sometimes houses of whites were burned. In some cases small towns were burned, as in Warren and Hamburg, Arkansas. Men, women, and children were killed in raids on "insurrectionary" communities and counties. Their deaths were reported as "killed trying to escape." There were Union League barn burnings and other destruction in every North Carolina County. During a single week of 1869 in Gaston County, North Carolina, nine barns were burned. In two months of the same year in Edgecombe County, two churches, several cotton gins, a cotton factory, and many barns and homes were burned. The Raleigh Sentinel reported on August 29th of the same year that ten Federal Army companies associated with the Union League had terrorized the Goldsboro area and committed violent depredations of all sorts. It reported the actions of the troops "so violent that it was unsafe for women to leave their homes." This was all part of the Reconstruction mandate to remake the South.

In Myrta Lockett Avary's 1906 book, *Dixie After the War*, she relates a tragic, but not untypical atrocity. In upstate South Carolina a group of Union League federal soldiers marching and singing halted to discharge a volley of bullets into a country church during services, instantly killing a fourteen-year-old girl. At a nearby residence a squad of the same troops entered a home and bound the elderly owner as they ransacked his house and argued over who would first ravage his daughter. The girl, when approached, drove a concealed knife through the heart of her assailant. She was then beaten to death by the rest. But under corrupt military and carpetbagger rule, Southern whites had little recourse to justice. No federal justice occurred.

KKK

By 1870, the corruption of the carpetbagger governments and the violence of the Union League was becoming a concern to a significant minority in the U. S. Congress. As Klan activity increased in response to Union League and other Reconstruction misdeeds, the Radical Republicans formed a committee to investigate the Klan. A minority report by Northern Democrats and Conservative Republicans representing more than a third of the committee, however, noted that the Union League had "instilled hatred of the white race" and had "made arson, rape, robbery, and murder a daily occurrence." They also noted the role of corrupt government and Union League violence in driving whites to take law into their own hands.

A very stringent anti-Klan law was passed by the North Carolina legislature under the direction of Governor Holden in January of 1870. True to past Radical Republican despotism it gave the Governor power to declare counties in a state of insurrection and supersede practically all laws and Constitutional rights in its prosecution. Despite a vigorous attempt to enforce the law, Klan-like activity increased and a top black activist and leader of the League in Alamance County was found hanging in a tree. Shortly thereafter, Senator John Stephens, a ranking white operative for Governor Holden, seeking evidence for Klan prosecutions, visited a

Caswell County Union League meeting. There he handed to each of about twenty members a box of matches with the suggestion that they should be put to good use burning barns.

The next night seven barns, a row of houses, and the tobacco crops of several prominent citizens were burned.

A few days later Senator Stephens attended a rally at the Yanceyville Courthouse for the purpose of making notes on the speeches. He was quietly abducted, gagged, and brutally murdered in one of the Courthouse rooms with an open window to the crowd outside. His body was not discovered until two days later. It was not proven until 1936 that it was a well organized assassination by the KKK. The gruesome mystery and death of Stephens prompted Governor Holden and his advisors to launch a military campaign against the KKK in June. They hoped this would also be a political positive in the coming August elections.

Holden called upon black Union League militia regiments in eastern North Carolina and the white veterans of Union Colonel George W. Kirk's notorious bushwhackers from the mountains to score a decisive victory. Kirk was to be in charge. Kirk was a Confederate deserter who had been made a colonel in the Union Army during the war. During the war Kirk had commanded a combined force of Union Army regulars, Confederate deserters, and opportunistic criminals. A good size book could be written on the depredations and atrocities Kirk and his men inflicted on civilians in western North Carolina during the war. According to a report by a Union officer stationed in Yanceyville, Kirk lived up to his evil reputation in the service of Governor Holden. Kirk's troops were "an armed mob roaming the country, pillaging at will, insulting citizens with impunity, and even threatening to attack the United States troops." Many KKK suspects were arrested and imprisoned.

But on August 4 of 1870, the elections in North Carolina took place. Despite their despotic tactics the Republicans were very nearly routed. More than two-thirds of the legislative seats went to the Democrats. A growing number of whites had been able to register, and many blacks and even Union Army men had found the carpetbag corruption and tyranny so despicable that they voted for the Democrats. On August 6, U. S. District Court Judge George Brooks found that Kirk had no evidence against any of his prisoners and ordered their release. Thus ended the "Kirk-Holden" War. Kirk fled north, and within a few months, Governor Holden

General John Brown Gordon

was impeached by the North Carolina House for abuse of power, tried by the Senate, and removed from office. Within a year the Union League in North Carolina was disbanded and disappeared.

Former Confederate General John B. Gordon testified in 1871 to the Joint Congressional Committee on Affairs in the Insurrectionary States that:

"The first and main reason (for the Klan) was the organization of the Union League."

Gordon, who later became Governor of Georgia and then a U. S. Senator, also stated that even the burning of Atlanta and the devastation of Georgia during the war did not create a tenth of the animosity created by the Union League's treatment of the Southern people. Former Confederate General Nathan B. Forrest, a reputed founder of the Klan, testified before the same committee that:

"The Klan was intended entirely as a protection to the (Southern) people, to enforce the laws and protect the people from outrages."

Both men realized, however, that after a few years, the Klan, formed in a people's desperate cry for survival and justice, had itself become a lawless outrage. But it was the federally sponsored Union League that ranked first in time and violence. It should not be forgotten. The evils it inflicted on both black and white still live.

PLUNDERING THE SOUTH

At the end of the "Civil War" in the spring of 1865, the South had lost over 254,000 men killed in battle or died of wounds and disease. Of the 194,000 seriously wounded, at least half had some physical disability from lost limbs, eyes, or other crippling wounds and injuries. Destruction of public and private property was widespread. In the states of South Carolina, Georgia, and Mississippi where the North's total war policies had been most zealously carried out by Sherman, private property destruction exceeded 50 percent. In Virginia Sheridan's troops had laid bare the fertile

Shenandoah Valley. The loss in private property included not only homes and furnishings, but barns, livestock, crops, tools, and means of transportation. Confederate currency and bonds were worthless. Two-thirds of the South' railroads were utterly destroyed or severely crippled. Countless bridges and river transports had been destroyed. Many industries and businesses had been laid waste. Most of Columbia, Atlanta, and much of Charleston had been deliberately torched. In Oxford, Mississippi, only one commercial business was left standing. Many small towns in numerous states literally vanished with only a smoldering trace. General Sherman himself gave a vivid description of Southern devastation after the War:

> "Mourning in every household, desolation written in broad characters across the whole face of their country, cities in ashes and fields laid waste, their commerce gone…Ruin, poverty, and distress everywhere, and now pestilence…adding to their misery."

The South was utterly prostrate and destitute. In contrast to Lincoln's total war policy, with some exceptions the United States pursued a generally more benevolent policy towards civilians and private property during the Second World War. At the end of the War in 1945, the United States sought to secure future peace and the common good with massive assistance in rebuilding the economies of Western Europe, including West Germany and Italy. That was the Marshall Plan. Reconstruction after the "Civil War" was no Marshall Plan.

Reconstruction was not a plan to rehabilitate the Southern economy. It was a plan to remake the South into the ideological image of the North, plunder its resources and economy, insure Republican political power in Washington for the long term, and punish the South for its rebellion. The most intelligent and humane method of providing economic recovery is to cut taxes and government regulations, and to provide government assistance in rebuilding infrastructure and meeting urgent humanitarian needs. Instead, the North instituted punitive taxes and sent swarms of tax collectors and despotic government regulators to oversee the plunder and humiliation of the South. They were accompanied by swarms of political opportunists, shameless swindlers, and militant do-gooders.

The high tariff policies that touched off Southern secession in 1860-61 were instituted and kept in place until 1906. As feared, these high tariffs increased the costs of living and business in the South. This put its chief export, cotton, at a competitive disadvantage with Brazilian, Indian, and Egyptian cotton. The tax revenues, mostly collected in the South, were for the most part used to enrich and subsidize Northern industry and build Northern infrastructure.

One asset the South had left after the war despite all the destruction was five million bales of cotton. Prices were also at an all time high of 50 cents to a dollar per pound. The North confiscated three million bales of this cotton on the grounds of its association with owners who had previously sold cotton to the Confederate government. Cotton raised by slaves was also subjected to a 25 percent tax. It was up to the owners of cotton to prove the absence of any Confederate or slave taint, so U. S. Treasury agents frequently made some arrangements to clear the cotton by some means of bribery. Many Treasury agents were racketeers, using threats of total confiscation, if an appropriate bribe was not forthcoming. They also purchased cotton at low prices using this racketeering scheme. One Texas widow was forced to sell her 400 bales of cotton valued a $200 per bale for $75 per bale or have it confiscated for Confederate taint. Treasury agents took their payment in cotton. They were normally entitled to 25 to 50 percent of confiscated cotton as their fee, but their shameless greed exceeded their authority. They were willing to defraud the U. S. government as well as cotton owners. Some were caught red-handed in these schemes, but were released by the Army.

In addition, a three cents per pound export tax was put on cotton. This was to pay for the war, which according to the Northern party line, Southerners had started. When cotton returned to its normal price range of twelve to eighteen cents per pound, the three cent tax was a 20 percent burden. As usual, Treasury agents often settled for a bribe. A transportation fee of four cents per pound was also charged for the privilege of getting it to market. Cotton planters were forced to survive a gauntlet of numerous Treasury agents, racketeers, and swindlers in getting their cotton to market with any profit at all. Reconstruction governments dominated by opportunistic carpetbaggers with little sympathy for Southerners and with their own fingers deep into corruption, left white Southerners little legal recourse. They began to call on the KKK for justice. Usually only a Klan warning for the Treasury agent to leave town was sufficient for cotton producers to get their cotton to market. The cotton tax was removed in 1868 in response to falling cotton production and increasing embarrassment in Congress. Also, two-thirds of the Northern opportunists who bought cotton plantations at distressed prices, failed in the cotton business. One Florida failure in the cotton business was Harriet Beecher Stowe. Treasury Secretary, Hugh McCulloch, was by conscience finally forced to admit,

"I am sure I sent some honest agents south; but it sometimes seems very doubtful whether any of them remained honest very long."

The carpetbagger state legislatures were notorious for extravagant personal spending abuses, arranging legislation for personal or partisan profiteering, for bribe-taking, and for costly maladministration. Taxes were raised for property owners. For the average Southern state, property taxes were four times as high in 1872 as in 1865. In South Carolina, property taxes increased thirty fold. These tax increases were not really to repay spending deficits. It took Alabama and South Carolina almost one hundred years to pay off the deficit spending of the Reconstruction era. The principle reason was to force Southern property owners to sell their land at distressed prices. At one time over 20 percent of the land in Mississippi was for sale under property tax duress. Again, Southerners had little recourse to law. It was truly a case of taxation without representation. Most white Southerners had been disenfranchised, because they served the Confederate cause. In the present era we are again rapidly reaching the dangerous point where tax consumers can out vote taxpayers.

It is only in recent years that the South has been able to overcome the economic abuse of Reconstruction. In 1860, Louisiana ranked second in the nation in per capita income. South Carolina ranked third; Mississippi was fifth; and Georgia was eighth. In 1880, Louisiana ranked as number 37. South Carolina had fallen to number 45, Mississippi to 46, and Georgia to 40. These figures are only somewhat distorted because of the change in status of former slaves from 1860 to 1880. Contrary to popular opinion, according to Nobel Laureate economists R. W. Fogel and S. L. Engerman, both professed liberals, black slaves in the South had a higher living standard in nutrition, housing, leisure time, medical care, and old age security than did Northern factory workers. Their 1974 book, *Time on the Cross*, was not an apology for slavery, but a realistic look at the actual conditions of slavery, which were far less degraded than what most modern Americans imagine. Despite nominal legal improvements, black economic and political progress was substantially retarded by Reconstruction.

The bottom line is that Reconstruction further devastated the South and retarded its economic recovery by many decades. The primary economic beneficiary was the Northeast. The primary political effect of the War and Reconstruction was that we evolved from a philosophy of limited government to big, powerful, highly centralized unlimited government. The degree of corruption and despotism during Reconstruction may seem incredible, but they were the natural result of a collusion of big government and politically connected businesses unchecked by the consent of the governed.

Robert E. Lee had accepted defeat at Appomattox and encouraged his men to go home and be good Americans. But in 1870 after five years of Reconstruction, he privately told Fletcher Stockdale, former Governor of Texas, this:

"Governor, if I had foreseen the use those people designed to make use of their victory, there would have been no surrender at Appomattox; no, sir, not by me. Had I foreseen these results of subjugation, I would have preferred to die at Appomattox with my brave men, my sword in my right hand."

THE RISE OF THE KU KLUX KLAN

Few nations in the last millennium have been so devastated by loss of life and property as the South in 1865. Perhaps only the Russians, Ukrainians, Poles, Serbians, and in turn the Germans themselves in the Second World War endured such suffering. A Union general bragged that crows flying over the Shenandoah Valley of Virginia would need to pack their own lunches. The Union conquerors then proceeded with the reconstruction of the South by laying on heavy taxes, confiscating much of their remaining wealth in cotton and other goods, and forcing the sale of land under tax duress. They gave the right to vote to blacks, but took it away from Confederate veterans. They removed from Confederate veterans and their families all recourse to civil law and justice. They sent in swarms of Northern school teachers to teach their children to be ashamed of their fathers and their Southern heritage. They loosed upon them a reign of terror with a constant threat of depredations and outrages at the hands of the Union League. Political opportunists from the North constantly promised blacks that the properties of whites would be confiscated and given to them, if they voted Republican. Many of them also promised that Republican voting blacks would be given political and racial hegemony over the whites. The Union League regularly promised to hang blacks that did not vote Republican. Many blacks were, in fact, beaten or murdered for resisting Union League political objectives. These circumstances made forceful underground resistance to Radical Reconstruction inevitable.

Christmas Eve of 1865 was not a time of joy in Pulaski, Tennessee. But six young Confederate veterans meeting in a law office decided to lift the spirits of that town by forming a club or fraternity. Five of these six were Confederate officers during the war. Four of them were to become lawyers, one a circuit court clerk, and one a newspaper editor. Their first objective was to have some fun and lift the spirits of the town. To that end they devised the rituals of a secret fraternal society with mysterious code words, elaborate titles, and costume disguises. Starting with the Greek word for circle, *kuklos*, they came up with the name, Ku Klux, and then added Klan because they were all of Scotch-Irish descent. Their costume regalia for themselves and their horses was made up of available bed sheets. The next week at dark they rode into town to introduce their new club, show off their mysterious regalia, and amuse and serenade sweethearts and families. It was a roaring social success.

Their former slaves, however, thought they had seen the ghosts of dead Confederate soldiers. The next week the agitation that had been stirred among their former slaves by political opportunists from the North was considerably reduced. The six young members of the Ku Klux Klan now realized they had a powerful psychological tool to curtail the violence and outrages being suffered by Southern families. It could be a protective organization for beleaguered Southern whites as well as their black friends.

The original founders had strict character standards for membership. They wanted men of principle and reliability. They placed a high emphasis on the ideals of chivalry, patriotism, respect for the Constitution and legitimate law. They sought to protect the weak and defenseless, especially Confederate widows and their children, and to relieve the injured and oppressed. This included relief from the oppressive and hated cotton tax. Initiates pledged total abstinence from alcohol as long as they were members. They also pledged never to reveal that they were a member of the KKK or to reveal the names of any other members. They were not anti-black, but they were white supremacists. This advocacy of white supremacy must be seen in historical perspective to be fully understood. Living under a black dominated society was an intolerable prospect to them, but this prospect was constantly threatened by federal authorities, the Union League, and carpetbagger demagogues appealing for black Republican votes.

White supremacy was not a political idea that was confined to the South. In fact, Southern white supremacy retained a paternalistic view of blacks, whereas the equally prevalent white supremacy of the North was simply anti-black. Most Northern states did not want blacks within their borders, and Indiana, Ohio, Illinois, and Oregon had strict laws to enforce this bias.

Lincoln's attitude toward blacks was very typical of Northern whites, and he sometimes appealed to this sentiment in his political speeches. Lincoln was personally against slavery, but not at the cost of breaking up the country. Originally, before using emancipation as a military strategy, Lincoln favored a gradual, slave-owner compensated emancipation of African slaves, but favored their removal to Central America, the Caribbean, or back to Africa. Lincoln's thinking was very prevalent in the North. Before the war, Massachusetts was the only state in which blacks were allowed to be jurors. Even after Radical Reconstruction disenfranchised whites and enfranchised blacks in the South in 1867, voters in Ohio, Michigan, Minnesota, and Kansas refused to extend the franchise to blacks.

The situation in Tennessee was aggravated by its Radical Republican Governor, William P. Brownlow. Brownlow forced through the puppet Legislature a bill disenfranchising Confederate veterans in June of 1865, a full twenty-one months before such a measure was taken in ten other Southern states. Brownlow also provoked fear in Tennessee and the whole South with public pronouncements such as these:

"If I had the power I would arm...every negro in the South, every devil in Hell, clothe them in the uniform of the Federal Army and then turn them loose on the rebels of the South and exterminate every man, woman, and child, south of the Mason and Dixon line."

Brownlow also said this to a New York audience:

"I would like to see Negro troops under Ben Butler crowd every rebel into the Gulf of Mexico, and drown them as the devil did the hogs in the Sea of Galilee."

Brownlow disbanded the regular Tennessee Militia and replaced it with a force of black Union Army veterans and white bushwhackers to intimidate political opposition and resistance to his corrupt and tyrannical government. Thus Southern white supremacy was bolstered by constant threats of black supremacy and even wholesale white annihilation.

From Pulaski, Tennessee, the Klan spread to nearby Athens, Alabama, the scene of Union pillaging during the war. Still under the guidance of its original founders, it continued to spread, and its dens began to take on the role of regulators protecting the people from abuse by the Union League and racketeering U.S. Treasury agents. In response to Union League murders and outrages, they also began to engage in retributive guerilla warfare. By May of 1867 their numbers and role had grown so large that the founders decided that a leader of national prominence was needed. Meeting right under the nose of the Union Army at the Maxwell House Hotel in Nashville, they chose famed Confederate cavalry leader, Nathan Bedford Forrest of Memphis. The KKK thus advanced as a champion of the Southern people against the tyrannies of Reconstruction. But they would soon face a serious control problem. They did not have an enforceable patent on wearing white sheets.

THE INVISIBLE EMPIRE:
A RESPONSE TO FEDERAL TYRANNY

It is essential to understand that the Ku Klux Klan of the Reconstruction years of 1865 to 1877 has absolutely no connection to the various organizations calling themselves the Ku Klux Klan in the twentieth or present century. Nor is it likely that many of the original Klan members would be less than outraged by the indignities and atrocities committed by groups calling themselves the KKK beginning about 1915. The Klan of the Reconstruction years arose in response to Federal tyranny against which the Southern people were allowed neither political nor legal recourse. Armed resistance was made inevitable and necessary for their own protection, and especially the protection of their wives and children. The Klan can reasonably be credited with a significant role in breaking the back of Reconstruction and with it Radical Republican power and tyranny in the South. It could even be argued that they hastened the demise of Radical Republican hegemony in the North. A major problem the Klan faced during Reconstruction was keeping its organization under control. There is a public peril in any secret organization that attempts to administer justice. In addition, there was the problem of imitation by imprudent or unprincipled allies and by outright enemies such as the Union League. The KKK had no patent on white sheets and other disguises. Operating in disguise is a tactic anyone can imitate.

In fact, an enormous portion of the violence blamed on the KKK during Reconstruction was actually the work of the Union League. The League had found a way to disguise its violence and blame it on the KKK. The first two convictions under a Mississippi anti-Klan law in 1870 turned out to be two black Union League men who had been harassing a black Democrat. A U. S. Marshall in North Carolina also commented on the high number of Union League incidents using imitations of KKK disguise. According to KKK agents stationed in Washington, this imitation strategy came out of a meeting of Radical Republican Congressmen in Washington. The Radical Republican governments in the South made a concentrated effort to report as many incidents of white violence against blacks and white Republicans as possible. They went much further than honest reporting to keep Congress and Republican voters in the North stirred up against reputed Southern misdeeds. There was much distortion and fabrication involved. In several instances race riots were incited by Radicals for their propaganda value.

In April of 1866, in Memphis there were more than forty blacks killed in a three day race riot. This turned out to be a conflict between a garrison of black federal soldiers and Irish police of recent Northern importation.

In the summer of 1866 in New Orleans, Radical Republicans who had lost control of the Louisiana government because of Johnson's amnesty to Confederate veterans planned an illegal convention reinstituting

Radical government. Their objectives were to
depose the Conservative government, insure passage of the 14th Amendment, enfranchise blacks,
and disenfranchise Confederate veterans. This
coup d' etat plot had the indirect assurance of
support from Thaddeus Stevens himself in Washington. Two days before this convention, A. P.
Dostie, a Northern dentist, agitating for their support, promised a gathering of two to three thousand blacks that:

Edwin Stanton

**"...a hundred thousand good and true
Union white men"** would **"fight for and beside
the black race against the hell-bound rebels."**

Dostie advised them to **"come in your power"** on the day of the
coming convention. They did come, but as an angry and drunken mob that
essentially overwhelmed and disrupted the convention. A riot ensued as
New Orleans Police tried to disburse the mob. Thirty-four blacks were
killed as well as Dr. Dostie. Several other whites were killed including
one "disloyal" white. New Orleans Police reported their own casualties
of forty-two dead or wounded. Such incidents as these were played up
as Southern atrocities. News of Southern violence was of great political
value in the North. Secretary Stanton had been warned of the danger of
political violence by Federal Army commanders, but withheld notification
from President Johnson and other Cabinet members. Control of the state
reverted to Federal Army commanders until Radical power was imposed
by the March 1867 Reconstruction Act.

According to a current internet history source on the KKK, the Klan
was responsible for killing over 1,500 Republicans during the 1868 elections. This distorted number comes from taking as truth the trumped up
numbers compiled by corrupt carpetbagger governments and flagrantly
dishonest Radical politicians for the purpose of inflaming Northern voters
and Congress against the South. This had the dual purpose of perpetuat-
ing the corrupt and totalitarian carpetbagger governments in the South and
winning elections in the North. It also covered up the depredations of
the Union League. Within the Klan itself, however, there was growing

Gen. Nathan Bedford Forrest
Confederate Cavalry leader

concern that violence by its own members and of unrelated similar groups such as the White League, the White Brotherhood, and the Knights of the White Camellia, was escalating out of control.

One difficulty in studying the Ku Klux Klan during the Reconstruction years is that Klan members took very seriously their pledge never to reveal their own membership or the names of other members. It is generally acknowledged that General Nathan B. Forrest became the Grand Wizard or national director after a meeting held at the Maxwell House Hotel in Nashville in May of 1867. Although never specifically admitting even his membership, his statements indicated such knowledge of and an influence over the Klan that his leadership is reasonably certain. In my opinion the most authoritative source on KKK leadership was Susan Lawrence Davis, who published a history of the organization in 1924. Liberal and politically correct academics usually dismiss her book as being "discredited." But she alone, through family connections, knew personally many of the KKK leaders in Pulaski, Tennessee, and Athens, Alabama. She remembers as a child speaking with General Forrest, when he visited her family's home near Athens on "business." In preparing her book she had the unpublished manuscript of one of the Pulaski founders and interviewed several hundred men throughout the South that she knew to be KKK members. Furthermore, she appears to have been a well educated and highly principled woman. Her "discredited" status owes to her Southern sympathies.

Forrest had been a Confederate Major General during the war and the South's most famous and spectacular cavalry leader. Robert E. Lee acknowledged him to be the best soldier on either side. Forrest was highly principled and a strict disciplinarian. He possessed audacious courage and charismatic presence. He abstained from alcohol, gambling, and tobacco, and dismissed officers for immoral conduct with women. In respect to women he was chivalrous to an Arthurian degree. In camp his tent became a small church on the Sabbath, although a certain confession of his Christian faith did not occur until after the war. It is highly unlikely that Forrest ever donned KKK regalia, attended a KKK rally, or participated in actual KKK operations. He and the Grand Dragons that he personally appointed over each state apparently acted something like political strategists and consultant directors. The KKK was an "Invisible Empire." Forrest once told a reporter that he could summon 40,000 men in Tennessee alone. The reporter concluded that the KKK was 500,000 strong in the Southern states. The latter figure may be a wild exaggeration as other groups such as the Knights of the White Camellia were more numerous in some states than the Klan.   During the war and undoubtedly afterwards, Forrest frequently used numerical deception of his strength to his advantage.

Of the ten men who are reputed to be the first Grand Dragons of their states all were Confederate officers and five were Confederate Generals. At least four became governors of states, U. S. Senators, or both. Because of very strict Klan secrecy on membership, many of these names are in dispute, but they included many illustrious names, such as John Brown Gordon of Georgia, Zebulon B. Vance of North Carolina, and Albert Pike of Arkansas.

The leadership of so many distinguished Confederate officers gave the KKK formidable capacity for guerilla tactics. Among them were men of equally formidable political abilities. Forrest's demonstrated talents as a cavalry leader for deceiving the enemy as to his numbers and location undoubtedly proved valuable to the KKK. The rise of the KKK very soon caused a considerable reduction in Union League atrocities and indignities. Meanwhile much of the work of the KKK was political organization and influence. Forrest's talent for bluffing the enemy was undoubtedly of both operational and political advantage, but it also contributed to unwanted credit for the violent actions of others.

THE KLAN BATTLES AGAINST RECONSTRUCTION

At the end of war, the South had not only suffered tremendous human losses, but was also materially and economically devastated. Yet there was no Marshall Plan for her recovery put forth by the dominant faction of Northern political leaders. Instead, Reconstruction was a plan to punish the South and remake Southern society, while continuing and even increasing her ruthless economic exploitation for the benefit of Northern commercial and industrial interests. The total war policies of the Union Army and the exploitive policies of the Reconstruction governments had caused a famine in the South in 1866, while the North was enjoying economic prosperity and plenty.   Although many private relief agencies and churches in the North sent some relief, the U. S. government sent no aid and continued to force its destructive confiscation and tax policies on the South.   All this was related to maintaining the political dominance gained by the Republican Party in 1860 and furthering the agenda of the Radical Republicans.   If the South could not be remade into a region of political vassal states to the Radical Republicans, the Republicans would lose their national power.   Many politicians will do almost anything to gain and maintain power. The North had such men in Thaddeus Stevens, Benjamin Butler, Edwin Stanton, and others in the Radical Republican faction. Enfranchising and capturing the black vote was key to their strategy. Eliminating their political competition was a second key. That would perhaps be their most heinous political crime.

By March of 1867, they had disenfranchised Confederate veterans and former political leaders. Most white Southerners were then left without political power or any recourse to justice or relief from Reconstruction despotism. In addition, Radical Republicans seemed hell-bent on controlling the South through black dominance.

It was probably not encouraging to hear of the North's most acclaimed orator and most renowned and fervent of the radical abolitionists, Wendell Phillips, saying from the pulpit of Henry Ward Beecher:

"I do not believe there will be peace until 347,000 men of the South are either hanged or exiled."

Contrary to popular belief, most Christians North and South favored a gradual emancipation of slaves. Radical abolitionists wanted immediate emancipation of slaves despite the formidable ills it might bring on the slaves themselves and the Southern economy. The radical abolitionists were predominantly Unitarians or very liberal or apostate Congregationalists or Presbyterians. A few were allied to the Methodists, like lawyer Charles G. Finney. Finney was a powerful and manipulative persuader and not very orthodox in his theology. The radical abolitionists made up only about two percent of the population, but that included a substantial number of the Radical Republicans in Congress and considerable support in the Northern press led by Horace Greeley. Lincoln hated both the radical abolitionists and the Radical Republicans and wished to distance himself from them politically. They hated him in return until his assassination elevated him to a mythical status as the Great Emancipator. Lincoln's war was tyranny against the South, but his assassination was one of the worst things that could befall the Southern people. The Radicals would reign.

Radical Republican tyranny even extended to religion. A number of churches were closed and their clergy barred from preaching because they would not offer prayers for the President and government. Richard Wilmer, Episcopal Bishop of Alabama, was one who bravely suffered this fate. Wilmer insisted that the government had no authority in affairs of religion and worship, further stating that:

"No one can be expected to pray for the continuance of military rule."

This type of religious interference by Federal Army officers had also been a problem in Border States and occupied areas during the war. Fortunately, Bishop Wilmer had many Northern allies, and his case was eventually brought before a U. S. Supreme Court unsympathetic to the Radical Republicans. Wilmer's victory in Court was a major victory for religious freedom.

In such conditions the Ku Klux Klan became the hope of a powerless and beleaguered Southern people for relief from the intolerable tyranny of Reconstruction. The Klan of those years was quite different from later and modern imitators. Bedford Forrest described them in this way to a Congressional Investigation Committee in 1870:

"They admitted no man who was not a gentleman, and a man who could be relied upon to act discreetly; not men who were in the habit of drinking; boisterous men, or men liable to commit error or wrong."

In 1869 the Grand Dragon of Tennessee stated that it was essentially a protective organization with the purpose **"to protect all good men, whether white or black, from the outrages and atrocities of bad men of both colors, and who have been for the past three years a terror to society, and an injury to us all."**

General John B. Gordon, speaking of the violence perpetrated by the Union League, explained to a Congressional committee in 1871 that the Klan:

"...was therefore necessary to protect our families from outrage and preserve our own lives, to have something that we could regard as a brotherhood—a combination of the best men of the country to act purely in self defense."

By 1869, Reconstruction in some states had become intolerable, but the Klan was seeing considerable success against the Union League and in thwarting some of the more egregious conduct of Treasury and Freedman's Bureau agents. But they began to be gravely concerned that Klan violence was growing out of control. Much of the violence was by imitators, and even more by their enemies in the Union League, but there was a growing violation of discipline and principle in the Klan itself. A German survivor of Stalingrad and witness to many atrocities, when interviewed after the Second World War, probably put unchecked violence during and following particularly bloody wars or oppressions in perspective for all eras, when he told a reporter, **"Vengeance is a very powerful human emotion and motivation."** In October of 1869 General Forrest issued an order stating that:

"Whereas, the Order of the KKK is in some localities being perverted from its original honorable and patriotic purposes; ...and is becoming injurious instead of subservient to the public peace and public safety for which it was intended...It is therefore ordered and decreed, that the masks and costumes of the Order be entirely abolished and destroyed."

Forrest went on to declaim those who had used the KKK as an instrument of personal vengeance. He further stated that:

"This is not to be understood to dissolve the Order."

He went on to prohibit several actions such as the whipping of blacks or whites or interfering with any man on account of his political opinions. There are some academics that claim the Klan was disbanded at this time. But Major Robert Donnell, the KKK Grand Scribe in 1869, who gave Susan Lawrence Davis a copy of the order, stated to her that the Klan was not disbanded until 1877. There were several reports of the original KKK disbanding in the early 1870's, but at least one of these was only a ruse to confuse carpetbagger governments in the South. By 1877 they were still active and forming an alliance with the White League in Louisiana.

THE KLAN INTIMIDATES AND DEFEATS
THE UNION LEAGUE

The Klan was raised up primarily to protect the Southern people, both white and black, from the depredations and violence of the Union League. Had the Radical Republicans not commissioned the Union League to intimidate blacks into voting Republican and terrorizing any opposition by whites, there never would have been a Klan. The Union League's murders, beatings, burnings, and ravages created a climate of fear with no recourse to protection or justice by Federal authorities. Most of the League's murder and beating victims were other blacks who refused to comply with its ruthless political methods. Whites were sometimes murdered and their women ravaged, but most of the crime committed against them by the League was in the form of burned homes, barns, and crops. Southern men were, however, ever near their women and children. In some states the Reconstruction regimes did not allow Confederate veterans to own guns, but enforcement was not very effective.

The principal objective of the Klan was to defend against Union League atrocities, ravaging, and threats. The Klan proved very effective in its defensive measures and guerilla and psychological warfare against the Union League. Union League outrages and depredations were not eliminated, but they were considerably reduced and hampered. The Klan had succeeded in intimidating the League. A second objective of the KKK was protecting cotton farmers from the unscrupulous swarms of racketeering Treasury agents and carpetbag swindlers that plagued the South and to help them evade the oppressive and hated cotton tax. They accomplished this primarily by intimidation. Given the KKK's reputation for exacting regulatory justice, a single warning was usually sufficient to send a carpetbag predator or Treasury racketeer packing.   They also aided cotton farmers and cotton businesses by protecting secret cotton gins and cotton storage from Treasury agent, Union League, or Freedmen's Bureau discovery. The oppressive and predatory tax on cotton exports was phased out in early 1868, when the Republicans realized it was devastating the cotton wealth they hoped to exploit, and that their Treasury agents were swindling the government as well as farmers. The Klan's ultimate objective was to rid the South of corrupt and despotic Radical Republican dominated carpetbag state governments. This was a political objective that was finally achieved in the elections of 1876. In order to break an electoral impasse in the Presidential election, Republican Rutherford B. Hayes agreed to remove all Federal troops from the South. Consequently the last of carpetbagger governments fell in 1877 with the installation of Confederate war hero, Wade Hampton, as Governor of South Carolina. The Radical Republicans had completely failed in their effort to have a black dominated Republican South. They had created instead a solid Democratic South.

Unfortunately, once the Northern carpetbaggers and Radical Republicans had abandoned their black political constituency, Southern Democrats indiscriminately made second class citizens of all blacks, friend and foe, regardless of qualifications. The Southern experience with the widespread corruption, demagoguery, and oppression of Reconstruction caused in most whites a fear and revulsion of black participation in government that would take many decades to subside. Blacks were placed under the same type of "black laws" that still relegated blacks to second class citizenship in most Northern states. Several Northern states, such as Indiana, Illinois, and Oregon had laws that prevented blacks or mulattos from even entering their states. Because of the Reconstruction experience and the larger black population in the South, the residual of these "Jim Crowe" laws lasted longer in Southern states.

The Union League and Freedman's Bureau had failed in their purpose, but succeeded in doing tremendous damage to race relations in the South. Thus they were a strong contributory cause in retarding rather than advancing black political and economic progress. Donn Piatt, Washington newspaper editor, Union Brigadier General during the war, and personal friend of Lincoln editorialized that:

"All race antagonism in the South came from carpetbaggers using the Negro votes to get their fingers in the treasury."

Piatt was very pessimistic that the damage to race relations could ever be repaired. He believed race relations in the South had been permanently poisoned by Reconstruction. General Gordon told a Congressional committee in 1871 that:

"We never had any apprehension from the conduct of the Negroes until unscrupulous men came among them and tried to stir up strife."

It is probable that the immediate rather than gradual emancipation resulting from Lincoln's Emancipation Proclamation, which Lincoln admitted was a military move to divert Confederate armies from the field to protect their homes and families, doomed any real chance of a successful transition. Dealing with such a tremendous social revolution was bound to multiply problems and strife. The makeup of Union League militias also militated against future racial harmony. Sizeable components of the League militias were made up of the 100,000 Southern black soldiers who had served in the Union Army. Numerous Union Army communications indicate that very many of these were recruited into the Union Army at the point of bayonet. Yet at the war's end they were not welcome in the North and even excluded by law from entering many Northern states. They had to return south where they were strongly resented by the white Confederate veterans, whom they had fought against during the war. Most Union League militiamen, both Union veterans and ex-slaves, wore the Union Army uniform. They were essentially federal agency units of the War Department assigned to the military or carpetbagger governments for their political bidding and defense. Often the more resentful or vengeful Union League militiamen used their new and elevated status to insult and menace the now humiliated Confederate veterans and their families. The Union League militias were also notorious for their lack of discipline. In addition to their assigned political violence and bullying there was often wanton violence, destruction, confiscation, and thievery. They outnumbered regular Federal troops in most states. Despite their numbers, reputation for brutality, and connections to Federal power, the Union League was first intimidated and then defeated by the Invisible Empire of the Ku Klux Klan. The severely damaged racial relations that was the work of the Union League and Reconstruction policies still lingers, but modern political correctness generally assigns the South as the sole scapegoat.

THE ROLE OF THE KLAN
IN DEFEATING RECONSTRUCTION

Many thoughtful historians consider the Reconstruction era as the darkest and most disgraceful in the history of the American Republic. It certainly substantiated Lord Acton's famous dictum that **"power corrupts and absolute power corrupts absolutely."** For twelve years the South suffered every variety of tyranny and shameless exploitation at the hands of its conquerors. Arrogant, self-righteous, vengeful and pitiless despotism driven by merciless greed crushed their liberties and robbed the Southern people of their daily bread. Reconstruction had further impoverished the South following the wanton destruction of the Union's total war policies. White Southerners were a subjugated people, disenfranchised and denied the very fundamentals of justice under military and carpetbagger government. They were left with no political or legal recourse to exploitation, injustice, and violence. They feared even for the lives of their women and children. In their desperation there seemed not even a single star of hope. The hope that came was the Ku Klux Klan. The Klan was able to give them some protection from exploitation by Treasury and Freedman's Bureau agents and the violence of the Union League. Eventually the Klan, operating as an "Invisible Empire" across the South, became an effective political instrument for redeeming the South from the power of the Radical Republicans. It is important to realize that it was the Union League and the Freedmen's Bureau that deliberately stirred the passions of racial hatred to exploit the black vote. It is also extremely important to realize that the KKK of 1865 to 1877 was completely different in principles and motives from the imitation KKK that was founded in 1915. The earlier, original, and true KKK was primarily organized to protect both white and black Democrats from the Radical Republican sponsored violence of the largely black Union League. One of the terrible legacies of Reconstruction is racial distrust.

In addition to significantly increased racial turmoil, Reconstruction also engendered decades of regional distrust. As General Gordon commented to a Congressional committee:

"But to say to our people, 'you are unworthy to vote; you cannot hold office...your former slaves are better fitted to administer the laws than you are...this sort of dealing with our people has emphatically alienated us."

General Gordon also commented that Reconstruction was a betrayal of the terms of Lee's surrender at Appomattox and of Johnston's surrender of the Army of Tennessee. It is only in recent years that the South through its growing economic and political power has enjoyed some relief from Northern disdain. Still there are some that insist that the South should sit upon an eternal stool of repentance.

General Gordon later went on to hold the offices of Governor and U. S. Senator for Georgia. Gordon was a highly significant personality in redeeming the South from Reconstruction. He was revered for his courage and dedication demonstrated in the war. He had a sincere brand of Christianity very similar to that of Robert E. Lee, and was also noted for his wisdom and integrity. He was also a master of diplomacy and negotiation. Although he never admitted specifically to being a member of the KKK, he did admit to having been a member of an organization of its kind, and frequently sought to give Northern Congressmen a better understanding of the true nature of the KKK and why it was needed in its time. Theodore Roosevelt admired him as a soldier and a statesman, saying:

"A more gallant, generous, and fearless gentleman and soldier has not been seen by our country."

Gordon loved the South and its people and was tireless in every effort to rescue and redeem them from the ravages of war and Reconstruction. He once made this statement, with which every Southerner can identify:

"No people in the history of the world have been so misunderstood, so misjudged, and so cruelly maligned as the people of the South."

Gordon was crucial in the final redemption of the South from Reconstruction. He helped negotiate the agreement with Rutherford B. Hayes to withdraw Federal troops from the last Southern states in exchange for South Carolina's and Louisiana's contested electoral votes that gave

Wade Hampton

Hayes a majority of electoral votes in the 1876 election. He was also able to persuade Hayes to prevent any further, untimely Congressional attempts to coerce the South on social and political matters that might exacerbate racial or political tensions and erupt into violence. He advocated gradual and voluntary changes. Bedford Forrest is also alleged to have had a representative at that meeting.

Gordon was along with Bedford Forrest also allegedly ready to assist Wade Hampton with Klan support, if the Radicals tried by force to defeat Wade Hampton's election as Governor of South Carolina. Forrest was the more visible, promising 15 thousand armed Klansmen already in South Carolina to support Hampton if needed with more on the way from Georgia and Tennessee. This may have been another of Forrest's bluffs, but it worked. President Hayes' strongly worded advice and the threat of Klan assistance to Hampton's South Carolina Red Shirts to oppose Federal troops and Union League militia backed the Radicals down. The Radicals vacated the South Carolina legislative buildings and the Democratic majority assumed power, confirming the election of Wade Hampton. Wade Hampton's inauguration as Governor of South Carolina was the final and glorious victory in redeeming the South from the tyranny of Reconstruction.

A minority report from the Congressional Committee that investigated the Klan in 1871 is a good summary of its reason for existence. The majority report had simply condemned the Klan, which was the electioneering purpose of the committee in the first place. But the minority report of eight Northern Democrats and Conservative Republicans gave a more useful and fairer appraisal. Here is an excerpt of their report:

"...when the courts were closed and Federal officers, who were by Congress absolute rulers and dispensers of what they called justice, ignored, insulted and trampled upon the rights of the ostracized and disenfranchised white men while officials pandered to the enfranchised Negro on whose vote they rallied, in short, when people saw that they had no rights which were respected, no protection from insult, no security, even for their wives and children, and that what little they had saved from the ravages of war was being confiscated by taxation…many of them took the law into their own hands and did deeds of violence which we neither justify or excuse. But all history shows that bad government will make bad citizens."

The Ku Klux Klan was a critical influence in defeating Reconstruction and returning the Southern states to the sovereignty of her own people. Both Forrest and Gordon acknowledged that though the Klan was based on very noble principles and tried desperately to reign in unwarranted violence by its own members and its several allied imitators, the violence had escalated beyond the public good. The Klan was finally and truly disbanded in September of 1877, having accomplished its purposes, and wishing to return the South to peaceful enjoyment of her liberties. At that time, just weeks before his death, Nathan Bedford Forrest made this statement:

"There never was a time before or since its organization when such an order as the Ku Klux Klan could have lived. May there never be again!"

A U.S. Congressional Committee investigating the KKK was more political grandstanding than a search for the truth. **But here are the findings of a Minority Report in 1871, prepared by conservative Northern Republicans and Northern Democrats:**

The KKK arose as an inescapable response to Union League brutality and lack of legal redress under corrupt occupation governments.

Many crimes against blacks were committed by Union League men disguised as Klansmen.

Had there been no wanton oppression and tyranny against Southern whites by corrupt carpetbagger and scalawag governments, there would have been no KKK.

From the oppression and corruption of the carpetbagger governments and the violent actions of the Union League sprang the outrages of the KKK and its successors.

FROM A UNION LEAGUE CATECHISM:

Q: With what party should the colored man vote?
A: The Union Republican Party

Q: What is the difference between Radicals and Republicans?
A: There is none.

Q: Would the Democrats take away all the Negro's rights?
A: They would.

Q: The colored men then should vote with the Republican or Radical Party?
A: They should and shun the Democratic Party as they would the overseer's lash and the auction block.

Q: Is Mr. Sumner a Republican?
A: He is, and a Radical; so are Thad Stevens, Senator Wilson, Judge Kelley, Gen. Butler, Speaker Colfax, Chief Justice Chase, and all other men who believe in giving colored men their rights.

ORIGINAL KKK PRINCIPLES (1865-1877):

To be an institution of Chivalry, Mercy, and Patriotism.

To protect the weak, the innocent, and the defenseless from indignities, wrongs, and outrages of the lawless and violent.

To relieve the injured, oppressed, and suffering, especially the widows and orphans of Confederate soldiers.

To protect and defend the Constitution of the United States and all laws conforming to the Constitution.

To protect the States and people from all invasions from any source.

To aid and assist in the execution of all constitutional laws and to protect the people from unlawful seizure of property and trial without a jury of their peers.

CHAPTER 22

လင္သာ

The Impeachment of President Andrew Johnson

The Tribune of the People versus the Radical Congress

Andrew Johnson

President Lincoln chose Andrew Johnson, the Union Military Governor of Tennessee, to be his Vice Presidential running mate on the "National Unity" or Union-Republican ticket in 1864 in hopes of garnering the votes of pro-war Democrats in the November election. Johnson had been a Democratic Senator from Tennessee, but he refused to side with his state when Tennessee seceded in 1861. Politically he was a Jacksonian conservative. He believed strongly in states rights and limited constitutional government, but just as strongly rejected the concepts of state secession and nullification. In Tennessee politics he had identified himself with the interests of the common people and against the interests of the wealthy planter classes. Like most Democrats and conservative Northern Republicans he supported the constitutionality of slavery. Although his political beliefs were very close to other Southern Democrats except for secession, he was known for his severe and threatening criticisms of secessionists.

Because of Johnson's harsh and sometimes vengeful remarks about secessionists, the Radical Republicans assumed he would support their radical aims for reconstructing the South after the war. The Radical Republicans were very uneasy about Lincoln's March 4, 1865 inauguration speech in which he indicated a lenient plan for reconstructing the South.

Lincoln believed that a magnanimous policy on reconstruction would avoid further regional conflict and pave the way for rebuilding political alliances between Northern Republicans and Southern business interests. The Radicals, however, probably judged rightly that Southern politicians would not support the Whig-Republican policies of high protective tariffs and government subsidies for industry or a national bank (essentially fiat money). They believed that welcoming Southern States back into the Union without radically restructuring Southern society would only result in more Democrats in Congress, thus threatening continued Radical Republican dominance and control. The Radicals believed the South deserved to be severely punished and exploited and made into Republican states before reentering the Union. The latter objective was to be achieved by enfranchising black voters and disenfranchising Confederate veterans, thus giving the Radicals permanent political dominance in the South and thereby the nation.

When the Radicals realized that Johnson intended to follow the same lenient Reconstruction policies as Lincoln, they began to oppose him strongly and plot how they might limit his power and influence. The first confrontation between the Radicals and Johnson began when the Radical dominated Congress refused to seat the new Southern delegates elected in 1865. This left them free to impose their punitive policies on the South. Their excuse was that Southern states were trying to circumvent the abolition of slavery, instituting "black codes" to limit the civil rights of blacks, and failing to control racial violence. There was little truth to these excuses, but campaigning against the faults of the South was a successful political strategy in the North. Johnson pointed out the hypocrisy of Northern legislators, whose states (for example: Indiana, Illinois, Ohio, and Oregon) had far more restrictive "black laws" than any in the South, using this issue as an excuse to impose punitive measures on the South.

In February of 1866, Johnson successfully vetoed the first Freedman's Bureau Bill. This bill would have extended many civil rights to the newly freed blacks, but also authorized confiscation of land from whites for redistribution to blacks, established previously unheard of social-welfare programs for blacks but not for whites, and established an extra-constitutional military tribunal system for whites accused of violating the rights of blacks. Johnson noted in his veto message that:

"A system for the support of indigent persons in the United States was never contemplated by the authors of the Constitution; nor can any good reason be advanced why, as a permanent establishment, it should be founded on one class or color of our people more than another...The idea on which the slaves were assisted to freedom was that on becoming free they would be a self-sustaining population. Any legislation that shall imply that they are not expected to attain a self-sustaining condition must have a tendency injurious alike to their character and their prospects."

Congress would pass a modified and only slightly less heinous version of the Freedman's Bill in February 1867 and was then able to override Johnson's veto.

The next month Congress passed the Civil Rights Act of 1866. This bill duplicated many civil rights laws already passed by the states, but its real intent as seen by Johnson was to grant the federal government unlimited power to intervene in state affairs. It also granted revolutionary police powers to Freedman's Bureau officials to enforce all civil rights laws. Johnson feared it was so severe that it might resuscitate armed rebellion. Congress overrode Johnson's veto. Several provisions of this Act were later incorporated into the Fourteenth Amendment, which Johnson strongly opposed, rightly predicting that it would lead to a consolidation of power at the federal level—in effect turning the Constitution upside down.

In May of 1866, there was a race riot in Memphis. The conflict was between black Union soldiers and white Irish police of recent Northern origin, but the Radicals made good use of it as an example of Southern intolerance and violence.

By early summer of 1866, the new state government in Louisiana had elected state legislators, state executive officers, and a Mayor for New Orleans. Much to the displeasure of the Radical Republicans, Louisiana was returning to Democratic Party control, and it was only a matter of time before a Democratic Governor might also be elected. The Republicans immediately laid plans for overturning the newly elected government. They called for a reconvening of the 1864 Union Military Government appointed convention to amend the state constitution and hold new elections. Only those eligible to vote in 1864 (mainly Radical Republicans) would be allowed to vote for delegates. The plan was to void the recent

Democratic electoral victory, disenfranchise most Confederate veterans, and enfranchise blacks, thus establishing a sizable Republican political dominance.

Hearing of this revolutionary attempt to overthrow the legally-elected government of Louisiana, President Johnson demanded that the Radical Republican Governor, Madison Wells, halt this proceeding. Wells ignored the President and continued to pursue plans to displace the recently elected conservatives and establish a lasting Republican dominance. Outraged at this, Mayor Monroe of New Orleans and Lieutenant-Governor Voorhies called for Union General Baird, commanding federal forces in the city, to prevent the illegal Radical convention from taking place. Baird declined to interfere and only offered to protect the convention and the city from mob action.

On the Friday before the Monday, July 30, 1866 convention, the Radicals organized a mass meeting denouncing Johnson and urging blacks to arm themselves to protect their rights and any attempts by New Orleans authorities to break up the convention. A white radical threatened that "the streets will run with blood," if there is any interference with the convention, and urged the mainly black gathering of several thousand to come in force on Monday.

Alarmed at this, General Baird telegraphed the President for instructions. All telegraphs to the President, however, came through the War Department and Secretary of War Edwin Stanton.

On Monday, incited by the radicals, a variously armed and intoxicated mob of freedmen swarmed the convention and came in conflict with Democratic protestors and New Orleans police. About fifty people were killed in the ensuing riot and mayhem, most of them blacks. General Baird's Federal troops arrived after the fact.

President Johnson's telegram from General Baird was not received until the riot was over. Secretary Stanton, with no explanation, had deliberately withheld it from him. As news of the bloody riot was received in the North, the Radical Republicans and their allies in the press and pulpit exploded with inflammatory denunciations of the South and Johnson's lenient Reconstruction policies. By this time President Johnson was thoroughly disenchanted with Stanton.

In February of 1867, at the behest of Stanton, the Radical dominated Congress passed the Tenure of Office Act, prohibiting the President from dismissing any officer confirmed by the Senate without Senate approval. This act was primarily intended to keep Secretary Stanton, a sympathetic ally to the Radical Republicans and a strong proponent of stern Reconstruction for the South, at his very influential post. Congress promptly overrode the President's veto of the bill.

Stanton

In March of 1867, when most Southern states had rejected the Fourteenth Amendment, Congress passed the infamous Reconstruction Act, putting most Southern states under military governments, enfranchising blacks, disenfranchising most Confederate veterans, establishing corrupt carpetbagger governments, imposing debilitating taxes, and a tyranny over the South that would last until 1877. **Passing the Fourteenth Amendment was made a prerequisite for Southern States to reenter the Union.** Johnson's strong protest and veto were overridden.

In early August of 1867, President Johnson learned from the trial of John Surratt and a conversation with Col. William P. Wood, superintendent of the Old Capitol Prison in 1865, that Edwin Stanton had deliberately suppressed a petition of mercy from five officers on the Lincoln Assassination Tribunal that would have caused him to spare the life of Mary Surratt in July of 1865. Johnson knew that the Radical Republicans would try to impeach him for violating the Tenure of Office Act if he attempted to fire Stanton. But the very day he learned of Stanton's treachery regarding the trial and sentencing of Mary Surratt, he decided that justice and honor required him to dismiss Stanton.

The relationship between President Andrew Johnson and the Radical Republicans who dominated Congress was very strained in the two years following his assumption of office. He strongly opposed the harsh terms of Reconstruction imposed upon the South and vigorously resisted Congressional usurpation of power over the states. His relationship with his Secretary of War, Edwin Stanton, was particularly strained. Stanton had a clandestine alliance with the radicals even while serving under Lincoln and had become, in fact, not only a key ally of the radicals in Congress, but also one of their most influential leaders. He was among the most determined proponents of a punitive and repressive Reconstruction as a means

Benjamin Wade

of preventing conservative Democrats from regaining power in the South and the nation. Also having his own presidential ambitions, Stanton frequently used furtive and underhanded tactics to undermine Johnson.

During the 1867 trial of John Surratt, who was accused of conspiracy in the Lincoln assassination (as was his mother, Mary Surratt), it was revealed that Stanton had withheld John Wilkes Booth's diary from evidence during the previous 1865 conspiracy trial. There was also a controversy over missing pages of that diary, disputing whether more pages were missing when examined during John Surratt's trial than when recovered from Booth's body in April 1865. There were many embarrassing revelations that the War Department had used torture, threats, and bribery resulting in perjured testimonies in prosecuting its case against Mary Surratt. Most alarming to the public and to Andrew Johnson was the revelation that five officers on the military tribunal had submitted a plea for mercy for Mary Surratt, but that petition had been suppressed, resulting in her hanging on July 7, 1865.

Johnson called in his Chief of Secret Service, Col. William P. Wood (ironically appointed on July 5, 1865, the day Mary Surratt and three others were sentenced to death) to inquire as to his opinion on the matter. Wood was a close confidant of Stanton, but while commandant of the Old Capitol Prison during Mary Surratt's stay there, he had come to believe that she was innocent of any complicity in the assassination of Lincoln. Wood's background would seem incongruous with sympathy for Mary Surratt. She was a devout Roman Catholic, and he had rejected that church and turned to atheism. He was a radical abolitionist and had even helped to train some of John Brown's men before their infamous raid on Harpers Ferry, but he refused to approve of Brown's moving arms across a state border. Regardless of their contrasting worldviews, Wood had attempted to deliver a statement of his strong conviction of Mrs. Surratt's innocence to President Johnson before her hanging, but had been stopped by Stanton's Chief Detective, Col. Lafayette Baker, carrying a restraining order specifically directed to Wood and signed by Stanton.

Col. Wood's conversation convinced President Johnson that Mary Surratt was innocent of any significant wrong-doing and should not have been hanged. Though a close friend of Stanton, Wood admitted that Stanton's conduct regarding the investigation, trial, sentencing, and finally the hanging of Mary Surratt had been regrettable. On August 7, 1867, President Johnson addressed and signed a letter to Stanton, which read:

Ben Butler

"Sir: Public considerations of a high character constrain me to say that your resignation as Secretary of War will be accepted."

Stanton, however, refused to vacate his office, although on August 12, Johnson temporarily suspended him and designated General Grant as Acting Secretary of War. Congress was not in session at the time.

When Congress returned on January 13, 1868, the Senate refused to concur with Stanton's suspension by a vote of 35 to 16. President Johnson then formally dismissed Stanton, designating General Lorenzo Thomas as his replacement.

Led by Radical Republicans Thaddeus Stevens, Benjamin Butler, and John Bingham, the U. S. House approved an impeachment resolution by a vote of 126 to 47. Stevens of Pennsylvania was the House leader of the Radical Republicans and so powerful that some referred to him as "the Boss of America." Butler of Massachusetts was a former Union Army General whose conduct as commander of the Union forces occupying New Orleans during the war earned him the sobriquets "Beast Butler" and "Spoons Butler" for his outrageous order to treat Southern women who showed any disrespect to Union officers as prostitutes and for his infamous looting of Southern households. He also had a young man hanged for cutting down an American flag. Following the assassination of Lincoln, Butler, speaking on the floor of the U.S. House, accused President Johnson of complicity in the assassination. Bingham of Ohio had been one of the assistant prosecutors at the trial of Mary Surratt and other alleged Lincoln assassination conspirators in 1865. It was he who inscribed, per the directions of Stanton and Army Judge Advocate Holt, the military tribunal's petition requesting mercy for Mary Surratt, which was then by various means suppressed. Stanton had also made Bingham promise never to reveal what they knew concerning the Lincoln assassination and the trial of Mary Surratt.

Eleven articles of impeachment were presented to the Senate for trial. Ostensibly, the main issue was Johnson's violation of the Tenure of Office Act that Congress had passed in 1867 to protect Stanton. This Act was later ruled unconstitutional. The real issue was that the Radical Republican majority disagreed with Johnson's lenient plan to restore the Southern States to the Union. Their plans were to punish and loot the South severely and structure its electorate to assure long-term Republican dominance in the South and thus the nation. Johnson had also criticized the Radical Republicans and exposed their intent in public speeches. In truth, the Tenure of Office Act had been passed as a means of trapping Johnson into impeachment. With Johnson out of office, Radical Ohio Republican Senator Benjamin Wade, Speaker Pro-tem of the Senate, would become President, and the way would be cleared for unopposed social and economic revolution in the South—the key to long-term Republican power and national dominance. This would assure the perpetuation of high protective tariffs and government subsidies for Northern industry and the fiat money of a national bank.

On March 30, the impeachment trial of Andrew Johnson commenced in the Senate. A two-thirds majority was necessary for conviction. Acting as presiding officer and judge was Chief Justice Solomon Chase, a Radical Republican, who had been Lincoln's Treasury Secretary. The Senate floor leaders for conviction were Benjamin Wade and Massachusetts Senator Charles Sumner, the acknowledged leader of Radical Republicans in the Senate. Johnson was defended by Henry Stanbery, who temporarily resigned his position as Attorney General to defend his president.

The opening argument for impeachment was made by House impeachment manager, Benjamin Butler. The closing argument for impeachment was made by Thaddeus Stevens, and the closing argument for defense by Attorney General Stanbery. Thirty-six votes were required for the two-thirds necessary for conviction. On May 16, the House managers brought up Article XI regarding the President's speeches against the effort of Radical Republicans to impose outrageously harsh Reconstruction terms on the South. The vote was 35 for conviction and 19 against, one vote short of conviction. On May 26, the Senate failed to convict Johnson on Articles II and III by the same vote and abandoned further attempts at conviction. President Johnson was acquitted, and the Radical Republicans' dubious attempt to remove him from office (due to what were essentially policy disagreements) was frustrated. Six Republicans heroically defied the powerful and ruthless leadership of their party by voting to acquit Johnson. The Senate, however, retaliated against Henry Stanbery by shamelessly refusing to re-confirm him as Attorney General.

Perhaps the best summary of the Presidency of Andrew Johnson and his conflict with Stanton and the Radical Republicans came from Gideon Welles, Secretary of the Navy under both Lincoln and Johnson:

"The real and true cause of assault and persecution was the fearless and unswerving fidelity of the president to the Constitution, his opposition to central Congressional usurpation, and his maintenance of the rights of the states and of the Executive Department against legislative aggression…carried on by a fragment of Congress that arrogated to itself authority to exclude States and people from their constitutional right of representation, against an Executive striving under infinite embarrassments to preserve State, Federal and Popular Rights."

Secretary of War Edwin Stanton's star began to fall with Johnson's acquittal. The revelations of his conduct during the Lincoln conspiracy trials and especially that relating to the hanging of Mary Surratt no doubt figured in his failure to achieve his ambition to become President. Ulysses S. Grant was the successful nominee of the Republican Party in 1868. Grant did nominate Stanton to a Cabinet post, but after much persuasion by Congressional Republicans, the wary Grant finally nominated Stanton to the Supreme Court. He was quickly approved by the Senate, but Grant delayed in making the appointment.

In December of 1869, Stanton requested his old confidant, Col. Wood, to visit him and explain why Grant was delaying his appointment to the Court. Wood informed him of his opinion—which he never disclosed publicly. Stanton then lamented that **"the Surratt woman haunts me so that my nights are sleepless and my days are miserable."** He added that he wished that Wood had tried harder to stop her execution, though he admitted that he was personally responsible for blocking Wood's efforts. The next day, December 24, 1869, Edwin Stanton died at his home.

No Regrets in the Struggle for Liberty

"Nothing fills me with deeper sadness than to see a Southern man apologize for the defense we made our own inheritance. Our Cause was so just, so sacred, that had I known all that has come to pass, had I known what was to be inflicted upon me, all that my country was to suffer, all that our posterity was to endure, I would do it all over again"

—Jefferson Davis

CHAPTER 23

cs&o

Slavery in Fact and Fiction

A Historical Perspective on American Slavery

Ancient slavery

Slavery is one of those subjects of American history that is highly charged emotionally and wrapped in the sensitivities of both historical and modern political agendas. Any discussion of slavery is unfortunately very much bound by the chains of modern political correctness. This severely hinders a historically accurate and realistic perspective on American slavery. Unvarnished and uninhibited truth on this important aspect of American history is sorely needed.

The image of American slavery in the minds of most people today is one of chains, bullwhips, cruelty, and arrogant human abuse. This was largely true of the transportation of slaves associated with the slave trade, but was largely untrue of the practice of slavery on American shores. The actual practice of slavery in America was in the vast majority of cases considerably more benign than its modern image. There were, of course, many inherent flaws in slavery as a social and economic system that limited social and economic justice and opportunity. Some inexcusable human abuses did occur under American slavery and should not be condoned, but such abuses were far less common than generally assumed. Even Harriet Beecher Stowe's *Uncle Tom's Cabin,* based principally on accounts of runaway slaves, Southern newspaper records of *prosecuted* abuses by masters, and only very limited first hand familiarity with the South, gives a more balanced picture of slavery than the common modern image.

American slavery first needs to be seen in the perspective of world slavery. **The universal evidence of history indicates that the institution of slavery in various forms existed from the most ancient times in every recorded civilization. Until the last two centuries it was viewed as a completely normal and acceptable form of social and economic organization.** Its establishment among the nations was the rule rather than the exception. The physical abuse of slaves was considered evil in many societies, but not the institution of slavery itself. Violent, despotic, or predatory methods of obtaining slaves might be considered objectionable in many societies, but not slavery per se. Slavery itself was rarely looked upon with moral disdain. It seemed part of the natural hierarchy of human organization that often provided a degree of protection and security for those bonded to a competent and just master. Even though some masters might govern their slaves unjustly, this was not considered a flaw significant enough to undermine the institution of slavery itself.

Slaves were among the earliest commodities traded in the ancient civilizations of the Middle East and Egypt. Prisoners of war were a prime source of slaves in ancient and more recent times. To soldiers having been defeated or captured in battle, becoming a slave was one of the more merciful alternatives. Criminals were often made slaves. Depending on the society and the crime, slavery was one of the more lenient judicial punishments. In many societies debtors became slaves. Slaves were often given to subordinate military and political leaders and even to common soldiers as a reward for meritorious service. The acquisition of slaves was often the primary reason for military conquest and raiding. In the higher echelons of many societies, brides were given slaves as part of their dowry. Slavery was viewed as a great source of wealth for many nations and rulers of the past.

In some societies the rule of the monarch was so absolute that everyone was subject to forced labor at any time. One Chinese emperor of the seventh century AD drafted over five million of his subjects between the ages of fifteen and fifty to widen a canal between the Yangtse and the Huang Ho Valley. These were not technically slaves, but they had little or no freedom. But no man is completely free in any society. Varying forms and degrees of freedom or slavery have existed in the past. It is only in the last two centuries that the institution of slavery has been reduced to its present level.

Most of the great building projects of antiquity were built by slaves. The Great Pyramid of Gizeh in Egypt, built around 2900 BC, was roofed by 56 slabs of stone weighing 54 tons each. This work involved thousands of slaves. Perhaps millions of slaves were used in the construction of the great pyramids and temples of ancient Egypt. By 2000 BC Egypt was importing slaves from Nubia and exporting them to Iraq, where many great building projects were being undertaken by the Sumerians. Of course, many will recall from the Bible that Joseph was sold into slavery by his brothers. This was about 1900 BC. We might note from this history that the career potential of Egyptian slaves at the time might vary from forced labor to trusted overseer of the household of a powerful military commander. Probably within less than one hundred years, the Hebrews were enslaved by a Pharaoh, who had no appreciation for Joseph's achievements in Egyptian history and considered the Hebrews a threat to Egyptian security. As a result, the Hebrews endured hard forced labor in Egypt for about 400 years.

About 2000 BC, the Hebrew patriarch Abraham held many bondsmen. In most biblical contexts, bondsmen and servants were equivalent to slaves as opposed to hired servants. They certainly had more security than hired servants, and because they were also generally more trustworthy and dependable, held a higher social status. In the pre-Civil War South, it was not unusual for African slaves to draw a degree of status from their security and the social rank of their master. This was relative both to other slaves and to many free whites. While the Bible generally implies that freedom is preferable to slavery, it neither endorses nor condemns slavery. Biblical passages such as Leviticus 25 simply regulate slavery, indicating the circumstances in which it is permissible and emphasizing the necessity for fair and humane treatment of slaves.

As early as 1400 BC, the slave trade was the leading source of economic wealth in the Mycenaean kingdoms of Greece. **Three quarters of the inhabitants of Athens in its fourth century BC flowering of democracy were slaves.** The Greek geographer Strabo claimed that the Athenians traded 10,000 slaves per day at a great slave emporium on the island of Delos. Sparta, a model for totalitarian rather than democratic society, had an even higher proportion of slaves, called helots, who were often treated

Arab slavers taking slave boy

with ruthless disregard. Though many Greek slaves were captured in war, most were purchased. The Greeks imported slaves from around the eastern Mediterranean, but also from the Scythian or Slavic North.

In their territorial expansion beginning in the third century BC, the Romans began to accumulate millions of slaves. Their implacable enemy, Carthage, was said to be overpopulated with disgruntled slaves from all over the Mediterranean, and some historians have claimed that this contributed to her defeat. The victorious Roman General Marius brought back 60,000 German slaves to Italy. Pompey's victories in Asia Minor resulted in the acquisition of two million slaves. Slaves were a valuable trading commodity and made many Roman generals extremely wealthy. **By the second century BC slaves made up 75 percent of the population of Italy.** Julius Caesar possessed only modest wealth before he conquered Gaul. He returned with many Gallic slaves and became fabulously rich. After his victory at Alesia in 52 BC, he rewarded every one of his soldiers with at least one slave. In all, Caesar brought more than a million slaves to Italy.

Roman slavery was not always as harsh as depicted in American movies. Roman magistrates were bound by law to consider complaints of slaves against their masters. Killing a slave was considered murder. Roman justice for both slaves and citizens was greatest during the Republic and then declined during the Empire. Yet there remained many opportunities under Roman law for slaves to gain their freedom. During the first century, the time of Christ and the Apostles, slaves declined to less than 40 percent of the Italian population.

The Arabs were also notable slave traders, and slavery increased as the Arab world became largely Muslim. The Koran approves of slavery but limits it to non-Muslims and regulates their treatment. Most slaves were taken by the aggressive Muslim practice of Jihad, but many were also purchased. The Turkish Muslim Ottoman Empire enslaved many Christians in the Slavic Southeastern European nations of Serbia and Bulgaria for three centuries ending around 1650. Many Christian children were taken from their parents to become military slaves. Some Muslim nations also raided villages in Southern Russia to obtain military slaves. Many of the Mamluks, who became a powerful military caste, were of Slav Christian origin. Even the word "slave" is related to the large number of Eastern European Slavs that were enslaved under Ottoman rule. Slavery is not just history in many Muslim countries. Thousands of non-Muslim Christians are still being enslaved in the Sudan and Mauritania.

In Northern Europe, the Vikings raided the coasts of Britain and France and made expeditions into Russia and the Baltic lands not to destroy, but to gain wealth. The Vikings brought back many slaves from their raids, especially pretty females. Modern genetic studies of DNA indicate that about half of the female genes contributing to the present population of Iceland came from the British Isles. The Norwegian Vikings that settled Iceland brought back many female slaves from the British Isles and married them. There are also indications that significant Celtic genes were absorbed in Western and Southern Norway in the same way. Several years ago I visited a Viking ship that had been recovered and was on display in Oslo, Norway. I was surprised to learn that this now famous Viking ship was carrying a cargo of women's shoes. Perhaps some of these Vikings were under great pressure to keep their British wives happy. There is also considerable evidence that many Swedish Vikings brought back Slavic slaves and Slavic wives from Russia. This type of DNA is also surprisingly common in some parts of Norway.

Slavery and race do not have a very high correlation in history. In the long run of history there have probably been more white slaves than black slaves. Greeks enslaved Greeks, Arabs, Persians, and Slavs. Romans enslaved Italians, Greeks, Germans, Celts, and Egyptians. Turks enslaved Arabs and Slavs. Vikings went on slaving expeditions to Britain, France, and Russia. Many European forms of indentured service were a form of white slavery. In the seventeenth and eighteenth centuries, the British enslaved thousands of political prisoners, petty criminals, debtors, and paupers in the West Indies. There were over 21,000 on Barbados alone around 1645. Few survived. Poor white English children were slaves in the famous workhouses of London and other industrial English cities in the nineteenth century. In the South, free blacks, who made up six percent of the population, owned many slaves.

The practice of slavery varied in nature from tyrannical to paternalistic. The potential for upward mobility and freedom for slaves varied by nation and century. Though many were forced into slavery, some welcomed it as a means of security.

THE SLAVE TRADE AND EARLY AMERICAN SLAVERY

Slavery was an institution with the potential for many abuses. Human abuse inevitably accumulates when some men have too much unchecked power over others. But most Americans have little knowledge of the origins of American slavery and an exaggerated and sometimes highly distorted image of the actual conditions that characterized it. This is not surprising, since ending slavery became the ex post facto justification for a war that took the lives of 620,000 Union and Confederate soldiers and indirectly resulted in the deaths of an estimated 50,000 Southern civilians from malnutrition and disease.

The origin and actual conditions of Southern slavery have been buried under decades of propaganda. There are still many political factions in America that have a vested interest in keeping a misinformed and distorted historical perspective of American slavery alive and constantly before the public. There is thus a great gap between common beliefs and historical reality. This misinformed and exaggerated public image of American slavery is engendering mischievous academic, social and political influences in the United States. Facts and analyses that contradict the prevailing historical view of slavery are generally unwelcome. Honest, courageous scholars attempting to contradict widespread misinformation on the subject of slavery are frequently shouted down without a hearing.

It was the demand for sugar, rather than tobacco or cotton that first drove the economics of African slave labor in the New World. By 1503 both the Spanish and Portuguese were transporting African slaves purchased from West African kings and chieftains to the Caribbean and Brazil. The growing demand for tobacco and cotton would later drive the demand for African slaves in North America.

In 1637, the Massachusetts Bay Colony engaged in a war with the Pequot Indians. Many of the defeated and captured Indians were enslaved. Rather than trying to convert their Pequot prisoners to Christianity these Puritan entrepreneurs gave some to allied Indian tribes, such as the Mohegans, and found a ready cash market for most of the rest in the cheap-labor-hungry West Indies. Now, having a taste of easy money, Massachusetts began to build a fleet of slave ships.

Slave ships

The first American slave ship, *The Desire*, commissioned in 1638, brought back the first cargo of African slaves. The slave trading business soon proved irresistibly profitable. New England slave ships could sail to West Africa and trade less than $100 worth of rum for a slave that could be sold for $650 or more in the Americas. Unlike the way it was depicted in the entertaining but often historically inaccurate novel, *Roots*, by Alex Haley, it was never necessary to venture into the West African jungles to round up a cargo of slaves. They were simply purchased from West African chieftains, specialists in supplying human cargos for European and New England merchant shipping. The going price for a sturdy male slave was a hundred gallons of rum, less for females and children. The cost of building a sixty-foot, fifty-ton, slave ship was often repaid in just one trip.

The return trip from Africa known as the "Middle Passage," usually took from four to nine weeks, depending on the weather. Yankee ingenuity and economy insisted on compact quarters for its 250 or more prospective "guest-workers." They were confined to an under deck area only 42 to 46 inches high and allowing only about eight to nine square feet of floor space per person. For security purposes the males were usually kept chained.

Although it was in the economic interests of the New England entrepreneurs for their cargo to arrive at their destination in good, saleable condition, the brutal and crowded confinement exacted a heavy toll. Seasickness, dysentery, and contagious diseases combined to kill eight to ten percent of their human merchandise. Considering the fact that the death rate for the crew was the same as for their crowded human cargo, the stamina of the slaves in surviving this passage is remarkable.

Massachusetts legally recognized slavery in 1641 under a code of laws called "The Body of Liberties:"

"There shall be no bond slaves among us unless it be lawful captives taken in just wars and such strangers as are sold to us."
This law is actually biblical according to Leviticus 25, but their practice of it was far short of biblical, and their nefarious profiteering in the slave trade made it a roaring hypocrisy.

Between 1755 and 1776 over 23,000 African slaves were brought to Massachusetts. Most of these were later sold to Caribbean or Southern owners. Only about six percent of all African slaves brought to the New World wound up in North America. Most went to Brazil, Cuba, Jamaica, Haiti, Central America, and various other destinations in and around the Caribbean.

Massachusetts was joined by Rhode Island, Connecticut, and New York in the slave trade. **By 1750 Newport boasted a fleet of 170 slave ships. By 1787 Rhode Island had taken the American lead in slave trading.** Virtually all American slave trading was done by New England owned ships. After the Revolutionary War, these ships flew the U.S. flag. Even after the Constitutional ban on slave trading went into effect in 1808, New England shippers continued to engage in the slave trade right up until 1860. New England shippers found supplying slaves to Brazil, Cuba and other nations bordering the Caribbean too profitable to resist. Most New Englanders closed their eyes to this illegal trafficking in slave labor. The enormous flow of capital from the slave trade enabled New England to develop its strong industrial base.

Because the climate was not suitable to the scale of agriculture typical of Southern cotton, tobacco, and sugar plantations, relatively few slaves were kept in New England. There were about 20,000 slaves living in New York until about 1800. Between 1780 and 1799 the New England states, New York, and Pennsylvania all initiated gradual emancipation laws. Faithful to their Yankee ingenuity, they simply sold their slaves to Southern planters before actually having to emancipate them. There were just over 8,000 Africans in New Hampshire in 1787. Several years later there were fewer than two hundred. **New England's answer to slavery was to export their slaves to the South for cold cash.**

Until about 1665, most of the farm laborers in Virginia, the Carolinas, and Georgia were indentured English immigrants. Indentured servants were apprenticed and normally worked for a specified time, typically seven years, before they were free and received a grant of their own land. Up until then and peaking in 1655, thousands of English Royalists, also called Cavaliers, came to Virginia and the Carolinas to escape the political depredations of the Puritan victors in the English Civil War. Following them were many thousands more English yeomen, who were willing to serve an indenture period to establish themselves as farmers or tradesmen in the Southern colonies. By 1665, however, economic and political conditions in England had improved enough to provide comparable or better opportunities there. With vast agricultural lands available for very profitable tobacco farming and developing opportunities in cotton, but fewer English yeomen available to do the work, African slavery began to increase. In 1650 only 3 percent of the South's population were African slaves. By 1770 the figure had risen to 40 percent. This turned out to be its peak. The great Scotch-Irish immigration of independent farmers had begun to outpace the African slave trade.

The continuous rise in the African population to near 40 percent began to be viewed with alarm. In 1760, South Carolina protested to the English crown against further importation of African slave labor. The English sovereign, however, preferred not to cut off such a profitable business for the crown just because South Carolinians were nervous about the possible consequences of their being outnumbered by African slaves. Virginia also began to worry about the longer term consequences of slavery and demographic changes on such a grand scale. Consequently, between 1699 and 1772, the Virginia House of Burgesses passed twenty-three acts designed to impede the slave trade. North Carolina and Georgia joined Virginia in their prayer to the King to cease his dangerous policy of flooding the colonies with African slaves. But neither the King nor the British Parliament would listen, and this added yet another Southern grievance against British rule. **Virginia, having declared her independence in 1776, in 1778 became the first state to outlaw the slave trade.** Ironically, by 1808, Britain had become the international scourge of the slave trade and was determined to eliminate slavery from the British Empire.

In 1793, Eli Whitney invented a cotton gin that enabled one man to do the work fifty did before. This made cotton King in the South, displacing

Virginia slaves in 1862

tobacco as the chief cash crop. In 1791, the South had exported 9,000 bales of cotton. In 1804, it exported one million bales of cotton. Most Southern states continued their objection to the slave trade, but the new profitability and importance of cotton would make parting with the institution of slavery financially painful. Contrary to popular beliefs, the South was the richest section of the country in 1860, owing to their agricultural exports.

Despite the South's largely agricultural economy, fewer than 25 percent of Southern families actually owned slaves. Many people, including even prominent slave owners, saw slavery as extremely dangerous and inconsistent with liberty. Among these last were Washington, Jefferson, Patrick Henry, Richard Henry Lee, and John Randolph. A majority of Southerners would gladly have phased out slavery, but no one, North or South, could see how it could be done without causing extreme economic hardship on the South. The South's economy was overwhelmingly agricultural, and cotton exports to Europe and New England comprised the vast majority of its income. Because machinery for large-scale farming had not yet been developed, by about 1830 the South was dependent on slave labor. Any economic transition from slave labor would take time and likely prove costly. Any abrupt adjustment in Southern cotton production or costs would risk loss of its markets to Egypt, India, and Brazil. Certainly, the immediate emancipation being called for by the abolitionists threatened economic disaster for the South. The dangers of massive employment of slave labor, clearly foreseen by South Carolina, Virginia, North Carolina, and Georgia before 1760 had come home to roost. Cheap foreign labor is an alluring but dangerous addiction.

SOUTHERN SLAVERY AS IT REALLY WAS

As part of the Federal Writer's Project during the Great Depression, the Roosevelt Administration employed scores of journalists to interview former slaves and record verbatim (and in dialect) their memories of slavery. From 1936 to 1938 about 2,300 former slaves were interviewed, most of whom were delighted to tell about "slavery times." These systematically designed interviews also covered their experiences during the Reconstruction years (1865 to 1877) following the War. In 1941, these interviews were published by state in a multi-volume series called *The Slave Narratives*. These volumes, along with Fogel and Engerman's formidable academic study published in 1974 on the economics of Southern slavery, entitled *Time on the Cross*, are the two richest scholarly resources on what Southern slavery was really like. Besides being invaluable study material, *The Slave Narratives* are also very colorful and entertaining reading. Because these two sources combined give both statistical data and thousands of eyewitness testimonies, they are a historical gold mine. Unfortunately, because they both present a surprisingly benign historical account of Southern slavery opposed to what is now fashionable in university circles, they are now largely neglected by modern academics who seem increasingly bound by the chains of political correctness.

In reading *The Slave Narratives*, one is struck first by relief that slavery no longer exists, but secondly by the remarkable degree of mutual affection between slaves and masters, and thirdly by the astonishingly positive reminiscences of the actual conditions of slavery. These positive reminiscences are strongly supported by Fogel and Engerman's studies of Southern plantations. One is also struck by the degree to which strongly held Christian faith and forbearing kindness prevailed among both masters and slaves. Slaves were usually referred to as servants and were frequently treated as extended family. Many bore such titles of affection as "Aunt" and Uncle." It is also evident that these former slaves had been overwhelmingly loyal to their masters and sympathetic to the Southern cause. For example, in Volume 9, a small Mississippi collection of 26 interviews of former slaves, three of the ten men who were at least fifteen by the end of the war, were Confederate veterans. All three had been exposed to enemy fire and commented on the horrible battle scenes they had witnessed. The only Union veteran had been forced into service by the Union Army to dig ditches around Vicksburg. Several of these ex-slaves had negative comments about their treatment by Yankees during the war and especially during Reconstruction. None offered positive comments.

Slaves social gathering

A young female journalist was shocked to hear Clara Young, age 95, of Monroe County, Mississippi say this:

"What I think 'bout slav'ry? Well, leetle Miss, I tell you. I wish it was back. Us was a lot better off in dem days dan we is now. If dem Yankees had lef' us 'lone we'd been a lot happier. We wouldn't been on 'lief an' old age pension fer de las' three years."

Just as some parents abuse their children today, there were some masters who abused their slaves. However, a study of 331 references to the treatment of slaves revealed that 86 percent of former slaves described their masters as "good" or "kind." Decidedly negative descriptions probably run less than five percent. John Cameron, age 95, of Jackson, Mississippi commented:

"My old Marster was de bes' man in de worl'. I jus' wish I could tell, an' make it plain jus how good him an' old Mistis was...De overseers was made to un'erstan' to be 'siderate of us...Marse had two of de slaves jus' to be fiddlers. Dey play for us an' kep' things perked up. How us could swing an' step-'bout by dat old fiddle music always a-goin' on. Den Old Marster come 'round wid his kin'ly smile an' jov'al sp'rits. When things went wrong he always knowed a way. He knowed how to comfort you in trouble."

On the other hand, Charlie Moses of Brookhaven, Mississippi, who was twelve when the war ended, had this to say:

"My marster was mean an' cruel. I hates him, hates him!...We was treated no better than one o' his houn' dogs...His family was as scared o' him as we was...They lived all their lives under his whip...No Sir! No Sir! There warnt no meaner man...He done ever'thing he could 'cept eat us. We was worked to death."

The material conditions of Southern black slaves compared favorably to Northern industrial whites. Their caloric intake, for example, was ten percent greater than free whites. The vitamin content of the slave diet far exceeded that of whites and the recommended daily lev-

Slave cabins

els established in 1964. The protein content was 110 percent greater and the iron content 230 percent greater than the minimum daily requirement. According to testimonies in *The Slave Narratives*, it is very evident that slaves enjoyed abundant, varied, and much appreciated food. The reason the nutrient value of the slave diet exceeded that of whites so much was that the whites ate white potatoes, while the slaves enjoyed the much more nutritious sweet potatoes. Most slave families were also allowed their own small gardens, most frequently planted with sweet potatoes. John Cameron further commented that:

"De slave cabins, 'cross a valley from de Big House, was built in rows. Us was 'lowed to sing, play de fiddles, and have a good time. Us had plenty t' eat and warm clo'es an' shoes in de winter time. De cabins was kep' in good shape. Us aint never min' working for Old Marster, cause us got good returns. Dat meant good livin' an' bein' took care of right."

While most slaves were field hands or household servants, there were significant numbers in other occupations. Seven percent of slaves, almost all of them males, were essentially part of the plantation management staff. Such positions were foremen (or drivers), overseers, and even general managers. In fact, most field foremen were black slaves. Another twelve percent were skilled craftsmen such as carpenters and blacksmiths. About seven percent were semi-skilled, which included teamsters and many household servants.

Housing standards for Southern slaves in 1860 compared favorably to free whites. There were 5.3 persons per white household and 5.2 persons per slave household. Only rarely was there more than one family per slave cabin. Most slave cabins were about 360 square feet of ground space plus sleeping lofts for children and some porch space. This exceeded the average living space of New York City households in 1892.

Medical care for the average Southern slave was considerably better than for the white Northern factory worker. Most larger plantations maintained a substantial hospital. These were usually visited by the same doctor that treated the plantation owners and white employees. The largest plantations had full-time doctors. The hospitals were usually staffed with one or more full-time slaves acting as nurses and midwives. They were typically elderly slaves who could no longer perform physical labor. Other slave-women specialized in caring for the children on the plantation. Ike Stier, age 99, of Natchez, Mississippi commented:

"De slaves was well treated when dey got sick. My marster had a standin' doctor what he paid by de year. Dey was a horspital building near de quarters an' a good old granny woman to nuss de sick…When de war broke out I sho' stuck by my marster. I fit de Yankees same as he did. I went in de battles 'long side o' him an' both fit under Marse Robert E. Lee…Right now, I loves my marster an' his wife in de grave. Dey raised me and showed me kindness all dey lives. I was pround of 'em. At de present time I's under treatment o' young Dr. Stowers, my marster's gran'chil'. I trusts him an' he is sho' good to me."

Owners of smaller farms with fewer slaves usually provided the same healthcare for their slaves as they did for their own families. There is every indication that slave owners paid considerable attention to the health of their slaves. Owning slaves was a major economic investment. No rational slave owner neglected the health of his slaves. Also, contrary to the propaganda of Northern abolitionists and modern liberals, a compassionate Christianity pervaded Southern slave owners far more than most other segments of Southern or Northern society. Thus Southern slaves enjoyed a relatively high standard of medical care offering cradle to grave healthcare security. James Lucas, age 104, of Natchez, Mississippi, commented:

"Now-a-days folks don' live right. In slav'ry times when you got sick a white doctor was paid to git you well. Now all you gits is some no-count paten' medicine. You is 'fraid to go to de horspital."

The average slave lifespan was only 36 in 1850, comparable to Northern industrial workers and whites in France, Italy, and the Netherlands, but four years less than the average of all American whites. The maternal death rate of slaves in childbearing was 167 per thousand births. While this is very high by modern standards, it was slightly less for slaves than whites. The infant mortality rate for slaves was 183 per thousand, about three percent higher than white Southerners. The slave suicide rate was only one in ten thousand per year, only one third that of whites.

The standard issue of slave clothing was quite adequate. The clothing was not fashionable, but very sturdy. Slaves were generally issued two pairs of shoes per year made of high quality leather. According to Jim Allen, age 87, of West Point, Mississippi:

"Our clo'es was all wove and made on de plan'ation...We had a' plen'y er good uns. We was fitted out an' out each season, an' had two pairs of shoes."

Contrary to popular belief, slave owners generally relied on motivational incentives rather than the whip to increase the work efficiency of slaves. Some typical incentives were cash payments, time off, team bonuses, and the opportunity to make money selling produce from their own gardens and small plots of land. Many plantations worked on a task system. A slave was assigned tasks that could be easily accomplished in a day. They usually finished these tasks ahead of schedule and used the time to rest, visit, or work on their own accounts. Some were allowed to work off the plantation to earn additional money.

Another astonishing statistic derived from Fogel and Engerman's data is that when the cost of food, housing, clothes, and healthcare, plus various kinds of cash incentive pay are added, the total compensation of the average slave was fifteen percent higher than the pay of comparable free agricultural workers in the South. Fogel and Engerman also estimate that the owner share of slave production after expenses was only about 14 percent. Today almost all workers pay more than 14 percent of their income in various payroll taxes. Slave maintenance costs were from cradle to grave. It took slightly more than 21 years from birth to breakeven. Slave labor could not therefore be said to be irresistibly profitable. Slavery was probably a doomed economic system that could not have lasted another generation. Slavery was not the cause of the War and would have ended without the War, just as it did in all other countries.

Contrary to popular opinion, the slave family was usually kept together and had strong patriarchal rather than matriarchal features. They had de facto ownership of homes and gardens and were allowed to keep incentive and other entrepreneurial earnings for themselves. The unit of plantation distribution was the family. Marriage ceremonies were often performed, although many were de facto. One moral defect of the slave system was that slave families could be broken up. But on the average only one slave in 22 was sold in a year. At least a third of these were estate sale disbursements. Most family separations occurred because of westward migration.

Abolitionist propaganda claimed that there were many Southern stud farms for breeding slaves. Thousands of hours of professional research has not revealed a single case. Slave owners did encourage large families. Sexual exploitation of slaves by white masters was also comparatively rare due to the considerable social disgrace involved. Around 1860 about 7.7% of the slaves were mulattos. Genetic studies estimate Negro children of white fathers increased this number by only 1 to 2 percent per generation.

Prince Johnson of Clarksdale may have summed up the prevailing attitude and feelings of former Mississippi slaves with these words:

"Marster would let us work at odd times for outsiders an' us could use de money for anything us pleased. My gran'ma sol' 'nough corn to buy her two feather beds...Us always had plenty t'eat...Folks dese days don't know nothin' bout good eatin'...My folks was sho' quality...When Sund'y come us dressed all clean'an nice an' went to church. Us went to de white folks' church an' set in de gal'ry...I stayed dere (on the plantation) **all four years o' the war. I couldn't leave 'cause de men folks all went to de war an' I had to stay an' pertec' de women folks...I'se seen many a patrol in my lifetime, but dey dassent come on us place. Now de Kloo Kluxes was diff'ent. I rid wid' em many a time. 'Twas de only way in dem days to keep order...Maybe things is better lak dey is today. Mos' folks says so anyway. But if Old Marster were a-livin' I'd be better off. I know dat to be so."**

THE MATCHLESS DEVOTION OF
BLACK CONFEDERATES

A NEGLECTED CHAPTER OF AMERICAN HISTORY

At Appomattox Courthouse in April of 1865, an Alabama soldier by the name of Zeb Thompson stood, rifle by his side, within a stone's throw of General Robert E. Lee when he yielded his sword to General Grant. Thompson had participated in many of the greatest battles of the War during his service to the Confederacy and had been wounded three times. Thompson, like several other Confederate soldiers looking on, was a black man. Also there was Private John P. Leach, one of two blacks, and ten whites left in Company C of the 53rd North Carolina Regiment. These were just a few of at least 50,000 and as many as 100,000 black slaves and freemen who served the Confederate cause in some military or naval capacity. Thompson indicated in his 1917 interview with the *Birmingham Age-Herald* that he had attended every Confederate reunion and was very proud of his war record.

On May 15, 1861, Walter Bryson, a recent graduate of South Carolina Medical School in Charleston and son of a prominent Hendersonville, North Carolina, family, returned home to enlist in the Hendersonville Rifles. With him went 17-year-old George Mills, a slave belonging to his father, to serve as his body servant. Within a short time Bryson was elected by his fellow soldiers to serve as Captain of Company G of the 35th North Carolina Troops. Unfortunately, Captain Bryson, only 21-years-old, was killed by a Yankee sharpshooter at the Battle of Sharpsburg (Antietam) in Maryland on September 17, 1862.

George Mills recovered the body of his master's son from the battlefield and by an arduous journey obtained an iron casket and a wagon and returned Walter Bryson's remains to his grieving family in Hendersonville, thus faithfully fulfilling a promise to the Bryson family. Upon his return to Henderson County, George Mills served in the Home Guard until the end of the war. He eventually received a Confederate pension and was active in Confederate veteran affairs until his death in 1926. Both Walter Bryson and George Mills are now buried in Oakdale Cemetery in Hendersonville. The grave of George Mills is marked with a Confederate Cross of Honor and a memorial plaque placed by the United Daughters of the Confederacy in 1960. In April of 2006 the local Sons of Confederate Veterans in

Hendersonville renamed their camp the Captain Walter M. Bryson-George Mills Camp, honoring both men.

In late June and early July of 1863, a force of 2,000 Confederate cavalry, consisting of Kentucky, Texas, and Alabama regiments under the command of the daring and flamboyant Major General John Hunt Morgan, crossed the Ohio River and swept through southern Indiana and Ohio in a completely unexpected and startling raid. This panicked the state and local governments of Indiana and Ohio and diverted 60,000 Federal infantry and cavalry from more pressing military objectives. Morgan's raid was not authorized by his Confederate commanders, and he and his men were later captured, but their daring made a lasting impression. Indiana and Ohio civilians and local militia were also astonished to see dozens of black faces among these elite Confederate cavalrymen.

It was very late in the war, March 13, 1865, before the Confederate Congress reluctantly authorized President Davis to call on slave owners to provide the service of able-bodied servants for military service. Although some Confederate leaders, such as General Patrick Cleburne, had long advocated the move, many had resisted the idea. Many feared the loss of productive workers in the vital cotton and agricultural industries. Others were uncertain of the loyalties and fighting spirit of slaves essentially drafted into the army. By 1865 however, President Davis, General Lee, and a majority of the Confederate Congress believed the move was essential to win the war. They were also willing to give those slaves who served in the army their freedom at the end of the war as a reward for their service. (Most Southerners were quite willing to give up slavery to achieve their independence.)

However, many blacks both free and slave were already serving in the army by that time. Confederate government was by its very nature decentralized government with great flexibility left to the states. For example, the Tennessee Legislature authorized enlistment of "all male persons of color between the ages of fifteen and fifty" in June of 1861. In other states many free blacks joined local militia and Home Guard units. As the war continued, both free and bonded blacks began to fill in many needed occupations and positions in the Confederate Army. Many "body servants" accompanied their masters into the army. Early in the war most of these body servants supported their masters and their units in the rear. As the war progressed, it became more and more common for body servants to accompany their masters into battle armed to the teeth and fully participating in combat.

Blacks were especially common as teamsters of Confederate supply wagons. Great numbers were used for building fortifications and other engineering support or "sapper" (combat engineering) jobs. They were also enlisted as nurses, ambulance drivers and attendants, railroad firemen, cooks, buglers, drummers, fifers, and all sorts of musicians, barbers, messengers, blacksmiths, and other support positions. One Tennessee regiment even had a much appreciated black chaplain. These support troops were often exposed to enemy fire in accomplishing these activities.

Many blacks became integrated through one means or another into regular infantry and cavalry regiments and artillery batteries. Many accounts indicate they were frequently used as sharpshooters. Considerable anecdotal evidence seems to place more blacks in cavalry and artillery units than others, perhaps because of past responsibilities and skills learned such as shoeing and caring for horses, repairing and maneuvering heavy wagons, and other plantation and farm experience also very necessary to keeping armies in the field. A Union Army observer estimated that at least 3,000 of 64,000 Confederate troops that moved through Frederick, Maryland, on their way to the battle of Sharpsburg (Antietam) in 1862 were fully armed and equipped blacks, many on horseback.

Blacks were also common in the Confederate Navy from the very beginning of the war. Photographic evidence indicates that black sailors served on the Confederate Navy's most distinguished warship, the C.S.S *Alabama,* commanded by Captain Raphael Semmes. The Alabama terrorized and frustrated Yankee merchant shipping around the world.

Contrary to fashionable academic opinion, Confederate blacks were generally more enthusiastic and dependable supporters of the Southern cause than were their Federal counterparts to the Union cause. In the vast majority of cases there remained a strong bond of affection between master and slave, and Southern blacks identified more with the South, their homes, and familiar and friendly relationships than with Yankee promises. Late in the war, according to a letter to General Richard S. Ewell from F. W. Hancock, a group of slaves working at a Confederate hospital were asked if they would be willing to take up arms against an impending attack by Federal forces. Sixty out of 72 responded that they "would go to the trenches and fight the enemy to the bitter end."

It is true that over 500,000 of 3,500,000 black slaves crossed over to the Union lines as Federal armies arrived in their area, but many of these had nowhere else to go. Sherman and Sheridan's total war tactics were devastating farms, homes, food, and all means of survival. According to several reports, most of these preferred to return to their masters within weeks. Elizabeth Keckley, seamstress and friend to Mary Todd Lincoln in the White House, in her autobiography, commented on the disappointment and despair of newly emancipated slaves arriving in the North during the war:

"In visiting them...they would crowd around me with pitiful stories of distress. Often I heard them declare that they would rather go back to slavery in the South and be with their old masters than to enjoy the freedom of the North. I believe they were sincere in their declarations."

Union records indicate that forcing Southern blacks into the Federal Army at bayonet point was commonplace. About 135,000 of 186,000 blacks in the Union Army were from Southern states. Many were enthusiastic for their new cause and new masters, but many were not. Many were very conflicted by the ordeal. The March 21, 1864, issue of the *Fayetteville Observer* carried a story of a black Union soldier that refused to fire into a Confederate regiment, saying:

"My young master is thar; and I played with him all my life and he has saved me from getting a many whipping I would have got, and I can't shoot thar, for I loves my young master still."

This sort of behavior perplexed Union troops, who had come to believe they were liberating blacks from terrible oppression. It fully exasperated Northern abolitionists. One Northern journal, shocked by Union losses inflicted by black Confederates at Manassas in 1861, editorialized:

"The war has dispelled one delusion of the abolitionists. The Negroes regard them as enemies instead of friends. No insurrection has occurred in the South—no important stampede of slaves has evinced their desire for freedom. On the contrary, they have jeered at and insulted our troops, have readily enlisted in the rebel army and on

Sunday at Manassas, shot down our men with as much alacrity as if abolitionism had never existed."

Slave church in SC

Post war and modern propaganda has buried an important part of American history, the matchless devotion of most Southern blacks to their masters and to the Southern cause of independence. White Southerners have great reason to appreciate the steadfast loyalty that black slaves and freemen showed them during the terrible ordeal of the Civil War. Blacks faithfully watched after their farms and families during the war. They fought side by side with them and supported them with the last drop of sweat and blood on many fields of honor. Black Southerners have as much reason to take pride in their Southern and Confederate heritage as their white compatriots. Why not do so together? There is nothing sinful about mutual affection and respect. Indeed, the Bible says that Christians will be known for their love for each other. Slavery is gone now, and no one outside of a madhouse regrets it. But what have we gained if freedom and mutual affection are lost? Let the Southern Cross be a symbol of liberty and brotherhood.

TIME ON THE CROSS

SPIRITUAL AND RELIGIOUS ASPECTS OF SOUTHERN SLAVERY

The remarkable prevalence of Christian faith and affectionate bonds between master and slave in the South can be seen in the words of former slave, Adeline Johnson, of Winnsboro, South Carolina, as recorded by a Federal government researcher in the 1930's and published in the *Slave Narratives* in 1941:

"I hope and prays to get to heaven. I'll be satisfied to see my Savior that my old marster worshiped and my husband preached about. I want to be in heaven with all my white folks, just to wait on them, and love them, and serve them, serta like I did in slavery time. That will be enough heaven for Adeline."

Those who have been led to see the relationship of master and slave in the South as one of cruel tyranny by masters and suppressed resentment on the part of slaves may be stunned to read such remarks, but they are so numerous in the *Slave Narratives* that they make an immediate impression on the reader. Gabe Emanuel, age 85, of Port Gibson, Mississippi, gave a government researcher some insight with these words:

"De mistis used to teach us de Bible on Sund'ys an' us always had Sund'y school. Us what lived in de Big House an' even some o' de fiel' han's was taught to read an' write by de white folks...Lawdy! I sho' was happy when I was a slave...When de time comes to go I hope to be ready. De Lawd God Almighty takes good care o' his chillun if dey be's good an' holy."

Fanny Smith Hodges, a former slave from near McComb, Mississippi, gave this testimony:

"No, Marse Cassedy didn't have no church fer de slaves. Dey went to de white folks' church...I can't stay here long but God won't low me to starve. Bless God, he's comin' fer me some day."

This was not the universal experience, however. Gus Clark, age 85, gave this report:

"Slav'ry was better in some ways 'an things is now. We allus got plen'ty ter eat, which we doan now...My Boss didn' 'low us to go to church, er to pray er sing. Iffen he ketched us prayin' er singin' he whupped us. He better not ketch you with a book in yo' hand. Didn't 'low it. I doan know what de reason was. Jess meanness, I reckin. I doan b'lieve my marster ever went to church in his life, but he wa'nt mean...'cept fer doin' things he doan 'low us to. He didn' care fer nothin' 'cept farmin'."

But the experience of Gus Clark was the exception rather than the rule. The evidence is overwhelming that the vast majority of Southern masters not only treated their slaves well, looking after their health and medical needs even when they were too old to work, but also took a keen interest in their spiritual welfare.

Many wills from the era of Southern slavery testify to the high degree of moral obligations masters felt toward their slaves. For instance, when Jacob Weaver, a Virginia planter, died in 1821, his eldest children are recorded as assuming responsibility for several aged slaves who were listed as having no monetary value but for whom Jacob Weaver had obligated himself "by the law of God and of Virginia" to feed, clothe, house, and care for until they died.

A common criticism of Southern slavery is that some states passed laws forbidding the teaching of reading to slaves. However, the *Slave Narratives* make it clear that these laws were often ignored. A closer look at their history will reveal the tragic reason for their existence.

In 1791, inspired by the French Revolution, Haitian slaves overthrew the French colonial government, slaughtering several thousand white colonists in the process. When Napoleon Bonaparte took control of the French government in 1804, he sent 45,000 troops to restore French sovereignty. But these were largely wiped out by disease and Haitian resistance. The defeat of the French resulted in the slaughter of virtually all of the 20,000 remaining whites in Haiti. There were also other slave revolts in the Caribbean during the first half of the nineteenth century, twelve in Cuba alone.

Though slave revolts were rare in North America, Virginia experienced a bloody and far reaching uprising in August of 1834. Nat Turner, a semi-literate slave and self-styled preacher, influenced by several visions and celestial signs, gathered six of his friends and slaughtered his master's entire household while they slept. They preceded from house to house gathering a total of over 40 slaves and slaughtering every white family they came upon. Before they were defeated, captured, tried, and hanged they had butchered 55 whites, of whom 18 were women and 24 were children.

The "Nat Turner Rebellion," as it came to be known in history, could not have occurred at a worse time. The Virginia Legislature had been considering a plan to emancipate Virginia's slaves over a number of years and to compensate slave owners for their losses. Because of fears raised by the Nat Turner Rebellion, this emancipation plan was narrowly defeated. It was also a time when Northern abolitionists had begun to sneak inflammatory tracts into the South urging slaves to revolt and even to slit the throats of their masters. To the dismay of the South, this radical behavior was even being supported from Northern pulpits. Rev. W. J. Sloane of the 3rd Reformed Presbyterian Church in New York publicly declared that:

"It is better that six million white men, women, and children in the South should be slaughtered...than that slavery should not be extinguished."

The Southern reaction was a severe tightening of state regulations governing slaves. Some states forbade the teaching of reading to slaves. According to prominent Southern political economist and theologian, Rev. R. L. Dabney, in his famous 1865 book, *In Defense of the South and Virginia,* Virginia was one state that never had such a law.

In any case, these laws were not really intended to prevent slave owners from teaching their slaves to read and understand the Bible. Their intent was to prevent outsiders, especially abolitionists, from doing so as a means of fomenting rebellion. Besides, the very nature of the Southern mind resists regimentation. Most Southern slave owners continued to do whatever they wanted to do. The Christians, especially, were going to ignore any law they felt conflicted with their Christian responsibilities. The literacy rate for Southern slaves remained in the 30 to 40 percent range.

The slavery issues of the 19th century are now very much misunderstood by the general public and most academics. It is politically and intellectually fashionable to distort the history of slavery in order to create a whitewashed version of American history that glorifies abolitionist radicalism and Northern aggression against the South, while covering up the strongest underlying motivation for Northern opposition to the extension of slavery to new states. Northern whites did not want competition from black labor and wanted to keep the Northern states purely white. Lincoln, himself, stated this very clearly on October 16, 1854, in Peoria, Illinois:

"The whole nation is interested that the best use shall be made of these territories. We want them for the homes of free white people."

The religious issues surrounding slavery have also been very much distorted, making the predominantly Unitarian, Transcendentalist, and apostate abolitionists look like heroic Christians and Southern Christians look ignorant, hypocritical and mean spirited. The denominational conflicts that split the Baptists in 1843, the Methodists in 1844, and the Presbyterians in 1857, along regional lines, have also been distorted. The Northern side of the issue was about slavery, but the Southern side was about the authority of Scripture.

Many Christians today, not being well-read in the Bible, assume that all slavery was a heinous sin. This type of abstract morality is isolated from actual human conditions and needs. The Bible recognizes that there are many degrees of freedom and many conditions which make some forms of servitude a temporary necessity for individual and social survival. Consider what might have been the advantages of being one of Abraham's several hundred bondservants as compared to facing life alone in a hostile and bandit filled environment. The Bible regulates various degrees of servitude emphasizing fair treatment of servants and respect for masters. There are numerous versus in Scripture that touch on the moral obligations of both servant and master. Leviticus 25: 44-46 (NIV) is an eye opener for many:

"Your male and female slaves are to come from the nations around you; from them you may buy slaves. You may also buy some of the temporary residents living among you and members of their clans born in your country, and they will become your property. You can will them to your children as inherited property and can make them slaves for life, but you must not rule over your fellow Israelites ruthlessly."

There are many other important passages that could be quoted and their complexity and applicability debated, but that is beyond the scope of this article. Suffice it to say that the Bible does not condemn the institution of slavery per se, but sets forth the moral obligations and accountability for both master and slave.

Southern pastors and theologians, who often favored the gradual emancipation of slaves and other slavery reforms, would not condemn or discipline slave owning church members except for mistreating their slaves or failing to meet their obligations to them. They were not about to condemn what God had not condemned. The real issue of the interdenominational conflicts was the moral authority of Scripture versus the moral fashions of men. To a great extent, this battle line still exists today across a wide range of issues touching the authority of Scripture versus the changing morality of man-centered philosophies.

One often hears the complaint that "Sunday is the most segregated day of the week." But that was the choice of the newly liberated blacks. Many Northern denominations sent missionaries south to recruit blacks into their denominations even though Southern churches would have been glad to keep them. At the same time it is understandable why blacks wanted their own churches. They had developed their own style of preaching, teaching, and worship on the plantations, and they did not want to be supervised by Northern or Southern denominations.

A distorted view of the history and actual conditions of slavery is a malignant and dangerous infection that must be checked by the healing balm of truth. Certainly there were many social ills attendant to slavery, and we can all be glad that its time is past. But we must also recognize that in the mysterious providences of God, Southern slavery was most often characterized by the moderating influences of Christianity. Between master and slave there generally prevailed a remarkable degree of mutual affection and kindness. Most importantly, because of God's providence in pairing their "time on the cross" with so many benevolent Christian masters concerned not only with their physical well being, but their spiritual welfare, millions received the benefits of the Christian gospel.

The true history of American slavery is a taboo subject, fettered by many chains of past and current political correctness. Yet there are few subjects in American history that deserve more scholarly attention. We are living in an age of mandatory ignorance, rigid restrictions of thought and speech, and obligatory social and political lies. If there is to be a real and lasting healing among races and regions in America, it must be based on a common recognition and understanding of truth.

CHAPTER 24
Gone with the Wind

Margaret Mitchell, author, Gone with the Wind

"There was once a land of Cavaliers and cotton fields called the Old South. Here in this pretty world, gallantry took its last bow. Here was last ever seen the Knights and their Ladies Fair, master and slave. Look for it only in books because it is no more than a dream remembered, a Civilization Gone with the Wind."

Gone with the Wind, first published in June 1936, is according to many sources, the most successful and widely read novel ever published in America. The author, Margaret Mitchell of Atlanta, received a Pulitzer Prize in May of 1937 for her sweeping historical novel of the Old South set during the War for Southern Independence and Reconstruction. The novel was also wildly successful internationally. By 1965 it had been published in twenty-five different languages in twenty-nine countries.

The movie, premiered at the Loew's Grand Theater in Atlanta on December 15, 1939, in what may have been the grandest event ever held in Atlanta. It went on to set records that have not yet been matched even by *Titanic*. The film, produced by David O. Selznick, starred some of Hollywood's and Britain's most acclaimed and unforgettable actors and actresses: Clark Gable, Vivien Leigh, Leslie Howard, Olivia de Havilland, and

Vivien Leigh as Scarlet O'Hara

Hattie McDaniel. It swept the Academy Awards, receiving Oscars for Best Picture, Best Director, Best Screenplay, Best Cinematography, and Best Actress (Vivien Leigh as Scarlet O'Hara).

For her truly unforgettable supporting role as "Mammy," Hattie McDaniel became the first African-American to receive an Oscar. Who can forget her famous line when Scarlet tells Mammy how famished she is and how much she could eat as Mammy prepares her for an important dinner and social event where she will encounter her romantic favorite at the time, Ashley Wilkes (played by Leslie Howard). Mammy rebukes her in a firm tone:

"Oh no you ain't! If you don't care what folks says about this family, I does. And I done told you and told you, you can always tell a lady by the way she eats in front of people like a bird. And I ain't aimin' to see you go over to Mista John Wilkes' house and eat like a field hand and gobble like a hog."

Another classic pair of lines were delivered by British actress Vivien Leigh as Scarlet and Clark Gable as the dashing Rhett Butler. In a very authentic Old Atlanta dialect, Vivien Leigh delivers her line as Scarlet:

"Rhett…if I go…where shall I go? What shall I do?"

As Rhett, Clark Gable shocked movie audiences of the time with:

"Frankly, my dear, I don't give a damn."

Scarlet's final line symbolized the Southern people's determination to survive the destruction of War and Reconstruction:

"After all…tomorrow is another day."

The movie has become an American classic.

Margaret Mitchell was born in 1900 into an Atlanta family with strong ties to the Old South and the struggle for Southern Independence and Southern Rights. As a small girl she listened as relatives told many stories of the War and Reconstruction. She did not discover that the South had actually lost the War until she was ten years old. Her devoutly Irish-Catholic mother encouraged her to read the classics and to write her own stories. Her mother also impressed upon her the precariousness of life and the necessity of a trained mind and dogged determination to survive, just as had her family during the War. Her father, an Atlanta lawyer, also encouraged her in reading and the importance of honesty and originality. Growing up, her favorite authors were Sir Walter Scott and Charles Dickens. No doubt she was strongly influenced by the romanticism of Scott and the vivid character descriptions and development of Dickens.

Margaret Mitchell was a small woman, but quite attractive and very vivacious. She could also be very head-strong. She was popular with boys and had many suitors. In the summer of 1918 she met, fell in love with, and became engaged to Lieutenant Clifford Henry. He was killed in battle a few months later. In 1919, her mother died of flu and pneumonia. After attending Smith College for a year, she returned to Atlanta to take care of her father, and at the age of nineteen became mistress of the house. She made her social debut into Atlanta society the same year. Despite being lovely, engaging, and intelligent, she was snubbed by Atlanta's Junior League because she and a young man had performed a "scandalous" Apache dance during an Atlanta ball.

In September 1922, she married Berrien Upshaw despite the objections of her father and brother. Upshaw proved a violent and dangerous man, who deserted her after only a few months of marriage. She was granted a divorce in 1924. In 1922, she had begun working for the *Atlanta Journal Sunday Magazine*. She wrote 129 feature stories over the next four years, learning to love Atlanta and developing her writing skills. In 1925, she married John Marsh, an old friend, fellow journalist, and her literary mentor. In 1926, she began the historical research and writing of *Gone with the Wind*. It took her ten years to complete it. No one but she and her husband ever saw the manuscript until it was given to Macmillan Publishing in 1935.

Just one month after publishing, *Gone with the Wind* was selected as the July 1936 Book of the Month, and sales skyrocketed. David O.

Selznick bought the movie rights for $50,000. This was, at the time, the highest amount ever paid for movie rights. By the time of the movie premier in Atlanta in 1939, Margaret Mitchell had already become a literary legend. *Gone with the Wind* was Margaret Mitchell's first and only novel.

On August 11, 1949, Margaret and her husband, John, were on their way to see a movie only a few blocks from their house. As they were crossing Peachtree Street, a speeding driver slammed on his brakes, but not in time to avoid hitting Margaret. She died five days later on August 16, never having regained consciousness.

There is a wonderful full-face photograph of Margaret Mitchell on the wall of the Grove Park Inn in Asheville, North Carolina. She was a strikingly attractive woman. But few remember now that Margaret Mitchell was also a compassionate and generous supporter of the Red Cross or that she was very active in supporting America's war effort in the Second World War. Fewer still know that she inspired the building of the first African-American hospital and worked with Morehouse College to establish fifty scholarships for African-American medical students.

All Atlanta and all of Georgia mourned on the news of her tragic death. Her love story, so vivid in character development, and set in the Georgia of the Old South, centering on real and familiar places in Atlanta, Decatur, Jonesboro, and Fayetteville, had not only fascinated and entertained millions, it had educated them. The South that she portrayed may in many respects be gone with the wind, but her fictional novel portrayed the South and Southerners as they were, not according to modern standards of political correctness. For that especially, the nation owes her a debt of gratitude.

It is for this last reason, the cause of truth, that we ought to come to a higher appreciation of both the novel and the movie, *Gone with the Wind*. There are truths and virtues that must not be forgotten or discarded. They must be preserved and honored.

CHAPTER 25

The Faith of our Fathers

Jefferson Davis
Confederate President

Biblical Christianity pervaded the Old South perhaps as much as any society in history. Although authentic faith was by no means universal and nominal Christianity and lapsed moral standards were common enough, a genuine Christian faith and Christian worldview permeated and substantially influenced every level of society and almost every institution. In his comprehensive biography of Stonewall Jackson, Southern historian James I. Robertson Jr. emphasized that Jackson could not be understood without understanding his Christian perspective. Neither can the Old South, nor even the modern South, be fully understood without understanding the degree to which Christian faith and worldviews have pervaded its culture and society for more than two centuries.

It should not be surprising then, that Confederate President Jefferson Davis, the man Confederate Postmaster General John H. Reagan later called "the most devout Christian I ever knew" and who was acknowledged throughout the South to be a man of sincere Christian confession, character, and conduct, concluded his February 18, 1861, first inaugural remarks in Montgomery, Alabama, with a humble appeal to divine guidance and protection:

"Reverently, let us invoke the God of our fathers to guide and protect us....With the continuance of His favor ever gratefully

acknowledged, we may hopefully look forward to success, to peace, and to prosperity."

Two months later on April 29, Davis elaborated:

"We feel that our cause is just and holy; we protest solemnly in the face of mankind that we desire peace at any price save that of honor and independence; we ask no conquest, no aggrandizement, no concession of any kind from the states with which we were lately confederated; **all we ask is to be left alone**; that those who never held power over us shall not now attempt our subjugation by arms. This we must resist to the direst extremity. The moment that this pretension is abandoned the sword will drop from our grasp, and we shall be ready to enter into treaties of amity and commerce that cannot but be mutually beneficial. So long as this pretension is maintained, with a firm reliance on that Power which covers with its protection the just cause, we will continue to struggle for our inherent right to freedom, independence and self-government."

A year later in Richmond, on February 22, 1862, commencing a full six-year term as President of the Confederate States, Davis concluded his second inaugural speech with a similar appeal to heaven:

"

...Our faith and perseverance must be tested, and the chastening, which seemeth grievous, will, if rightly received, bring forth its appropriate fruit. It is meet and right, therefore, that we should repair to the only Giver of all victory, and humbling ourselves before Him, should pray that He may strengthen our confidence in His mighty power and righteous judgment..."

Then he laid his prepared remarks on the table, raised his hands to heaven, and exclaimed:

"To thee, O God! I trustingly commit myself, and prayerfully invoke thy blessings on my country and its cause."

He then called the Southern people to a day of fasting, humiliation, and prayer. According to one observer, the effect of his speech on the crowd was "thrilling" and "electric."

Several months earlier, in the summer of 1861, one hundred prominent Southern ministers from various denominations signed a statement entitled, "Address to Christians throughout the World." In this document they stated why the vast majority of Southern ministers and Southern Christians supported the Southern cause as fully consistent with their commitment to Christ and his Church. Some of their stated sentiments are quoted in the following paragraphs:

"The war is forced upon us. We have always desired peace. After a conflict of opinions between the North and the South, in Church and State, of more than thirty years, growing more bitter and painful daily, we withdrew from them to secure peace—they sent troops to compel us into re-union! Our proposition was peaceable separation, saying, 'We are actually divided, our nominal union is only a platform of strife.' Their answer was a call for troops to force submission to a government whose character, in the judgment of the South, has been sacrificed to sectionalism."

"We are aware that in respect to the moral aspects of the question of slavery, we differ from those who conceive of emancipation as a measure of benevolence, and on that account we suffer much reproach which we are conscious of not deserving."

"With all the facts of the system of slavery before us, as eye witnesses and ministers of the word, having had perfect understanding of all things on this subject of which we speak, we may surely claim respect for our opinions and statements."

"Most of us have grown up from childhood among the slaves; all of us have preached to and taught them the word of life; have administered to them the ordinances of the Christian Church; sincerely love them as souls for whom Christ died; we go among them freely and know them in health and sickness, in labor and rest, from infancy to old age. We are familiar

266   The Un-Civil War | Shattering the Historical Myths

with their physical and moral condition, and alive to all their interests, and we testify in the sight of God, that the relation of master and slave among us, however we may deplore abuses in this, as in other relations of mankind, is not incompatible with our holy Christianity, and that the presence of the African in our land is an occasion of gratitude on their behalf, before God; seeing that thereby Divine Providence has brought them where missionaries of the Cross may freely proclaim to them the word of salvation, and the work is not interrupted by agitating fanaticism. The South has done more than any people on earth for the Christianization of the African race. The condition of slaves here is not wretched, as Northern fictions would have men believe, but prosperous and happy, and would have been yet more so but for the mistaken zeal of abolitionists. Can emancipation obtain for them a better portion? The practicable plan for benefiting the African race must be the providential plan—the scriptural plan. We adopt that plan in the South, and while the State should seek by wholesome legislation to regard the interests of master and slave, we as ministers would preach the word to both as we are commanded of God. This war has not benefited the slaves. Those that have been encouraged or compelled to leave their masters have gone on to no state of society that offers them any better things than they had at home, either in respect to their temporal or eternal welfare."

"We regard abolitionism as an interference with the plans of Divine Providence. It has not the sign of the Lord's blessing. It is a fanaticism which puts forth no good fruit; instead of blessing, it has brought forth cursing; instead of love, hatred; instead of life, death—bitterness and sorrow and pain and infidelity and moral degeneracy follow its labors We remember how the Apostle has taught the minister of Jesus upon this subject, saying, 'Let as many servants as are under the yoke count their own masters worthy of all honor, that the name of God and his doctrine not be blasphemed. And they that have believing masters, let them not despise them, because they are brethren; but rather do them service, because they are faithful and beloved, partakers of the benefit. These things teach and exhort. If any man teach otherwise, and consent not to wholesome words, even the words of our Lord Jesus Christ, and to the doctrine which is according to godliness, he is proud, knowing nothing, but doting about questions and strifes of words, whereof cometh envy, strife, railings, evil surmisings, heresies, disputing of men of corrupt minds and destitute of the truth, supposing that gain is godliness; from such withdraw thyself' This is what we teach."

"The Christians of the South, we claim, are pious, intelligent, and liberal. Their pastoral and missionary work have claims of peculiar interests. There are hundreds of thousands here, both white and colored, who are not strangers to the blood that bought them. We rejoice that the great Head of the Church has not despised us. We desire as much as in us lieth to live peaceably with all men, and though reviled, to revile not again."

"Our soldiers were before the war our fellow-citizens, and many of them are of the household of faith, who have carried to the camp so much of the leaven of Christianity that amid all the demoralizing influence of army life the good work of salvation has gone forward there."

"Our President, some of our most influential statesmen, our Commanding General, and an unusual proportion of the principal Generals, as well as scores of other officers, are prominent, and we believe consistent members of the Church. Thousands of our soldiers are men of prayer."

"In conclusion, we ask for ourselves, our churches, our country, the devout prayers of all God's people—the will of the Lord be done."

After four years of war, the South was finally overwhelmed by superior numbers and resources. The South suffered tremendously during the war. One-fourth of Southern adult white males were killed or died of disease. Widows and orphans were often left in dire circumstances. Tens of thousands of Confederate veterans were left with disabling wounds or injuries. Forty percent of private property had been destroyed, including crops, livestock, and farms. Its public and transportation infrastructure was severely damaged and interrupted. Poverty, starvation, and disease threatened almost every family. The South was then subjected to twelve years of political tyranny and economic exploitation.

Yet there is another perspective. In the midst of catastrophic suffering, the South received one of the most phenomenal spiritual blessings in history. It was called "The Great Revival in the Southern Armies." A great Christian revival swept through the Southern armies, beginning in the Army of Northern Virginia in the summer of 1861 and spreading to almost every Confederate regiment by the end of the war. According to Rev. W.W. Bennett (*The Great Revival in the Southern Armies*, 1877), there had been 150,000 new conversions in the Confederate Army by January 1865. Some chaplains estimated that over 25 percent of the men in the Confederate Armies were converted during the war. Nearly 20,000 conversions occurred in the Army of Tennessee while it was at Dalton, Georgia, in 1863-4. These added to the ranks of the many devout Christians who brought their faith to the army. Bennett estimated that fully one-third of all Confederate soldiers in the field were "praying church-members" at the end of the war. Some estimates run higher. An estimated one million men in all served some time in the Confederate armies. The aftereffects of this great revival continued for many decades, aided in consequence of so many Confederate soldiers entering the ministry after the war. Indeed, the widespread Christian influences that characterize the Southern people today owe much to the great army revival of 1861-5.

Although first manifested in the camps of the Army of Northern Virginia in the summer of 1861, the Great Revival in the Southern Armies really began with prayer in the home churches. As companies and regiments formed in local communities, there was great patriotic fervor. Local churches prayed for the cause of Southern Independence — which they almost universally believed was righteous and just — and for success in battle against their enemies. But the most passionate focus of prayer in these churches and the small prayer groups and homes that made up their Christian communities was for the safety and spiritual welfare of the men and boys, many of whom were close relatives and friends, now marching off to face the hazards, deprivations, and temptations of war.

At the beginning of the war, despite the essentially religious nature of the Southern people, many of the army camps were becoming virtual schools of vice. According to Bennett, they were filled with profanity, intemperate drinking, lewdness, gambling, irreverence, malice, greed, envy, pride, self-seeking ambition, favoritism, and brutality. To both the physical dangers of war and the moral dangers of such camps, the home churches and families reacted with a mighty outpouring of prayer and fervent campaigns of evangelism in what had become a critical home mission field affecting almost every family. They sent more chaplains, evangelists, missionaries, Bibles, New Testaments, letters, tracts, religious books and literature, and Christian periodicals into the field.

Millions of pages of evangelistic literature were delivered to the camps by "colporteurs," supported in the field by meager salaries from churches and evangelistic societies. Perhaps the most widely read and effective tract was one entitled, "A Mother's Parting Words to Her Soldier Boy." Written by Dr. J. B. Jeter of Richmond, it appealed for spiritual and moral faithfulness and a high sense of duty and honor. Others most remembered were "Prepare for Battle," "I am a Soldier," and, "Why Do You Swear." These colporteurs became very effective evangelists. They regularly visited the camps, distributing new supplies of tracts, testaments, and literature, and stayed with the soldiers for long periods, befriending them and sharing their hardships and concerns. They prayed with the men both individually and in small prayer groups that became an integral part of camp life. Churches nearby the camps often took on considerable responsibility for the spiritual welfare of soldiers away from home.

The Army chaplains concentrated on basic Christian evangelism, doctrines, and teachings. Denominationally distinctive sermons, politics, and social agendas were generally minimized or avoided. A shortage of chaplains was frequently met from the ranks with soldiers ranking from private to colonel stepping in to meet the need for spiritual leadership in companies and regiments. Many regiments formed Christian Associations whose membership was non-denominational but whose leaders encouraged church membership. These often reported conversions, baptisms, and new church memberships that included a mix of Baptists, Methodists, Presbyterians, Episcopalians, and other denominations. These Christian Associations not only preached and taught the Gospel but also held their members accountable for moral discipline.

There were many Roman Catholic as well as Protestant chaplains. In fact, although Jefferson Davis was a devout Episcopalian, he was the first American President to have Catholic and Jewish as well as Protestant members in his cabinet. One Tennessee regiment elected a black Confederate soldier as their chaplain.

As the war progressed, the spiritual and moral environment of most camps changed dramatically. They became schools of prayer and Christian fellowship rather than vice. It was not unusual in the camps to have several nightly prayer meetings per week. Some regiments had them every

Robert E. Lee

night. Soldiers returning to their regiments after long recovery periods from sickness or wounds were often astonished at the changes in language, conduct, and spiritual environment.

At services by chaplains, evangelists, and missionaries—in prayer groups and sometimes spontaneously—soldiers lifted their voices to God in hymns of praise. "How Firm a Foundation" was a favorite and General Lee's personal favorite. "There is a Fountain Filled with Blood" was often heard and was the personal favorite of Stonewall Jackson.

In addition, local churches, colporteurs, missionaries, and evangelists found the hospitals serving wounded soldiers to be a ripe mission field. Many soldiers were ministered to in the last hours and minutes of their lives. Many private homes also took in wounded soldiers and ministered the Gospel as well as comfort and medical care.

Southern women were remarkable in their persevering support for the Southern cause and in their ministry to Confederate soldiers. They supplied socks, gloves, scarves, many other clothing items, and food to the troops. Passing troop trains were met by scores of women with delicious food, refreshments, encouragement, testaments, tracts, and religious books and literature. They were among the most remarkably effective evangelists as they nursed and ministered to sick, wounded, and often dying soldiers.

One important reason for the tremendous success of evangelism in the Southern armies was the strong support of both the South's political and military leadership. For example, in late March of 1864, President Davis and the two houses of the Confederate Congress called for a day of fasting, humiliation, and prayer on April 8. General Robert E. Lee responded with General Order 21, dated March 30, 1864. In that order he *invited* (rather than commanded) the Army to join in observing the day. But he pleaded with great passion for their participation:

"Soldiers, let us humble ourselves before the Lord our God, asking through Christ the forgiveness of our sins, beseeching the aid of the God of our forefathers in the defense of our homes and our liberties, thanking him for his past blessings and imploring their continuance upon our cause and our people."

The South was blessed with an unusual number of prominent Christian generals and officers, but the most revered by the Southern people was Lee. At a Memorial meeting in Richmond on November 3 following Lee's death on October 17, 1870, Jefferson Davis addressed what was probably the largest gathering of Confederate Generals and officers since the end of the war. In the course of his speech, he gave this fitting praise of Lee:

Gen. Stonewall Jackson

"This good citizen, this gallant soldier, this great general, this true patriot, had yet a higher praise than this or these: he was a true Christian."

A few of the more prominent Christian generals serving the Confederate cause were Stonewall Jackson, Jeb Stuart, John B. Gordon, Patrick Cleburne, W. N. Pendleton, D. H. Hill, T. R. Cobb, Kirby Smith, Braxton Bragg, M. P. Lowrey, and Leonidas Polk. In addition, a number of prominent Confederate generals were converted during the war: Ewell, Pender, Hood, R. H. Anderson, Rodes, Paxton, and Baylor. Confederate cavalry leader, Nathan B. Forrest, encouraged the spiritual feeding of his troops and confirmed the Christianity he practiced after the war.

In addition, the South was blessed with an unusual number of gifted pastors, theologians, and chaplains: Robert L. Dabney, James H. Thornwell, Daniel Baker, Benjamin Morgan Palmer, John L. Giradeau, J. William Jones, William W. Bennett, J. A. Broadus, Moses D. Hoge, Joseph C. Stiles, A. E. Dickinson, J. L. Burrows, Abram Joseph Ryan, Beverly T. Lacy, E. M. Bounds, and hundreds of others.

During the course of the war, Confederate conversions occurred at an increasing pace. These conversions were generally accompanied by persevering faith and altered life styles that had an enormous impact on Southern society and culture far beyond the years of War and Reconstruction. Many soldiers were converted by the sermons of chaplains, evangelists, and missionaries. Others were converted by letters from home, or the tracts, Bibles, testaments, and literature of colporteurs, but far more were the result of individual or small group interactions over time. These occurred in camp, on the battlefield, and in the hospitals, typically only one or two at a time as the result of individual or small group relationships.

There were many different paths to effective evangelism, but the most effective evangelism, supported by many tiers of prayer and sacrificial effort, was soldier to soldier. Yet in the end, it was an astonishing work of God's sovereign grace accomplished by the Holy Spirit and little understood by modern secular historians.

Though little remembered or acknowledged today—probably because it conflicts with the politicized myth that the "Civil War" was fought by a righteous Union to end slavery in the South—the Great Revival in the Southern Armies, with its staggering numbers and far more enduring impact, may rank as a spiritual milestone of more sweeping significance than the First (1730-1750) and the Second (1790-1850) Great Awakenings.

Did such a revival occur in the Grand Army of the Republic, too? Religious revival was not confined to the Confederate Armies, but in the North it fell on generally less fertile soil. It was more evident in the western half of the Union but was of a lesser scale and more confined to the lower ranks. Neither did it have the political and high-ranking military support it had in the South. The South was generally more faithful and attuned to the cardinal doctrines of Christianity, while many Northern churches were being influenced by Unitarianism, universalism, and Biblical skepticism. There are fewer records of religious revival in the Union Army.

Yet many instances and examples of Christian faith and commitment in the North can be seen in the actions of individuals and churches. For example, Christian individuals and churches in Chicago were active in trying to relieve the suffering of Confederate prisoners of war at Camp Douglas. Their efforts, however, were eventually prohibited by Federal authorities in Washington. The records of the U.S. Sanitary Commission contain numerous instances of compassionate Christian commitment and actions. Even in the very un-Christian burning of Columbia, South Carolina, by Sherman's troops, individual Union soldiers stepped forth to protect Southern homes, women, and children. Union General George B. McClellan, for awhile the highest ranking field commander in the Union Army, became a committed Christian about the time he married, but his insistence on conducting the war according to Just War Doctrine and his preference for a negotiated peace were not embraced by Lincoln or Secretary of War Edwin Stanton. This may be the real underlying reason for his disfavor with Lincoln and Stanton. The hero of Little Round Top, Joshua Lawrence Chamberlain, was also an unwavering Christian, and it showed in his every action. There were others, such as Major General Don Carlos Buell, whose conduct strongly suggested an underlying Christian commitment. These officers, however, were a brave minority who risked the displeasure of Lincoln and Stanton.

The Great Revival in the Southern Armies left a strong Christian legacy to the Southern people. That legacy has been eroded by modern secularism, but it still exists and forms an important Southern cultural distinctive that spills over into its politics and almost every aspect of Southern society, both black and white. The South, Southern history, and leaders like Jefferson Davis, Robert E. Lee, Stonewall Jackson, and John B. Gordon cannot be understood outside the framework of their Christian worldview.

For more information and detail on the Great Revival in the Southern Armies, I strongly recommend two astonishing histories: W.W. Bennett, *The Great Revival in the Southern Armies* (1877) and J. William Jones, *Christ in the Camp* (1887). Both are being re-published by Sprinkle Publications in Harrisonburg, Virginia. These volumes contain many touching and encouraging anecdotes of Southern Christianity in the camps, on the battlefields, in the hospitals, at the gravesides, and on the home front of what Ludwell H. Johnson has called "The American Iliad."

Generally, their defeat did not embitter Southerners against God. They understood that though God's providence is often inscrutable, it always works for the good of his people. Stonewall Jackson's favorite verse was Romans 8:28:

"And we know that for those who love God all things work together for good, for those who are called according to his purpose."

In May 1865, while a prisoner in chains, former Confederate President Davis reminded them that:

"The principle for which we contended is bound to reassert itself, though it may be at another time and in another form."

In a December 1868 article, "The Duty of the Hour," Rev. Robert L Dabney counseled the Southern people that:

"It is only the atheist who adopts success as a criterion of right. It is not a new thing in the history of men that God appoints to the brave and true the stern task of contending, and falling, in a righteous quarrel."

On the death of Jefferson Davis, December 11, 1889, his former pastor in Richmond during the war, Dr. Charles Minnigerode, gave this tribute to him, which seems an appropriate end to this treatise:

"He loved the truth; he served God and country. Let us go and do likewise."

APPENDIX CHAPTER 1

⋘⋙

Just War Doctrine

The nineteenth century concept of Just War was derived principally from Biblical roots, but both Greek and Roman thought and especially Roman experience undoubtedly influenced Augustine (354-430 AD) in what is generally recognized as the first systematic treatment of Christian doctrine as it applies to the State, its citizens, and its soldiers in time of war. First of all, Augustine recognized that war is often a necessity to defend the State and its citizens from aggressive enemies and that Christians may justly bear arms in that defense. Categorical pacifism is unrealistic, unloving, and unbiblical.

Augustine outlined three main criteria for a just war: it must be initiated by properly constituted authority (Congress, in the case of the United States), it must be for a just cause, and it must be conducted by just means. To Augustine, the just end to war should be a just peace. Who then determines what is proper authority, just cause, and just means? Augustine's answer: God, as revealed in Scripture. Practically, those who constitute proper authority decide these issues on behalf of the citizenry, but these authorities are also ultimately accountable to God and therefore the teachings of Scripture. Thomas Aquinas and many others since have attempted to flesh out a more comprehensive Just War Theory, but the tragedy of war always generates many ethical loose ends.

Most Frequently Listed Principles of a Just War:

- Just Cause—Generally defensive or correcting a grave wrong.
- Initiated by Properly Constituted Authority (Congress in the case of the U.S.).
- Just Means and Conduct—A distinction must be made between combatants and non-combatants. Senseless cruelty and wanton destruction are prohibited.
- Goal must be a just peace. (Therefore allied nations should not be abandoned to slaughter or brutal tyranny.)
- Proper Jurisdiction—Evils corrected must be within legitimate sovereignty.
- Last Reasonable Resort—Reasonable exhaustion of attempts to settle differences peacefully.

Most Frequently Listed Principles for "Conducting" a Just War:

- Non-combatants should never be deliberate or primary targets of military action.
- Prisoners of war must be treated humanely and respectfully.
- Torture of prisoners of war or non-combatants is prohibited.
- Force used must not be disproportionate to objectives, harm done, or threats.
- Avoidance of senseless cruelty and all evil means (even for a just cause).
- As much as possible, the enemy must be treated in good faith to keep open the possibility of reconciliation.
- In achieving a just peace, allied nations must not be abandoned to slaughter or brutal tyranny.

The Geneva Conventions of 1863, 1906, 1929, and 1949 evolved substantially from Just War Theory. The United States was not a signer of the 1863 Geneva Convention.

APPENDIX CHAPTER 2

ᘓ৪৹

The Un-Civil War in Missouri

*William Quantrill
Missouri Partisan leader*

Following the Kansas-Nebraska Act of 1854—which allowed Kansas to allow or reject the institution of slavery by popular sovereignty—a destructive and sometimes bloody border war between Kansas and Missouri partisans raged for six years. The grizzly Manson-style murder of five settlers from Missouri in Pottawatomie, Kansas, in 1856, by the radical abolitionist, John Brown, helped fuel a growing flame of regional distrust. Brown was later hanged in 1859 after an unsuccessful attempt to capture the U.S. arsenal in Harpers Ferry, West Virginia. He had planned to start a bloody slave insurrection. The fact that Brown was praised in many of the pulpits and hustings of New England greatly alarmed the South and added more fuel to the already smoldering issues of states rights and unfair tariffs.

In 1860, about 80 percent of Missouri's population was made up of first or second generation immigrants from other Southern and Border States. Except for St. Louis, a city of 160,000, where new German immigrants made up a considerable portion of the population, Missouri was solidly conservative and Democrat in its political leanings. Lincoln ran fourth in the 1860 presidential election, capturing only 10 percent of the vote.

In those days Democrat and conservative were practically synonyms, and the new Republican Party favored big government, high tariffs (disproportionately paid by the South), and subsidies to railroads and large manufacturing companies. The Democrats favored strict constitutionalism and limited government, while the Republicans felt the Constitution limited industrial growth and the prospects for national greatness. The Republicans wanted to confine slavery to the Southern and Border States and preserve new states for free white labor. More importantly, they wanted to preserve and increase their political power by Republican dominance in new states. The Republicans wanted Kansas to be a western extension of New England, and immigration from Democrat-leaning and pro-slavery Missouri threatened that ambition.

Only about 13 percent of Missouri households owned slaves. Thus the percentage of households owning slaves was only about half that of the South as a whole, and the number of slaves per household was much lower than in South Carolina and the Gulf States.

For most Republicans of that era, slavery was primarily an issue crucial to free white labor and Northern political dominance rather than any moral reservations about the institution. Actually, most Northerners and Southerners favored the gradual emancipation of slaves, giving the economy, freed slaves, and slave owners time to adjust to a new labor paradigm. It was only the radical abolitionists who favored immediate emancipation regardless of its impact on the Southern economy or the immediate welfare of the slaves themselves. Like John Brown, many of the more radical abolitionists favored violent means to achieve their ends.

Despite their sympathies with the South, the delegates to Missouri's convention to consider the secession question held on February 28, 1861, voted overwhelmingly against it. The results were the same in Kentucky, North Carolina, Tennessee, Arkansas, and Virginia. But on April 15, following South Carolina's capture of Fort Sumter in Charleston harbor, Lincoln called for troops from each state to put down Southern secession. Such military coercion of their fellow states by the federal government was repugnant to Southern thinking. Missouri's Governor Claiborne Jackson immediately and harshly rejected Lincoln's request:

"Your requisition, in my judgment, is illegal, unconstitutional, and revolutionary in its object, inhuman and diabolical, and cannot be complied with. Not one man will the State of Missouri furnish to carry out any such unholy crusade."

The Governor of Kentucky sent a similar wire to Lincoln:

"I say emphatically Kentucky will furnish no troops for the wicked purpose of subduing her sister Southern states."

Lincoln immediately moved Federal troops into Kentucky, Missouri, and Maryland to make sure they had no opportunity to secede. But Virginia, North Carolina, Arkansas, and Tennessee quickly moved to secede by now overwhelming votes.

St. Louis County was one of only two in Missouri that cast a majority of votes for Lincoln in 1860, largely due to the large number of recent German immigrants. But even there the Republican Mayor had been swept out of office on April 1, and Lincoln's effective declaration of war against the Confederacy was unpopular.

The local U.S. Army garrison in St. Louis had not yet been reinforced, but its commander, Connecticut-born Captain Nathaniel Lyon acted immediately to prevent secessionists from seizing weapons at the Federal arsenal there. He quickly augmented his small force to over 6,000 with German Unionist volunteers and on May 10 marched on Fort Jackson, where 689 members of the Missouri militia had gathered for annual training. The militia units commanded by Brigadier General Daniel Frost were themselves flying the U.S. flag and were uncertain as to the issue that had brought Lyon's advance on them. Outnumbered more than eight to one, they had no choice but to surrender their arms as demanded. Lyon then marched his dejected and bewildered prisoners through the streets of St. Louis led by a band playing "The Star-Spangled Banner."

Gathering along the sides of the streets, outraged citizens booed the Germans and began throwing rocks. Some of the Germans fired warning shots over their heads, but perhaps in confusion, others lowered their rifles and began to fire into the crowd. It was later claimed that some in the crowd returned pistol fire. When the firing finally ceased, 28 civilians lay dead. Included were two women and four children. In addition, three of the prisoners and two soldiers, probably accidental victims of friendly fire, were dead. At least 75 others were wounded.

Lyon recruited and armed another German regiment the next day, and there was more bloodshed. Lyon reported that ten civilians and two of his soldiers were killed. Over the next few days 10,000 people fled the Federal violence in St. Louis. Uriel Wright, who had voted against secession as a Convention delegate, articulated his new thinking:

"If Unionism means such atrocious deeds as I have witnessed in St. Louis, I am no longer a Union man."

One week after the St. Louis massacre, Lincoln issued orders promoting Lyon to brigadier general. This was one of the first of many forthcoming indications that Lincoln favored and would generously reward aggressive suppression of any secessionist sympathies. Any suspicion of resistance to the Lincoln government would be met with harsh measures.

Lyon next marched his troops on the capitol at Jefferson City. Governor Jackson and other elected officials were forced to flee. The Union military quickly occupied the rest of the state, and a Lincoln approved regime was installed in office. The people of Missouri were now at the mercy of Federal occupation forces and the Union regiments recruited by them.

The Union occupiers laid on all manner of decrees and fines persecuting any family suspected of Southern sympathies. These included double taxation and property confiscation with little opportunity to appeal. Every able bodied man was commanded to enroll in loyal Union militia. Federal Order 19 forbade any citizen of Missouri not a member of loyal militia to own a gun for any reason. Loyalty oaths often had to be accompanied by huge performance bonds. All freedom of the press and speech not loyal to the Union cause meant arrest and jail without due process. Twenty-two newspapers were shut down. Extortion, corruption, and arbitrary and vengeful justice were common. Missouri men commissioned in the Confederate Army were declared outlaws subject to immediate execution. The wives and daughters of many Confederate partisans were jailed for aiding and abetting the rebellion. Nevertheless, fewer than 4,000 Confederate guerilas in Missouri were tying up nearly 60,000 Union troops badly needed elsewhere.

In November 1861, the Seventh Kansas Cavalry (nicknamed "Jayhawkers") under the command of Union Col. Charles Dennison raided the town of Independence, Missouri and removed everything of value in wagons to their headquarters in Lawrence, Kansas. In January 1862, Jayhawker Cavalry burned 87 buildings and 170 homes and murdered nine local residents in Dayton, Cass, and Johnson counties. That summer wanton destruction and murder of civilians and Missouri partisan prisoners became commonplace. Union Brigadier General James H. Lane, also a radical abolitionist Republican U.S. Senator from Kansas, stated:

"We believe in a war of extermination. I want to see every foot of ground in Jackson, Cass, and Bates counties burned over—everything laid waste."

In 1862, three mass executions of a total of 36 civilian hostages and prisoners of war occurred in Missouri. The most famous of these was the Palmyra Massacre on October 18, 1862 in which ten civilian and partisan hostages were executed by firing squad in retaliation for the disappearance of a single Union informer. Despite some public outrage, six weeks later Lincoln promoted the Union officer in charge, Col. John McNeil, to brigadier general.

By August 1863, the second floor of the three-story Thomas building on Grand Avenue in Kansas City had become a Federal prison for women accused of Confederate sympathies. Most of the 27 women there were jailed for aiding their Missouri partisan relatives. None of the girls were over the age of 20. On August 13, the building suddenly collapsed killing or fatally wounding five women. Many others were badly injured. Three of the girls were Josephine, Mary, and Martha Anderson, sisters of Missouri partisan leader, Bill Anderson. Josephine was killed and thirteen-year-old Martha had her back and both legs broken and her face disfigured by lacerations. Also killed were twin sisters Susan Vandiver and Armenia Gilvey who had a brother serving with Missouri partisan leader William C. Quantrill. They were also cousins of partisans Cole and James Younger who were serving with Quantrill.

A rumor quickly spread that Brigadier General Thomas Ewing had ordered the building undermined. The Federals immediately shifted the blame by claiming that the girls had undermined the building themselves by digging a tunnel—an extraordinary feat from the second floor! The real cause was later found to be gross negligence. When news of the tragedy reached Quantrill's men in the field, they became wild with rage.

When the three-story Thomas building in Kansas City collapsed on August 13, 1863, eleven Southern girls between the age of 13 and 20 were

being held on the second story, which was being used as a Union deten-
tion center for women. As many as 27 women had been held there in early
August, but fortunately many had been removed. According to what I believe to be the best records, five of the girls were killed or died of injuries
shortly thereafter. Five others were seriously injured, and only one was
unscathed.

The cause of the Thomas building collapse is known, but the intention of the Union soldiers involved is not. The Thomas building was attached by a joint wall and common floor joists to the Cockrell building.
The first floors of both buildings were supported by outer foundation walls
and internal wooden pillars in the basements. The Cockrell building was
used as a guardhouse. The first floor of the Thomas building was occupied
by Jewish grocers. The second floor housed the women's prison, and the
third floor was vacant. For reasons unclear, Union soldiers began removing several of the internal pillars that supported girders running the entire
length of both buildings in order to make a passage through a foundation
wall from the Cockrell building to the Thomas building. Some say they
were planning a large barracks area. Others say that prostitutes were sometimes held in the basement of the Thomas building, and the guards wanted
easy access to them. Why they would remove the supporting pillars in the
latter case seems a mystery.

Several days before the collapse of the Thomas building onto the
guardhouse, the merchants on the first floor noticed that the building
seemed to be sinking and that large cracks were appearing along the walls
and ceilings. Consequently, they moved out.

The girls on the second floor also noticed that large and sometimes
groaning cracks were forming on the walls and ceiling. In expressing their
fear to the guards, they were only taunted and teased that they were going
to be killed. The landlady of a boarding house where many of the soldiers
stayed heard them talking about their work and was so alarmed that she
visited the Union headquarters and demanded that the girls be removed.
The provost marshal, the captain of the guards, and a military surgeon all
notified Union Brigadier General Thomas Ewing that the Thomas building was unsafe. In fact, an inspector had previously reported it was unsafe.
Ewing, however, sent his adjutant, Major Harrison Hannah, to investigate,
but he assured Ewing that the building was safe. Ewing then sent a second

inspector who also assured him that the building was safe. Meanwhile, even the guards evacuated both buildings.

The rest of the story we have already told. On the morning of August 13, 1863, the Thomas building came crashing down on the guardhouse resulting in the death or fatal injury of five young girls between the ages of 13 and 20. General Ewing never investigated the cause of the collapse or disciplined any of the men involved. It was only because Union General George C. Bingham owned the building and sued for damages that we know so much about the structural cause of the collapse. We do not know whether the Union soldiers who undermined the building did so foolishly or malignantly. At the time, Quantrill's men and most of western Missouri thought it was intentional. But in any case, there was gross negligence on the part of General Ewing and several of his subordinates.

Bill Anderson lost his fourteen-year old sister, Josephine, as an immediate result of the collapse, and his thirteen-year old sister, Martha, had sustained severe injuries. In March 1862, Anderson's father and uncle had been hanged by raiders belonging to the Eighth Kansas Jayhawker Cavalry. All of the dead girls had relatives serving in Quantrill's Rangers, and two were also cousins of Cole and Jim Younger. The Younger brothers' father had been murdered by Missouri Union militia in July 1862. Both Bill Anderson and Cole Younger were key Quantrill lieutenants, and Anderson would later earn the sobriquet "Bloody Bill."

Besides the collapse of the Thomas building and the death of five Southern girls, approximately 221 Missouri men had been murdered and over 200 homes had been burned by Kansas Jayhawkers, Missouri Union militia, and "Redlegs" in the summer of 1863. The "Redlegs" were a particularly vicious company of Kansas guerillas organized by Kansas Republican Senator Jim Lane and led by George Hoyt. They were so named because of the knee-high dyed leather or sheepskin leggings they wore. Their number included the afterwards famous "Wild Bill" Hickock, Kit Carson, and William "Buffalo Bill" Cody. According to Mary Ethel Noland, a first cousin of President Harry S. Truman, the Kansas Redlegs were not proper soldiers but a band of desperados who sometimes "would come over and they would shoot a harmless old man because he was a Southern sympathizer, or sometimes they would even hang one; and sometimes they would shoot a young boy who was almost too young to bear arms..."

Frank and Jesse James were also serving under Quantrill in August 1863. In May 1862, the James Brothers' stepfather, Dr. Reuben Samuel, had been tortured by Union soldiers seeking the whereabouts of Confederate Frank James. They beat up fifteen-year old Jesse and then attempted to force information from Dr. Samuel by hanging him to a tree and strangling him. (This type of torture by strangulation was frequently used by Union soldiers to discover the location of money and valuables during Sherman's March through Georgia and South Carolina in 1864-65.) If Dr. Samuel knew of Frank's whereabouts, he did not tell them. He survived the torture, but may have sustained some brain damage.

Quantrill's men had favored a raid on Lawrence, Kansas, ever since Kansas Jayhawkers destroyed Osceola, Missouri, in 1861, killing nine men by execution and leaving only a few buildings standing. Lawrence was the seat of radical abolitionism in Kansas and the home of Jim Lane and other leading Jayhawkers. It was also headquarters for the hated Redlegs. Most of the goods stolen or confiscated by Jayhawkers and Redlegs were auctioned off to Kansas abolitionists in Lawrence. It was especially around Lawrence that land cleared by Missouri settlers had been claim-jumped by New England settlers, thus launching a string of grievances, terrorism, and retaliations that flamed into the Kansas-Missouri Border War five years before the Union and Confederate confrontation at Fort Sumter in 1861.

As the guerilla war against Union occupation of Missouri was met with more and harsher measures against the civilian population, Quantrill's men had become increasingly bitter about the barbarity shown to Southern women and children. The death of these young women in the hands of Union soldiers was a strong catalyst to reap vengeance on Lawrence.

Col. William Quantrill, however, was a brilliant and careful planner. One of his lieutenants described him as "the smartest man he'd ever met." He and a small cadre of his lieutenants had been planning a Lawrence raid for months. But still, he did not intend to ride into Lawrence until his plans and intelligence gathering were complete. He also wanted to wait until he could catch Jim Lane there. Quantrill knew that he must get his expedition of 400 men through a series of Union outposts without being detected and then get them back to Missouri safely. Lawrence was a town of 1,200 people, and every able-bodied man was a member of the militia. At least a company of regular Union troops would also be there. In addition, Jayhawker Cavalry units were stationed nearby and individuals and small detachments of Jayhawkers and Redlegs would be in and out of town. He knew his Partisan Rangers and a small detachment of Confederate regulars must rally undetected, travel undetected at night, and arrive before dawn to execute a swift surprise attack against potentially superior forces. As it turned out, there would be about 500 Union fighting men in Lawrence, making surprise and near flawless execution absolutely essential.

Quantrill relied on two of his most trusted men for the reconnaissance of Lawrence. The first out was, surprisingly, a black man, John T. Noland. Noland has been described as a "brave and resourceful fellow," especially loyal to Quantrill and the Missouri Partisans. The second was Fletcher Taylor. Taylor was sent out only when Quantrill feared that Noland had been captured or killed. They both arrived back about the same time and brought details of all the buildings, their uses, and their occupants. A death list was prepared of all the Redlegs, radical abolitionists, Jayhawker leaders, and identified war criminals that might be in Lawrence. A detailed, step by step plan, to accomplish their mission was thus set in motion. Some notorious war criminals were to be killed in route to Lawrence.

William Quantrill's appearance and demeanor completely contradicted the monster psychopath portrayed in the abolitionist press in Lawrence and New England. Only a few years before, he had been a respected school teacher. Only twenty-six years old, he was slightly above average height and slender in build, with a kind and handsome face and calm blue eyes that suggested a noble spirit. Home-schooled by loving and well educated parents in Ohio, he graduated from Union College when he was only sixteen. Like his father, he was extraordinarily gifted at math and a lightening-calculator. He had a studious love of books, but he could ride and shoot as well as any man in Missouri. He was morally high-minded and consistently fair and courteous. He was respected and trusted by his men and loved by the people of western Missouri, who considered him their protector. Yet he was a terror to Kansas Jayhawkers and Redlegs.

PAY BACK

On August 18, 1863, only a few days following the collapse of the Thomas building in Kansas City that had resulted in the death of five

young Southern girls, William Quantrill began to assemble his Missouri
Partisan Rangers near Oak Grove, Missouri, where there was plenty of
water, and the terrain and heavy woodlands facilitated concealment of a
large number of horses and men. He waited impatiently there for the return of John Noland and Fletcher Taylor. One of the secrets of Quantrill's
remarkable success in guerilla warfare was accurate and timely intelligence, and he made extensive use of spies and scouts. During any military
operation he was continually calculating the odds for success and rapid
escape. Objectives, routes, communications, and means of concealment
were planned and timed in detail. A raid on Lawrence—the very capital of
Kansas Jayhawkers, Redlegs, and radical abolitionists—would be extraordinarily daring and hazardous. As always, he would carefully orchestrate
as many details as possible to reduce his risks and enhance his probability
of success.

Posing as a land speculator, Fletcher Taylor lodged at the Free State
Hotel in Lawrence. Through lavish spending, generous hospitality, and
friendly conversation he uncovered a wealth of important information.
Noland, being black and supplied with a large amount of bribery money,
easily loosened the tongues of former Missouri slaves living in Lawrence.
He was also an astute observer in all matters of military, financial, political,
and personal associations in his intelligence gathering. Returning from his
reconnaissance mission, Noland was stopped by Union soldiers but somehow allayed their suspicions, even though he was carrying a large sum of
money. After hearing from these two trusted intelligence men, Quantrill
finalized his plans and called a meeting with his captains.

On the same day, Union Generals Schofield and Ewing issued General Order Number 10 to remove all Southern sympathizers and their families from four counties in West Central Missouri.

Once Quantrill's captains were assembled around his campfire, he
outlined the plan of attack on Lawrence. These ten captains, who usually
rode with about 30 men each, were Bill Anderson, Andy Blunt, Ben Estes,
William Gregg, John Jarrette, Oliver Shepherd, George Todd, Harrison
Trow, Dick Yeager, and Cole Younger. Many of these men would gain
fame as guerilla warriors, and some would gain fame as outlaws after the
war.

Contrary to the portrait of Quantrill painted by many Northern authors, he was by no means an autocrat. His discussion with his captains

drew on their knowledge and opinions and took place over a 24 hour period. At last he gathered them again, and Noland and Taylor gave full reports and answered questions. Then Quantrill explained his plan once more and spoke to them about the risks, which he considered to be very high.

"I do not know if anyone of us will get back to tell the story," he stated frankly.

One by one — starting with Bill Anderson, who had just lost a sister in the Thomas building collapse — he asked for their vote. Many of them had had homes and farms burned and close relatives murdered by Jayhawkers and Redlegs. Each man answered in the affirmative, briefly recounting the sufferings of his own family.

"Where my house once stood there is a heap of ruins. I haven't a neighbor that's got a house. Lawrence and the torch," was Dick Yeager's answer.

Finally all agreed, including Col. John D. Holt, who had just arrived with a small contingent of regular Confederate cavalry.

Quantrill was still determined, however, to execute vengeance without harming women and children. He emphasized that every man in a Federal uniform should be killed but no harm should come to a woman or child.

With his officers unanimously behind him, Quantrill then addressed the men, pointing out the extreme hazards of the mission and warning that many could be lost. According to William Gregg, he added:

"Hence, I say to one and all, if any refuse to go, they will not be censured."

Quantrill then ordered an inspection to make sure every man had adequate weapons, supplies, and ammunition. But the most important requirement was a fast and well trained cavalry horse. On this raid, each man would lead an extra horse. Most riders carried a carbine with them, but pistols were to be their main weapons, and each man carried several, some as many as six.

As they began their march on August 19, Quantrill's Missouri Partisans plus a small force of Confederate cavalry totaled about 250 men. That night they rode through blackened fields and past many burned homes, the work of Jayhawker Cavalry. By prearrangement, another 50 Partisans from Cass County joined them on the morning of August 20. In addition, Confederate Col. Holt had managed to enlist 100 new recruits in Clay County. These new recruits increased the total force to about 400. The new recruits would be used for less exacting responsibilities during the entry into Lawrence, leaving the most crucial objectives to the most experienced men.

When they reached the Kansas border about noon, they were about 45 miles from Lawrence. Most of Quantrill's men then donned Federal blouses. Underneath they wore their specially decorated brown or red Partisan shirts, which would be needed to distinguish friend from foe in combat. Units with Federal blouses were put at the front of the column and carried U.S. flags. After a brief rest, they headed southwest with Gregg and his men acting as vanguard about a quarter mile in front of the column. Todd's men made up the rear guard. On the flanks were scouts and vedettes. These units communicated to Quantrill every few minutes.

At 7 p.m. a unit of the Ninth Kansas Jayhawkers spotted an unidentified column, believed to be moving northwest. But they reported it to Kansas City rather than alerting Union forces farther west. General Ewing, who was spending the night in Fort Leavenworth, would not receive the message until late morning the next day, at which time he belatedly gathered 300 men and headed for Lawrence.

Several hours later that night a farmer also spotted the column and noted that many riders had tied themselves to their saddles in case they fell asleep. The column encountered a few Union soldiers at Spring Hill, but these soldiers did not suspect anything. As the Partisans came nearer Lawrence, several Jayhawkers were recognized along the way and promptly killed. They came upon the home of Jayhawker Joseph Stone and shot him in the head. Quantrill detailed two men to find Sam Snyder, a Jayhawker lieutenant who had been with Jim Lane at the burning of Osceola and was responsible for looting several churches in Missouri. They found Snyder milking his cow and shot him.

Near dawn they reached the outskirts of Lawrence, and Quantrill turned to his men and said:

"Boys, this is the home of Jim Lane and Jennison; remember that in hunting us they gave no quarter. Shoot every soldier you see, but in no way harm a woman or child...Molest no women or children. Kill every man in Federal uniform."

Quantrill then removed his Federal blouse and threw it to the ground. The rest of his men did the same. They would now be recognized by their unmistakable Partisan Ranger shirts. Turning his horse toward Lawrence, Quantrill drew his pistols, gave a Rebel Yell, and galloped to the head of the column.

The vanguard first encountered a Union company quartered in about 40 tents along the main road. They charged through the tents meeting little resistance at first, but bullets soon began to fly from every direction. Eighteen of the 21 Union recruits in the camp were killed. Other Union soldiers retreated to a store but then surrendered. They were promptly shot. The Partisans then encountered the tents of a small troop of new black recruits who immediately scattered. Most were chased down and shot. Quantrill then ordered an assault on the main part of town. They charged through the wide streets five or six abreast, yelling like demons and gunning down every blue coat that appeared. Many shouted a battle cry as they blazed away: "**Remember the girls and Osceola!**"

But when they came to the bank of the Kansas River, a hail of bullets from about 400 men of the Eleventh and Ninth Kansas Jayhawker regiments poured into them. Yet the Jayhawkers on the other side of the river did not come to the aid of their comrades. They cut the ferry rope, not only preventing the Missourians from reaching them but also their own crossing to save Lawrence.

The Mayor of Lawrence, General George Washington Collamore, had made the mistake of storing all the local militia arms in a central armory. As men in Union uniforms rushed to fetch their arms, they were shot down by Partisans. Meanwhile, Quantrill's men were searching and burning the houses of those Jayhawkers on their death list.

Next the Partisans surrounded the Free State Hotel. In this case, Quantrill allowed Captain Alexander Banks, a regular Union Army officer who was staying at the hotel, to surrender the 60 occupants and gave his word that they would not be harmed. He honored his guarantee by promising to put bullets into anyone who harmed the prisoners. They were moved to another hotel owned by an old friend of his. The Free State Hotel was then burned.

The Missourians then surrounded the Johnson House Hotel, a known hangout for Redlegs. Fourteen men were there. Realizing their imminent danger, several slipped out the windows, but a few of these were gunned down. The remaining seven asked for quarter. Quantrill reminded them that they had given no quarter to hundreds of elderly men they had killed in Missouri. Nevertheless, they were taken prisoner. Of these, one notorious Redleg, Joe Finley, was immediately recognized and shot. The other six men were interrogated and also found to be Redlegs. These were pushed into an alley and promptly executed.

LAWRENCE IN PERSPECTIVE

Following their fearsome charge through the main streets of Lawrence, Quantrill's Partisan Rangers quickly captured the armory and the major Jayhawker and Redleg hotels. The remaining Federal resistance collapsed and scattered. Squads of Missouri Partisans with maps and long death lists continued through the town door by door seeking the Jayhawkers and Redlegs who had wantonly murdered their kin, scorched their farms, and pillaged and burned their homes. They were also looking for the leading abolitionist politicians and editors who had spewed out so many venomous lies and so much burning hatred to justify the crimes and depredations visited on Missouri. In addition, their lists included the leaders of the New England Emigrant Aid Society, an organization responsible not only for bringing thousands of radical abolitionists to Kansas but also for supplying them with thousands of guns, swords, and other weapons. The Manson-style murderer and radical, John Brown, had been one of their key agents and catalysts for violence against Southern sympathizers in Kansas and Missouri.

Quantrill's last major objective was the home of Jayhawker Brigadier General and Republican U.S. Senator Jim Lane. Lane was not only the principal leader of Jayhawker cavalry but also a founding organizer of the despicable Redlegs. He had led several raids on Missouri and had commanded the 1,500 man force that destroyed the beautiful little town of Osceola in September 1861. Lane, a former Indiana Congressman, was near penniless when he had come to Kansas in 1855, but his charismatic speaking style and disregard for principle quickly gained him wealth and power. Political influence, graft, and plundering Missouri farms enabled him to own the largest, finest, and most lavishly furnished home in Lawrence.

Accompanied by scout John McCorkle and several other men, Quantrill rode to Lane's house on the west side of town. On arriving, he dismounted and boldly strode up to the front door and knocked. When Lane's wife came to the door, Quantrill politely addressed her:

"Give your husband my compliments, Madam, and tell him I should be most happy to meet him."

Mrs. Lane replied that he was not at home. But just a few minutes before, on seeing the approach of Partisan cavalry, the senator had leaped out a window in his nightshirt and hid in a cornfield. According to some sources, Quantrill planned not to kill Lane but to take him captive and hold him hostage. The Partisan leader made no search for him but ordered the house burned. Before it was torched, John McCorkle—whose sister Charity had been killed in the collapse of the Thomas building in Kansas City—looked inside and recognized three expensive pianos that had been stolen from Southern families in Jackson County, Missouri. Senator Lane escaped.

Another man Quantrill hoped to find in Lawrence was former Kansas Governor Charles Robinson, the abolitionist leader who was responsible for bringing the New England Emigrant Aid Society to Lawrence. The Robinson house, however, could not be approached because of gunfire from the Jayhawker regiments isolated on the other side of the Kansas River. Ironically, Robinson was a bitter political enemy of Lane and had published statements in the local papers complaining that Lane's method of warfare was "pouncing upon little unprotected towns and villages and portraying their capture as splendid victories."

Like Lane and Robinson, many of the highest ranking abolitionist leaders and Jayhawker and Redleg Cavalry officers escaped. But the Mayor of Lawrence, General George Washington Collamore, along with a friend, suffocated from the smoke of his burning home when they tried to hide in his well. Another man fell into the well and was killed trying to rescue them.

The Partisans found about 40 flimsy shacks near a ravine across from Massachusetts Street, which were filled to capacity with stolen goods from

Missouri. Included were expensive rugs, mahogany furniture, and several pianos valued at over $1,000 each—a small fortune in those days. The Partisans reluctantly put them to the torch.

About 9 a.m., after four hours of killing and burning, Quantrill's men gathered near the south end of town. Behind them much of downtown Lawrence was in flames, and stocks of gunpowder that had been stored for its defense began to explode. Quantrill formed his men to get an accounting of all those present or missing. He knew that any man left behind would be summarily executed. As it turned out, only one man was lost.

Summary execution of all captured Partisans had been Union policy in Missouri since late 1861 and was reemphasized by Major General Henry Halleck's General Order Number 2, the so-called "No Quarter Order" on March 13, 1862. This General Order also allowed Union commanders to take whatever action was necessary against Partisan guerillas or civilians to restore the authority of the U.S. Government.

As Quantrill's Partisan Rangers left Lawrence, their lookouts on nearby Mount Oread observed a distant blue line approaching from the east. It was General Ewing and 300 Union cavalry from Kansas City. But Quantrill and his men successfully evaded any Union opposition in withdrawing to Missouri.

In Lawrence, 148 Union men had been killed and 87 of approximately 300 buildings destroyed. No women or children were killed. Some of the men were as young as fourteen, but they had been in uniform. Several of Quantrill's raiders were also that young, and one was only twelve at the time. Despite his order to kill all men in Federal uniform, Quantrill spared nearly a score that could have been killed. Cole Younger saved at least a dozen lives. John Jarrette saved five prisoners because they were Masons. George Shepherd rescued a wounded man and two children from a burning house because one of the children had given him a rose. Andrew Blunt spared a man because his daughter offered him a cup of coffee. One Union solder was spared because he had a Southern accent. The Partisans were on a hunt primarily for political radicals and war criminals, but they killed many soldiers and local militiamen in the process, some of them ruthlessly.

Most of the people of Lawrence refused to admit that there was any guilt attached to profiting from Jayhawker and Redleg looting, burning, and killing in Missouri. Their attitude seemed to be that anyone who owned a slave or sympathized with the South deserved such rough treatment. This sort of arrogant self-righteousness was typical of many abolitionists. A notable exception was former Governor Robinson who admitted that the plundering of Western Missouri by Jim Lane had triggered an awful retribution.

Most Lawrence residents and the Eastern newspapers did everything possible to sensationalize and exaggerate Quantrill's "massacre" of Lawrence. Eastern newspapers featured front page drawings of Quantrill's men brutally killing women and children, although none were killed. Some claimed that the whole town had been burned and almost every inhabitant killed. Many claimed Quantrill's men were in a drunken frenzy; yet Quantrill always insisted that his men be keen in body and mind. According to several of his captains and journalist John Edward Newman, he had a horror of unnecessary violence. But he could be remorseless with armed or dangerous enemies and those he considered to have violated the rules of honorable warfare—especially those who abused civilians, the elderly, women, or children.

In my opinion, sensationalism was particularly prevalent in abolitionist newspapers before, during, and after the war. I would even say that irresponsible journalism was a major cause of the war.

The Lawrence raid retains a prominent but degraded place in U.S. history, while the deeds of Unionists like Senator Jim Lane have been buried to protect the myth of a righteous Union cause. But by comparison, Lane and his lieutenants inflicted far more destruction of lives and property in Missouri than did Quantrill at Lawrence.

Osceola, Missouri was a picturesque town of 3,000 before Lane's Jayhawker Cavalry sacked and burned it on September 23, 1861. All but three of 800 buildings were left in ashes. Nine civilian men were rounded up, taken to the town square, and executed. Most of the rest of the men were away in Confederate service or riding with various Missouri Partisan units. Lane's men left with 150 wagons of loot, forming a caravan more than a mile long. The plunder included 350 horses, 400 head of cattle, and 200 kidnapped slaves. The slaves were sent to work on Kansas farms for whatever food they could scrounge during their labor. Osceola's women and children were left to fend for themselves. At the end of the war only 183 people lived in Osceola.

In January 1862, the Seventh Jayhawker Cavalry under the command of Charles Jennison and his deputy, Daniel Anthony, looted and burned all 47 houses in the village of Dayton, Missouri. In the next few weeks they pillaged and burned the villages of Columbus, Pleasant Hill, West Point, Morristown, and Rose Hill. At Chapel Hill they burned 150 homes and left the women and children, many of whom were sick, standing in the snow. At Kingsville they burned 160 homes and executed nine male hostages. Prior to the Lawrence raid, hundreds of older men and young boys had been indiscriminately murdered during Jayhawker and Redleg raids on Missouri farms and villages.

The depredation of Western Missouri by Kansas Jayhawkers and Redlegs was the inspiration for the 1976 movie, *The Outlaw Josey Wales*, starring Clint Eastwood.

Four days after Quantrill's raid on Lawrence, on August 25, 1863, Union General James Ewing signed the infamous General Order Number 11—the most repressive action ever taken against civilians by the American Government.

GENERAL ORDER NUMBER 11

General Order Number 11 has been called the harshest measure ever taken by an American government against civilians. The order was signed by Union Brigadier General Thomas Ewing on August 25, 1863—four days after Quantrill's raid on Lawrence, Kansas—and called for the forced evacuation of all civilians from most of four counties in West Central Missouri within 15 days. It also required all grain and hay in the district to be turned over to the Union Army. All remaining hay, grain, and crops in the area were to be destroyed. Those who could prove their loyalty to the Union would be given receipts for their crops.

The order affected about 20,000 people in Jackson, Bates, and Cass counties and part of Vernon County. It was backed by Ewing's commander, Major General John M. Schofield, and the highest levels of the Lincoln Government as a measure to suppress civilian support for pro-Southern guerilla activity against Union troops in Missouri and Kansas. *The Kansas City Western Journal of Commerce* estimated that about nine-tenths of the people of Jackson, Cass, and Bates counties were pro-Southern and actively engaged in supplying and aiding Confederate guerillas.

General Order Number 11 would have been severe enough in it-self, but the lawless Jayhawker and Redleg Cavalry units under Senator/ Brigadier General Jim Lane in Kansas swarmed into Western Missouri to make the most of an opportunity for burning and looting homes and preying upon defenseless wagon trains to rob and murder. Many wagons of household valuables were redirected to Lawrence, leaving their former owners with nothing. There were numerous instances of Missouri men be-ing shot trying to defend their wagons and families. Quantrill's men were successful, however, in taking a heavy toll of Jayhawkers and Redlegs and scaring others off.

Many historians have wrongly concluded that General Order 11 was simply retribution for Quantrill's Missouri Partisan raid on Lawrence, but that sweeps far too much under the carpet. To uncover the full truth it is necessary to look at the escalating severity of the Union occupation of Missouri and the development of the Lincoln Administration's "Total War" policies.

As Union occupation troops poured into Missouri from Illinois, Iowa, Kansas, Indiana, and other states, Governor Claiborne Jackson and most of the Missouri Legislature were forced to flee south. On August 10, 1861, however, Union forces under Nathaniel Lyon were defeated at Wilson's Creek in southwestern Missouri by Confederate forces under Benjamin McCulloch and Sterling Price, a former Missouri Governor and hero of the Mexican War. Lyon, whom Lincoln had promoted to Briga-dier General following the St. Louis massacre, was killed. Despite their victory, McCulloch refused to support Price in attempting to retake the rest of Missouri. William Quantrill was at the time a sergeant in the Third Missouri Confederate Cavalry and was promoted to captain of a Partisan cavalry unit as a reward for his valor.

Meanwhile Union war crimes against civilians in Missouri contin-ued to increase. In Oklahoma, the misconduct of Union occupying forces in Missouri was cited in the Cherokee Declaration of Independence of August 21, 1861, as one of their reasons for declaring their independence from the United States and allying themselves with the Confederate States:

"But in the Northern States the Cherokee people saw with alarm a violated constitution, all civil liberty put in peril, and all rules of

civilized warfare and the dictates of common humanity and decency unhesitatingly disregarded..."

The Cherokee Declaration is enlightening reading for those who have been taught only the Northern version of the Un-Civil War. The Cherokees were joined by the Creeks, Choctaws, Seminoles, and Chickasaws in Oklahoma. Together they were able to raise about 7,000 cavalry and mounted infantry to frustrate and bedevil far greater numbers of Union troops in the West.

On October 31, 1861, the exiled Government of the State of Missouri, operating from Neosho, seceded from the Union, and on November 28, the Confederate Congress recognized Missouri as the twelfth Confederate State.

Confederate President Jefferson Davis was reluctant to approve of guerilla warfare, but Price persuaded him that Missouri Partisan companies were needed to defend their homes and farms against the escalating crimes of Federal troops and Unionist Missouri State Militia units against Southern sympathizers. They would also be useful for intelligence and support when Confederate forces could return in strength to Missouri. Most Confederate Missouri Militia units were renamed Missouri State Guard units and later incorporated into Missouri regiments of the Confederate Army. President Davis authorized the commission of officers who could raise at least ten men in their home counties for Missouri Partisan Ranger units. The Partisans quickly grew to 60 cavalry companies totaling about 4,000 men. They turned out to be extraordinarily successful in tying down 60,000 Union troops in Missouri.

Lincoln at first envisioned that the Southern "rebellion" would be quickly put down for lack of sufficient public support in the seceded states. This proved to be a significant miscalculation. No crowds welcomed the Union invaders. Union officers in the field soon realized that they were fighting not only the Confederate Army but a whole people. The President's champion for total warfare, General William Tecumseh Sherman, put it bluntly:

"This war differs from other wars, in this particular. We are not fighting armies but a hostile people, and must make old and young, rich and poor, feel the hard hand of war."

By late in 1861 it had become common practice for U.
execute captured Partisans. General Henry Halleck made the ⊦
ficial on March 13, 1862 with General Order Number 2, the "No
Order" branding all Partisans as outlaws subject to immediate exec.
on capture. Even Confederate recruiting officers were shot. The Partisa.
in return also "raised the black flag" of no quarter warfare on Union military units—but not civilians.

But even Halleck complained about the depredations of Jim Lane's
Kansas Jayhawkers and Redlegs on Missouri civilians. Halleck complained to General George B. McClellan, commander over all Federal
Armies, that Lane's atrocities and crimes against civilians had turned Missouri against the Union and resulted in 20,000 men joining Sterling Price
in the Confederate Army. McClellan in turn complained to Secretary of
War Edwin Stanton and ultimately to Lincoln himself, but no action was
ever taken against Lane. Lincoln and Stanton continued to favor Lane and
to advocate severe measures against anyone who supported the Confederacy or openly opposed the Lincoln Administration. Both Halleck and
McClellan were soon replaced.

In 1862, three towns in Northeastern Missouri were the sites of mass
executions of Partisan prisoners of war and in some cases partisan civilians. In August, sixteen prisoners of war were executed in Kirksville. In
September, ten men who refused to take the Union Oath of Allegiance
were executed in Macon. On October 18, Col. John McNeil ordered the
execution by firing squad of ten hostages including one older man when
a Union informer was not returned to Union hands. The Union oriented
Palmyra Courier editorialized the next day that:

"The madness of rebellion has become so deep seated that ordinary
methods of cure are inadequate."

Despite great controversy as far away as London, Lincoln promoted
McNeil to Brigadier General. In August of 1862, Lincoln had also promoted Col. Ivan (John) Turchin to Brigadier General after his troops taught the
town of Athens, Alabama, a lesson in pillaging and rape. Total war against
civilians—which included burning, pillaging, torture, and sometimes

rder and rape—had become meritorious conduct in a strategy to defeat whole people.

General Order Number 11 was not just retaliation for Lawrence. It was part of a growing "total war" against Southern civilians that culminated in Sherman's devastation of Georgia and South Carolina in 1864 and 1865. In scope, it exceeded the Cherokee "Trail of Tears" in which 17,000 Cherokees were removed from Georgia and North Carolina to Oklahoma in 1838. It was only surpassed during World War II, when 120,000 Japanese Americans were forcibly removed to internment camps.

Ironically, General Order 11 was not effective in reducing Partisan warfare against Union forces. Enough stray cattle and hogs were left in the affected counties to feed thousands of Partisans. Quantrill withdrew to Texas only when winter came.

While they were in Texas, Bill Anderson quarreled with Quantrill over disciplinary issues and split off from him. In September 1864, Sterling Price was gathering a Confederate army in a desperate plan to influence the 1864 U.S. Presidential election by capturing St. Louis and Jefferson City. Price's Confederate Missouri Guard was to be supported by Partisan Rangers. On the morning of September 27, Anderson and about 30 of his company of 80 men rode into Centralia, Missouri, to intercept a Union passenger train. After a brief resistance by some of the Union soldiers, the Partisans boarded and forced the 125 passengers off the train. Twenty-three men in Union uniforms, most on furlough from Sherman's Army, were separated from the rest. Anderson chose the highest ranking, a sergeant, for a possible prisoner exchange. Still seething with anger because six of his men had recently been scalped by a Union patrol, Anderson told the others why, despite their pleading, they would not be spared. He gave the order to "muster them out," and all 22 were shot down, but none were scalped or mutilated as Union propagandists later charged.

In the afternoon a force of about 155 men commanded by Union Major A.V.E. Johnston of the newly formed 39th Missouri Mounted Infantry Regiment arrived in pursuit of Anderson's Partisans. Despite warnings that there were hundreds of Partisans gathering in the area, they followed Anderson right into an ambush by a combined Partisan force of 225 men. Armed with new but only single shot Enfield rifles, Johnston's men dismounted and formed ranks for a volley into the Partisans just as they began their cavalry charge. The Partisans rode low in their saddles—Comanche style—and only three were hit and killed before their horses knocked down or trampled almost every Union soldier. Before the Union riflemen could recover and reload, the Partisans reversed their direction and charged into them, each horseman blasting away with two pistols. After a few more gun-blazing passes, Major Johnston and 123 of his men lay dead on the field. More than a dozen others were pursued and shot while trying to escape on horseback. None of the bodies were scalped or mutilated. According to Frank James, his brother Jesse fired the shot that killed Major Johnston.

The end of the war did not bring peace to members of the Partisan Rangers. They were still counted as outlaws. Those who stayed in Missouri were forced to live as outlaws.

Thus began the outlaw careers of the James brothers and the Younger brothers.

QUANTRILL AND HIS MEN

It is often said that the victors write the history of wars. In so doing, they declare the heroes, brand the villains, and rationalize the causes and the conduct of the conflict. This is the reward of armed might, but arms can never establish truth.

Before his death in 1864, Irish-born Confederate General, Patrick Cleburne, exhorted his officers with these words:

"Surrender means that the history of this heroic struggle will be written by the enemy; that our youth will be trained by Northern school teachers; will learn from Northern school books their version of the War; will be impressed by all the influences of history and education to regard our gallant dead as traitors, and our maimed veterans as fit subjects for derision."

There are few better examples of historical distortion in war and its subsequent politics than the demonization of William Clarke Quantrill and his Missouri Partisan Rangers. Nations often demonize their enemies to wage war. In the case of Quantrill, the distortions of war propaganda have persisted and even increased to justify modern political fashions. Behind the demonization of Quantrill, the Missouri Partisan Rangers, and the Confederate cause lies not only an ongoing agenda to justify and glorify the Northern cause, but also a relentless effort to cover up Union despotism and war crimes. This is all part of a greater picture in which perversions of history and science are orchestrated to justify profound social change — embracing multiculturalism, egalitarianism, humanism, socialism, and quasi-religious Statism.

Northern propaganda during and after the war was designed to justify the Union cause and to discredit the Confederate cause. Discrediting Quantrill was essential to defeating Partisan guerilla warfare against Union forces and for rallying the people of Missouri, Kansas, many wavering Union States, and the Northern press to the Federal cause. In regard to Quantrill and his Missouri Partisan Rangers, no lie in the pursuit of Federal victory was too big, too vicious, or too far from the truth. Quantrill and other Partisans were depicted as psychopathic killers. Every Partisan victory was described as a massacre. Every vile practice and atrocious deed of Kansas Jayhawkers and Redlegs were turned around and attributed to Missouri "bushwhackers" and "border ruffians." This did not end with the War or Reconstruction. Much of this same propaganda still pervades the politically correct version of Kansas and Missouri history.

The most outrageous propaganda was later picked up and sensationalized by Kansas historian, William Elsey Connelley (1855-1930). Many later historians used him as a source and thus compounded the distortions and outright lies. Connelley claimed that Quantrill's father was a thief and embezzler, that there was no love in the Quantrill family, that Quantrill was a fiendish child who skinned his neighbors' cats, and that he shot pigs in the ear just to hear them squeal. He claimed that Quantrill courted women with suggestions of sadism and was a shiftless thief and bloodthirsty killer.

No historical evidence supports these claims. In fact, the evidence from close childhood friends and later acquaintances in Missouri and Kansas completely contradicts Connelley. But many modern historians would rather have Quantrill the monster than Quantrill the protector and hero of the people of western Missouri. The internet, including many government websites, is rampant with Connelley influences and a desire to project a whitewashed version of the conduct of Federal forces in Missouri during the War.

The best source of information on the real William Quantrill is Paul R. Petersen, author of *Quantrill of Missouri*, who grew up in the parts of Jackson County, Missouri, where Quantrill lived and recruited his men. In addition, Petersen is a highly decorated retired Marine Master Sergeant with experience in guerilla warfare in Vietnam. Another good source can be found by searching for "Missouri Partisan Rangers" on the web.

Quantrill was extraordinarily bright and exemplified high ethical standards. He strongly believed in adhering to the established rules of civilized warfare. He always preferred chivalry to the "black flag warfare" forced upon him and other Missouri Partisans by General Halleck's 1862 General Order Number 2, commanding "no quarter" for Missouri Partisans. Quantrill was consistently adamant that no women or children should ever be harmed or molested. He was generally soft-spoken, but his orders were always clear and firm. He was scholarly, particularly gifted at math, and a meticulous planner. He cared deeply for his men and was dedicated to protecting the people of western Missouri from the depredations of Kansas Jayhawkers and Redlegs.

Quantrill's leadership style was consultative, and he placed great emphasis on timely and accurate intelligence. Much of his knowledge of guerilla warfare was learned from reading Revolutionary War and early British Colonial history. He revered the Revolutionary War "Swamp Fox," Francis Marion and the French and Indian War guerilla leader, Major Robert Rogers, and his famed Rogers' Rangers. But Quantrill had often lived with Cherokee, Shawnee, and Delaware Indians and learned much of his guerilla tactics and superb horsemanship from them. He usually trained his men personally in both horsemanship and pistol marksmanship—shooting with a gun in each hand. He was said to be the best shot and best horseman in Missouri. John Newman Edwards—who was known to exaggerate a little at times—stated in a *Kansas City Times* article in 1872, that Quantrill, even with his horse at a gallop, could swoop down from his saddle and pick up a pebble on the ground. Both his men and the people of western Missouri loved and respected him.

The most frequent attack on Quantrill's character involves his story of how he turned from the abolitionist sentiments of his parents in Ohio and his early days as a school teacher in Kansas to a pro-Southern leader of Missouri Partisans.

When Quantrill first came to Kansas, although not involved in politics, he sided with the "Free Soil" settlers in Kansas. Initially, he even believed Republican politician and Redleg-Jayhawker leader, Jim Lane, was a good man. But in 1858, he took a job as a "bull whacker" on a wagon train heading west. The company of Russell, Majors, and Waddell was out of Westport, Missouri, and he found himself for the first time mostly in the company of Southerners who had a different view of politics. The company was unusual in that the principal partner, Presbyterian Alexander Morgan, paid seven days wages for six days work and observed the Sabbath. Along with two Colt revolvers, he also issued his employees a Bible and required them to attend a Scripture reading and the singing of a few hymns after Sunday morning breakfast. Quantrill subsequently began to measure the words and deeds of Missouri men versus the words and deeds of the Kansas Free Soil militias. By the time he returned to Kansas, he had a different view of politics.

Sometime in 1859 or 1860, using the alias of Charley Hart, Quantrill was acting as a private detective for the Delaware Indians, who felt that Jim Lane and other Jayhawker politicians had been swindling them out of their lands.

From Lawrence, Kansas, on July 30, 1859, Quantrill wrote to his mother that he and a friend were attacked by a band of Jayhawkers on the banks of the Little Cottonwood River and robbed of their horses and all their possessions. He told her that his friend was wounded but did not mention any wounds to himself.

However, sometime in 1861, Quantrill told William H. Gregg, his Adjutant, and other followers that he and "his older brother" and a free black boy were attacked by James Montgomery's Jayhawkers near the Kaw (?) River. According to this account, his "older brother" was killed, the boy was taken by the Jayhawkers, and he himself was badly wounded. His life was saved by an Indian couple who nursed him back to health. Sometime later he joined Montgomery's band to seek revenge on the men who had killed his "brother."

Some critics of Quantrill claim the whole thing was an outright lie because Quantrill had no older brother. Yet why would he have written his mother about the incident in July 1859, if it were totally fabricated? Granted, he wrote his mother a softer version. But what of the "older brother?" This still remains a mystery, but could it be that the "brother' was one of the Shawnee, Cherokee, or Delaware Indians that he had befriended and to whom he had become a blood-brother? Additionally, there is the question of whether his "brother" died or recovered. Moreover, it could be true that Quantrill tended to exaggerate some aspects of his story when telling it to men who had lost family members to Jayhawker raids. Whatever the exact truth, Quantrill considered the experience a deep personal injury and felt robbed of his dignity. Despite his otherwise noble and exemplary character, the trauma of this event may have bent him toward an obsession with vengeance against all moral wrongs.

On January 26, 1860, Quantrill wrote his mother in Ohio that according to his firsthand experience, the outrages that Northern newspapers claimed were committed by Southerners in Kansas were false. He told her that, in fact, it was the opposite party that was causing all the trouble and indicated his disgust for people who could sympathize with John Brown, the brutal abolitionist murderer. He further implied in that letter that he had some business to finish before he came home.

According to Petersen, as soon as Quantrill joined Montgomery's band of Jayhawkers, he began to murder them one by one—leaving a telltale .36 caliber Blue-Point Navy Revolver bullet hole in the forehead of each victim. He took revenge on all of Montgomery's 32 men except for a group who left for California. According to Petersen's accounting, that would mean that Quantrill personally dispatched 20 or more of Montgomery's men. Some of the circumstances, however, indicate that Quantrill had help.

In November 1860, Quantrill completed his vengeance against Montgomery's men by betraying three of them who were attempting a raid on the Missouri farm of Morgan Walker. From there he emerged as a pro-Southern protector of western Missouri and leader of a company of Partisan Rangers in Jackson County.

Where did Quantrill recruit his so-called "border ruffians"? The core members of his original company were members of the Blue Springs Baptist Church. Most of them were Bible-believing church-goers who simply wanted to defend their homes and families.

"But Quantrill and his men were no more bandits than the men on the other side. I've been to reunions of Quantrill's men two or three times. All they were trying to do was protect their property on the Missouri side of the line…"—President Harry S. Truman

The Second American Revolution

"If we were wrong in our contest, then the Declaration of Independence of 1776 was a grave mistake, and the revolution to which it led was a crime. If Washington was a patriot, Lee cannot have been a rebel."

—Lt. Gen. Wade Hampton, CSA

Slavery and the Spirit of Salem

Slavery is a part of world history, and it is an important part of American history. But slavery is one of the subjects Americans cannot have a frank discussion about. It is too wrapped in emotional, political, and ideological chains. On the subject of slavery, many Americans, especially in the media and academia, have succumbed to a form of hysteria comparable to the Salem Witch Trials. If you say anything that contradicts the usual, required extreme image of Southern slavery, you are likely to be shouted down without any consideration of the facts. If you say anything that contradicts the heroic image of the "abolitionist" movement in pre-Civil War and Reconstruction America, you are also likely to be shouted down without regard to the facts. This leaves us in a dangerous intellectual, moral, and political straightjacket. But if we value truth and freedom, we need to look at unadulterated and un-white-washed truth no matter how loud the screaming. LMS

APPENDIX CHAPTER 3

ᎤᏒᎤ

Fighting Joe Wheeler

EXTRAORDINARY CONFEDERATE CAVALRY LEADER

Gen. Fighting Joe Wheeler
Confederate cavalry
leader

There lingers to this day a romantic vision of Confederate Cavalry that brings forth the images of Sir Walter Scott's gallant knights of old. To a considerable degree, this reputation is well deserved. Confederate Cavalry quickly gained a reputation for valor, gallantry, horsemanship, bold tactics, and esprit de corps that persisted throughout the "Civil War" and can be validated in the many histories of that conflict.

Many Southern cavalrymen, and to a certain extent the whole Confederate Army, were strongly influenced by the romantic novels of Scott, which were very popular reading in the South. Furthermore, many successful cavalry exploits had an electrifying effect on Southern morale early in the war and were causes for hope late in the war.

"Every morning brought a noble chance, and every chance brought out a noble knight." — Tennyson

Yet the reality of cavalry success, and especially Confederate General Joe Wheeler's success, required much more than knightly valor and gallantry. It required dogged, often sweaty perseverance and long, physically exhausting days and nights, enduring many hardships and deprivations.

Joe Wheeler was characterized by Robert E. Lee as being one of the two best cavalrymen in the war. This will be sure to provoke considerable debate, but a strong case can be made that Wheeler was, in fact, the most effective cavalry leader of the war on either side. This was despite his youth and modest appearance and manner. Wheeler was without doubt brave and gallant, but he was very unlike the colorful Jeb Stuart, the flamboyant John Hunt Morgan, and the fierce Nathan Bedford Forrest. In point of fact, Morgan and Forrest were at one time both under the command of Wheeler. Wheeler's effectiveness lay in his utterly selfless and single-minded devotion to duty. Given an order, Wheeler's extraordinary sense of duty and honor drove him to persist and persevere and innovate until he had overcome any obstacles to meeting his assigned responsibilities.

Wheeler was most effective at the cavalry basics. These were such routine duties as protecting the rear and flanks of the main infantry forces from surprise, collecting intelligence, slowing and frustrating enemy advances, acting as a rear guard for retreating forces, and disrupting enemy communications and supply lines. Due to the numerical and material advantages of the Union forces, Wheeler was often called on to protect the Army of Mississippi and the Army of Tennessee during retreat, a duty which he performed with consistent and remarkable proficiency. He was less successful at daring raids, but extremely effective at disrupting and destroying Union supply and communication lines. In addition, Wheeler proved astonishingly successful in combating Union Cavalry.

Wheeler entered West Point in 1854 at the age of seventeen. The young Georgian was only about five foot five and weighed only about 120 pounds. His appearance was rather mild and youthful, but he had a dignified presence that seemed to command respect. Everyone who ever knew him remarked on his extraordinary personal energy. His West Point classmates gave him the nickname, "Point," because he had neither height, nor width, nor thickness. Like the Superintendent of West Point at that time, Robert E. Lee, he had a strong sense of duty. The quick-thinking military brilliance and the scholarly brilliance of his future Congressional career were not especially evident at West Point. He graduated 26th out of 29 cadets, completing the then five-year course in 1859, ironically making his lowest grades in Cavalry Tactics.

After completing Cavalry School, Second Lieutenant Wheeler was assigned to a regiment of mounted rifles at Fort Craig, New Mexico. The rule of warfare and scouting there was to travel light and range far. This experience was formative in his career as a Confederate Cavalry Commander.

In June of 1860, Wheeler was assigned escort duty for a wagon train traveling from Hannibal, Missouri, to points in New Mexico. Several days into the trip, he was detailed to escort an ambulance that had to be left behind until a young mother delivered her baby. As the ambulance—carrying the mother and new baby, along with an accompanying surgeon and wagon driver—proceeded to catch up with the wagon train, it was attacked by a small group of marauding Indians. Wheeler and the wagon driver were its only defense. With the surgeon taking the reins of the wagon, the driver downed one attacker with his musket. Wheeler then charged the attackers on horseback, knocking down one horse with a shot from his musket. Then throwing his musket down, with arrows flying everywhere, he continued the charge blazing away with his Colt pistol. With the driver now also firing into the attackers with his pistol in support of Wheeler, the marauders were put on the run. When the ambulance overtook the main wagon train and the story was told, the soldiers began to call Wheeler, "Fightin' Joe." Thus the polite, little fellow with a soft Southern accent and dignified manner received the nickname that would follow him all of his life. He was serious and usually mild mannered, but he would prove many times over on the battlefield and later as a member of Congress that he possessed an indomitable fighting spirit. As one of his men said after the war, "Joe Wheeler warn't afraid of nuthin' or nobody."

Like most of the officers in his mounted rifle regiment, young Wheeler sympathized with the South. When his home state of Georgia seceded from the Union on January 9, 1861, he immediately resigned his commission in the U. S. Army and headed home to Augusta, hoping to receive a commission in one of the newly forming Georgia regiments. There he received a commission as a First Lieutenant and was assigned as an artillery officer in Pensacola, Florida. One of the ironies of Wheeler's career as a Confederate officer is that he first distinguished himself as an artillery officer and then as an infantry officer before receiving a Confederate Cavalry command. This demonstrates the great breadth of abilities that Wheeler possessed and would manifest in combat and later in Congress.

Wheeler's courage, demonstrated consistently throughout his life, was much deeper than a purely physical courage. Physical courage is often a temporary self-confidence in physical or weapons prowess or even a misapprehension of danger. Wheeler's courage was born of his highly developed sense of duty and honor. Once Wheeler saw his duty, no arrows, gunfire, grapeshot, flashing sabers, danger or hardship mattered. He exerted all energy and resources to his strongly felt obligations to duty and honor. Wheeler was wounded three times during the course of the war. He had sixteen horses shot from under him! Six of his staff officers were killed by his side and another 30 were wounded.

Wheeler's initial duty as an artillery officer demonstrated his innovative ability to get things done under difficult circumstances. This gained him the favorable attention of General Braxton Bragg and Confederate politician and General Leroy Pope Walker. In September 1861, Walker succeeded through his connections in the Confederate Congress in getting Wheeler promoted to the rank of full Colonel, a rather controversial jump of four ranks. He was then made the commander of the 19th Alabama Infantry Regiment, where he proved himself an able trainer and organizer in preparing the regiment for combat.

On April 6-7, 1862, Col. Wheeler and the 19th Alabama distinguished themselves at the Battle of Shiloh. Wheeler and the 19th wound up in the center of the battle and found himself in effective command of his whole Brigade. During this time Wheeler's men captured 2,000 Union soldiers including a Union General. He was highly praised in dispatches for his personal valor, quick thinking, and cool presence and leadership under heavy fire. As the numerical superiority of Union forces increased, the Confederate Army of Mississippi retreated first to Corinth and then to Tupelo. Wheeler further distinguished himself commanding the 19th Alabama and three other infantry regiments (the 25th and 26th Alabama and the 4th Mississippi) in conducting rear guard actions against advancing Union forces.

On August 28, 1862, Col. Wheeler was put in command of three cavalry regiments and assigned to the command of fellow Georgian, General William J. "Old Reliable" Hardee. During September and October on an advance into Tennessee and Kentucky, Wheeler performed well in protecting Hardee's flanks and gathering intelligence. His cavalry also succeeded in destroying much of Union General Don Carlos Buell's railroad and telegraph lines north of Nashville and in frustrating his movements and attempted advances. On October 13, Wheeler was appointed Chief of

Cavalry for the Army of Mississippi, followed on October 30 by his promotion to Brigadier General at the age of only twenty-six. On November 14, the new Brigadier General was ordered to take charge of all cavalry under General Joseph E. Johnston, including the forces under the famous Nathan Bedford Forrest and John Hunt Morgan. During this time Wheeler developed tree-felling tactics in delaying Union Army advances, gaining his men the nickname, "the Lumberjack Cavalry."

In December 1862 and January 1863, Wheeler's Cavalry wreaked havoc with Union General Rosecrans' supply lines in Tennessee, burning over 450 Union supply wagons and capturing over 2,400 prisoners. This left Rosecrans at least temporarily ineffective and utterly frustrated.

February 1863 brought still another nickname to Wheeler's Cavalry. Operating along the Cumberland River in Tennessee, Wheeler's forces burned bridges and managed to capture and destroy a Union gunboat and four transports. This resulted in the capture of 400 prisoners. Hence they gained the name, "Horse Marines." That Spring, Wheeler also published a manual entitled *Cavalry Tactics*, which proved particularly valuable in systematizing Bragg's cavalry. It was also adopted by General Johnston's Army of Tennessee. The manual advocated mounted infantry over heavy cavalry.

The fame of Wheeler's Cavalry continued to grow and was a household name in the Middle South. On May 1, 1863, Wheeler was promoted to the rank of Major General by the Confederate Congress.

The months of June and July 1863 would prove difficult for Wheeler and for the Confederate cause. On June 27, Wheeler experienced a near disaster trying to rescue Forrest and his 3,000 men from being cut-off by Union forces at Duck River, near Shelbyville, Tennessee. Wheeler personally led 600 men in a cavalry charge to drive Union forces back across the bridge at Duck River. He and about 50 men, however, found themselves cut-off and had to plunge 15 feet down into the strong current on horseback while under fire to escape. Meanwhile Forrest managed to extricate himself and his men from cut-off.

On June 13, Wheeler gave permission to the restless John Hunt Morgan to take 2,000 men on an expedition against Union forces and facilities in the vicinity of Louisville, Kentucky. Their objective was to disrupt Union supply, transportation, and communications systems supporting Rosecrans' forces in Tennessee. Morgan, however, went further than his orders. The daring and flamboyant Morgan took his famous raiders across the Ohio River and raided across the states of Indiana and Ohio. This threw Union forces and the state governments of Indiana and Ohio into panic and diverted more than 60,000 Union troops to defend against the unexpected intruders. This spectacular raid also had the potential of diverting Union troops from opposing Lee's advance into Pennsylvania.

The result, however, was that Morgan and most of his men were captured. Morgan had hoped to escape across the Ohio River into West Virginia at Buffington Bar (Isle), but heavy rains upstream made the river extremely difficult to ford. In addition, the high level of the river made it easy for two Union gunboats, the *Moose* and the *Allegheny Belle*, to get in position to bombard Morgan's cavalry as it gathered on the Ohio side. Morgan's men were caught between advancing Union cavalry and infantry on one side and deadly naval bombardment from the Ohio. Major John McCreary, a future Governor of Kentucky, described the desperate position of the Confederates:

"Shells and minie balls were ricocheting and exploding in every direction, cavalry was charging, and infantry with its slow, measured tread moved upon us, while broadside after broadside was poured upon our doomed command from the gunboats."

Years ago, my grandfather described part of this chaotic scene to me as my great grandfather had described it to him. My great grandfather and one of his brothers were members of an Alabama company (G) of Morgan's original Second Kentucky Cavalry.

As the gunboats poured their deadly exploding shells into the mounted Confederate cavalry trapped on Buffington Isle, their horses became wild with fear and difficult to control. One gunboat shell exploded next to my great grandfather, and his horse reared, threw him off, and then fell on him, breaking his right leg. His brother stayed with him until they were overrun and captured by Union infantry. They spent the rest of the war as POWs at Camp Douglas, near Chicago.

About half of Morgan's men were captured at Buffington Bar on July 19. Most of the rest were captured further north in Ohio by the end of July. Only about 300 who managed to ford the river were able to escape. This reduced Bragg's cavalry by almost 20 percent at a critical time.

In the meantime, Bragg, badly outnumbered by the ever-increasing forces of Rosecrans, was forced to retreat from Middle Tennessee to Chattanooga on July 3, the very same day Lee's invasion of Pennsylvania was halted at Gettysburg. The next day on July 4, Vicksburg and 30,000 troops under Pemberton surrendered in Mississippi, giving Union forces effective control of transportation on most of the Mississippi River.

September of 1863, however, brought more favorable developments. On September 19-21 Confederate forces under Bragg, reinforced by Longstreet from Virginia, defeated Union forces under Rosecrans at Chickamauga, Georgia, just south of Chattanooga. Wheeler's cavalry protected Bragg's flanks and gave Rosecrans' forces considerable harassment in their disorderly retreat to Chattanooga. On October 3, Wheeler's cavalry dealt a devastating blow to Rosecrans' forces, destroying, according to official Union estimates, at least 500 supply wagons. Many historians believe the official Union estimates are far understated. The number of supply wagons destroyed was probably nearer 1,800, leaving a smoking corridor of destruction from Chickamauga to Chattanooga—probably a "Civil" War record.

On December 27, General Joseph E. Johnston replaced Bragg as Commander of the Army of Tennessee and retained Wheeler as his Cavalry Commander, supporting Hood's and Hardee's Corps. On February 22, 1864 Wheeler turned back federal forces at Tunnel Hill, Georgia, frustrating their plans for assaulting Atlanta and delaying them until May.

In May, Wheeler again broke the federal movement into North Georgia and slowed Union General Sherman's movement toward Atlanta. With the death of Lee's Cavalry Commander, Lt. General J. E. B. Stuart on May 12 in Virginia, Wheeler became the highest ranking cavalry officer in the Confederate Army. On May 24, he received personal congratulations from General Johnston for destroying 80 Union supply wagons and capturing 100 prisoners at Cassville, Georgia, and continued to be a major nemesis to Union forces. Every Union effort to turn the Confederate flank and drive to Atlanta was met and successfully thwarted by Wheeler.

On July 17, the aggressive John B. Hood replaced Johnston as Commander of the Army of Tennessee. On July 29-30, Wheeler's Cavalry force of 5,000 men dealt Sherman's cavalry forces of 9,000 men a series of stunning, one might even say astonishing, defeats. Wheeler routed divisions of Sherman's cavalry at three different points. He mauled and defeated

McCook at Newnan. He routed and captured Stoneman and five of his Brigadier Generals at Macon, and turned Garrard to flight northeast of Atlanta. In all, the Confederates took 3,200 prisoners and numerous supply wagons and artillery batteries. This was the worst and most disastrous defeat ever inflicted on Union cavalry during the entire war. Unfortunately, the overwhelming manpower and material resources of the Union would be able to replace Sherman's losses within months and supply them down to the last tent peg.

In August, General Hood ordered Wheeler to take 2,000 cavalry on a raid into Central Tennessee. But Wheeler returned demoralized and with less than one thousand men. According to Forrest, only about 500 of them were effective for combat. Meanwhile the reduction of cavalry in the Atlanta area left Hood unable to gather intelligence effectively or to successfully hinder the buildup of Union forces approaching Atlanta. At Jonesboro, just south of Atlanta, from August 30 to September 1, Hardee's Corps with portions of Stephen D. Lee's Corps and units of Wheeler's cavalry attempted to parry a death blow to the strategic city of Atlanta by defending the remaining railroad connection between that city and Macon. This valiant but unsuccessful endeavor was against odds of nearly three to one. On September 2, General Hood was forced to evacuate Atlanta.

On October 4, Wheeler's men felled trees near Dalton, Georgia, and used them as rafts to destroy the Chattahoochee Bridge at Resaca, Georgia. Hood headed for Tennessee in hopes of a surprise defeat of Union forces around Nashville. He left Wheeler to harass Sherman as he marched through Georgia. Although Wheeler's cavalry was successful in containing Sherman within a narrower swath of destruction than might have been, Sherman succeeded in leaving a 60-mile-wide path of dead livestock and burning towns, homes, farms, and crops—devastating the Georgia economy. On November 26, Wheeler nearly captured Sherman's infamous young cavalry commander—now transferred from Virginia—Judson "Killcavalry" Kilpatrick. Kilpatrick was the same age as Wheeler and graduated two classes behind him at West Point in 1861. He was quite a different personality than Wheeler and seemed to have a personal vendetta against him. Kilpatrick's nickname "Killcavalry" was given to him by Union officers for his recklessly aggressive tactics, not for the amount of casualties inflicted on Confederates. He was one of Sherman's most devoted subordinates.

In December 1864, Wheeler came under the criticism of Confederate Generals D. H. Hill and P. T. G. Beauregard. This criticism in turn came to the attention of President Davis. Wheeler's cavalrymen often had to travel very light and forage for food and supplies. Against very specific orders from Wheeler, however, some of his men had stolen chickens, small livestock, and food, and made similar depredations on an already hard-pressed civilian population. General Hardee came to Wheeler's defense and most of the charges were proven false. Responding to complaints, however, that Wheeler's forces were out of control, General Beauregard's Inspector General found Wheeler's Corp lacking in discipline, organization, leadership training, and proper records. He noted, however, that the same conditions prevailed in the commands of Bedford Forrest and Wade Hampton. No charges were made against Wheeler, but a recommendation was made that the 28-year-old Wheeler be placed under the command of the 48-year-old South Carolinian, Wade Hampton. Beauregard stated that while Wheeler was a modest, gallant, zealous, and indefatigable officer, he was unable to control such a large cavalry force. In the meantime, on February 11, 1865, Wheeler was successful in driving back Kilpatrick's cavalry at Aiken, South Carolina.

On February 17, Wheeler was officially placed under the command of Lieutenant General Wade Hampton. His responsibility was reduced by about half, but he continued to serve without complaint or bitterness. When Hampton personally informed Wheeler of the change in command, he is said to have responded, "Certainly, General, I will receive your orders with pleasure." Many officers on both sides would have resigned their commissions in bitterness and fury rather than take an apparent demotion or any sort of slight. Wheeler's response sheds light on his character and selfless concept of honor. His was not the kind of honor that sought personal glory or spent much time sulking about being unappreciated or slighted. To Wheeler, honor was about doing the right thing regardless of personal recognition or personal cost.

On November 15, 1864, Sherman's Army of 62,000 men departed the ruined city of Atlanta singing the "Battle Hymn of the Republic" and began to pillage and burn their way to the sea. Hood's 40,000 Confederates of the Army of Tennessee were already headed to Nashville in a desperate attempt to cut Sherman's supply lines and divert his attention from devastating Georgia. Only Hardee's Corp with scarcely 10,000 men and

3,000 cavalry under Wade Hampton and Joe Wheeler were left to oppose Sherman's relentless destruction of farms, crops, livestock, and homes as he advanced toward Savannah. By the time Sherman captured Savannah on December 21, Hood had suffered devastating casualties at Franklin and Nashville in Tennessee and was retreating to Mississippi.

Sherman's depredations on South Carolina would exceed his handiwork in Georgia. By February 17, 1865, Sherman's troops had cut through half of South Carolina and burned Columbia and ten other towns. Wheeler's cavalry continued to dog and harass Sherman's marauding forces as they continued to loot and burn their way towards North Carolina.

Brigadier General Judson Kilpatrick had become the leader of Sherman's cavalry forces after Atlanta. Sherman had this to say about his new cavalry commander:

"I know Kilpatrick is a hell of a damned fool, but I want just that sort of man to command my cavalry."

On February 28, the Confederate Congress promoted Wheeler to the rank of Lieutenant General. On March 9, General Wheeler again forced his archrival, Kilpatrick, to flee in the night—much to his embarrassment, this time in his nightclothes.

On April 26, following the surrender of Lee at Appomattox, Virginia, on April 9, Johnston—now in command of the Army of Tennessee again—was forced to surrender at Bentonville, near Durham, North Carolina.

Wheeler issued a farewell to his cavalry command before departing to assist Confederate President Jefferson Davis. His address included these words:

"During four years of struggle for liberty you have exhibited courage, fortitude, and devotion. You are the sole survivors of more than two hundred severely contested fields; you have participated in more than a thousand successful conflicts of arms. You are heroes, veterans, patriots... In bidding you adieu, I desire to tender my thanks for your gallantry in battle, your fortitude under suffering, and your devotion at all times to the holy cause you have done so much to maintain. I desire also to express my gratitude for the kind feeling you have seen fit to extend toward myself and to invoke on you the blessing of our heavenly Father, to whom we must always look in the hour of distress. Pilgrims in the cause of freedom, comrades in arms, I bid you farewell."

With the Confederate Armies collapsing all around him and with the North in a frenzy because of the assassination of Abraham Lincoln, "Little Joe," as his men often affectionately called him, embarked on one last knightly quest. He headed south to Georgia with a small volunteer escort to try to rescue President Davis. Such is the final tribute of knights to whom duty and honor and loyalty mean everything. President Davis and his family were, however, captured on May 10, at Irwinsville, Georgia, before Wheeler and his small escort could reach him. About three days later Wheeler was himself captured.

Now prisoners, President Davis and his family, Vice President Alexander H. Stephens, Postmaster General Reagan, other cabinet and military staff, and now Wheeler were taken to Augusta. There they were loaded on a prison boat for Savannah, guarded by about 50 German speaking Union soldiers and accompanied by Union gunboats. During this time Wheeler saw that Mrs. Varina Davis was under much stress and volunteered to assist with caring for the Davis baby daughter, Winnie. Thus, Lieutenant General Wheeler was not too proud to walk the deck of the prison boat holding an infant on his shoulder. True to his chivalrous, always resourceful, and energetic nature, Wheeler also devised a plan for President Davis to escape, but it was foiled before it could be put into action. From Savannah, Wheeler was taken as a prisoner of war to Fort Delaware and was not released until June 8, 1865. So ended the Confederate Cavalry career of "Fighting Joe" Wheeler. President Davis described him as "**one of the ablest, bravest and most skillful of cavalry commanders.**"

Wheeler's dedication to the cause of liberty did not end, however, with the War in 1865. While encamped near Muscle Shoals, Alabama, in October 1863, he met and began to court his future wife, the recently widowed, Mrs. Daniella Jones Sherrod, the daughter of Col. Richard Jones. They married after the war on February 8, 1866. In 1870, after a brief time as a partner in the carriage business in New Orleans, Wheeler and his wife returned to North Alabama. Starting out as a planter and later becoming a self-taught lawyer, Wheeler was elected to Congress in 1880, serving nearly 20 years representing his North Alabama district in Washington.

In the U. S. Congress, Wheeler continued to fight for States Rights, Constitutional liberties, and against unjust tariffs. Wheeler also had a respect for all soldiers and for justice and honor no matter what the color of the uniform. In 1882, Wheeler defended one of his former instructors at West Point, former Union General Fitz John Porter, before the U. S. House against accusations made by Union General John Pope, trying to make Porter the scapegoat for losing the Second Battle of Manassas. Porter was acquitted and commended by Congress.

On July 13, 1894, Wheeler gave a speech on the floor of Congress educating his colleagues on the causes of the War of 1861 to 1865. This scholarly speech pointed out much of the hypocrisy of attributing the cause of the War solely to slavery. Wheeler first touched upon the role that other issues — States Rights, the South's devotion to limited Constitutional government, the Northern Republican Party's inclination to favor majoritarian democracy over Constitutional principles, the heinous Morrill Tariff, and the fanaticism of abolitionist radicals — had played as causes of the War. Then he also gave an extensively researched account of the origins of slavery in America. He cited the enormous profits that New England had accumulated from the despicable slave trade. He then pointed out that the Southern States had initially resisted the introduction of slavery but were eventually seduced by New England slave traders appealing to a growing planter lust to profit from cheap labor. He noted that anti-slavery agitation began in the North only after slavery had proved unprofitable there and the slave trade had been officially closed in 1808 as specified by Article I Section 9 of the 1787 Constitution. In addition, he reminded them that the issues that divided the North and South were essentially the same issues that divided the Republican and Democratic parties in 1860. His speech was printed in the *Richmond Dispatch* on July 31, 1894, and may be read today on the internet.

Wheeler was a scholarly and gentlemanly Congressman, but he was as always full of energy and sometimes gave fiery, sharply worded speeches. One of Wheeler's passions was Cuba. He was an outspoken opponent of Spanish misrule in Cuba and an advocate for Cuban independence. Following the outbreak of the Spanish-American War in 1898, he petitioned President McKinley to serve in the U. S. Army to liberate Cuba. McKinley made him a Major General of Volunteers in the U. S. Army. His dismounted cavalry, which included Teddy Roosevelt's "Rough Riders," took San Juan Hill near Santiago and forced the Spanish to negotiate a peace treaty. Wheeler returned a hero and symbol of a reunited nation.

Joseph Wheeler, famed Confederate Cavalry leader, respected Alabama Congressman, and hero of the Spanish-American War, died on January 25, 1906, while on a visit to Brooklyn, New York. The whole nation, North and South mourned. He is one of the few Confederate officers buried at Arlington Cemetery in Virginia. His life and character could very well be summed up by the West Point Motto: ***Duty, Honor, Country.***

Veritas

"Truth crushed to the earth shall rise again; the eternal years of God are hers."

William Cullen Bryant, 1794-1878

"An honest man's the noblest work of God."

Alexander Pope, 1688-1744

"Wisdom is found only in truth."

Johann Goethe, 1749-1832

"Those who have no concern for their ancestors will, by simple application of the same rule, have none for their descendents."

Richard Weaver, 1910-1963

APPENDIX CHAPTER 4

Find the *Alabama*

Raphael Semmes
Captain of the CSS Alabama

In October of 1862, Secretary of the Navy Gideon Welles was in a state of apprehension and baffled frustration. In this, he was joined by President Lincoln, Secretary of War Stanton, and many high-ranking officials in Washington. In only two months since the British-built Confederate cruiser, the *CSS Alabama*, slipped out of Liverpool on her maiden voyage, she had wreaked havoc on the U.S. merchant and whaler fleets in the North Atlantic. In September, she had captured and burned ten U.S. commercial vessels. On October 3, the *Alabama* took two more prizes in a single day. The *Emily Farnham* was carrying English cargo and was therefore released on bond. The 839-ton *Brilliant* was carrying U.S. cargo from New York to London, so after her crew, passengers, and supplies were taken aboard the *Alabama*, the magnificent two-year-old ship was set ablaze at sea.

It was standard practice for Confederate commerce raiders to take the crews and passengers of captured Yankee ships aboard their own ship and transport them to a convenient port or another ship bound for port. Although the *Alabama* had so far captured eleven Yankee ships and sunk them in a fiery spectacle, there was not a single loss of life. Union commercial losses were, however, substantial.

After Captain George Hagar of the *Brilliant* arrived back in New York on the *Emily Farnham* on October 16 to tell his story, Northern newspapers were filled with indignant editorials expressing dismay that a single Confederate warship could disrupt the seaborne commerce of one of the greatest naval powers in the world. The *Alabama* had brought the war home to the Union. The Lincoln Administration was seriously concerned about both the economic impact of the merchant marine losses and their potential to weaken public support for the war. The *Alabama's* exploits, of course, raised Southern morale and sent cargo insurance on U.S. merchant ships soaring. As the increased risks and costs of merchant shipping began to have a significant impact on Northern shipping companies, they began to sell their ships to British buyers who would not be affected by Confederate commerce raiders.

Although Britain was officially neutral, most of her middle and upper classes favored the Southern cause. Britain was probably the leading anti-slavery nation in the world at that time, but most of the British commercial, intellectual, and governing classes saw through the Union propaganda that the war was about slavery. In December 1861, English author Charles Dickens, who was a strong opponent of slavery, wrote:

"The Northern onslaught upon slavery is no more than a piece of specious humbug disguised to conceal its desire for economic control of the United States."

Karl Marx, who favored the Union cause, summarized the opinion of the major British newspapers in 1861:

"The war between the North and the South is a tariff war. The war, is further, not for any principle, does not touch the question of slavery, and in fact turns on the Northern lust for power."

In 1860, the U.S. did not have an income tax. Over 95 percent of Federal Revenue came from tariffs on imported goods. Although the tariffs protected and profited Northern industry, they resulted in higher costs to produce and export cotton and other agricultural products in the South, significantly lowering Southern income and living standards.

In 1860, Northern Republicans pushed through a tariff bill more than doubling the average tariff from an average of about 15 percent to 37 percent. This bill, called the Morrill Tariff for its sponsor, Vermont Representative and steel man-ufacturer Justin Morrill, also

CSS Alabama famed Confederate commerce raider

contained an escalation clause which would raise the tariff to 47 percent within three years. Under the existing tariff, the South was already paying 87 percent of all U.S. tax revenues but receiving the benefit of only 20 percent of Federal spending. The bill passed the U.S. House 105 to 64, but with only one of forty Southern Congressmen voting for it. The Senate passed the bill with no Southern votes two days before Lincoln's inauguration on March 4, 1861, and it was immediately signed into law by outgoing President James Buchanan. Lincoln, who had campaigned hard for the tariff, endorsed its firm enforcement in his inaugural speech. A more blatant case of majoritarian tyranny and commercial partisan greed than the Morrill Tariff can hardly be found in history. It had calamitous results.

Facing this unjust and staggering increase in taxes imposed upon them by the Northern majority in Congress, South Carolina and the Gulf Cotton States had no economic choice but to leave the Union. Britain, whose vast textile industry was the primary export market for Southern cotton, also stood to suffer from the high American tariffs on its exports as well as from the resulting higher costs of Southern cotton. The Morrill Tariff thus helped to tilt British sympathies toward the Confederacy.

It should not be surprising then to find that the British were quietly violating their proclaimed neutrality by building the *Alabama* and two other cruisers destined for the Confederate Navy. The project was supervised by Confederate Navy Captain James D. Bulloch, a maternal uncle of future U.S. President Theodore Roosevelt. Built by Henry Laird, the *Alabama* was 220 feet long and only 32 feet wide. She rode low in the water and had the sleek appearance of a yacht. She had three slightly swept-back masts of English yellow pine and a 300-horsepower steam engine with a two-blade propeller. Her funnel was low and black, making identification difficult. Her hull of copper-sheathed English oak was built for speed and easy repair rather than battle armor. Six stationary cannon firing 32-pound shells graced her side gun ports. On her forward deck was her most formidable weapon—a rifled Blakely pivot gun firing 100-pound projectiles. On the aft deck was an unrifled pivot gun firing a 68-pound shell. Capable of 13 knots by sail and more than 15 knots using sail and steam, the *Alabama* was one of the fastest ships in the world. She was built for speed, stealth, easy maintenance, and long voyages. Her Captain, already a Confederate Naval hero, would be the slight, scholarly, but fiercely determined and daring Raphael Semmes.

By early 1863, the reputation of the *Alabama* was reaching mythical proportions in the Northern press. She appeared everywhere and anywhere, burning and sinking one Yankee merchant ship after another. Consequently, Navy Secretary Gideon Welles had 18 of the Navy's most formidable warships in pursuit of the *Alabama*. But where was she? The *Alabama* would appear out of nowhere, running up her Confederate ensign for the pursuit and capture of yet another Union prize.

When the *Alabama* captured the *Ariel,* carrying 140 U.S. Marines and gold from Panama to New York, such gold shipments fell 70 percent. The capture of 140 Marines was, of course, an extreme embarrassment for the Navy Department. Then the *Alabama* unexpectedly arrived off Galveston and easily sank the Union Navy gunboat *Hatteras*. In addition, a new Confederate cruiser, the *Florida*, began marauding in the Gulf.

Scores of U.S. merchant marine owners were now selling their ships to the British.

The Union Navy also began to lose its stranglehold on Southern ports. Its success rate at intercepting blockade-runners dropped from 27 percent in 1862 to 13 percent in 1863. Meanwhile 18 of the Navy's best ships were kept busy chasing a phantom around the world.

At the beginning of the War, the Confederate Navy, with only ten serviceable warships, was less than one-ninth the size of the Union Navy. How could a single Confederate commerce raider, the *CSS Alabama*, so terrorize U.S. merchant shipping companies and utterly frustrate one of the most powerful navies in the world?

By the end of February 1863, the Confederate cruiser *Alabama* was operating off the coast of northern Brazil. That month her crew boarded 31 ships that her Captain, Raphael Semmes, believed to be Yankee merchants, but only five of them turned out to be of U.S. registration. He burned three of these, bonded one, and ransomed one. The U.S. merchant captains had learned to avoid the busiest sea lanes where the *Alabama* might be lurking like a wolf for her next prize. After re-coaling at a Brazilian port, Semmes set sail for Cape Town, South Africa, a rich British colony and a more likely location for intercepting Yankee merchant ships.

Meanwhile, Secretary of the Navy Gideon Welles kept sending his interception squadrons to the last place the *Alabama* had struck rather than trying to anticipate what rich sea lane she might try to attack next. By the time the Union Navy was on the scene of the Alabama's latest plundering spree, Semmes was somewhere else. Welles, his staff, and the Lincoln Cabinet—distressed over the *Alabama's* continued disruption of U.S. shipping—sometimes allowed the latest rumors and hearsay in Washington to influence naval tactics. Because of continual political interference in military and naval affairs, especially during any crisis or following a setback, Confederate agents found it easier to influence Union Navy operational decisions by spreading misinformation and false rumors.

Captured ships were Semmes' principal way of getting news of shipping and the progress of the war. On March 2, the *Alabama* captured and burned the *John A. Parks* out of Maine. From Northern newspapers confiscated from her captain, Semmes and his crew learned that the *Florida*, the second Confederate cruiser built by the British in Liverpool under the supervision of James Bulloch, had burned the *Jacob Bell* and a cargo valued at $1.5 million, the largest trophy of the entire war.

The officers of the British-built Confederate cruisers were mostly Confederate Navy personnel, but their crews were largely British volunteers. Late in the war the *Alabama* and the *Florida* would be joined by a third Confederate Cruiser built in Liverpool, the *Shenandoah*. When the *Shenandoah* finally lowered her ensign at Liverpool on November 6, 1865, more than six months after Lee's surrender at Appomattox, she had captured 34 U.S. merchant ships and whalers, most of which were burned at sea.

When the *Alabama* arrived at Cape Town, South Africa, in the summer of 1863, she was the most famous ship in the world and the most dreaded ship in the counsels of Union government and the U.S. shipping industry. Just before coming into the harbor at Cape Town, in the full view of many on the shore, the *Alabama* raised her Confederate ensign and chased down and captured the Union merchant, *Sea Bride*. Semmes decided, however, that the *Sea Bride* would not join the 43 ships the *Alabama* had burned at sea. After transferring the *Sea Bride's* crew to the *Alabama*, he assigned a small crew to bring his prize into Cape Town for sale. Word traveled fast in the British governed Anglo-Dutch city that the famous *Alabama* had arrived with a Yankee prize in tow.

As the *Alabama* anchored in Cape Town harbor, her executive officer, John Kell, described the scene in a letter to his wife:

"It was really wonderful to behold the people congregated on shore, the hillsides covered with an excited populace....Hundreds crowded on board. Their enthusiasm was beyond description and their hearty welcome and sympathy expressed for our cause was truly gratifying."

The jetties and streets near the harbor area were thronged with people there to welcome these famous sea-knights and their storied ship. From upper windows, ladies waved their handkerchiefs as if to fair knights resplendent on their chargers. Many people stood on the roofs of houses to get a better view. Disregarding even the pretense of official British neutrality, the crowd gave three great cheers for the *Alabama*.

Captain Charles White of the captured *Sea Bride*, when interviewed by a local newspaper, was resigned to his loss and remarked:

"What can't be cured must be endured. I had not the remotest idea of a capture at this end of the world. I never supposed that she was in this direction."

Another Confederate ship followed the *Alabama* into Cape Town harbor. She was the *Tuscaloosa*, formerly the U.S. bark *Conrad* taken by Semmes off Brazil. Semmes had made her a tender for his own ship. Equipped with two guns and a small crew of fifteen, she was effectively a small Confederate cruiser.

After four days of celebration and re-supply at Cape Town, the *Alabama* steamed out of Table Bay. She was already the most successful commerce raider in naval history.

But 2,200 miles to the northwest, the Union warship *Vanderbilt*, commanded by Charles Baldwin, was just arriving at the island of St. Helena. She was the biggest and fastest vessel in the U.S. Navy. Her mission was to find and destroy the *Alabama*. Captain Baldwin's instructions were personally delivered to him by Assistant Secretary of the Navy Gustavus Fox, a personal confidant of President Abraham Lincoln. On August 15-16, a U.S. consul and a Danish schooner confirmed that both the Confederate cruisers *Georgia* and *Alabama* were operating out of Simon's Bay just east of Cape Town.

Arriving at Simon's Bay, the *Vanderbilt* found she had missed the *Georgia* by just 18 hours. The *Alabama* was operating off the west coast of Africa about 600 miles to the north and in route back to Simon's Bay. Semmes had no idea that the powerful *Vanderbilt* was there. Luckily, weather delayed his arrival until the *Vanderbilt* had left. Now the chase was on and both crews knew that deadly combat might be just hours or even minutes away.

One night about 10 p.m. in thick weather, the watch on the *Alabama* heard a nearby vessel strike four bells. Through night field glasses they identified her as the *Vanderbilt*. The low-riding, black-painted *Alabama*, her crew in hushed silence, stole away from the larger Union warship and headed due south for two days. Baldwin guessed wrong and headed north. The elusive *Alabama* had disappeared again. With the *Vanderbilt* lurking around the Cape, Semmes set sail for Singapore.

In New York, news of the *Alabama's* exploits and escape in the Cape of Good Hope inspired a dime novel. Published in the fall of 1863, it was entitled: *The Track of Fire; or A Cruise with the Pirate Semmes*.

By early 1864, the war news from home was not good, but Semmes continued raiding in the Indian Ocean and had a narrow brush with the Union warship *Wyoming*. But the *Alabama's* steam engine and water condenser had begun to fall into disrepair. Since there were no dependably friendly ports where major repairs could be made, Semmes headed back to Cape Town. On March 25, 1864, after re-supplying, he set sail for Brazil but found only two prizes. By this time he realized his ship's speed and efficiency were deteriorating. She would need serious repairs in a friendly port with the proper materials and skilled labor. Besides her diminished steam power, her decks were leaking, some of her beams were splitting, and her copper hull sheathing was stripping below the waterline. In May 1864, the *Alabama* took two more prizes, but two more outran her. As Semmes expressed it, his ship was "crippled and limping." The *Alabama* was coming apart.

Because the war was going badly, the South had fewer open friends. Under U.S. pressure, British ports were beginning to be less open to Confederate ships. Semmes decided to head to the French port of Cherbourg in Normandy. Emperor Louis Napoleon was sympathetic to Southern independence, and the *Florida* and the *Georgia* had recently found refuge and repair facilities at French ports.

On June 10, the *Alabama* entered the port of Cherbourg. There was little chance of it remaining a secret. Within hours the U.S. minister in Paris, William Dayton, sent a telegram to the Union gunboat *Kearsarge*, cruising off the Dutch port of Flushing. By late morning of June 14, the *Kearsarge,* commanded by Captain John A. Winslow, had also arrived at Cherbourg. The rules of neutrality forbade combat in French waters, but Winslow intended to engage and sink the *Alabama* if she attempted to leave Cherbourg.

At the time she arrived in Cherbourg, the *Alabama* had burned 52 Yankee merchant ships and whalers and had bonded, ransomed, sold, or put into Confederate service 12 more. She had also sunk the Union gunboat *Hatteras* off Galveston. Because of the increased risks and costs she posed to U.S. merchant shipping, over 900 U.S. merchant ships were sold to foreign owners, mostly British. She had also seized more than $5 million dollars worth of U.S. shipping cargos (a vast amount of money back then). Along with other Confederate cruisers—especially the *Florida* who took 60 prizes—she helped reduce the effectiveness of the Union blockade of Southern ports by about 50 percent.

When the *CSS Alabama* arrived at the French port of Cherbourg for repairs on June 11, 1864, she had traveled 75,000 miles in the 22 months since her launch in Liverpool. On Monday the 13th, Semmes wrote to his superior in Paris that the *Alabama* needed more than two months of extensive repairs, including recoppering her hull, refastening some of her beams, and overhauling her boilers. Many of Semmes's crew were in marginal health. Exhausted from nearly three years of almost continuous hard duty at sea, first on the *Sumter* and then the *Alabama*, Semmes himself was suffering from a cold and fever. Consequently, he asked to be relieved of command. The arrival of the Union warship *Kearsarge* at Cherbourg on June 14 changed all that.

Hostilities were unlawful within the three-mile territorial limits of a neutral nation, but the *Kearsarge* was now in a position to intercept and destroy the *Alabama* if she left Cherbourg and crossed into international waters. The *Kearsarge* steamed into Cherbourg harbor and passed within yards of the *Alabama,* allowing both crews to eye each other and compare their ships. Rather than anchoring, the *Kearsarge* then steamed out of the harbor and took up a position beyond the breakwater.

Semmes knew that if he did not face the *Kearsarge* now, she would be reinforced by other Union warships in a few days or weeks. He and his officers resolved to come out fighting.

The two ships were remarkably similar. They were both long and narrow and about the same size. Each had three masts, a black-painted hull, a single funnel, steam machinery, and a screw propeller. The *Alabama* had eight guns to the *Kearsarge*'s seven, but two of the Union warship's guns were the giant Dahlgrens that threw eleven-inch diameter shells weighing 164 pounds each—about twice the size and penetrating power of the *Alabama's* two pivot guns. However, the bottle-shaped Dahlgrens were, smooth-bored, more unwieldy, and less accurate than the *Alabama's* rifled, pivot mounted Blakely. About a third of the *Kearsarge*'s hull was ironclad (protected by sheet anchor chains hung over the sides and covered with black-painted boards). The *Alabama* had no such additional protection.

The *Kearsarge* had just undergone an overhaul in London. With a clean hull, two new sails, and a refurbished boiler, she was in peak shape and ready for action. The *Alabama* would have to join battle still needing serious repairs to her boiler and structure. A major concern to Semmes and his officers was that after 22 months at sea, much of their gunpowder and fuses had become unreliable. In April, the *Alabama* had practiced her gunnery on a captured Union prize, the *Rockingham.* During that practice, one-third of the *Alabama's* shells had failed to explode.

The *Alabama's* poor condition and unreliable ammunition and the Union ship's better protected hull and two huge Dahlgren guns made the contest somewhat uneven except in the eyes of the dauntless Semmes. Semmes hoped that by out-maneuvering the *Kearsarge* he could avoid serious damage from the Dahlgren guns. If he could disable her cannons on one side, Semmes planned to take the *Kearsarge* by boarding her and subduing her crew by pistol and cutlass in hand-to-hand combat. Then he might switch ships and go back to sea with a combat ready vessel. It was a bold, perhaps desperate plan, but it fit the Southern tradition and necessity for daring invention and improvisation.

Semmes decided to fight exclusively from his starboard (right) side, so he had his three port (left) guns moved to that side, doubling his effective firepower. This caused the ship to list to starboard, presenting a smaller target on his combat side. He also had his ship loaded with extra coal to help protect his steam machinery. Meanwhile, his crew practiced combat-boarding techniques.

On the evening of Friday, June 17, the British steam yacht *Deerhound*, anchored at Cherbourg. She was owned by Confederate sympathizer, John Lancaster of Lancashire.

Built in Liverpool by Henry Laird, she looked like a small unarmed version of the *Alabama*. Captain Evan Jones and other officers on the *Deerhound* met several times Saturday with Semmes and his officers aboard the *Alabama*. Several boats transferred records and valuables from the *Alabama* to the *Deerhound*. Other valuables were carried to the British yacht *Hornet* also at Cherbourg. A British publishing agent arrived to secure Captain Semmes's records and personal journal. The Alabama's last payroll, bonding documents on Yankee prizes not destroyed, and five bags containing 4,700 British gold sovereigns were left with French officials for safekeeping.

By Sunday, June 19, more than 1,300 spectators had arrived from Paris in anticipation of witnessing a great naval battle. *The Alabama's* executive officer, John Kell, had his ship ready for combat. The decks were scrubbed, and the brass was polished. Sand was spread on the deck to absorb blood and prevent slipping. On the lower deck surgeons stood by with their instruments. The crew were dressed in their muster uniforms.

At 9 am, the *Deerhound* left the harbor and ran near the *Kearsarge*. Then she returned and passed near the *Alabama*, apparently exchanging some signals. At 10:30 a.m., the *Alabama* steamed out of the harbor and headed straight for the *Kearsarge*. With the French ironclad *Couronne* patrolling nearby, Winslow took his Union warship farther out in the Channel to make certain that he was beyond the French three-mile territorial limit. Behind the *Couronne* trailed the *Deerhound* at a safe distance.

As the *Kearsarge* turned back toward shore, she was heading straight for the oncoming *Alabama*. When the two ships were about a mile apart, the *Alabama* suddenly sheered to port and opened fire on her adversary with a starboard broadside. Semmes hoped to make some disabling hits, but at least to get the *Kearsarge* leaning away so he could run up alongside and grapple and board her. But the Confederate gunners overcompensated for their ship's starboard list, and the shells exploded harmlessly overhead the *Kearsarge*.

The *Kearsarge* waited until she was within a thousand yards, and then she began to fire. Because the *Kearsarge* was faster and more maneuverable, the *Alabama* was unable to get in close. Now the ships were firing starboard broadside to starboard broadside, circling clockwise around a common center. The range tightened from 900 to 400 yards, but the *Alabama* could not close on the Yankee warship. They circled seven times in this dance of death, booming away the whole time. The echoes reverberated for seventy miles across the English Channel, even as far as Bristol.

The eleven-inch Dahlgren guns began to take a heavy toll on the *Alabama*, splintering and slicing its wooden bulwarks and causing many casualties. A direct hit to the aft pivot gun, one of the two most potent Confederate weapons, killed or wounded all but one of its gun crew.

A shell from the *Alabama's* Blakely ripped through the *Kearsarge's* aft quarter, causing an explosion that shook the entire ship. Another shell pierced the Union warship's funnel and exploded but did no damage to the steam equipment. Yet another shell zipped through the engine room but fell harmlessly on the other side of the ship. Two sailors and a gunner were wounded when a shell passed through the starboard bulwark and exploded just below the main rigging. Yet the Union gun crews kept firing with cool, mechanical discipline.

As Semmes feared, the *Alabama's* damp powder charges resulted in weakened shell impact. Several of her shells bounced off the enemy's ironclad hull. Many shells failed to explode, and one shell that could have seriously crippled the *Kearsarge* lodged in the rudder post without exploding. Another shell hit the rail of the *Kearsarge's* forward pivot gun but failed to explode.

Meanwhile, the big Dahlgrens wreaked havoc on their target. A flying splinter wounded Semmes in the right hand, but he wrapped the wound and continued to command his ship. One eleven-inch shell crippled the *Alabama's* rudder, making the ship difficult to steer. Another Dahlgren shell hit near the waterline and exploded in the engine room. When the ship rolled, water poured into a hole nearly three feet in diameter.

At noon, seeing his situation was hopeless, Semmes set his fore-and-aft sails in an attempt to get the *Alabama* back into French waters. But Winslow easily positioned the *Kearsarge* to cut him off.

Rising water soon disabled the *Alabama's* boilers and pumps. As the ship began to settle perceptibly at the stern, Kell went below to assess the damage and reported that she would founder within ten minutes. The *Kearsarge* continued to rake the *Alabama* with volley after volley.

As the bow began to rise, Semmes ordered the colors to be struck, but before the forward gunners got word, two unauthorized shots were fired. In outrage, the *Kearsarge* pounded the *Alabama* with another five shots. Two *Alabama* crewmen managed to raise a white flag and the firing stopped. Kell ordered all hands to abandon ship and swim away to avoid being sucked under as the ship went down. Only two of the *Alabama's* lifeboats remained intact. One, under the command of George Fullam, was sent to the *Kearsarge* with the Confederate wounded.

With her fore-and-aft sails still set, the *Alabama* began to drift away. At ten minutes past noon, as seawater began to pour through the gaping three-foot Dahlgren wound in her starboard side, she began to sink by the stern. Within minutes her bow, with fore-and-aft sails still spread from her bowsprit, rose to a near vertical position. Her mainmast snapped in two, and then she hesitated a few groaning moments before plunging straight down beneath the bone-chilling waves of the English Channel. She was about six miles off the coast of Normandy, near Cherbourg.

A few minutes following this appalling spectacle, the British steam yacht Deerhound came up from behind the victorious *Kearsarge* and asked if they could help rescue the Confederate sailors struggling in the numbing waters. The *Kearsarge* had already launched its two surviving lifeboats, so they readily agreed to the assistance. **"For God's sake do what you can to save them,"** was their answer.

George Fullam's lifeboat, filled with wounded Confederates, reached the *Kearsarge* shortly thereafter. Fullam announced the surrender of his ship and requested permission to go and rescue more men. This was also readily granted, and Fullam returned to the dreadful and chaotic scene and picked up as many additional shipmates as he could find. He did not return these men to the *Kearsarge,* however. He took them to the *Deerhound*.

A lifeboat from the *Deerhound* picked up a number of survivors in the water including the *Alabama's* captain, Raphael Semmes, and his executive officer, John Kell. But she did not return her rescued Confederate seamen to the *Kearsarge*. The *Deerhound* immediately steamed off for Southampton. She arrived there several hours later with 41 crewmen of the *Alabama* including Semmes, Kell, and 12 other officers, a substantial proportion of the Confederate raider's crew of 145.

The *Alabama* had lost 10 men killed in action or died of wounds and another 16 drowned or lost at sea, a total of 26 dead. Another 21 had been wounded, bringing her combat casualties to 47, nearly a third of her company. In addition, approximately 57 of her rescued crew became Union prisoners of war. The 41 men rescued by the *Deerhound* were returned to Confederate service after a comfortable recuperation in England. Several of these men became officers and sailors aboard the *Alabama's* Liverpool-built sister ship, the *Shenandoah*, launched in October 1864.

Only one of the *Alabama's* officers was lost, Assistant Surgeon David Llewellyn, who had heroically refused to leave the ship until he was certain that all wounded men had been put aboard a lifeboat. Llewellyn, who could not swim, was a British subject dedicated to the Confederate cause.

The *Kearsarge* sustained only moderate damage during the battle. Of the three wounded seamen, one later died of wounds. The *Kearsarge's* victory has been attributed to her recent boiler maintenance and consequently superior speed and maneuverability, her partial ironclad protection, and of course, to the enormous destructive power of her 11-inch Dahlgren guns. But we must also add the superior gunnery and remarkable discipline of her crew. Additionally, it must be said of her captain and officers that they showed gallant compassion in allowing the pro-Confederate British steam yacht *Deerhound* to rescue many of the Confederate seamen struggling in the frigid waters off Cherbourg.

After a good rest and stay with close friends in England, Raphael Semmes returned home to his family in Mobile and much public acclaim as the Confederacy's most famous naval war hero. He had captured or destroyed 19 U.S. ships as captain of the *Sumter* and 65 as captain of the *Alabama*. Semmes was made a Rear Admiral and an honorary member of the Confederate Congress and the Virginia legislature.

Confederate Navy Captain James D. Bulloch, the Confederate government agent who coordinated and supervised the building and launching of the Confederate cruisers *Alabama, Florida, and Shenandoah* in

Liverpool is not a household name among Civil War buffs, but his accomplishments in building a formidable Confederate fleet of commerce raiders in England must be ranked among the most remarkable achievements for the Southern cause.

It was largely due to Bulloch's adroit diplomatic relationship with the British government and shipbuilding industry that the Confederate Navy was able to put to sea three of the most successful commerce raiders in naval history. He was also instrumental in acquiring what became the Confederate commerce raider *Georgia* in Scotland. Bulloch's four British-built commerce raiders are credited with capturing or sinking 170 U.S. merchant ships and helped to substantially reduce the effectiveness of the Union blockade of Southern ports. These and four other Confederate commerce raiders captured or destroyed a total of 236 Union ships. In addition, they caused American shippers to sell as many as 1,800 merchant ships to British and other foreign owners in order to avoid the risk of capture by Confederate cruisers. By the end of the war, only eight Confederate commerce raiders had caused more than half of the U.S. merchant fleet to disappear. Seldom in history have so few ships and men had such an enormous impact for the cause of their country.

Bulloch's younger brother, Irvine, was an officer on the *Alabama* and after her sinking at Cherbourg became the navigator on the *Shenandoah*. These two brothers were much revered uncles of a future President of the United States, Theodore Roosevelt. Roosevelt had both Union and Confederate family connections and was proud of them both.

In recent years, the spinal disorder of political correctness and its distorting influence on history have significantly affected many American politicians and caused them to distance themselves from any connection to the Confederacy. Teddy Roosevelt's unabashed pride in his Confederate ancestry puts this modern trend to shame. Speaking to a crowd of well-wishers in the Bulloch home town of Roswell, Georgia, in 1905, Roosevelt beamed with Southern patriotic pride:

"It has been my very great good fortune to have the right to claim my blood is half southern and half northern, and I would deny the right of any man here to feel a greater pride in the deeds of every southerner than I feel. Of all the children, the brothers and sisters of my mother who were born and brought up in that house on the hill there, my two uncles afterward entered the Confederate service and served with the Confederate Navy."

Roosevelt went on to reveal a little known fact about the last minutes of the *Alabama*.

"...when at the very end the *Alabama* was sinking and the *Kearsarge* passed under her stern and came up along the side that had not been engaged hitherto, my uncle, Irvine Bulloch, shifted his gun from one side to the other and fired the two last shots fired from the *Alabama*."

(Irvine Bulloch had not received word that Semmes had just ordered the Confederate colors struck. This confusion caused the *Kearsarge* to pound the *Alabama* with another five shots after she had struck her colors.)

Another fascinating aspect of the story of the *Alabama* and her sister commerce raiders is the appreciable sympathy of the British for the Southern cause. There are several cultural, political, and economic reasons for this, but among the foremost was the considerable British displeasure with the Morrill Tariff and Northern protectionism versus the free trade policies favored by both Britain and the South. The very anti-slavery British dismissed Northern pretensions that the war was about slavery. **"The contest is really for empire on the side of the North and for independence on that of the South,"** wrote the *London Times* in 1861.

British distaste for Union economic and political policies was further exacerbated by the "Trent Affair" in late 1861. This was a major diplomatic clash between the U.S. and Britain over an incident in which a U.S. Navy ship intercepted and boarded the British steamer *RMS Trent* at sea and forcibly removed two important Confederate diplomats bound for England. This nearly provoked British naval and military intervention against the United States.

In October 1861, Confederate President Jefferson Davis had appointed James Mason of Virginia and John Slidell of Louisiana as envoys to Britain and France respectively with the mission of securing their recognition of the Confederate States government. Official British and French recognition of the Confederate States was strongly contrary to the interests of the United States. Consequently, Secretary of the Navy Gideon

Welles ordered interception of the diplomats should they attempt to leave Charleston. A Confederate blockade-runner, however, was able to slip them out of Charleston and take them to Cuba to await a British steamer — the *RMS Trent*— bound for England.

Learning that Mason and Slidell had left Havana on the British *Trent*, Captain John Wilkes of the U.S. Navy's 11-gun warship *San Jacinto,* nevertheless, made plans to intercept them. On November 8, the *San Jacinto* forced the *Trent* to heave to and allow a boarding party to search for the two diplomats. Despite strong protest from the British ship's captain, the *San Jacinto's* executive officer and a contingent of Marines forcibly removed Mason, Slidell, and two associates from British protection. The Confederate envoys were then carried to Boston, where they were incarcerated at Fort Warren. The news of this arrest at sea was joyously received by the Northern public and the U.S. Congress. Secretary Welles accordingly presented Wilkes with a gold medal.

British newspapers and public opinion were, however, thoroughly outraged that an American ship had arrogantly violated international maritime law, British sovereignty, and British honor. Her Majesty Queen Victoria's government considered the incident to be a provocation to war. Presiding at an emergency cabinet meeting, British Prime Minister, Lord Palmerston, threw his hat on the table declaring:

"I don't know whether you are going to stand for this, but I'll be damned if I do."

The British government did not want war but immediately sent 11,000 troops to Canada and began to make other naval and military preparations. Although war fever was running high in the public, press, and Parliament, Queen Victoria's consort, Prince Albert, managed to soften the seven-day British ultimatum for an apology. Lincoln's cabinet immediately realized that they could ill afford a war with Britain while trying to subdue the Southern Confederacy. U.S. Secretary of State Seward managed to persuade the Lincoln cabinet that Mason and Slidell should be released immediately and that the U.S. should admit that Captain Wilkes acted without authorization.

This was done but without a formal U.S. apology. Nevertheless, after the release of Mason and Slidell in January, the heat of the "Trent Affair" subsided and war was averted. But British feeling toward the Lincoln government remained strained, and public sympathy for the Southern cause thrived.

The *Alabama's* record as the most successful commerce raider in naval history still stands, notwithstanding German submarine warfare in two world wars. During the Battle of the Atlantic from 1939 to 1945, 863 operational German submarines sank 2,827 allied merchant ships. Allied shipping losses totaled about 3,500 from all enemy causes resulting in a loss of over 30,000 men. The German U-Boat Captain who sank the most allied ships was Otto Kretschmer with 47. Nine other German submarine commanders sank 26 or more allied ships. The *Alabama*, in contrast, destroyed 53 Union ships and spared 12 more for various reasons, bringing her total prizes to 65. Except for sinking the Union warship Hatteras, there was no loss of life. (Such chivalry is not a practical option in submarine warfare.)

The last line of a well known sea shanty, **Roll Alabama Roll**, is "Off the three-mile limit in '64, the *Alabama* was seen no more."

But in November 1984, the French Navy minesweeper *Circe,* while on a training mission, discovered a wreck at a depth of about 200 feet, about 7 miles from Cherbourg. It was the *Alabama*—found again after more than 120 years! About 300 artifacts have been removed from the ship.

The Bonnie Blue Flag

We are a band of brothers and native to the soil,
Fighting for our Liberty, with treasure, blood, and toil.
And when our rights were threatened, the cry rose near and far,
Hurrah for the Bonnie Blue Flag that bears a single star!

Chorus:
Hurrah! hurrah!
For Southern rights, hurrah!
Hurrah for the Bonnie Blue Flag that bears a single star.

As long as the Union was faithful to her trust
Like friends and like brethren, kind were we, and just.
But now, when Northern treachery attempts our rights to mar,
We hoist on high the Bonnie Blue Flag that bears a single star.

First gallant South Carolina nobly made the stand.
Then came Alabama and took her by the hand.
Next, quickly Mississippi, Georgia, and Florida,
All raised on high the Bonnie Flue Flag that bears a single star.

Then here's to our Confederacy, strong we are and brave,
Like patriots of old we'll fight, our heritage to save;
And rather than submit to shame, to die we would prefer,
So cheer for the Bonnie Blue Flag that bears a single star.

****

These verses are particularly rich in imagery of the causes of the war, sung while on the march. Verses 3, however, contains a historical inaccuracy. It was Mississippi that first took South Carolina's hand. See page 64 for secession order.

APPENDIX CHAPTER 5

ᜣᝈᜭ

Exploding a Mountain Myth

It is commonly believed that Western North Carolina was a hotbed of Union sentiment and that a large minority of her native sons chose to serve in the Union Army rather than the Confederate Army during the War Between the States. Terrell T. Garren's new book, *Mountain Myth: Unionism in Western North Carolina,* based on more than sixteen years of detailed research of Union and Confederate military records, completely debunks that myth.

Garren's research documented that 27,282 men from 21 Western North Carolina counties served in the Confederate forces and only 1,636 served in the Union Army. Garren rounds down his Confederate estimate to an even 26,000 to allow for duplication and generously rounds up his Union estimate by 200 to 1,836 to allow for possible omissions. That means that those who served in the Union Army represent less than 7 percent of the total serving in both armies.

Rounding down the Confederate estimate for duplication was primarily necessary because, of the 1,636 men who Garren documents on the Union rolls, a substantial majority were Confederate deserters. Of the 1,372 North Carolina men who served in the Union 2nd and 3rd North Carolina Mounted Infantry and the 13th Tennessee Cavalry, Garren estimates that close to 90 percent were Confederate deserters, as was their leader Union Col. George W. Kirk. He also documents 161 North Carolina men who joined the Union Army to escape the high death rates in Northern prisoner of war camps. These were sent to serve on the Western frontier. Of these, 28 percent promptly deserted the Union Army.

338 The Un-Civil War | Shattering the Historical Myths

Garren also notes that 97 percent of the Western North Carolina men who enlisted in various Union regiments did not do so until after the Battle of Gettysburg in July of 1863. Approximately 42 percent enlisted in the last nine months of the war, and of these, more than half (22 percent) did not enlist until after January 1, 1865. In contrast to their fellow North Carolinians in Confederate regiments, most of the estimated 1,836 men in Union regiments saw comparatively little combat as Union soldiers. The regiments under George Kirk did, however, gain a reputation for robbery, rape, pillage, and wanton destruction. Kirk also gained fame as a rogue during Reconstruction.

Those who served in Confederate regiments saw a considerable amount of combat. A total of 5,840 or about 23 percent were killed in battle or died of wounds or disease. Of these, 976 died in Union prisoner of war camps. Nearly 34 percent of Confederate soldiers from Cleveland County and 33 percent from Catawba County lost their lives. Wilkes County suffered a 32 percent loss, and nearly 30 percent from McDowell County died.

Many people point to the fact that only about 30 percent of Western North Carolinians voted for secession before Fort Sumter as proof of strong Union sentiment in the region. But after Lincoln's call for 75,000 troops to "put down the rebellion," secession sentiment rose to about 95 percent. This was true of many areas in the South, even northern Alabama.

What then lies behind the myth that Western North Carolina was a fervent hotbed of Union sympathies? First of all, it seemed natural for many Northern observers to conclude that Western North Carolina should be more Unionist than the rest of the state, because slave ownership, which they automatically equated with Confederate sympathies, was less common in the mountains. Mountain agriculture was based more on animal husbandry and food crops rather than cotton. Slavery was, however, still commonplace, especially among the wealthier families. Approximately 25 percent of Southern families owned slaves in 1860. My own estimate, based on data from 17 of 21 counties, is that between 11 and 12 percent of Western North Carolina families owned slaves, but many of these families could be classified as at least conditionally Unionist before Fort Sumter. All things considered, slavery did not seem to be an issue that divided Unionist from Confederate sentiment in Western North Carolina.

Secondly, many Northern observers automatically equated West-ern North Carolina with eastern Tennessee, which was the home of many politically powerful Unionists, including Andrew Johnson and politician-preacher William Brownlow. But the Great Smoky Mountains divide the two regions, and they have never been political twins.

Most importantly, however, Alexander Hamilton Jones, a leading Henderson County Unionist and the successful Republican candidate for Congress in 1866, in a 38-page campaign biography, asserted that there were 5,790 Western North Carolina men sympathetic to the Union, of whom three-quarters or approximately 4,342 joined the Union Army. But Jones had little way of knowing such a precise figure, especially that soon after the war. Jones's main campaign theme was that he was a true Unionist from the beginning—a safe campaign tactic when most Confederate vet-erans had been disenfranchised. Despite his advertised Unionism, Jones and the newly elected Senators and Congressmen from 11 Southern states were refused seats in the new Congress as a Reconstruction measure. To implement their heinous Reconstruction plans, the Radical Republicans refused the credentials of even the most loyal Southern Unionists. Follow-ing President Johnson's amnesty for Confederate veterans in late 1868 and a subsequent increase in Confederate veterans registered to vote again, Jones was defeated during the Democratic sweep of 1870 that toppled Reconstruction Governor William Holden. Unfortunately, until Garren's research, Jones's figures were cited by many historians without critical examination.

There were several factors that spawned resentment against the Con-federate Government during the war, turning many mountain people who were not really Unionists into what Garren calls "anti-Confederates." The draft was not popular, but there was no widespread public protest. Harsh treatment of Confederate deserters late in the war, however, did increase resentment toward the Confederate Government among many mountain families.

During the war, there were thousands of deserters on both sides. Union desertions peaked shortly after the Emancipation Proclamation at the beginning of 1863. Southern deserters typically left their units with-out permission to relieve some problem at home and then returned to the ranks. Toward the end of the war Southern desertions were having a decid-ed impact on combat effectiveness and the ability to resist the increasing numerical superiority of Union forces. In a desperate attempt to instill some discipline, Confederate General Joe Johnston had 14 Western North Carolina soldiers stationed in nearby North Georgia executed for desertion. This drastic measure backfired and caused an increase in anti-Confederate Government sentiment. Finally, as the prospects for the survival of the Confederacy began to crumble, many men found it expedient to desert and join the Yanks rather than suffer the hardships of a collapsing Confederate Army or to be thrown into such desperate, high-casualty battles as Franklin, Tennessee.

Yet despite all the deprivations and discouragements suffered during and especially near the end of the war, it is amazing how fiercely Western North Carolina Confederate regiments continued to fight.

Garren makes his point still another way in his discussion of Confederate monuments in Western North Carolina. His book includes photographs of sixteen Confederate monuments erected after the war. There is only one Union monument, and it was not erected and dedicated until very recently (1985). This small monument, recognizing the 130 Henderson County men who served in the Union Army, is located on the grounds of the Etowah branch of the Henderson County Library.

The county distribution of men who enlisted in the Union Army at some time during the war is rather surprising. Yancey was the most Union county with Union enlistments reaching nearly 27 percent of total belligerents by the end of the war. Second was Buncombe with over 14 percent. Mitchell County ran third with just under 11 percent, and Henderson County was fourth with nearly 10 percent. Surprisingly, Madison County ran less than 7 percent. Wilkes County, a reputed Union stronghold, had just over 9 percent. Again, most Western North Carolina Union soldiers enlisted late in the war, and a large majority were Confederate deserters.

Garren also points out the political correctness of one of the North Carolina's historical markers. The Shelton Laurel Massacre marker in Madison County reads:

"Thirteen men and boys suspected of Unionism were killed by Confederate soldiers in early 1863."

Unfortunately, they were massacred by men of the 64th North Carolina (Confederate) Infantry as a revenge for a raid of about 50 Shelton

Laurel men on the town of Marshall in Madison County. This raid is reputed to have involved the rape of the wife of a Confederate officer and to have contributed indirectly to the death of their two children. What the marker fails to say is that most of the massacred men were in the Confederate Army in 1862. The Shelton Laurel families may have become anti-Confederates by 1863, but they did not become Unionists until after the massacre.

Garren's book may be debated for many years. Cherished myths die hard, but as far as I am concerned, he has obliterated the myth that Western North Carolina was a Unionist stronghold.

Terrell Garren is from Henderson County, North Carolina, and is also the author of two historical fiction books: *The Secret of War: A Dramatic History of Civil War Crime in Western North Carolina* and *The Fifth Skull: A Historical Novel of the Civil War and the American West*. Garren makes more tangible and personal some of the issues discussed in *Mountain Myth* and in this book. I strongly recommend all three books.

Defining the Confederate Battle Flag

"The right to define the meaning of the Confederate Battle Flag or any flag belongs to those who by their history and shed blood own its heritage. Radical and lawless groups often display the United States flag, but this does not change its true meaning to fair-minded people. Nor should fair-minded people rightly associate the Confederate Battle Flag with evil because the very same groups expropriate and display it. No media or self-appointed social designers have the right to define the meaning of the Confederate flags. The base impropriety of redefining and slandering someone else's heritage and symbols is incredibly arrogant and stirs up needless strife. Honorable people pursuing a just and civil society do not seek to dishonor and marginalize the heritage and symbols of others. The Confederate Battle Flag ought to be the honored heritage of every Southerner and every American. No cowardice or indifference should allow it to be trampled under the heels of uninformed busybodies and political correctness police."

—Mike Scruggs

APPENDIX CHAPTER 6

ᴄ୭ଯ୭

H. K. Edgerton and the Pursuit of Truth

Mike Scruggs

August 19, 2005

H.K. Edgerton

A few days ago I had lunch with H. K. Edgerton at Hannah Flanagan's Pub in Hendersonville, North Carolina. H. K., as almost everyone calls him, is a graying, 56-year-old African-American whose photo often appears in the news. In fact, his photo was on the front page of *The Asheville Tribune* that very day. What is remarkable to some is that very often he is carrying a Confederate Battle Flag, defending Confederate monuments or Confederate heritage. H. K. is Chairman of the Board of Advisors for the Southern Legal Resource Center, but it would be a serious mistake to think that was all he is about. He is very knowledgeable on a very wide variety of political and social issues.

H. K. had the chicken wings, a favorite dish for him. I had the shepherd's pie. One of the things I like about Hannah Flanagan's is that they have a good choice of authentic Irish meals on their menu. One of the things I like about H. K. is that he himself is an authentic Southern style, American patriot.

H. K. is an energetic advocate of truth and right. It might seem strange to some that a former NAACP officer speaks so fervently for Confederate heritage. But H. K. is not bound by the chains of political correctness. He is a zealous advocate of truth, wherever it is found and however unpopular.

H. K.'s internal drive seems to be based on a strong belief in the transcendent and eternal truths taught in Scripture. The outward manifestation of that faith is his zealous drive for truth in all things, including history. His zeal for truth in all things often brings strong opposition, but he persists with courage and grace. Truth is not a popularity contest to him. He possesses that remarkable, all-weather brand of courage without which no other virtue can long survive.

H. K. was using a cane that day. He had just returned from Memphis where there has been a political attack on Southern heritage centering on Confederate monuments in Memphis parks. During his travel through Tennessee he hurt his leg and back mowing a lady's lawn. That in itself is a portrait of H. K. He is filled with a courageous zeal for truth, but he is the soul of grace, compassion, courtesy, and helpfulness. He is in every respect the model of the Christian gentleman whose devotion to duty, honor, courage, grace, and selfless patriotism, Robert E. Lee sought to instill in his students as Superintendent at West Point before the Civil War and as President of Washington and Lee after the war.

H. K. and I talked about of lot of things from home-schooling, property rights, the Constitution, and the moral tail-spin of American society to the tidal wave of illegal immigration that is engulfing the Carolinas and other Southern states. He is saddened that many black leaders have chosen to preach victimhood and aggravate racial grievances in the name of justice and that so many white business and political leaders kowtow to them. At the same time he mourns that most public schools have distorted Southern history so much that young students are ashamed of their Southern heritage. Every day brings forth some new instance of the very descendents of Confederate soldiers and patriots trampling the honor and courage of their forefathers to the ground to gain respectability with the vicious slanderers of Southern heritage. Such is the advanced state of political correctness even in the South. Of course, political correctness is not about the truth. It is about shouting down the truth, and it feeds on an environment of obsequious moral cowardice.

H. K. Edgerton doesn't put on any righteous or self-important airs. He is as human and vulnerable to human frailties as the rest of us, but somehow his extraordinary courage, grace, and a zeal for truth shine through. A lot of people, both white folks and black folks and others as well, love and admire H. K. He would probably make a great preacher, but his life is a pretty good sermon itself. I wish we had about 50,000 teachers like him. I would rest more comfortably about the future of our country.

H. K. showed me a letter he had written to President Bush, asking for a meeting with him. I know the letter was hand delivered to the President by a friend. The President would do well to meet with H. K. and listen keenly to what he says. I am sure the White House can fix up some chicken wings, and America would be far better for it.

Post Script: September 10, 2009. President George W. Bush never met with Edgerton who is now trying to meet with the current president.

REFERENCE RESOURCES

The Southern heritage articles appearing in *The Tribune* papers from 2005 to 2008 were the result of research consulting over 100 books and articles and about two score tape cassettes over a period of five years.

The study of the causes and conduct of the "Civil War" is still governed by the partisan myths of the Union victors and modern political correctness. If you visit the large national bookstores, you will not find many of the books I have listed here, although they will generally order them for you. With the development of the internet and advances in computer publishing, however, more scholars are producing books that dare to break the chains of whitewashed and highly politicized history. Truth crushed to the ground is still the truth, and modern technology is assisting in its resurrection. Older books, too, closer in time to the events and published in eras less politically and socially restrictive, are being republished. An appreciation for the Southern Cause is making a comeback, but the going is still uphill. The Southern Heritage articles published in *The Tribune* papers and these books provide conservatives with what Stonewall Jackson would have called a flanking action to bring truth to high ground.

I have not listed all the books and tapes here, only the best and most essential. They are arranged here by category, the first category being books that are either most comprehensive or essential to understanding the Civil War. Next follow more specific categories such as the Morrill Tariff, Constitutional Issues, Union Total War, Reconstruction, Fort Sumter, Slavery, et cetera. Many books are recommended in several categories.

Best General or Essential Books on Causes and Conduct of the War

Charles Adams; *When in the Course of Human Events*, 2000. Essential reading, the best short introduction to the causes and conduct of the war and Reconstruction.

Walter Brian Cisco; *Taking a Stand: Portraits from the Southern Secession Movement*, 1998.

Frank Conner; *The South Under Siege 1830-2000; A History of the Relations Between North and South*, 2002. Very comprehensive and easy to read.

R. L. Dabney; *A Defense of Virginia and the South*, 1867. A very articulate defense of the South.

Jefferson Davis; *A Short History of the Confederate States of America*, 1890.

Thomas J. DiLorenzo; *The Real Lincoln, A New Look at Abraham Lincoln, His Agenda, and an Unnecessary War*, 2002. Absolutely essential reading on Lincoln, the war and Reconstruction.

Clifford Dowdey; *The History of the Confederacy 1832-1865, 1955.*

Greg Loren Durand; *America's Caesar: The Decline and Fall of Republican Government in the United States of America*, 2006. Two volumes of invaluable research.

John S. Dwyer; *The War Between the States: America's Uncivil War*, 2005.

This recently published, easy-to-read, magnificently illustrated volume in my opinion gives the most comprehensive view of the causes and conduct of the war.

Shelby Foote; *The Civil War: a Narrative,* 1958, 1986. This three volume narrative of the war is comprehensive in its coverage and insight.

Eugene D. Genovese; *The Southern Front, History, Politics and the Cultural War*, 1995.

Jeffrey Hummel; *Emancipating Slaves, Enslaving Free Men*, 1996.

Ludwell H. Johnson; *The American Iliad 1848-1877*, 2002 edition.

James Ronald Kennedy and Walter Donald Kennedy; *The South Was Right! 1996.*

James M. McPherson; *For Cause and Comrades-Why Men Fought in the Civil War*, 1997. McPherson is famously pro-Union, but his research on thousands of letters from soldiers on both sides gives valuable insight into their thinking and motivation.

Mildred Lewis Rutherford; *Truths of History, 1907.* Reprinted with added material as *Truths of History: a Historical Perspective of the Civil War from the Southern Viewpoint,* 1998.

Otto Scott; *The Secret Six-John Brown and the Abolitionist Movement,* 1979. You really cannot fully understand the war until you read this book!

John Spence; *The American* Union, 1862. An inquiry into the causes of the war by a British observer.

Francis W. Springer; *War for What?* 1990

John S. Tilley; *The Coming of the Glory*, 1949. One of the best short and easy-to-read books on the issues.

Howard Ray White; *Bloodstains: An Epic History of the Politics That Produced the American Civil War*, Several volumes, 3 of 4 volumes complete in 2006. Invaluable detailed research.

Field Marshal Viscount Garnet Wolseley (1833-1913), edited by James A. Rawley; *The American Civil War: an English View*, 2002.

THE MORRILL TARIFF

Charles Adams; *For Good and Evil: The Impact of Taxes in the Course of Civilization*, 1993.

Charles Adams; *When in the Course of Human Events: Arguing the Case for Southern Secession*, 2000.

John Chodes; *Destroying the Republic: Jabez Curry and the Re-education of the South*, 2005. See Special Documentation Notes.

Frank Conner; *The South Under Siege 1830-2000; A History of the Relations Between North and South*, 2002.

Thomas J. DiLorenzo; *The Real Lincoln: A New Look at Abraham Lincoln, His Agenda, and an Unnecessary War*, 2002.

Frank William Taussig; *The Tariff History of the United States*, 1888, 2005.

Mark Thornton; *Tariffs, Blockades and Inflation: The Economics of the Civil War*, 2004

John G. Van Deusen; *Economic Bases of Disunion in South Carolina*, 1928.

Howard Ray White; Bloodstains, 2006.

CONSTITUTIONAL ISSUES

H. Lee Cheek, Jr.; *Calhoun and Popular Rule: The Political Theory of the Disquisition and Discourse*, 2001.

Marshall L. DeRosa, Editor; *The Politics of Dissolution: The Quest for a National Identity & the American Civil War*, 1998.

John Remington Graham; *A Constitutional History of Secession*, 2002

Ludwell H. Johnson; *North Against South: The American Iliad 1848-1877*, 1992 edition.

James Ronald Kennedy and Walter Donald Kennedy; *Was Jefferson Davis Right?* 1998.

Ross M. Lance, Editor; *Union and Liberty: The Political Philosophy of John C. Calhoun*.1992.

Donald W. Livingston; *Secession and the Modern State*, League of the South Institute, 1998. Many excellent tapes on Civil War issues are available through Apologia Bookstore on the internet.

Forrest McDonald; *States Rights: Imperium in Imperio 1776-1876 (American Political Thought)*, 2002.

William Rawle; *A View of the Constitution*, 1825. The legality of secession was taught at West Point prior to the war!

Mildred Lewis Rutherford; *Truths of History, 1907*. Reprinted with added material as *Truths of History: a Historical Perspective of the Civil War from the Southern Viewpoint*, 1998.

John S. Tilley; *The Coming of the Glory*, 1949.

Clyde N. Wilson; *From Union to Empire: Essays in the Jeffersonian Tradition*, 2003.

THE CHEROKEES

Vernon H. Crow; *Storm in the Mountains: Thomas' Confederate Legion of Cherokee Indians and Mountaineers, 1982*.

Frank Cunningham; *General Stand Watie's Confederate Indians*, 1959

E. Stanly Godbold, Jr., and Mattie U. Russell; *Confederate Colonel and Cherokee Chief: The Life of William Holland Thomas*, 1990

John C. Inscoe and Gordon B. McKinney; *The Heart of Confederate Appalachia: Western North Carolina in the Civil War*, 2000.

Emmett Starr; *History of the Cherokee Indians*, published by the Warden Company, Oklahoma City, Oklahoma, 1921. Reprinted by Kraus Reprint Company, Millwood, New York, 1977.

FORT SUMTER AND THE WAR CONSPIRACY

Shelby Foote; *The Civil War: a Narrative*, 1958, 1986.

Ludwell H. Johnson; *The American Iliad 1848-1877*, 2002 edition.

H. W. Johnstone; *The Truth of the Conspiracy of 1861*, 1921.

John S. Tilley; *Lincoln Takes Command: How Lincoln Got the War He Wanted*, 1941, 1991.

UNION TOTAL WAR POLICIES

David Aiken, introduction, editor: William Gilmore Simms; *A City Laid Waste: The Capture, Sack, and Destruction of the City of Columbia*, 2005.

John Chodes; "The Battle of New York City," *Southern Partisan*, Volume XXIV, April 2005. The amazing story of Lincoln's war on Northern Democrats.

Walter Bryan Cisco; *War Crimes Against Southern Civilians*, 2007. This book was not available when I was writing the chapter on Union Total War Policies, but it is highly recommended.

Burke Davis; *Sherman's March*, 1988.

Henry Clay Dean; *Crimes of the Civil War*, 1869.

Thomas J. DiLorenzo; *The Real Lincoln: A New Look at Abraham Lincoln, His Agenda, and an Unnecessary War*, 2002.

George Edmond; *Facts and Falsehood Concerning the War on the South*, 1904.

Jeffrey Rogers Hummel; *Emancipating Slaves, Enslaving Free Men: a History of the American Civil War*, 1996.

Thomas Bland Keys; *The Uncivil War: Union Army and Navy Excesses in the Official Records*, 1991.

Jeffrey Mamber and Neil Dahlstrom; *Lincoln's Wrath*, 2005. This book details much of the suppression of free press and civil rights during the Lincoln Administration.

Hunter McGuire & George L. Christian; *The Confederate Cause and Conduct in the War Between the States*, 1907. Dr. McGuire was Stonewall Jackson's surgeon.

Paul R. Petersen; *Quantrill of Missouri: The Making of a Guerilla Warrior—The Man, the Myth, the Soldier*, 2003. A thoroughly researched rebuttal of common myths about Quantrill and essential reading for understanding Union Total War Policy. The author is a native of Quantrill country and an experienced veteran of the guerilla war phase of the Vietnam conflict.

William Gilmore Simms; *The Sack and Destruction of Columbia, South Carolina*, 1865.

John S. Tilley; *Facts the Historians Leave Out*, 1951. This very short book is an excellent summary of the causes and conduct of the war.

Cole Younger; *The Story of Cole Younger*, 1903. Yes, this is the famous Missouri Confederate guerilla fighter and post war bank robber.

UN-CIVIL WAR IN KANSAS AND MISSOURI

Albert Castel; *Civil War in Kansas: Reaping the Whirlwind*, 1958, 1997.

Nicole Etcheson; *Bleeding Kansas: Contested Liberty in the Civil War Era,* 2004. A largely Kansas Unionist point of view, but informative.

Thomas Goodrich; *War to the Knife: Bleeding Kansas 1854-1861,* 1988.

Missouri Partisan Rangers website—Virtual Museum and Archives: www.rulen.com/partisan.

Jay Monaghan; *Civil War on the Western Border, 1854-1865.1955.*

Paul R. Petersen; *Quantrill of Missouri: The Making of a Guerilla Warrior*—The Man, the Myth, the Soldier. 2003.

Otto Scott; *The Secret Six: John Brown and the Abolitionists Movement,* 1979.

UNION AND CONFEDERATE PRISONS

George Levy; *To Die in Chicago: Confederate Prisoners at Camp Douglas 1862-1865.*

James Madison Page; *The True Story of Andersonville Prison*, 1908. The truth from a Union soldier held at Andersonville.

J. H. Segars, editor; *Andersonville: The Southern Perspective*, 2001.

Lonnie R. Speer; *Portals to Hell: Military Prisons of the Civil War,* 1997.

RECONSTRUCTION

There are two warring schools on Reconstruction today. Up until about 1960 the Dunning school prevailed. William A. Dunning and his students viewed Reconstruction as the most corrupt, tyrannical, and disgraceful period in American history. Most conservatives and moderates after looking at the facts would be appalled at the scandalous injustices of the times.

It is now the Foner school that dominates. Eric Foner is a Marxist, Columbia University professor, who believes Reconstruction did not go far enough. Harsher methods should have been used to remake the South into a more liberal society. Foner's facts are usually right, but his solutions are generally big government despotism with a liberal flavor.

One difficulty in writing about Reconstruction is the role of the Klan. The Dunning school is willing to look at the Klan in the perspective of Radical Republican and Union League violence against and suppression of white Southerners after the war, while the modern Foner school is unforgiving. I have made a distinction between the two Reconstruction schools below.

TRADITIONAL OR CONSERVATIVE
RECONSTRUCTION VIEW (DUNNING SCHOOL)

Charles Adams; *When in the Course of Human Events: Arguing the Case for Southern Secession, 2000*.

Myrna Lockett Avary; *Dixie after the War*, 1906.

Charles G. Bowers; *The Tragic Era*, 1929.

John Chodes; *The Union League: Washington's Klan*, 1999. Essential reading.

Frank Conner; *The South Under Siege 1830-2000: A History of the Relations Between North and South*, 1996.

E. Merton Coulter; *The South During Reconstruction 1865-1877*, 1947. In my opinion the best book on Reconstruction.

Susan Lawrence Davis; *Authentic History of the Ku Klux Klan 1865-1877*, 1924.

Thomas J. DiLorenzo; *The Real Lincoln: A New Look at Abraham Lincoln, His Agenda, and an Unnecessary War*, 2002.

Thomas J. DiLorenzo; *Reconstructing America: Consolidation and State Power1865-1890*, cassette tape, 2001.

William A. Dunning; *Reconstruction, Political and Economic 1865-1877*, 1907.

Robert S. Henry; *The Story of Reconstruction*, 1937.

Stanley F. Horn; *The Invisible Empire; The Story of the Ku Klux Klan 1866-1871, 1939*.

Jeffrey Rogers Hummel; *Emancipating Slaves, Enslaving Free Men: A History of the American Civil War*, 1996.

Ludwell H. Johnson; *North Against South: The American Iliad 1848-1877, 1978, 1993, 2002* printing.

Richard Taylor; *Deconstruction and Reconstruction: Personal Experiences of the late War*, 1879.

Alfred B. Williams; *Hampton & His Redshirts: South Carolina's Deliverance in 1876*, 1935.

Clyde N. Wilson; *Reconstruction in the Experience of the Southern People*, cassette tape series, 2001.

Clyde N. Wilson; *An Overview of Reconstruction*, cassette tape, 2002.

These and many other tape sets may be ordered though Apologia Bookstore on the internet.

Other Reconstruction References of Modern Revisionist Slant (Foner school)

Eric Foner; *Reconstruction: America's Unfinished Revolution, 1883-1877, 1988, 2005.*

Kenneth M. Stamp; *The Era of Reconstruction 1865-1877*, 1965. (A much milder revisionist than Foner).

Slavery in Truth and Fiction

Charles Kelly Barrow, H. H. Segars, and R. B. Rosenburg, Editors; *Black Confederates,* 2004.

Lerone Bennett Jr; *Forced into Glory: Abraham Lincoln's White Dream*, 2000.

Bennett nails Lincoln but lauds infamous radicals John Brown, Charles Sumner, and Thaddeus Stevens. Well researched and well written, but his hostility toward the Southern cause is as strong as his criticism of Lincoln.

Jonathan Blanchard & Nathan L. Rice; *A Debate on Slavery*, 1846.

E. Merton Coulter; *The South During Reconstruction 1865-1877,* 1947.

Robert L. Dabney; *A Defense of Virginia and the South*, 1867.

John J. Dwyer; *The War Between the States; America's Uncivil War*, 2005.

Anne Farrow, Joel Land, and Jennifer Frank; *Complicity: How the North Promoted, Prolonged and Profited from Slavery.* 2005. Truth about slavery from a surprising source. All are journalists with the *Hartford Courant* in Connecticut.

Robert William Fogel and Stanley L. Engerman; *Time on the Cross: The Economics of American Negro Slavery, 1974*.

Robert William Fogel; *Without Consent or Contract: The Rise and Fall of American Slavery*, 1989.

Eugene D. Genovese; *The Southern Front: History and Politics in the Cultural War*, 1995.

Belinda Hermence, Editor; *Before Freedom: When I Can Just Remember: Twenty-seven Oral histories of Former South Carolina Slaves*, 1989.

Michael A. Hoffman II; *They were White and They Were Slaves; The Untold History of the Enslavement of Whites in Early America, 1991*.

John Henry Hopkins; *A Scriptural View of Slavery*, 1864. This book was written by the Episcopal Bishop of Vermont.

Walter D. Kennedy; *Myths of American Slavery*, 2003.

John C. Perry; *Myths and Realities of American Slavery: The True History of Slavery in America*, 2002.

Slave Narratives: Arkansas Narratives (Volume II, Part 7), Work Projects Administration, Sponsored by the Library of Congress, Prepared by the Federal Writers Project 1936-1938, published 1941.

Slave Narratives: Mississippi Narratives (Volume IX), Work Projects Administration, Sponsored by the Library of Congress, Prepared by the Federal Writers Project 1936-1938, published 1941.

Gary C. Walker; *The Truth about Slavery*, 1997.

BIOGRAPHICAL, RELIGIOUS, AND SPECIAL INTEREST

Felicity Allen; *Jefferson Davis: Unconquerable Heart*, 1999.

W. W. Bennett; *The Great Revival in the Southern Armies*, 1877. This book describes the incredible and inspiring revival in the Confederate armies that left a permanent mark on the South.

Thomas J. DiLorenzo; *Lincoln Unmasked*, 2001. DiLorenzo addresses both the real nature of the Lincoln Administration and the Lincoln Cult of modern academia.

John P. Dyer; *From Shiloh to San Juan: The Life of "Fightin' Joe" Wheeler*, 1941, 1961.

Ralph Lowell Eckert; *John Brown Gordon: Soldier, Southerner, American*, 1989.

Douglas Southall Freeman; *Lee* (abridged version by Richard Harwell), 1961.

J. William Jones; *Christ in the Camp, 1887*.

Terrell T. Garren; *Mountain Myth: Unionism in Western North Carolina, 2006*.

Garren is an in-depth researcher and an entertaining writer.

Douglas Kelly; *Preachers with Power: Four Stalwarts of the South*, 1992. This book is worth owning for its preface alone (The Old South: an Introduction), sixteen pages of which describe the religious background of the South during the Civil War.

Charles Pitts; *Chaplains in Gray, 1957*.

James I. Robertson; *Stonewall Jackson, the Man, the Soldier, the Legend*, 1997.

This is a masterful biography of Jackson, also worth owning for its preface alone.

J.Steven Wilkins; *Call of Duty-The Sterling Nobility of Robert E. Lee*, 1997.

This biography is short and easy to read. Everyone that reads it is touched by it. It is a good character and integrity building book for young men and women, older ones, too.

J. Steven Wilkins; *All Things for Good: The Steadfast Fidelity of Stonewall Jackson*, 2004.

MARY SURRATT AND HENRY WIRZ

Understanding the story of Mary Surratt, her trial, and hanging is essential to understanding the police state justice administered by Secretary of War Edwin Stanton after the assassination of the president. Witnesses were bribed, tortured, coerced, and threatened with death to obtain a conviction. It also shows Stanton's ambitious and devious nature. Combine the trials of Mary Surratt and Henry Wirz, and the patterns of outrageous injustice become clear.

Francis X. Busch; *Enemies of the State*, 1954.

Otto Eisenschiml; *Why Was Lincoln Murdered? 1937*.

John Chandler Griffin; *Abraham Lincoln's Execution*, 2006.

Kate Clifford Larson; *The Assassin's Accomplice: Mary Surratt and the Plot to Kill Abraham Lincoln*, 2008. Larson tries to make the government's case against Mary Surratt. Refer to the Foreword and Chapter 2 of this book.

Mildred Lewis Rutherford; *Andersonville Prison and Henry Wirz Trial, 1921*.

Elizabeth Steger Trindal; *Mary Surratt: An American Tragedy*, 1996. In addition to the well researched story of Mary Surratt, this book contains an accurate overview of many critical issues of the war.

NAVAL AND BLOCKADE WARFARE

John Baldwin and Ron Powers; *Last Flag Down: The Epic Journey of the Last Confederate Warship*, 2008.

Tom Chaffin; *Sea of Gray: The Around-the-World Odyssey of the Confederate Raider Shenandoah*, 2007.

Hamilton Cochran; *Blockade Runners of the Confederacy*, 1958, 2005.

Stephen Fox; *Wolf of the Deep: Raphael Semmes and the Notorious Confederate Raider CSS Alabama*, 2007.

Chester G. Hearn; *Gray Raiders of the Sea: How Eight Confederate Warships Destroyed the Union's High Seas Commerce*, 1996.

Philip Van Dorn Stern; T*he Confederate Navy: A Pictorial History*, 1992.

Stephen R. Wise; *Lifeline of the Confederacy: Blockade Running During the Civil War*, 1988.

SPECIAL DOCUMENTATION NOTES

Morrill Tariff: Nearly 80% of federal tariff revenues disbursed in the North.

From a November 21, 1860 letter from then U.S. Congressman J. L. L Curry to Jonathan Haralson of Selma, Alabama, on the eve of Alabama secession: "but of the 1,100 millions of dollars collected in customs in the last seventy years the South has paid two-thirds of the sum, while nearly four-fifths have been disbursed in the North..." The customs, or tariff, was the source of almost all U.S. tax revenues in that era. John Chodes; *Destroying the Republic: Jabez Curry and the Re-education of the South,* 2005, Algora Publishing, New York, pages 9-10.

Morrill Tariff: 87-90% of federal tariffs paid by the South.

Thomas J. DiLorenzo; *The Real Lincoln*, Random House, 2002, pages 236-240.

Even before the 1860 Morrill Tariff, the South was paying 87% of federal tax revenues. The Morrill Tariff effectively more than doubled the tariff. By 1862, it was up to an average of 47.06%. DiLorenzo's principal source on tariff statistics is Frank Taussig, *The Tariff History of the United States*, Putnam, New York, 1931. DiLorenzo cites pages 166-7. DiLorenzo also notes that because more items were covered by the 1860 Morrill Tariff than the 1857 Tariff, the effective tax burden on the South may have nearly tripled.

Morrill Tariff: Tariff rate more than doubled from 1857 average rate 18.84% to 46.56% by 1865.

Frank Conner; *The South Under Siege: A history of the Relations between the North and the South 1830-2000*, page 94.

Morrill Tariff: "Doubled the 1857 rate to about 47%,"

Charles Adams; *For Good and Evil: The Impact of Taxes on the Course of Civilization*, Madison Books, Lanham, MD, 1993. Chapter 29, "Was It Taxes Rather than Slavery that caused the Civil War?" Page 330.

Southern Civilian Casualties: 50,000 civilian deaths in the South, 200,000 homeless refugees.

Jeffrey Rogers Hummel; *Emancipating Slaves, Enslaving Free Men: A History of the American Civil War*, Open Court Publishing, Chicago, 1996. Page 279. Some noted historians believe the numbers are much higher.

Many blacks forced into Union Army without consent: Union Army recruiting reports from Louisiana, Tennessee, Alabama, North Carolina, and Kentucky.

Thomas Bland Keys; *The Uncivil War: Union army and Navy Excesses in the Official Records*, Beauvoir Press, Biloxi, MS, 1991. Louisiana, page 64; Tennessee, page 71; Alabama, page 72; North Carolina, forced labor, page 106. Kentucky, page 134, letter from Lincoln to Lt. Col. John Glenn CO of 120th Colored Infantry dated 7 Feb. 1865, regarding inappropriate coercion and torture of Blacks to "extort their consent."

THE AUTHOR

Leonard M. Scruggs

Leonard M. (Mike) Scruggs is a real estate broker living in Hendersonville, N.C. Previously, he was an investment executive with a major Wall Street firm. He holds a BS from the University of Georgia and an MBA from Stanford University. A former USAF intelligence officer and navigator, he is a decorated combat veteran of the Vietnam War (Distinguished Flying Cross, Purple Heart, Air Medals) and until recently was Chairman of the Board of a Classical Christian School. He is the author of *The Un-Civil War: Truths Your Teacher Never Told You* (2006) and *Lessons from the Vietnam War: Truths the Media Never Told You (2009)*. and writes a weekly commentary for *The Asheville Tribune* and *The Hendersonville Tribune* in North Carolina and the *Times Examiner* in Greenville, South Carolina. In addition, he is a contributor to Vdare.com. He was awarded the prestigious D. T. Smithwick Award in 2008 by the North Carolina Society of Historians for the excellence of his newspaper and magazine articles on the Un-Civil War. He is a member of the Walter M. Bryson-George Mills Camp 70 of the Sons of Confederate Veterans in Hendersonville, North Carolina and an associate member of the Fighting Joe Wheeler Camp 1372 in Birmingham, Alabama.